The Politics and Policies of Sub-Saharan Africa

Edited by
Robert Dibie

University Press of America,® Inc.
Lanham · New York · Oxford

4720 Boston Way
Lanham, Maryland 20706
UPA Acquisitions Department (301) 459-3366

12 Hid's Copse Rd.
Cumnor Hill, Oxford OX2 9JJ

Printed in the United States of America
British Library Cataloging in Publication Information Available

Library of Congress Cataloging-in-Publication Data

The politics and policies of Sub-Saharan Africa /
edited by Robert Dibie.
p. cm.
Includes bibliographical references and index.
1. Africa, Sub-Saharan—Politics and government—1960-
2. Africa, Sub-Saharan—Economic conditions—1960-
3. Democracy—Africa, Sub-Saharan. I. Dibie, Robert A., 1956-

JQ1879.A15 P644 2001 320.967—dc21 2001041571 CIP

ISBN 978-0-7618-2093-2 (cloth : alk. paper)
ISBN 978-0-7618-2094-9 (pbk. : alk. paper)

™ The paper used in this publication meets the minimum requirements of American National Standard for Information Sciences—Permanence of Paper for Printed Library Materials, ANSI Z39.48—1984

Contents

Tables and Figures

PREFACE

In the middle of the 20th century several former European colonies in Africa, became independent nations. The uniqueness of the former colonies' political problem results largely from the precipitous shift of sovereignty from governments in Europe to inexperienced colonized people. This shift of sovereignty created administrative problems for the new leaders who at best had a brief apprenticeship in political responsibility. Another problem was the imposition of European political culture, policy institutions and economic development models that were largely alien to the indigenous cultures. These former European colonies have been classified as Third World nations because of their low economic and political development. In this text we examine the basic political and economic problems of sub-Saharan Africa, and the relationship with their former colonial regimes. The text is based on the premise that some degree of instability and political underdevelopment within and among sub-Saharan African nations should be regarded as part of the colonial legacy. The book sets out both to reconsider the analytical premises on which we Africanists operate and to offer one possible interpretation of contemporary Africa politics. It is also a product of innumerable discussions with Africans both in Africa and elsewhere.

This book attempts to correct the impression created by western media that sub-Saharan Africa is in a state of anarchy. This notion further predicts that sub-Saharan Africa is going to be marked by diseases, overpopulation, scarcity of resources, refugee migrations, increasing erosion of nation-state and international borders, and empowerment of private armies, security firms and international drug cartels. The book further analyzed Economics reform measures and political liberalization initiatives in sub-Saharan Africa. From one perspective, recent events in Africa appear to confirm this pessimist prediction. Some chapters in this book to argue that all African nations must not be lumped together and pronounced a disaster. Just as it is frequently misleading to generalize about Europe or Asia, so it is virtually impossible to generalize about Africa. Africa is a massive continent of over 54 nations, occupying an area more than three times the size of the United States. Sub-Saharan Africa is home to over 600 million people who speak more than a thousand different languages. Indeed, the defining feature of contemporary Africa is the increasing divergence of the paths being taken by different nations on the continent.

This book analyzes and shows that while many sub-Saharan Africa nations are experiencing the worst time of their independence history, others are enjoying their best times. From Senegal to Uganda and to South Africa, hope and real success are transforming the continent. Significant improvement in political stability and the shift to democracy have underpinned social peace in much of sub-Saharan Africa. We noted that while in 1996 the aggregate economic growth rate for the 34 Sub-Saharan Africa nations that have implemented major economic reform topped five percent, many observers of Africa decried the media's negative approach to the continent. Because war and famine provide far more dramatic television images than functioning economies and parliamentary debates, the image of sub-Saharan Africa to which Americans and Europeans are exposed are sharply skewed and discouraging. Therefore, we present two contradicting trends symbolizing contemporary sub-Saharan Africa. Sub-Saharan Africa is a continent of crisis; and it is also the site of major new experiments in governance, peace-building and free-market reform. Both of these trends are exemplified by nations examined in this book.

To what extent can new regime change resemble democratization? To what extent do processes of regime change resemble democratization? We believe that these concepts can be applied in sub-Saharan Africa, and we disagree vigorously with the view that their usage in the sub-regional context is both arbitrary and terribly premature. We argue instead that the efforts of African citizens to hold their leaders accountable for providing for common good are, at heart, a quest for democracy. We further contend that the innovative trend to install leaders by means of competitive elections, while far from democratization, is an indispensable first step. Moreover, to view recent sub-Saharan Africa's political development through the lens of colonial legacy provides a useful point of comparison both within the continent and with other world regions. Indeed, instead of adding to sub-Saharan Africa's marginalization by asserting its cultural uniqueness, we see value in situating our study within the ambit of mainstream analysis. In considering sub-Saharan Africa's cases of regime transition in the context of rich literature on democratization, we are able to highlight their singularity – but also their similarity – in relation to political reforms that have swept the rest of the late twentieth century.

Furthermore, the enlarged size of the postcolonial political community in sub-Sahara Africa and the complexity of development policy issues necessitate representative forms of governance. At the same time, citizen control of elected representatives is imperfect in all modern democracies. It is particularly elusive in sub-Saharan Africa, where many citizens have limited levels of formal education and live in remote rural areas; not surprisingly, they tend to regard central government as remote and inscrutable. Democratic principles can be expressed in a variety of institutional forms, including forms that embody cultural preferences derived from African traditions. But for ordinary people – in sub-Sahara Africa as elsewhere in the world – the challenge of democracy concerns how to obtain accountability from officials of the state. Note that this approach to democracy does not depend on proving that contestants for power are "true" democrats. It does not presuppose the existence of a political culture of democracy among either elites or masses. It requires only that incumbents and opponents acknowledge, however reluctantly, the acceptability of electoral contests for leadership.

In examining the prerequisite for political development in sub-Sahara African nations, we focused on colonial legacy, economic and ethnic factors, indigenous institutions, and other persistent forces. The erosion of these factors as well as the civilian order often provide both a prime reason for military intervention, and the means of justifying the breach of legality after it has taken place. Hence in the text we analyzed the role of military in state building in sub-Saharan Africa. We also evaluated the effects of the World Bank and International Monetary Fund aid, and development policy assistance in sub-Sahara African nations. On one hand, some scholars see these institutions as instrumental to re-colonization of former colonies. On the other hand, others associate the World Bank and IMF as a source of imperialism.

The contributors to the text include political scientists, economists, historians, policy analysts, World Bank and IMF consultants, all of whom shed light on the multidimensional impact of sub-Sahara African politics and colonial legacies. This book is written for both practitioners and students of economic development and development administration. It is appropriate for use in a variety of upper division and graduate university courses. Although the mode of analysis introduced in the text applies only to African problems, it could be applicable to a wide variety of international political economy issues. It is my hope that all those engaged in analyzing development problems, particularly those wrestling with the challenging task of developing and maintaining successful political and economic development in sub-Sahara African nations will find this text informative and helpful.

This book has benefited from the comments of valued colleagues. Special thanks are due to those who read and evaluated the entire manuscript, including Andrew Conteh, Leonard Gadzekpo, Babatunde Agiri, Sharron Herron,

Saliwe Kawewe, and Nelson Dibie and reviewers appointed by American University Press. They help us to rethink and amend the presentation of key ideas. I also wish to acknowledge grants from the Indiana State University Research Committee that have help to make this volume possible.

The book is organized as follows: Chapter 1 provides a brief premise of political and economic development in sub-Saharan Africa. The chapter overviews some theories of political and economic development and how they could be applied in sub-Saharan Africa. It links political and economic development process to the colonial legacy. International factors such as type of previous European regimes that controlled a territory prove helpful in explaining the present pattern of politics.

Chapter 2 surveys the prodigious literature on the origin of modern politics in sub-Saharan Africa. It addresses the question of why democracy has not been sustained in Africa south of the Sahara.

Chapter 3 describes in detail the extent to which Nigerian colonial political parties and post – independence parties have performed the task of national integration, and the variety of ways in which Nigeria's citizens have participated in politics.

Chapter 4 discusses the beginning, internal dynamics, and outcomes of the cold war, and the impact of the Cold War on political activities in sub-Saharan Africa. It also focuses on political liberation that took place in sub-Saharan Africa between 1988 and 1993, and its distinctive characteristics.

Chapter 5 examines the past and current trends of economic and political relations between Liberia and the United States. The dialectics of these relations will help us comprehend the nature of politics and class relation in Liberia, especially as they have related to various processes of capitalist economy and civil war.

Chapter 6 discusses the meaning and dimensions of democracy in Kenya. It analyzes Kenya's political system during the colonial era, and under the leadership of Jomo Kenyatta and Daniel arab Moi. The main thesis of this chapter is that whether one looks at Kenya from the standpoint of democratic activists or from the vantage point of the merchants of political pluralism the idea of democratic governance in the nation within the rubrics of existing socio-economic, political constitution structure is, in fact, an illusion of the epoch.

Chapter 7 critically examines the nature of Africa's opposition parties. It contends that as a rule, democracy in sub-Saharan Africa should be responsive to the will of the people, and permit people to organize parties as they please. People should be free to organize and support a political party that opposes the government, provided the party is committed to promoting of human rights. However, if people form an opposition party they should be free to vote it into office and thus oust the government party. This is an essential condition for government accountability that seems to be minimal in sub-Saharan Africa.

Chapter 8 focuses on the politics in Uganda. It argues that since independence Uganda has suffered decades of civil war and terror. However, under the leadership of President Yoweri Museveni, Uganda is becoming symbolic in news. The major variables that are key to the regime's successes are limited political liberalization – No party system, extensive economic liberalization, substantial external aid and international legitimacy and pragmatic but repressive political leadership.

Chapter 9 examines the struggle for ethnic control of access to social rewards such as political power, wealth and prestige in Nigeria, Rwanda, and South Africa. It argues that inter-ethnic or inter-racial (in case of South Africa) conflict might be due to duality of citizenship in these nations during post-colonial era.

Chapter 10 discusses methods that can be used to resolve race and ethnic problems in sub-Saharan Africa. The chapter commends the government of South Africa for the way they have handle the transition program from apartheid regime to democratic political system.

Chapter 11 examines economic reform policies in Cote D' Ivoire, Niger, Guinea, and Senegal. It argues that current structural adjustment programs lack coherent linkages between the short-term objectives of attaining balance-of-payments equilibrium and improving allocative efficiency and the long-term objective of sustainable development in sub-Saharan Africa. Thus, the economic reform policies prescribed by the IMF and World Bank has a hidden agenda of neo-colonialism.

Chapter 12 discusses the politics in the Democratic Republic of Congo (former Zaire). It argues that the struggle for democracy is one of the longest predicament sub-Saharan African nations have waged in the most recent time. The chapter reviews the political development of the nation from the era of Belgium colonial regime to those of Kasavubu and Lumumba, and further to Joseph Mobuto. It analyzed the regime of Laurent Kabila from 1997 till January 2001, when he was killed. The chapter also examines the philosophy of the new president of DRC, General Joseph Kabila.

Chapter 13 presents an argument that pan-Africanism is a direct result of the colonial partition of Africa. It contends that Africa could have not achieve regional cooperation or dreamed of continental unity if Europeans had not come to divide up the continent. The chapter also analyzes what accounts for the willingness of numerous political leaders in sub-Saharan Africa to run considerable risks by initiating dramatic changes that their predecessors did not dare to embrace. Finally, the chapter examines how colonialism has influenced sub-Sahara African nations' post independence politics. Two aspects of this legacy noteworthy: the first is the patterns of public administration, education, education and legal system. The second is what we will refer to as the economic legacy – IMF, World Bank, multinational corporations, GATT and various regional integration treaties.

Robert Dibie

Chapter 1

Premise of Sub-Sahara African Politics

Robert Dibie

INTRODUCTION

The foundation of the twentieth century's sub-Saharan Africa nations was indeed laid on the nineteenth century industrial revolution, globalization of trade, technological development and severe competition among European states on several issues which unfortunately led to the two world wars. However, once the industrial revolution launched the great transformation in the method of production and the associated reorientation in human life that continues, the limits of the state as a structure for rational economic life became gradually more apparent. The world wars also divided the globe into two ideological segments that in turn kept the world for half a century under fear of nuclear holocaust. The sudden demise of one side of the World left the other side at full bloom of the star war and technology for domestic and ordinary business purposes. Looking into all these technological revolutions, one can easily get fascinated to assume a twenty first century world foundation would be laid on electronic revolutionary advances.

The countries of the world are generally grouped into three broad regions - the West (First world or the North), the East (Second World), and the Third World or the South or developing nations. The first world or North comprises the industrialized states of North America, Western Europe, Australia, New Zealand and Japan. Nations of the North are economically prosperous with a moderate degree of governmental direction in their economies. The East comprises Russia and other east European nations. These countries are prosperous, although not as well off when compared to the West. They are marked by massive governmental direction in their economies. Third World or the South nations are neither the West nor the East. Third World nations range from communist nations like Cuba to conservative monarchies like Saudi Arabia. Generally, African, Latin America, the Middle East and Asian nations are classified as Third World or developing countries. Two-thirds of the world's population lives in the Third World. Most Third World or nations in the South are poor, but a number of them have great mineral wealth like Nigeria, Democratic Republic of Congo, Kuwait and other oil producing countries. Some Third World nations such as Argentina, Brazil, South Korea, Indonesia, and Singapore have become heavily industrialized, and they are sometimes referred as developing nations. Most sub-Sahara African nations are classified as either Third World or South or developing nations and they generally have all had dictatorship or bureaucratic-authoritarian political structures, sometime during their post independence history, and their citizens are generally not popularly involved in politics.

The major actors in Western politics, economic development and other revolutionary fields of the information system of the past two decades have been trying to create a New World order. An order without anticipated war and horrendous nuclear war. The order, where more than one dozen new nations are on the screen to play a game without knowing what posture they will take. Since the world for all political and economical purposes is divided into two, for example, the North and the South, the North has an agenda to go advance and higher. The men of this world contribute and share their labor, money and dreams. There are eight hours a day and life is sincerely devoted to those hours. On the other hand, the men in the South have not found any agenda or their agenda is limited to making a daily living. There is no political guidance, nor equal participation and distribution of the resources of their nations in their plans. They are not provoked, directed or shown the path of progress and achievements. They are still covering the shell of ethnic cleansing and ethnic nationalism.

The foundation of sub-Saharan Africa politics in the 21st century is going to be built on two pillars; one is a concrete, solid, and strong plan to support multidimensional progress on one hand. On the other hand, the second pillar is weak, full of cracks, unprepared to give support to the first pillar. This is indeed a signal to the people and government who are riding the strong pillar that if they ignore their other weak leg, they cannot build sustainability in the 21st century. The Northern and Southern nations comprise more than one hundred and eighty-five nation-states. Within the nation-states, are several ethnic groups and "nationalities", such as Igbos, Sikhs, Irish, Kurds, Yorubas, Native-Americans, Hausas, Kikuyus, Hutus, Tamils, Kashmiries and so forth. Each of its nationalities has their own identity.

The purpose of this book is to discuss the selected national politics and economic development processes in sub-Saharan African countries. Several scholars will diagnose and examine the causes of sub-Saharan African political and economic turmoil, and advance suggestions for possible solutions. Some of the chapters argued that unless the people of sub-Saharan nations find a way to reconcile the concept of nationalism and the imperative of political unity and order, nationalist and subnationalist (ethnonationalists) ideologies may lead to the disintegration of political and economic development. The main question is; can we find a new ideology to counter and accommodate subnationalism and keep the respective sub-Saharan Africa nations united? Before the different scholars discuss and examine the situation in a profile of Sub-Saharan African nations, let us review the theoretical framework about Africa's politics and economic development.

COLONIAL EXPERIENCE

An examination of the colonial experience is a necessary prelude to an analysis of sub-Saharan politics. Africa, Asia and Latin America do not share a single common culture like Europe. According to Ali Mazrui (1986) different ethnic groups and civilization shaped the people of Africa nations. Africa suffered from the debilitating effects of the slave trade until well into the nineteenth century. This tied it into the world market and when the slave trade came to an end, European merchants sought other commodities for which a market could be found. Palm products were the main exports for some time, but as Europe industrialized, there was a growing need for raw materials or foodstuff that could be cultivated in the climate of Africa. The scramble and partition of Africa that followed the Berlin conference of 1884/5 further facilitated colonization in the continent.

The economic impact of Sub-Sahara African nations on Western industrialization took several forms. Colonization was part of the search for new sources of raw materials from Africa nations. The colonies provided new opportunities for some individual citizens of the imperial powers. These opportunities led the settlement of Europeans in the colonies. The problem of white or European settlers was born in countries that ranged from South Africa to Algeria, from Zimbabwe to Kenya, from Nigeria to Morocco. The colonies also provided potential markets for goods produced in Europe. While colonizing African countries provided wealth and prosperity for European nations, it was more effective in destroying indigenous sub-Sahara African structures and culture. Legitimate indigenous institutions were designed for societies with the same political tradition before the Europeans invaded and imposed colonial borders and laws. Indeed, the colonial boundaries often encompassed a variety of societies with greatly different political traditions. The tension between new imported structures and old resilient cultures is part of the post-colonial conflict of cultures in the Africa. Mahmood Mamdani (1996) and William Tordoff (1997), contend that European colonizers shifted from their zeal of humanitarian and civilizing mission to a calculated preoccupation of holding power, from rejuvenating to conserving society, from being the torch bearers of individual freedom to being custodians protecting the customary integrity of dominated tribes. This shift took place in older colonies, mainly Nigeria and Ghana, but its lessons were fully implemented in Africa, Europe's last colonial possession.

It is interesting to note that virtually all-African countries have close links with the industrialized west. On one hand this link was a result of colonial conquest, and on the other hand, some African nations gravitated towards the former Soviet Union out of military and economic need. The extent, to which the industrial world continues to have interest in the affairs of sub-Sahara African countries however, depends on the geographical location and strategic importance of the nation. Nations in West and East Africa are particularly susceptible to external intervention from Portugal, Spain and to a lower extent Great Britain. China, the United States and the former Soviet Union have all pursued perceived interest in South Africa. The adoption of opposing values and ideologies of development by the different colonial regimes and their subsequent imposition of these ideologies in the form of policies sometimes complicated the implementation. This often resulted in failed development processes in African nations' as well as less industrial advancement. African, nations experienced foreign domination and ideologies during colonial period. Their contact with modern institutions and western values, especially the institutions of capitalism gravitated towards the demand for independence. While the Asian colonial experience has stimulated the desire to become technologically advanced, African nations are still being engulfed in political turmoil, ethnic conflict, corruption, military dictatorship and illegitimate governments.

Much of the discourse on colonization focused on the negative aspect of its impact; however, we should not fail to realize that there were some positive legacies. On one hand, the negative aspect includes massive exploitation of Africa in terms of resource depletion, labor exploitation, unfair taxation, lack of industrialization, the prohibition of inter-African trade, and the introduction of fragile dependent one-crop economies. According to Vincent Khapoya (1994) and Ali Mazrui (1986) the exacerbation of ethnic rivalries by the British, especially through the implementation of the colonial policy of "indirect rule," continued to echo in post-independence conflicts in Africa and Asia. One significant political consequence of indirect rule was that it reinforced separate ethnic identities and stunted the development of a national or colony-wide political consciousness. The alienation and undermining of traditional African authority patterns, through the use of chiefs for colonial duties, made the task of nation-building that much difficult. The creation of artificial boundaries has been the basis of much suffering in African nations as political conflicts have flared up from time to time because of territorial claims and counterclaims. The destruction of African culture and values through imposition of alien religions, and the relentless attack on African values mounted by missionary schools contributed to a mentality of dependency and the loss of confidence sub-Sahara African nations had in themselves, their institutions, and their heritage. The denial of political participation to colonized Africans and

Latin Americans have retarded post-colonial political development, as the excessive use of force in addressing political problems has been carried to the post-colonial period. It is therefore, unrealistic for anyone to expect ethnic groups that had been played one against the other for so long to know suddenly how to forge one nation overnight when independence came. Incidences of inter-ethnic political violence in former British colonies can be partly traced to indirect rule.

On the other hand, the positive legacy of the colonial regimes that many scholars are likely to agree on are: (1) Clonialization has shortened the process of nation formation by imposing arbitrary boundaries in Africa because countries were created with the stroke of a pen; (2) the introduction of Western medicine has made an incredible difference in the survival rates of the African population; (3) the introduction of Christianity and Islam to the African people greatly simplified their spirituality and created a new basis for the people to come together, despite their diversity; (4) the limited infrastructure that colonial authorities established became the foundation upon which new African leaders built their post-independence national institutions; and (5) the introduction of formal education deserves mention in helping to broaden sub-Saharan Africa's outlook and to unlock the hidden potential of its people. Thus, although colonialization created much pain and suffering, it also promoted literacy, health care and self help.

An important question to ask at this point is: Could it have been possible for sub-Sahara African nations to enter the international or global state system without suffering the agonies of the slave trade, exploitation of colonialism and the humiliation of European racism? One possible answer to this question could be drawn from Japanese history. Japan is now a major power in the world political economy and has for sometime been a major figure in the international political system without having undergone the agonies of European colonization and imperialism. Japan was able to acquire Western tools without succumbing to Western subjugation. In essence Andre Gunder Frank (1969) sees underdevelopment as the effect of the penetration of modern capitalism into the archaic economic structures of the third world. He contends that the development of the underdeveloped nations will be stimulated by indiscriminately transferring capital institutions and values from developed North to the Southern nations that have been tremendously exploited.

NATIONALISM

Nationalism is the devotion to or concern for one's nation, race, religion, language, economics and historical factors. All these factors serve as a base for people to be divide into nations. Nationalism provides for a sovereign independence, set territories and boundaries, a single national and unified culture (Snarr and Snarr 1998). In sub-Saharan Africa nationalism is a feeling based on shared cultural norms, traditional institutions, racial heritage and a common historical experience. Along with this sense of shared identity is a collective desire to maintain one's own cultural, social, and political values independent of outside control. One enduring historical experience shared by nearly all-African nations is colonial oppression. Nationalists tend to focus on their country, no matter how good or bad it is. No moral principle is higher; no religious principle is higher; no other standard is higher or better than those in their country. This notion is associated with nationalism or the right to self-determination of peoples. All nationalists appeal to the right of self-determination of people, arguing in many cases that "we don't like the decisions that are being made on our behalf, we want to make them for ourselves." Dawa Norbu (1992, 29) has observed that nationalism is society's claim to political participation in the state's affairs. Culturally, in his point of view, nationalism is the concretization of collective conscience embedded in a given tradition. Its diffusion in the lower levels of society is accompanied by corresponding demand for power distribution. Thus, national consciousness spreads fairly rapidly from sector to sector, from class to class until the entire society is engulfed with its complex and composite political consciousness, at which stage the terms nation and nationalism may be employed.

Nationality also denotes an ethnic and cultural identity that is based on common values. A state, on the other hand, is a political organization holding and exercising supreme power through its various agencies over a given people within a given territory. A state may include a number of "nationalities" (Renan and Kohn 1929). A state, in other words, may be "multinational" as is the case in Nigeria, Kenya, Ghana, South Africa and so on. A nation-state, in contrast to nationality (which is not a state) and to a state (which is not necessarily based upon a common nationality), is supposed to be both a state and a nationality.

Roy Macridis (1991, 191) explains the concept of nationality and nationalism in terms of two theories, i.e., objective and subjective. Under objective theory, he stresses the most common traits with which nationality is associated as: (1) language; (2) religion; (3) a consciousness of common traditions and history and a will to maintain them; and (4) a common territory. When no common territory exist, as was the case with the Jews, the Greeks and Polish, it was the memory of the common territory they occupied in the past that kindled their desire to regain or reclaim it. The same is true today of Kurds or Tamils in Sri Lanka and many other nationalities. Nationalism becomes an ideology and a movement only when it translates this self-consciousness into a demand to form a state under subjective theory. The subjective element is the element of will and purpose (Macridis 1992; Snarr and Snarr 1998). According to the subjective theory, nationalism asserts the validity of the objective factors of nationality for certain political purposes; it affirms their uniqueness and often their exclusiveness. It is not only the will to live together but to have a government; a sovereign government. It is the assertion that such a purpose has an inherent claim to be heard and to realize itself; it is a purpose that is presumed to be morally just. In this sense, according to Elie Kedourie (1971), it holds that humanity is naturally divided into nations, that nations are known by their characteristics and the only legitimate type of government is a national self-government, a sovereign government.

Radical nationalism is associated with the national liberation movements that fought for independence in the emerging national states of Africa. Nationalism and anti-colonial fervor erupted all over African colonies almost as soon as the Second World War ended. Barely fifteen years after the end of WW II the bulk of the African continent nations had attained formal political sovereignty. As nationalism began to take shape, the immediate goal of its spokesmen seemed to be to take over the administration from the expatriate civil servants whose superiority as a ruling bureaucracy was based upon educational qualifications, and not upon the ownership of property. Nevertheless, the political power that they wielded ensured the prerogatives and privileges of the European firms who effectively controlled the commanding heights of the economy. European business community, with its network of relationships with powerful firms at home, formed an exclusive group that African nations could not penetrate.

The growth of the nationalist's movement in African nations and increasing international pressure to promote development in the colonies compelled the administration to consider internal development more positively and to bring indigents into decision making. It became clear that independence could only be a matter of time while, in this changing situation, the national elites in sub-Saharan Africa nations became increasingly self-conscious and politically organized. In the African context the elites had some specific features which helped to account for their subsequent behavior. Emerging from the ranks of prosperous peasantry, for example, ruling families and rich business people, the elites acquired Western education.

Although African elites were united in the fight for self-determination there were also strong regional and ethnic loyalties and rivalries. Politically the members of the national elites were pragmatic, moderate and at times revolutionary. They generally retained a respect for European education and the Western way of life as exemplified by the colonial civil servants and teachers. African elites desiring social improvement and economic advancement, for which they saw political independence, as a necessary first step had to adopt the European models. These African elites tended to be suspicious of the powerful foreign corporations that held sway over the economy, but they had no viable alternative in the short run to the continuation of the existing organization of trade and production just after independence.

European colonizers had some racial and economic motives for seizing African territories, but the African people simply wanted their territories back, and the freedom to live their lives as they saw fit. This surge in Africa nationalism was fueled by several factors. Besides the oppressive colonial experience itself: missionary churches, colonial education, the exposure to the world through World War I and II, the ideology of Pan-Africanism, and the forum provided briefly by the league of Nations and later by the United Nations.

When African nations started to achieve independence from the colonial administration, they continued along the capitalist line of ideology. Although phrases of "socialism" featured in their respective political history, it was no more than populist rhetoric for improving the welfare of the masses. Other African nations did not take coherent action planning serious programs that would lead forwards developing their economy or promoting industrialization under the umbrella of the state. The members of the elite, as they took over the levers of power, accepted the values of capitalism. As a result of the fact that they were already privileged economically and educationally, the elites accepted personal advancement and enrichment as vital goals, modeling their expectations very much upon the life-style of Europeans in colonial times. The way was thus open for cooperation and collusion between politicians and civil servants on the one hand and indigenous entrepreneurs, of whom there was no lack of aspirations, and foreign businessmen on the other. Peculation and corruption became endemic in the new nations, intertwined with regional and ethnic rivalries and favoritism.

POST-COLONIAL POLITICAL SYSTEMS

The tortured history of African nations offers insight into the difficulties of operating a democratic system in a setting where democratic values are not yet firmly established. The previous narrative of the legacy of colonial authoritarianism gives us the impression that the first four decades of post-independence politics in sub-Saharan Africa has been marked by personal despotism, single-party autocracy or military dictatorship. African nations' political leaders only partially internalized the rules and roles associated with a proper functioning of a democratic system, and their replacement by military regimes in some countries is not surprising or unique. The integration of several ethnic groups with different cultures in Africa's nations by European colonial administration resulted in a long history of conflict among the various cultures.

The majority of the African nations achieved independence under a democratic type of political system. Some became independent under a federal and presidential system, a unitary parliamentary system or a semi-presidential system. The nature of their political system was vividly spelled out in their respective constitution. A unitary parliamentary political system gives the central government strong powers, while the federal system of government is more decentralized. Since these democratic systems do not remain constant in all the Sub-Saharan Africa countries and are covered in the subsequent chapters, we shall briefly mention them here. From our analysis of the three political systems in Africa nations it is very difficult to choose a parliamentary, presidential or semi-presidential system of government. One problem is that all of the alternatives have their advantages and disadvantages. No obvious winner has emerged from their practice in African nations.

At independence, African nations inherited some form of democratic political system. The choice of political system mostly depended on the model in practice by the European country from which they achieved independence. For example Ghana, Nigeria and other former British colonies adopted the parliamentary system. Senegal, Ivory Coast, Algeria and other former French colonies equally adopted a semi-presidential system. National political leaders only partially internalized the rules associated with the democratic system. The political relations between the regional and sub-ethnic groups grew tense after the attainment of independence in sub-Sahara African nations because there were perceived imbalances in wealth and opportunities. This fear has led in some cases to post-independent restructuring of the political system.

Political legitimacy brings us to one of the crucial political problems in many sub-Saharan African countries, namely the problem of governance, or the ability of a civilian government to maintain order and simultaneously solve the problem that confronts it without the necessity of a military intervention. An expanded system-transforming role of the military emerged after the coups in Brazil (1964), Argentina (1966), Peru (1968), Chile and (1973). The military has held the formal reins of government in Nigeria, Burkina Faso, Ghana, Liberia, Benin, Niger, Uganda, Zaire, Rwanda, Egypt and Libya.

When civilian regimes fail to govern effectively they are often replaced by the military. In Africa the military has tried to operate as a single ruling party. Before 1965 for example, the military was contented to act as a moderator or arbitrator in politics of African nations, but today powerful factions within the armed forces are more likely to become exasperated with corrupt political parties. Further, the military are fearful of the internal security threat posed by rural and urban guerrillas, and oppositions to military rule. The military are also confidence that they possess the wisdom to play a permanent political role in producing more rapid development. The main reason for military intervention, namely, taking temporary control of government in order to restore order and work for a speedy return of civilian rule, in some African nations has become inadequate justification for military intervention. The experience in some nations in Latin America and Africa has shown that the military cannot decree economic growth, higher farm production, honesty in administration, higher labor productivity, an end to capital flight abroad, and higher rates of investment. Nor can order be simply decreed or maintained by high levels of repression. The evidence from Brazil, Argentina, Chile and Peru in the 1960s and Nigeria, Liberia, Ghana, Sierra Leone, Democratic Republic of Congo (former Zaire) and Burkina Faso between 1970-1990s shows military juntas have not learned that they cannot create a conducive environment for economic development. By isolating themselves from interest groups in order to make policy unhindered by private demands, the military only increases distrust of the policy making process and encourages resistance to their decisions.

The ethnic complexity of African nations has often generated intense political conflict and an irrepressible social pluralism that cannot be effectively managed by a military regime. Despite the various reasons for military intervention in Africa political system, all nations are concerned not only with political stability, but also with positive economic performance. While the forces of nationalism may serve the cause of development, a theory of nationalism and development is not clearly discernible.

The problem of illegitimacy also prevails everywhere in sub-Saharan Africa post-independence politics. Legitimacy is a major requirement to political development, institutionalization, order, and stability. Popular or democratic nationalism should entail mass identification within the state, as well as participation in the affairs of the state. The point is if the people of sub-Saharan Africa believe that they own their state, then they will have a greater emotional attachment to it and a greater responsibility to support it. The process of getting people to become emotionally connected to the state invariably entails transference of supreme authority from rulers to the people. In most sub-Sahara African nations where such transference does not exist, where the political system fails the democratic test fails. In this regard, the people are unresponsive to the government's mobilizational endeavors of any sort. Further, the only way that government change hand was by military coup or in the relatively rare cases when a ruler died in office or natural causes.

In the case of the Republic of Benin, Brigadier Mathieu Kerekou, after 18 years of military rule, become the first African leader to be voted out of office. In February 1991, after multiparty elections, new governments took over in two small island nations off the West African coast, Cape Verde, and Sao Tome and Principe. In February 1993, President Dideir Rasikara of Madagascar, who had been in office since 1975, went down to defeat at the polls. In Senegal, Abdou Diouf, who had been president since 1981, finally lost power to the Senegalese opposition leader, Abdoulaye Wade in general elections of march 2000.

Malawi presents an interesting political trend. Kamuzu Banda was the tyrannical leader of the nation for 30 years. Banda's regime ended in 1994 when he was defeated in multiparty elections. Kamuza Banada declared himself president for life during his tenure. He oversaw the elections to Parliament, and he could dissolve Parliament as well as dismiss his Cabinet at will. Those who opposed him were assassinated, forced into exile, or thrown into jail (Wiseman, 1998).

In Nigeria after three and half decades of domination by the military, the army eventually handed over power to an elected political leader. It will be recalled that soldiers ruled the nation for all but nine years since it gained independence from Britain in October 1960. Over the years, the promise to restore civilian rule, and the retraction of it, alternated with a frequency that prompted Wole Soyinka to observe that "the military had perfected the art of contradictions until it became a mark of consistency (Soyinka, 1993).

In 1993 General Babangida annulled the presidential elections held on June 12. This annulment prevented the winner of the election Moshood Abiola from being sworn in as president. General Sani Abasha, who seized power in a military coup in November 1993, imprisoned Moshood Abiola, the winner of the election, because he declared himself president elect in a rally in Lagos. On July 6, 1993, tens of thousands of people protesting the nullification of the election were fired upon and scores of them killed in Lagos. While Abiola remained incarcerated, his wife was assassinated. In 1994, in the face of a precipitous decline in the nation's per capita income and widespread perception that Nigeria had become one of the world's most corrupt nations, Abacha promised a quick transition to a democratic government that would not include him. Barely four years later, the name Abacha coerced all of Nigeria's five Legal political parties to choose him as their nominee in presidential elections. On June 8, 1998 Abacha suddenly died from heart attack. His death saved the nation from another meaningless stage-managed transition from military to civilian rule. Few months after the death of Abacha, Moshood Abiola died in prison. General Abdulsami Abubaker assumed the leadership of Nigeria after the death of Abacha.

In May 1999, Nigeria's military ruler General Abdulsalami Abubaker turned power over to the winner of the country's general elections. Formal military leader, retired general Olusegun Obasanjo was elected as Nigeria's new democratic leader. President Obasanjo became the first democratically elected President after the toppling of Shehu Shagari in December 1983.

In Ghana, Flight Lieutenant Jerry Rawlings, in the wake of over twelve years military rule ran and won presidential elections that took place in 1992. This victory at the polls by Rawlings despite several charges of improprieties, led to a boycott of parliament by the opposition parties over the next four years. Unperturbed by dismal tales of governmental corruption and mounting social and economic crises of every hue, Rawlings set out in 1996 to run for yet another term and once again, as a matter of course ended up the winner. At the end of his second term in 2000, another political leader won the elections in the nation. Ghana now has a new breed political leader.

The political leadership in Uganda posed another interesting search for democratic development in sub-Saharan Africa. Yoweri Museveni has been the President of Uganda for the past ten years. On May 1996, Museveni swept the presidential election victory in Uganda. It will be recalled that Museveni became the leader of Uganda in 1986, against charges of massive rigging, multiple voting and counts exceeding the number of registered voters. Chapter 8 will discuss the political trend in Uganda in detail.

Gambia is another nation in sub-Saharan Africa that has experienced military rule. Two years after seizing power in a military coup that overthrew one of Africa's longest functioning democracies Yahya Jammeh organized elections. The election that was held in September 1996, was said to have been manipulated in favor of Yahya Jammeh (French, 1996).

Sudan is Africa's largest country, but since its independence from Britain in 1956, the nation has not known peace. Sudan has been faced with a civil war. This civil war is known to be Africa's longest-running civil war, and it goes back to the nation's accession to independence from British rule in 1956. The civil war in

Sudan is said to have killed more than a million people in 1998 alone (New York Times, 1998). The civil war motivating force is the determination to Islamize and Arabize Sudan whose majority is African traditionalist or Christian. It's Muslim citizens who believe that Sudan is geographically in Africa but is Arab in its aspirations and destiny has galvanized the civil war. These Muslim citizens of Sudan argue "we consider ourselves the Arab spearhead in Africa, linking the Arab world to the African continent" (Aguda, 1973). The stakes in the conflict suddenly got higher in 1999 with the marketing of oil that had been discovered decades ago. There is widespread suspicion in diplomatic quarters that the Sudanese government will use the windfall to buy more weapons to keep the war, and its devastating policies geared toward shoring up The National Islamic Front, going.

Sierra Leone has also experienced a civil war. This civil war started in 1991. Among the catalogue of horror emanating from the civil war, is the forcible conscription of children, some as young as seven years old. Kidnapped by rebel forces or drawn into the government's army, they were forced to become soldiers, human shields, spies, porters, and sex slaves. By some estimates, children made up between 40 and 50 percent of the insurgents' total force strength of around 15,000, while representing a fifth of the government's 25,000 strong Civil Defense Forces (Goodard, 1999). Diamond smuggling has been at the root of the war. Sudan's deep social inequities, despite the potential wealth of its diamonds, have been the rallying cry for the rebels who call themselves the Revolutionary United Front (Onishi, 2000). The categories of victims in this war are endless. Norimitsu Onishi (2000) pointed out that people whose hands, arms or feet were hacked off have become the war's symbols of suffering, other kind of victims are more numerous.

In sum the majority of sub-Saharan Africa's post-independence leaders have occupied the political stage with personal ambition rather than the general good for their people. These African Leaders have shown recklessness with the lives of defenseless civilians than is hallmark of men grown accustomed to unaccountable people (Berkeley, 2000). It is rather unfortunate that while all the stock exchanges in the world are preoccupied with sub-Saharan Africa's gold, diamond, uranium, platinum, copper, iron and petroleum the majority of the citizens of Africa are certified as disinherited and broken indigent. From all this, it is axiomatic that a new tangible strategy of integration in sub-Saharan Africa needs to be based on societies that reserve their highest respect and their highest prizes for those whose life and work demonstrate the greatest service, not the greatest personal acquisition of wealth.

INTEGRATION AND ECONOMIC DEVELOPMENT

International integration and dissimilarities in economic development are the characteristics of the world political economy today. The post-independent era of African nations has experienced disputes over appropriate models of development. These models include functionalism, trickle down development, dependency, neoclassical approach and so on. The trickle down model shows that the effects of rising incomes and output would ultimately trickle down to the poor nations so that they would benefit as well as the rich industrialized countries.

Sub-Saharan Africa nations, however, argued that their economic shortfall is primarily due to external neocolonial dependency, over exploitation by international economic regimes that extracted crops and mineral resources from the continent at low prices and then sell refined products back to Africa at very high prices. European countries, Japan, and the United States also blocked the entry of finished products from Africa to their markets. These Northern nations also monopolized modern production technologies, and denied Africa nations access to investment funds and foreign assistance in sufficient quantity and on reasonable terms (Frank 1972; Amin 1976; Udogu 1999). Western industrialized nations, in contrast, tend to attribute the economic failures of African nations to internal factors such as discouraged private enterprise, subsidized consumption, under motivated departments and enterprises in the public sector and perverse economic policies (Nafziger 1997; World Bank 1985). The World Bank believes that African nations could have capitalized on opportunities in the expanding international economy like their successful partners in Indonesia, Malaysia, Thailand, Taiwan and Korea.

International integration refers to the process by which supranational institutions come to replace national ones (Goldstein, 1994). This involves the gradual shifting upward of sovereignty from the state to regional or global structures. Integration processes are making state borders more permeable to people, goods and ideas. One question that emerges from this is: Under what circumstances could international cooperation among nations result in economic development? In an attempt to answer this question we shall discuss the functionalist, dependency, neo-classical, realist, idealist and liberal institutionalized approaches to integration and economic development.

Functionalist Approach:

The most prominent approach to our understanding of the creation and growth of international cooperation is that of the functionalist. This approach stresses that growth in non-political issues i.e., technology, trade, cultural exchange, education and so on, will create pressures for states to cooperate in international organization (Haas 1964, 1970; Mitrany, 1975). The functionalist contend that technological and economic development lead to more supranational structures as states seek practical means to fulfil necessary functions such as delivery of mail or phone calls from one country to another or coordinating the use of rivers that cross borders. Increasing interdependence leads states to cooperate in order to solve common problems and to take advantage of greater efficiency from such cooperation. Functionalist contends that nations begin cooperation in technical and relatively non-controversial areas because these are often low political issues. The organizations formed are very specialized and generally have limited membership. On the long run, cooperation in this limited areas may expand or spill over into more controversial political issues (Nye, 1974). This spill over into political issues is referred to as neofunctionalism. Neofunctionalists argue that economic integration generates a political coordination in order to operate effectively and eventually lead to political integration. Neofunctionalism is a modification of the functional approach in explaining these developments. The European Community (EC), Economic Community of West African States (ECOWAS), and Southern African Development Coordination Conference (SADCC). In 1992 SADCC was transformed into the Southern African Development Community (SADC). The new SADC explicitly added market integration SADCC. In 1993, the member states of the Preferential Trade Agreement (PTA) signed a new treaty to establish the Common Market of Eastern and Southern Africa (COMESA). The objectives of COMESA go beyond the creation of a customs union and include the free movement of capital and persons and formation of a customs monetary union. COMESA includes the possibility of supranational elements in decision-making. Also in 1993 the ECOWAS Treaty was revised. The Association of South East Asian Nations (ASEAN) is an example of integration among Asian nations (Bach 1999). The recent link of Argentina, Brazil, Paraguay and Uruguay in MERCOSUR suggests that economic cooperation may be possible at the sub-regional level. The temptation for individual countries to break ranks and tie themselves to developed country blocs is exemplified in Mexico's entry into North America Free Trade Agreement (NAFTA), with Canada and the United States.

The notion of economic development, in the case of integration among African nations, means the extent to which the integrationist measures contribute to the development of the participants. Since it is assumed that such measures will not be carried out for the purpose of achieving total integration, it may consist of partial or intrinsic benefits. Integration should therefore be seen as a supplement to national development efforts, rather than a panacea capable of solving all the problems of African nations.

Dependency Theory

African nations have passed through three types of dependency: (1) colonial dependency, evident in trade monopolies over land, mines and labor; (2) financial dependency accompanied by imperialism and the expansion of big capital at the end of the nineteenth century; and (3) the new dependency, characterized by the capital of multinational corporations in industry oriented to the internal market of African nations after the Second World War.

Dependency theory views modernization in African nations as simply the adoption of economic and political systems developed in Western Europe and North America. Celso Furtado (1973) contends that the global change in demand resulted in a new international division of labor in which the peripheral countries of Africa, Asia, and Latin Africa specialized in primary products in an enclave controlled by foreigners while importing consumer goods that were the fruits of technical progress in the central nations of the West. The increased productivity and new consumption patterns in African nations benefited a small ruling class and its allies who cooperated with developed nations to achieve modernization. Dos Santos (1970) described dependency theory as conditioned by the relationship of dominant to dependent nations so that the expansion of the dominant country could have a positive or negative impact on the development of the dependent one.

Andre Gunder Frank (1969), a major dependency theorist argued that underdevelopment does not mean traditional economic, political, and social institutions but the subjection of Third World nations to colonial rule and imperial domination. In essence Gunder Frank sees underdevelopment as the effect of the penetration of modern capitalism into the archaic economic structures of the Third World. More plainly stated, the economic development of the rich countries contributes to the underdevelopment of African nations. Gunder Frank suggests that, the following economic activities have contributed to underdevelopment, not development of Third World nations: (1) Replacing indigenous enterprises with technologically more advanced, global subsidiary companies; (2) Opening the economy to trade with, and investment from developed countries; (3) Workers migrating from villages to foreign-dominated urban complexes; (4) Recruiting highly educated youths for junior posts in the colonial administrative service; and (5) Forming an unskilled labor force to work in factories and mines and on plantations. He feels that the development of the underdeveloped countries will be stimulated by indiscriminately transferring capital institutions and values from developed countries.

Some policies geared towards reducing dependence in Africa have not had the anticipated result. Dependence has taken new forms in the last quarter of the twentieth century (Nafziger, 1997). Beginning in the mid 1970s, Nigeria took several steps that, on the face of it, should have reduced its dependence on the West. The military government of Nigeria under General Olusegun Obasanjo cut substantially the share of its trade with the colonial power, Britain. Nigeria acquired majority equity holdings in local petroleum extracting, refining, and distribution and promulgated an indigenization decree shifting the majority of ownership in manufacturing from foreign to indigenous hands. But these measures did not greatly reduce dependence on the West.

Kenya, Tanzania, Zaire, Malawi, and Cote d' Ivoire made even less progress than Nigeria in using indigenization requirements to reduce external dependence. Kenya, Tanzania, Zaire, Malawi, and Cote d' Ivoire were probably hurt by excessive economic dependence on the United States and other Western Nations (Nafziger, 1997). But the solution to these problems is not withdrawal from the world capitalist system but rather, a more selective policy in dealing with capitalist nations.

Dependency theory, however, fails to distinguish between regional powers in the Third World, such as Brazil and OPEC countries, Venezuela, Libya, Saudi Arabia, Indonesia and Nigeria, and some more dependent nations, such as Niger, Nepal, Lesotho, Uganda, Haiti and Senegal. Most developed nations i.e., Belgium, Canada, and Switzerland are also dependent on foreign economic ties.

The Neoclassical Approach:

Neoclassical scholars argue that slow or negative growth result from poor resource allocation from non-market prices and excessive African State intervention. They contended that promoting competitive free markets, privatizing public enterprises, supporting exports and free international trade, liberalizing trade and exchange rates, allowing exchange rates to attain a market-clearing rate, removing barriers to foreign investment, rewarding domestic savings, reducing government spending, and monetary expansion, and removing regulations and price distortions in financial, resource, and commodity markets will spur increased efficiency and economic growth (Nafziger 1997).

The governments of United States, Japan, Britain, France, Germany, Canada, Australia and New Zealand, the high income members of the Organization for Economic Cooperation and Development (OECD), are largely supportive of the market, privatization, supply-side economics and other neo-classical positions. According to Wayne Nafziger (1997), neo-classicist dominated policy positions in the World Bank and the International Monetary Fund (IMF), and even had substantial influence in the United Nations Development Program (UNDP) and the regional development banks in Africa, Asia, and Middle East. The World Bank and IMF point to Indonesia, Malaysia, South Korea, Taiwan, Singapore, Hong Kong and Thailand as examples of the free market approach.

The neo-classical economic ideology is what the World Bank and the International Monetary Fund (IMF) adopted as their structural adjustment program (World Bank, 1985). The objective of the structural adjustment programs is to establish a market-friendly set of incentives that can encourage the accumulation of capital and more efficient allocation of resources.

Neo-classical scholars generally favor comprehensive change to liberalization, an immediate solution, rather than a gradual adjustment in price decontrol, market creation, reduction in government spending, monetary restriction, deregulation, legal changes, and privatization. Douglas North (1994) contends that the neoclassical approach is simply an inappropriate tool to analyzing and prescribing policies that will induce development in African nations. Even where privatization is desirable, African nations might want to proceed slowly to avoid a highly concentrated business middlemen being created from newly privatized firms falling into a few hands, as was true in Nigeria and many other African nations during the 1970s. As a result of harsh economic necessity and renewed openness to pragmatic measures, we may be witnessing the emergence of a new era of development in African.

Realist, Idealist and Institutional Approaches:

Realism is a school of thought that explains international relations in terms of power. Hans Morgenthau (1948, 1985) in his book Politics Among Nations, promoted the realist approach. Realists tend to treat political power as a sphere separate from, and predominant over, morality, ideology, and other social and economic aspects of life. For realists ideologies do not matter much, nor do religions or other cultural factors with which states may explain their actions.

The emergence of global interdependence in the 1970s led to a reassessment of the relationship between politics and economics. The differences in the global outlook resulted in diverging the views about the relative importance of economic and political factors in determining the distribution of rewards in the international system. On one hand, the neorealists stress that power has always been distributed unequally, and that the interaction of the most powerful states, each trying to maximize its national interests within the system, determines the general characteristics of international relations at a particular time. Stephen Krasner (1985) contends that neorealists acknowledge the increasing importance of interdependence and economic questions in world politics, but argue that each state's policies in all areas continue to be determined by a desire to maximize its relative power.

On the other hand, the idealists think that human nature is basically good and that with good habits, education, and appropriate international structures, human nature can become the basis of peaceful and cooperative international relationship. Idealists see the international system as one based on a community of states that have the potential to work together to overcome mutual problems, just as neighbors in a small town might do (Goldstein, 1994). The liberal approach is the third way of explaining the relationship between economics and politics.

The liberal institutionalized approach stresses the need for states to coordinate their policies if they wish to truly maximize their national interests in an international system that is becoming increasingly interdependent. Institutionalists now contend that there are a variety of international regimes. These are cooperative arrangements which involve principles, norms, rules, and decision-making procedures for collective action in regard to particular issue areas such as the foreign mails, telephone calls, oceans and monetary affairs. Some of these issues may be fully institutionalized and some may be more of mutual agreements between states. Thus, interdependence compel states to work together to promote their individual interests more efficiently.

CONCLUSION

Sub-Sahara African politics can be analyzed usefully with the substance of colonial legacy. This first chapter presents a discussion of concepts and issues affecting the entire African political system and its people. Nationalism, conflict, ideology and fundamentalism, technology, interdependence, integration, poverty, development, the world economy, ethnicity, human rights and cooperative global politics were all addressed. Despite the theoretical compatibility between political sovereignty and economic autarky, no contemporary African nation is economically self-sufficient. All are in some measure dependent on outside sources for some share of their economic goods, or they require external markets to sell their products. In some cases colonialism made several African nations to be over dependent on European capitalism.

Despite the differences between dependency, neoclassical theorists, realists, idealists and institutionalist approaches to the study of economic development, they have modified their original positions, resulting in something of a convergence. Since all people today have economic goals, the differences in physical, political, and economic circumstances lead to different and often conflicting economic policies by governments. What most distinguishes Western industrialized nations and their government is not their culture, nor their natural endowments, nor the availability of capital, or rationality of public policies, but precisely the capacities of their institutions and the skills of individuals, including those of management. Together these reflect their differential capacities to utilize resources, capitalize on opportunities, and adjust to changes. It is therefore critical to the future of Third World nations that substantial energies and resources be dedicated to and invested in the enhancement of the human resources and institutional capacities that determine the ability of societies to achieve and sustain economic development. The main focus of convergence is the increased role of the state in directing and promoting economic as well as political development in a legitimate manner.

Military governance is not compatible with ruling African nations as well as promoting economic development. Evidence of military regimes show that they are not better in governing than the civilian party governments they ousted. Military regimes are often based on fear of populism, left-wing subversion, rampant inflation, corruption, and disorder. They also disintegrate when they encounter the hard choices and inevitable failures of governing. As the military regimes in African nations confront policy failures, growing hostility from the civilian sector, and expanding internal problems concerning how they would reward and promote officers for the military and political activities, they often face pressure from within the military to withdraw from the direct control of government.

In spite of the many plans that the colonial powers had for civilizing and modernizing African nations, none of them seem to have included modernization. Indeed, in light of our discussion of colonial practice, it would have been a contradiction in terms if Europeans in Africa had actively pursued industrialization. Raw materials like coffee, cotton, and cocoa were badly needed for processing in the factories of Europe. This pattern of Africa producing raw materials to be processed in Europe, and then of re-exporting finished products to African nations at prices that they could ill afford, has continued to characterize a substantial portion of economic relations between Africa nations and Europe to this very day. However, when it became clear following the end of the World War II that colonial rule might be nearing its end, colonial powers began to think of ways to revitalize the economies of the colonies. Ali Mazrui (1986 & 1996) and Vincent Khapoya (1994) argued that this limited economic development was undertaken in order to persuade newly emerging leaders that colonialization had benefited Africa nations, and somehow to allow an amicable departure from Africa that would preserve colonial interests.

As we deal with the problems of African politics, we should not forget that we are engaged in something that matters in the here and now, as well as in the awful scales of truth. We should be logical, scientific, rigorous, objective, and honest, but we should never forget that we are a part of the global political system.

REFERENCES

Adams, Ian. 1993. Political Ideology Today. Manchester: Manchester University press, pp.82-83.

Aguda, O. 1973. "Arabism and Pan-Arabism in Sudanese Politics," The Journal of Modern African Studies, Vol. II, No. 2, 1973, p. 199.

Amin, S. 1976. Unequal Development. New York: Monthly Review Press.

Andre, Gunder, Frank. 1969. Latin America: Underdevelopment or Revolution? New York: Monthly Review Press.

Apter, David. 1965. The Politics of Modernization. Chicago: University of Chicago Press.

Bach, Daniel. 1999. (ed.). Regionalization in Africa: Integration and Disintegration. Bloomington, IN: Indiana University Press.

Berkeley, Bill. 2000. "A Good Time for Candor about Africa's Leaders." The New

York Times, January 17, p. A16.

Bernstein, H. (ed). 1973. Underdevelopment and Development. Boltimore:Penguin Press.

Chilcote, R.H. and Johnson D. L. (ed). 1983. Theories of Development: Mode of Production or Dependency? Beverly Hills: Sage Publications.

Dos Santos, T. 1970. "The Structure of Dependence". American Economic Review #60, pp. 231-6.

Esman, Milton. 1991. Management Dimensions of Development. West Hartford: Kumarian Press.

French, Howard. 1996. "Military Ruler in Gambia Defeats Rivals in Election." The New York Times, September 28, p. 7.

______1995. "Nigerians Lament Locust, that Pick Nation Bare." The New York Times, October 12, p. A4.

Furtado, Celso. 1970. Economic Development of Latin America: A Survey from Colonial Times to the Cuban Revolution. Cambridge University Press.

Gellner, Ernest. 1983. Nations and Nationalism. London: Oxford University Press

Goldstein, Joshua. 1994. International Relations. Harper Collins College Publishers, pp. 392-93.

Goodard, Jan. 1999. "Sierra Leone is No Place to Be Young." New York Times Magazine, February 14, Section 6, p. 48.

Haas, Ernest. 1970. International Organization Vol. 24, #4. Berkeley: University of California.

Haas, Ernst. 1964. Beyond the Nation-State: Functionalist and International Organization. Stanford: Stanford University Press.

Kautsky, John. 1968. "Nationalism" in Kebschill Harvey (ed), "Politics in Transitional Societies: The Challenge in Asia, Africa and Latin America. New York: Appleton-Century-Crafts, pp.112-113.

Khapoya, Vincent. 1994. The African Experience: An Introduction. Englewood Cliffs, N.J.: Prentice Hall.

Kodourie, Elie. 1971. Nationalism. London: Longman.

Kohn, Hans. 1929. A History of Nationalism in the East. London: Longman.

Krasner, Stephen. 1985. Structural Conflict: The Third World Against Global Liberalism. Berkeley: University of California Press.

Macridis, Roy. 1992. Contemporary Political Ideology Movements and Regimes. New York: Harper Collin Publishers, p. 191.

Mazrui, Ali. 1986. The Africans: A Triple Heritage. Boston: Little Brown and Company.

Mitrany, David. 1975. The Functional Theory of Politics. London: The London School of Economics Press.

Mitrany, David. 1966. A Working Peace System. Chicago: Quadrangle Books.

Morgenthaus, Hans and Kenneth Thompson. 1985. Politics Among Nations: The Struggle for Power and Peace 6th ed. New York: Knopf.

Nafziger, Wayne. 1997. The Economics of Developing Countries. Upper Saddle River: Prentice Hall Press.

New African, July/August. 1996, p. 24.

Norbu, Dawa. 1992. Culture and the Politics of Third World Nationalism. London: Routledge Press, p. 29.

North, Douglass. 1994. "Economic Performance Through Time". American Economic Review #84, (June Issue), pp. 359-68.

Nye, Joseph. 1975. "International Interdependence and Integration" in Fred Greenstein and Nelson Polsby (ed). Handbook of Political Science, Vol. 8. Addison Wesley Publishing Company, pp. 363-414.

Pye, L. 1966. Aspects of Political Development. Boston: Little Brown and Company.

Onishi, Norimitsu. 1999. “Anger Still Fires the Hell that was Sierra Leone.” The New York Times, March 31, p. 3.

The New York Times. July 26, 1998, p. 1.

Renan, Ernest. 1929. "What is a Nation? in Hans Kohn (ed), Nationalism: Its Meaning and History. London: Longman.

Rostow, Walt. 1970. The Stages of Economic Growth. Cambridge: Cambridge University Press.

Snarr Micheal, and Neil Snarr. 1998. (ed.) Introducing Global Issues. Boulder, CO: Lynne Rienne.

Soyinka, Wole. 1993. "The Babangida Watch." The New York Times, July 1, p. A19.

Tordoff, Williams. 1997. Government and Politics in Africa. 3rd ed. Bloomington, IN: Indiana University Press.

Udogu, Ike. 1999. "The Issues of Ethnicity and Democracy in Africa: Toward the Millennium." Journal of Black Studies. Vol. 29, (6), 790-808.

Wiseman, John. "Malawi: The Contended Legacy of the Ngwazi." Round Table, April 13, P.1.

Chapter 2

Indigenous and Foreign Influence on Sub-Sahara African Politics

Leonard Kodzo Gadzekpo

INTRODUCTION

Africa south of the Sahara gained political independence from Europe partitioned and retaining the various artificial boundaries and groups of peoples, nations that grew out of European colonial machination. What then is the political character of these nations? How did that character develop? Answers to these two questions may be used as the foundation for a discussion of Africa's political condition at the dawn of the Twenty-first Century. The political culture of the various nations as well as their economic, social, and cultural developments and international factors and influences that inform them are all integral parts of the African political condition. Questions arise as to the nature of political systems employed in the governance of African nations, especially the presence of a democratic process or lack of it. Why has democracy not been sustained in Africa South of the Sahara? What part does the military play in sustenance or instability and disruption of democratic processes? How does ethnic diversity in each nation factor into democratic practices? Are social and cultural conditions responsible for success or failure of a democratic system in sub-Sahara African nations? What are the internal and external economic and political pressures that drive and uphold democracy in Africa? These questions do not only bring into focus sub-Sahara African political conditions but also point to future developments in fifty-three independent states, territories, island states, and dependent island groups, all of which, except for Ethiopia and Liberia, saw their birth and growth in the last half of the Twentieth Century.

Africa South of the Sahara and sub-Sahara Africa are interchangeable terms used to designate all nations that are geographically located partly in the Sahara Desert and south of it. They are also sometimes designated Black Africa.

INDIGENOUS AFRICAN POLITICAL SYSTEMS

The search for African political heritage and its philosophical base is a complex undertaking in that one would have to look back at indigenous African political systems, which were numerous, and as diverse as the ethnic groups. It also implies a thorough examination of evidence found in cultural forms and products that include oral traditions, art, especially royal art, linguistic patterns, and archeology as well as the travel narratives of foreigners in Africa. The evidence may be used to distill a concrete understanding of the political systems prior to the ascent of Arabo-Islamic and European influences and control. Scholars have presented systems that were diverse but also had many underlying commonalties (Khapoya, 1998, Isichei, 1997, Iliffe, 1995, Curtin et al. 1994; Ayittey 1991). The organizational structure of each system was designed with community having an overriding importance. For that matter, the objective of the indigenous system was preservation, protection, and sustenance of community and all the systems "were generally based upon kinship, ancestry and survival in much the same way as social organizations were"(Ayittey 1991). Each ethnic group, however, had its peculiar system, which was indicative of the pluralistic character of the African indigenous political landscape. Modes of food production, artistic expression, lineage and inheritance patterns, and socio-religious practices reinforced each system (Herskovits 1967). While there were two general political systems, states and "stateless" societies, each type had many variations ranging from small chiefdoms to huge empires (Ayittey 1991). Within these two general systems existed three kinds of authority patterns which were segmental, hierarchical, and pyramidal. A segmental system was decentralized and mostly found in "stateless" societies in which power was defused and shared. A hierarchical system was highly centralized and controlled by a very powerful king supported by an efficient bureaucracy and/or a military; while a pyramidal system was a conglomeration of different levels of segmental groupings which were not completely autonomous (Khapoya 1998). George P. Murdock writes: It is almost as though all of Africa south of the Sahara were permeated, as it were, by a mental blueprint of a despotic political structure (Murdock 1959). The statement is erroneous and its arrogance lies in the fact that it uses one broadstroke to paint a wide spectrum of complex political systems that have networks of checks and balances from the lowest level of power to the apex. Indeed, just like in all political systems, European included, there were rulers who abused power and were despotic, but each African society had a democratic process as expressed by the Ewe of West Africa when they say: Three heads are better than one. A proverb from the Sotho of South Africa goes: A chief is a chief by the people; a people are a people through their chief. Jomo Kenyatta writes of the Gikuyu of East Africa:

> "In the eyes of the Gikuyu, the submission to a despotic rule of any particular man or group, white or black, is the greatest humiliation to mankind. The spirit of "itwika", namely, the changing of government in rotation through peaceful and constitutional revolution, is still engrained the minds of the Gikuyu people" (Kenyatta 1938).

Reaching a consensus after opposing viewpoints were expressed discussed, and decisions made in each African society. The structuring of the decision-making process may vary from group to group. There was, however, a general consensus at the core of governance. The arrival at first of islamizing forces and then European colonizers were to bring drastic and traumatic changes that would reshape the African political landscape.

ISLAMIC INFLUENCE

Islam etched its mark on the political system of societies that were overrun by the islamizing forces that swooped south across the Sahara forcing them initially to use Islamic tenets. These tenets were with the passage of time africanized. Islamic political structure found in the Mali Empire and later in Songhai and Kanem kingdoms of West Africa was hierarchical with the emperor, emir or caliph at the apex (Curtin et al. 1994). The overlapping of the Islamic paternal inheritance system over mostly indigenous maternal ones would be the source of internal conflict over succession to office. Civil wars fought over succession were indicative of the political disruption, adjustments or shifts that had to be made when a foreign political system met an indigenous well-entrenched one. Such a shift made it possible for Mali to last well into the nineteenth century (Curtin et al. 1994), only to be overrun by French colonialism. British colonial control in the Sudan disrupted complete Islamic control in the Sudan and its political influence in East Africa, until Sudan gained independence in 1956.

EUROPEAN COLONIAL SYSTEMS

The arrival of the European in Africa as a political force was heralded by a tremendous show of military power, use of violence and coercion, that changed the African political landscape on a broader and more pervasive scale than the Arabo-islamic intrusion and imposition of political course. Africa was partitioned among the British, the French, the Germans, the Belgians, and the Portuguese at the Berlin Conference of 1884 - 85 attended by fourteen European nations, and then followed by a scramble for African colonies and military occupation by European colonial armies (Iliffe 1995). The very nature of the institution of colonial rule meant the democratic systems practiced in the colonizing nations were not carried over to the colonies. A despotic hierarchical system that had a governor appointed from a colonizing nation served by an army of bureaucrats and buttressed with awesome military force was imposed upon the colonized who did not have a say in political or other matters in their land. Democratic processes did not exist in the colonies.

The French, Portuguese, and the Germans administrated their colonies using a highly centralized system called "direct rule." The French African colonies were federalized, not politically but structurally, into French West Africa and Equatorial Africa consisting of twelve territories. Each federation, French West Africa made up of eight territories and Equatorial Africa four, was administered by a governor-general and each territory had a territorial assembly under the control of a governor (Khapoya 1998). The territorial assemblies were only nominal in that their decisions were frequently over-ruled by governors and governor-generals. The overriding control came directly from Paris completely detached from the colonized nations in Africa. The extent of control from the metropolis was manifested in blatant coercive colonial state behavior such as military conscription and compulsory labor (Conteh-Morgan 1997).

The Portuguese had a harsher and stricter centralized administration than the French. They considered the colonies "Overseas Portugal." Antonio de Oliveira Salazar, the Portuguese dictator from 1932 to 1968, declared Portugal and her colonies constituted "one state, one territory, one people, one citizenship, and one government" (Khapoya 1998). There was no room left for the colonized to undertake any political activity, let alone aspire towards a democratic system. Whatever traditional system existed was violently stamped out.

German rule in Africa was brief ending with the defeat of Germany in World War I. The German system was also highly centralized. German governors were assisted by African appointed subordinates and officers. Traditional rulers were completely disregarded and German military officers and private entrepreneurs, who were given power and responsibility by the German Chancellery in Berlin, quickly and violently, suppressed any resistance. The "Maji Maji Rebellion" (1905 - 1908) in Tanganyika was ruthlessly crushed costing approximately 120,000 Africans their lives (Khapoya 1998).

The Belgians operated the most brutal colonial system in Africa: company rule. King Leopold II of Belgium made Congo Free State his personal property. It was in no way free and Belgium businessmen were allowed to exploit its natural resources using forced labor. The colonized were virtually slaves enduring the most severe deprivations and were mutilated or killed if they resisted. A coalition of Belgian businessmen, administrators, and the clergy of the Catholic Church (Khapoya 1998) controlled the administrative system. Africans had no rights whatsoever under such a system.

In Southern African, another version of company rule was employed under the leadership of Cecil Rhodes: indirect company rule. After using trickery to acquire mining rights from traditional rulers, Rhodes set up the British South African Company, got a royal charter that gave him the right to administer the land he got mining rights for, and then made them British colonies. European settlers streamed into the region taking up the land and met African resistance. The rebellions that ensued were brutally crushed using a

European mercenary army and the British colonial army. Rhodes used through the British South African Company the "indirect rule" employed by the British elsewhere in Africa (Khapoya 1998).

The British administered their colonies through "indirect rule." Lord Lugard developed the system in his dealing with Hausaland in northern Nigeria and was adopted throughout British colonies in Africa. The colonial administration identified the local power structure, especially the chiefs and elders, and incorporated them into the colonial power hierarchy. The chiefs were at the bottom of the hierarchy and passed on demands, such as taxes and forced conscription for the colonial army or labor, down to the citizens. Where there were no chiefs, "warrant chiefs" (Khapoya 1998) were appointed to be the links between the colonial administration and the colonized. The colonial army and police force were always at hand to enforce demands and decrees should the chiefs and elders refuse to carry out the demands. Pan-ethnic activities that opposed colonial policies were thus hindered or put under severe constraint.

Three conditions can be identified in the discussion of European colonialism in the context of democracy in Africa. The first was the destruction of whatever democratic processes existed in African societies. A look at the colonial administrative systems mentioned above clearly indicates that Africans were not allowed to practice any form of political system that drew from the indigenous or colonizer's democratic systems. Where indigenous rulers were used as subordinates in colonial administration, they were either appointed or under such pressure that whatever democratic mandate they had from their people was undermined. The second was the social fabric of the colonized communities was stretched to the limit and in most cases they snapped causing friction and sometimes-outright decay. Traditional rulers no longer embodied the vitality of the indigenous political system since they had to take orders from despised despotic foreigners who inflicted injustices on the people. The breakdown in the social fabric was also linked to economic changes that were ushered in by the colonial system. The loss of livelihood, taxation, forced labor or starvation wages hastened the social condition. The third was the introduction of mercenary colonial armies made up of mostly Africans under the command of European officers. The soldiers were sometimes forcibly conscripted or enticed by wages, given the destruction of indigenous financial opportunities. These soldiers were then used to oppress other Africans, thus generating distrust and hatred among peoples who before the arrival of the European had co-existed, to a great extent, peacefully. In any given colony, mercenary soldiers from the south would be used in battles against the north, those from the north in the south, or westerners used in the suppression of resistance in the east, or vice-versa. It was divide, conquer, and rule using one group against the other. The relationship between African soldiers and the citizenry as the struggle for independence ensued would be tenuous and continues to be a problem for Africa's democratic project.

DEMOCRACY AT INDEPENDENCE

The struggle for independence in Africa was predicated on the realization by the colonized that within a given colony the oppression they suffered, regardless of their ethnicity, could only end when pan-ethnic efforts were consolidated into one voice that demanded an end to European colonialism. Areas that would become modern African nations came into being not through the usual development found in the formation of nation-states in Europe, but through the development of nationalistic demands within borders that were artificially imposed upon various kingdoms and peoples in total disregard of the political, cultural, and socio-economic conditions that existed before the arrival of the European colonialists. If the indigenous traditional political systems were destroyed or disrupted, it meant new systems had to be put in place for the modern nation to be viable. The traditional ruler was no longer capable of giving far-reaching direction in the political sphere as he was part of the colonial system in the British "indirect rule," eliminated in the French, Portuguese, and German "direct rule," and in the Belgian "company rule" silenced and discarded. Political activity among the colonized, therefore, found expression in new institutions that had their genesis in the political and socio-economic developments and conditions caused by colonialism. Early forms of nationalism were manifested by religious associations as Christianity became africanized. Christian nationalists broke away from European-dominated churches as they considered Christian missionaries to be the first wave of the colonial armies (Tordoff 1997). Christian nationalists saw them and their churches as Trojan horses. At grass-root level in rapidly expanding urban areas, the basic need to associate with others from the same ethnic group or region far away from home led to the formation of the social clubs. In Nigeria, for example, some of the social clubs developed into politically conscious groups that would be part of the vanguard in the independence struggle. Another institution was the trade unions, which became politically active, although colonial authorities prohibited their political involvement in all the colonies. In the rural areas across Africa, those who were displaced by land-hungry European settlers, especially in East Africa, would organize into militant groups to fight for the return of their land. This agitation became violent as the settlers and the colonial authorities resorted to the use of brutal military force. With the flight of settlers, the struggle was expanded to a demand for independence. The "Mau Mau" Movement in Kenya exemplified such a development (Shillington 1995). On national and international levels, a new breed, the African elite who was educated in Africa, especially in Christian mission schools, and in universities in Europe and America gave voice to nationalistic fervor. The education that was to prepare them for careers in the colonial system and make them accept western culture, was the very one that exposed them to racism and the discrepancy between what was being taught to them and how they were treated. They also saw the political systems and practices in the colonizing countries and were aware of the tyranny of the colonial system at home. The educated African elite introduced the western democratic political system into Africa.

If European colonizers operated a despotic system that had the main goal of exploiting Africans, I argue that such a system could not have prepared Africans for modern democratic processes that operated in the colonizers' home countries. The only group of people who had any knowledge of such a system and had genuine interest of Africans at heart would be the educated elite. The term decolonization has often been used in the context of Africa's struggle and attainment of political independence. The colonizers did not decide on their own accord to end colonization but were forced to leave. They were not only armies of occupation but also economic exploiters, cultural chauvinists, usurpers of power, and disrupters of political growth in Africa. That is why the use of the term decolonization should be pointed out as denying Africans of the historic agency in their consciousness, political activism, and rejuvenation and reorganization of political life, given the severe oppressive conditions under which the political phenomenon, the attainment of independence, occurred. Africans made their own political boots and then bootstrapped them.

Formation of political parties was indicative of various political positions among the colonized, even though the universal-unifying goal was independence. The parties generated pressure that forced colonial administrations to inch reluctantly towards granting independence. They were the main vehicles of political activity in the independence struggle and responsible for introduction of modern democratic processes into the colonies at the national level. The African middle-class and educated elite founded the parties. As early as 1897, when a British colonial army occupied the area now called Ghana, then the Gold Coast, the Aborigines' Rights Protection Society was founded to safeguard African rights to land (Tordoff 1997). After World War II, the educated elite, lawyers, other professionals, and merchants mainly living in urban areas, led in the formation of political parties across Africa. These parties initially had minimal followers among the grassroots people. Further, through activism they brought under their umbrella trade and co-operative unions and farmers' organizations. It is interesting to note that despite an atmosphere of deteriorating conditions and the brutal colonial oppression, they gathered more followers and swelled into expressions of mass movement. This achievement on their part spelled the doom of colonialism. Protest marches, strikes, and mass insurrections were the tools used by the parties to force the colonial administrations to the negotiation table. Constitutional committees were established to draft constitutions that would be used for the would-be politically independent democratic nations. Internal constitutional democratic practices of the parties represented the first signs of the process that would be replicated at national levels across Africa at independence. Ghana was the first African nation south of the Sahara to gain independence in 1957 after a democratic election in 1956. South Africa was the last nation in the same region to gain its independence in 1994 from an internal colonial system that replaced British colonial rule after a democratic election was held in the same year. The constitutions of African nations at independence guaranteed multi-party democracy and were the foundation of elected legislatures and the heads-of-state. In thirty-seven years, the euphoria of independence and democratic aspirations of the large majorities of African countries have been replaced by repressive governments and disappointments. As democratically elected government became more centralized and autocratic; some gave up multi-party democracy; and others were overrun by the military with dictators at the apex of the hierarchy.

At independence, every African nation had a democratic system in place within a unitary or federal framework. Most elected leaders after coming to power turned their country into one party states through constitutional amendments, became autocratic, and used the police and armed forces to suppress resistance. While a semblance of the democratic process may be practiced within even the single parties, the heads-of state and the autocratic political machinery they ran made it impossible for such a process to be of any meaning to the countries as a whole. Ghana's example may be used as a model of what happened in most African countries. Kwame Nkrumah, the president, appropriated power, had the constitution amended to have a one-party system with him as the party leader, president, and supreme commander of the armed forces. He became autocratic, a dictator. He was overthrown in a military coup d'etat. The military dictatorship that was established was overthrown and replaced by another, and then by others thrice with two elected governments in between. Finally in 1993, a former military dictator, Jerry Rawlings, who overthrew a military government and democratically elected government, was elected president. Nigeria, a federation, had a similar development, including a civil war fought between 1966 and 1969 after the first democratically elected government was overthrown in a military take-over. Military dictators, an elected government, and then another set of military dictators followed. In 1999, a former military dictator, Olusengun Obasanjo, was elected president. Military dictators in Africa, like the colonizers before them, are usurpers of political power and use brutal oppression to hold on to it. An examination of the pendulum-swing of African nations between democracy and military dictatorship points to an inherited colonial military cadre that has no tradition of serving under an elected government coupled with the unresolved ethnic diversity problems, all of which are heightened by socio-economic devastation that followed independence and continues to plague Africa. The vacillation is not only a result of the internal search for political stability but also reflective of the external pressures and interference.

POST-INDEPENDENCE POLITICAL DILEMMA

While one may claim the colonial legacy is to a great extent responsible for the political condition of African nations south of the Sahara, it is not enough explanation for political developments in post-independence Africa. If after independence the former colonial nations still influenced political life in Africa, Africans themselves were also agents of change and stability or instability. The character of institutions within each given country sheds light on how political stability was maintained or disrupted. Constitutions of all African nations, except for Botswana, are based on European or American models, and, therefore, were not drawn from the traditional democratic pluralistic norms, especially the checks-and-balances, that were required by the socio-cultural realities of the peoples of Africa. Some countries choose socialism, which is also foreign, and modeled their constitutions accordingly. It means political institutions that grew out of the constitutions, or were maintained by them, would be transparently superimposed on traditional ones. The dualism and discrepancies that arose would be the first signs of the African political condition.

Group leadership, be it ethnic, tribal, or clan group leadership, as a political institution did not lose its importance among Africans even though they accepted Western the governmental system in modern African nations. In fact, traditional group leadership is nationalistic in nature because before the coming of the European some of the groups were sovereign nations or kingdoms. The term "tribe," in general use by several scholars, does not recognize the kingdoms and the nation-state character of the pre-colonial African societies, which indeed had tribes, but as smaller components of far larger ethnic groups and kingdoms. Basil Davidson explains that African nations and kingdoms came to be called tribes because the British and other Europeans preferred to think of pre-colonial Africa as a kind of savage backwoods instead of nations as was the case of a Scottish nation or a Welsh nation, although that notion had long become an antiquarian absurdity to average English opinion (Davidson 1992). The African being a citizen of two nations, one modern, and the other ancient with entrenched traditions, meant the African would have to negotiate constantly his participation in the political lives of both nations, the modern more powerful and visible in all spheres of public political action, the traditional subordinated but prevalent and directing the very essence of each individual and community within the modern n one.

The dualism that Africans had to negotiate would be at the core of personal and societal conflicts as to how to live in a society that was in a flux at all levels. W.E.B. DuBois analysis of the African-American personality and the conflict that may be within that personality, the "twoness" or "double-consciousness, the sense of always looking past one's self through the eyes of others, of measuring one's soul by the tape of a world that looks on in amused contempt and pity," is applicable to the African (DuBois 1990). Nkrumah presented to independent African nations consciencism, an ideological framework within which to fully synthesize their "triple heritage" (Mazrui 1986), aware that failure to do so, the new societies would be racked by "the most malignant schizophrenia" as a result of colonialism (Nkrumah 1964). He writes:

> "The philosophy that must stand behind this social revolution is that which I have once referred to as philosophical consciencism; consciencism is the map in intellectual terms of the disposition of forces which will enable African society to digest the Western and Islamic and the Euro-Christian elements in Africa, and develop them in such a way that they fit into the African personality. The African personality is itself defined by the cluster of humanist principles which underlie the traditional African society. Philosophical consciencism is that philosophical standpoint which, taking its start from the present content of the African conscience, indicates the way in which progress is forged out of the conflict in that conscience" (Nkrumah 1964).

"African Personality" was an essential element in nationalism at independence of all African nations, however, political expediency and desire to hold onto power would drive some African rulers to play on ethnic sentiments in order to garner support for policies and programs leading to what is termed "tribalism" (Mamdani 1996). Threats of subordination and oppression by particular ethnic groups were sometimes used to awaken allegiance to political leaders. In some cases, traditional rulers of ethnic groups or subgroups and tribes were called upon to drum-up old ethnic nationalism, the result being the fracturing of the delicate balance within artificially constructed countries. Civil wars in Nigeria in the 1960s and in Rwanda in the 1990s did not have their origins in ethnic conflicts, but "ethnicity became above all a vehicle of expression for 'a brutal political struggle, in which ethnicity was manipulated by a small clique who sought to avoid losing control of state' " (Tordoff 1997). In post-independence Africa, political leadership at modern universal national and traditional or regional levels was skewed to undermine democratic processes. Ironically, the very people, i.e., the educated elite and the traditional ethnic ruling elite, who should have maintained the pan-ethnic nationalism that won independence are those who now undermine the processes. Thus, these educated Africans continue to disrupt the normal direction of governance that has resulted in instability and the concomitant national internal conflict.

The rise of "tribalism" has its roots not only in faulty democratic processes but also in colonial legacy, inefficient or failed economic policies, and internal national social dysfunction. That ethnic groups were forced to exist within borders not of their own choosing attests to the legacy of colonialism. The formation of political parties, elections, and majority rule which were essential for Western democracy became the genesis of "tribalism," because political representation, power-sharing, as well economic and social equity were perceived to benefit a particular group or groups to the detriment of others. The affected groups may be minorities in a given country, although majority groups without the majority political power also have such perceptions. For example, the white minority formerly ruled South Africa, which has a large black majority.

Political power won through elections, the one-man-one-vote democratic elections, generates winner-take-all majority rule. Whichever model was adopted in Africa, Westminster or American or any other Western model, majority rule and minority rights had to be balanced to assure equity in all spheres of national life. George Ayittey's (1992) argument concerning the American model is germane and applicable in the discussion of how majority rule operates in Africa and the resultant disregard of minority rights that has been the cause of internal political mistrust and instability. Ayittey argues that "because they do not necessarily recognize the salience or intensity of minority interests, winner-take-all majoritarian systems do not give minority groups a reason to support the ultimate bargain or to believe the outcome is public-regarding or legitimate" (Ayittey 1992). She also points to marginalization that includes "techniques used to dilute or nullify the effects of votes cast by minorities or their representatives. Marginalization focuses on discrimination in the distribution of procedural resources such as votes, not on the specific outcomes of public policy debates such as the unfair or unequal distribution of resources, including jobs and promotions" (Ayittey 1992).

Across Africa, in parliaments and other forms of legislatures, such marginalization follows the path to the demise of democratic practices in the given legislature. I argue that if modern African nations came into being as a result of the rejection of colonial rule within artificially constructed borders, the pan-ethnic unity that forced the colonizer to leave can only be sustained if each group shares in political power in the legislature and has reasonable amount of equity in decision-making at the executive level. Ethnic trends or political formations are often presented as shortcomings, even pathological manifestations, in African politics. If political parties tend to follow ethnic lines, it is because each desires to protect group rights and demand equity. According to Donald Rothchild, "collective demands for political, economic and social equity must be viewed as natural and indispensable part of the political process, not as evidence of a malfunction or a negative attitude" (Rothchild and Olorunsola 1983). It means the democratic majoritarian system in each African nation has to be fine-tuned to be equitable, efficient, and be perceived as fair. It is especially important for the minority ethnic groups, to understand the need of sharing political powers that result from the discrepancies that arise out of the superimposition of a modern national universal political system over a traditional ethnic or regional one.

The failure of imported Western democratic processes that were not retooled to deal with the peculiarity of the African experience, the colonial legacy included, seems to give credence to those, especially declared socialist African heads of state, who claim Socialism would be the most appropriate system for Africa. Clearly, however, the single party socialist system would still have to deal with the same overlapping of the modern and traditional ethnic systems. The examples of Zambia, Tanzania, and Ghana indicate whatever tag was given to the socialist system, it tended to be a one-party system that was centralized, hierarchical, autocratic, and drew from charismatic leadership its initial appeal to the populace which faded in the face of repression and economic depression. Kaunda in Zambia, Nyerere in Tanzania, and Nkrumah in Ghana were charismatic leaders who created followership based on personal loyalty and acceptance of the ideology they espoused (Chazan 1979). The socialist experiments in Africa were nominal, in reality, a patchwork of socialist, populist, humanist, and even capitalist strands. In the case of Tanzania, "collectivization produced agricultural decline, peasant disaffection, and withdrawal into household self-sufficiency" and economic decline (Ramsay, 1999). Economic failure of socialist projects was not particularly different from those of Western-styled examples in Africa. The severe repressive character of such projects, however, stifled economic growth that was deepened by the external rejection and denial of economic support by the West. Support received from socialist and/or communist countries was marginal and did not alleviate the economic woes as these countries' economies were tied to those of industrial nations of the West. External support or pressures, therefore, play a major role in the success or failure of such experiments. The Western-styled political systems also fall under external pressures and, in some cases, direct intervention.

EXTERNAL FACTOR

Political independence in Africa was not accompanied by economic independence. One main feature of colonialism was the economic exploitation of Africa that led to underdevelopment of the colonies and economic dependence on former colonial powers after independence. Production of cash crops and its attendant monoculture promoted the exportation of raw materials to industrialized countries as against production of finished goods. The production processes continued to facilitate the dependence of African economic fortunes on the price fluctuations of their exports controlled by the industrialized countries. It is important to contend here that this production dynamics which seem to favor the western industrial nations and encourage Africa's economic dependence was fully developed during the colonial period. The legacy of European imperialism is closely linked with and etched into the close economic relations between the European Economic Community and Africa. The Yaounde and Lome Conventions that offered EEC-based transnational companies preferential treatment exemplified the relationship. These conventions also echoed the preferential access and tariffs given to companies from the metropole during the colonial period (Chazan 1979). The Soviet Union, its satellites, and America as well as China and Japan did not have a colonial past in Africa but also developed economic relations that were not based on equal economic benefits to Africa. The result is Africa's returns for exports, the sale of raw materials to the industrialized countries in the West and East, but more to West because of the larger volume of trade, are significantly small to defray ever-increasing cost of imports, manufactured goods and debt servicing; thus making African nations ever more indebted to these countries and international financial institutions, including the International Monetary Funds and the World Bank. By the 1990s, sub-Saharan Africa's foreign debt was 112 percent of GDP and almost all the countries in this region were spending at least over 50 up to 80 percent of their export earnings to service debt (Chazan et al. 1992). Africa's debt crisis has serious repercussion in all spheres. The inability of African governments to run independent economic systems and uphold the economic viability of their nations make them vulnerable to external pressures that undermine political independence. Economic depression that impeded development and the lack of private indigenous entrepreneurship, often destroyed by unfair competition from multinationals and restricted by insufficient support from the governments because of the conditions they agreed to in order to receive loans, undermine the sound economic foundation necessary for sustenance of democracy. If governments are unable to provide basic economic and social infrastructure, the political foundation of governance would be eroded and instability would set in. Sustaining democratic practices demand financial investment in elections, maintaining a virile legislature, and running an efficient bureaucracy that keeps institutions of governance well-oiled and operational. The deteriorated state of African economies means the citizenry would be deprived of proper socio-economic infrastructure and public institutions would not deliver the required services that are essential for democracy. Political instability, social unrest, and further deepening of the economic condition are often the result. A critical institution because it welds the most destructive force within any given country, the military, reacts to the instability in African countries by resorting to unconstitutional use of armed force to overthrow democratically elected governments putting the nations under military dictatorships. In most cases, by the time the elected governments are overthrown, they have become autocratic and repressive by maintaining a semblance of control through deployment of the very armed forces that later overthrow them.

MILITARY RULE

The modern military in all Africa has its origin in the colonial armies that conquered and buttressed colonialism. Since colonial armies were built to enforce European imperialist control over Africa, the African who was forcibly conscripted or enticed by monetary gain to join may be considered a mercenary because colonial armies did not serve the needs of Africans and were answerable to only European governments or private colonial entrepreneurs such as Cecil Rhodes. By the time of independence, former colonial armies which were filled with Africans under European officers, became the national armies with the replacement of European officers by a cadre of promoted rank and file Africans to commanding officers who were answerable to the newly elected leadership.

For example, Jean-Bedel Bokassa in the Central African Republic, Idi Dada Amin in Uganda and Etienne Gnassingbe Eyadema of Togo were non-commissioned officers, who at independence became commanding officers and later generals when they led coup d'etats and took over the reigns of government and promoted themselves to higher ranks. The transfer of the military as an institution from the European colonizer to the independent African leadership created the weakest point in African nation-building. The Angolan Civil War that has been going on for over three decades has its roots in that transfer. Togo experienced political turmoil in 1963, three years after its independence, when Togolese soldiers demobilized from the French colonial armies facing unemployment overthrew the democratically elected government under Sylvanus Olympio, who they assassinated. Patriotism and nationalistic motivations have been given as reasons for take-overs by military juntas, but the historical record and performance of the military governments across sub-Saharan Africa points to personal ambition and the corporate army considerations (Decalo 1990). I argue that if during the colonial period mercenary African soldiers were used to usurp power from traditional rulers, after independence, if the armies were properly demobilized and the soldiers retrained to fit the needs of democracy, they would still be operating in the colonial mercenary mode. In face of political instability, economic crisis, and/or social unrest, the power vacuum that may be created invites the attention and intervention of the army; an army often already deployed to control and suppress the turmoil.

The military in independent Africa has its umbilical cord still attached to European armies. African military officers still receive their training in staff colleges at Sanhurst in UK, Mons and St Cyr in France and others in Europe and America. Despite claims that Europe has no political or military interest in Africa, military technical aid programs between African and European nations suggest otherwise. French military technical aid involves military intervention when French interests are threatened in its former colonies. The French Foreign League has engaged in several missions to keep in power rulers who support French interests. When Eyadema called for French support under a military assistance treaty signed in 1963, French jets and 250 troops were sent in 1986 to buttress his show of force after crushing a mutiny (Decalo 1990). The British MI5 and American CIA intelligence agencies jointly warned the dictator of a mercenary attack earlier in 1977 (Decalo 1990).

Another form of aid comes in military hardware. Since there are no arms industries in sub-Saharan Africa, except in South Africa, the armed forces in the region are dependent on supplies from the industrialized world. Government priorities change under economic pressures and when budget cuts affect the military, the reaction ranges from requests for maintaining current levels of expenditure on the armed forces to overthrowing the government. Many democratically elected African leaders also create presidential guards that are better equipped than the regular armed forces. As these leader become more autocratic, the presidential guards become more powerful commanding more military hardware than the regular army. The presidential guards are in reality private mercenaries hired to protect their leaders and partake in their political and financial spoils (Chazan et al. 1992). Regular soldiers become demoralized and disgruntled leading to mutinies which in some cases escalate to coup d'etats and the establishment of juntas and military rule. Protracted military in-fighting spreads to national breakdown and civil war. Arms glut and political instability are a volatile mixture that could easily explode into a civil war.

During the Cold War period, Africa became the battle-field for super power proxy wars for the expansion of capitalism from the West led by the United States and for socialism from the East led by the Union of Soviet Socialist Republics and its satellites as well as China. Somalia's geographical location at the Horn of Africa made it strategically attractive to the super powers that flooded it with arms. The power vacuum left by military dictator, Siad Barre, resulted in a civil war in which the arms supplied by the super powers were used by the warring faction to destroy civil society (Ramsay 1999). The Angolan civil war and the human tragedy which has going on since 1975 have been created and sustained by the United States, the former Soviet Union, South Africa, Cuba, Zaire, other international political and commercial interest groups, and Angolans themselves (Ramsay 1999). The military aid given to Africa has destructive repercussions, which include the destruction human life, civil institutions, and Africa's political and economic development. Marauding armed Europeans who forced Africa into colonization did not lead her to democracy and the armed take-overs of political power since independence that in some cases degenerated into civil wars with marauding armed Africans hinder Africa's democratic growth. Economic and social problems of modern Africa are closely linked with the political instability. While democracy does not necessarily guarantee economic and social growth, Africa's condition is not helped by the lack of participatory governance and the public accountability that is inherent in democracy.

CONCLUSION

It is valid after examining the facts to argue that Africa's colonial legacy contributes to her present political instability, taking into account the artificial borders, the destruction of traditional democratic processes, the exploitative nature of colonial and neo-colonial economies, and the use of brutal force to appropriate and maintain power that has become part of military culture in post-independence Africa. However, one cannot put the blame solely on the colonial legacy in the face of the political and economic performance of African leaders and their governments, most of which are autocratic or simply dictatorial. That Africans were able to end colonialism, despite brutal oppressive methods of the European colonizers suggests that they could overcome their post-independence political and economic problems. If the military in Africa has the tendency to seize power, it is because as democratically elected leaders become autocratic and use the military to buttress their descent into charismatic dictatorships, the military is enticed into political involvement as it realizes its support is the only one the leadership could depend upon. Without the support of the populace and the accompanying social arrest that seizes the nation, the military rushes in to fill the vacuum. The military intrusion into the political life of African nations is a result of faulty transition of power from colonial military occupation to independent African governments, instability generated by the political and economic ineptitude of elected leaders, and the personal and corporate ambition and greed of cliques of military men. Military rule turns back the clock of African democratic development as well as economic and social well-being since military rulers have shown that they are unconstitutional, usurpers of political power, and inept in economic matters of the nations. If elected African leaders uphold constitutional democratic practices at all levels and follow through with sound economic policies, instabilities that require military intervention would be greatly minimized and the military would also have to uphold its professionalism that requires of it to protect and defend national sovereignty and the democratic constitutions of the various nations.

If artificial borders are reflective of Africa's colonial legacy, the manipulation of ethnic differences within African countries by elected and military leaders and their cohorts to maintain despotic power, "tribalism," is indicative of political excrescence and the leaders' impiety of constitutions that guarantee democratic practices and fair-play to all groups. That Africans lean toward ethnicity, tribe or clan is not the problem, because they have to protect and ensure their group rights. It is inequalities that grow out of corrupted democratic processes that are responsible for instability. Equity in power-sharing at legislative and executive levels, equal distribution of national resources, and the respect of each group's rights within any given border would ensure pan-ethnic unity in defense of democracy.

Pan-ethnic unity that underscored the struggle for independence suggests regional initiatives may help solve both political and economic problems African nations face. The Economic Community of West African States has proven the viability and validity of a regional approach to dealing with issues facing the various nations. If African countries are made up of ethnic groups, most of which before colonial rule were sovereign states; the partitioned groups in modern states may be the very source of Regional Corporation. Artificial borders that truncate communication and trade between kith and kin and neighbors would lose their colonial import and serve as administrative grids to work out models for regional development. Group rights may also be better addressed at regional level. For example, the Hutus and Tutsis of Central Africa, the Ewes, Fulanis, and Hausas of West Africa, or the Swahilis of East Africa, peoples partitioned among several nations may have their socio-cultural needs addressed without sacrificing the national sovereignty of each nation. It is the inability of governments to deal with ethnic tensions that rise out of genuine concerns that results in conflicts, only to be manipulated by power-hungry and unscrupulous politicians and military men causing countries to spiral down into civil wars and human tragedy.

The Economic Community Monitoring Group (ECOMOG), ECOWAS Monitoring Group, the military wing of the Economic Community of West African States (ECOWAS), has been able to stop the spread of civil wars in Liberia and Sierra Leone to regional conflicts within West Africa with reasonable success. Sovereignty questions arise when regional military interventions become necessary. The sovereignty of the nations engaged in civil wars is compromised by the very nature of war and that of their neighbors is threatened by the constant flow of refugees across their borders putting more pressure on the already economically strapped nations. If ethnic groups are partitioned among several nations, the danger of the spread of civil wars is real; thus the sovereignty of each nation in the region is at stake. Interventions such as those by ECOMOG, therefore, do not only preserve sovereignty and regional stability, but also foster the appropriate conditions to political and economic development.

Africa's economic condition also demands an approach that maximizes all the available regional resources. The former colonial ties did not wane after independence and Africa's dependence on the industrial products of the West makes it vulnerable to pressures and interests of multinationals. Individually, African nations could not surmount the daunting economic problems they face; so regional organizations such as the ECOWAS, the East African Community, EAC, the Common Market for East and Southern African, COMESA, and the Communaute Economique des Etats de l'Afrique Central, CEEAC, are the regional initiatives heralding the economic will of African nations to deal with their condition. If economic crisis breeds political instability, or vices versa, African realization of the importance of regional economic cooperation and formation of the organizations are pragmatic and also prudent political decision-making that would help sustain democracy.

Taking into account the facts of colonialism in Africa and its legacy, it suffices to mention that Africans have achieved more on all levels of human endeavor within the last half-century since attaining independence than during the hundred years of European colonial rule. The attainment of economic independence, a necessity for sustenance of political stability and democracy, however, keeps eluding African nations. Democratic elections have taken place in several countries with others moving steadily towards participatory governance. There are still autocratic leaders just as there are military juntas and dictators, who still operate with impudence; and civil wars continue or erupt. But the democratic wind sweeping across Africa south of the Sahara through the 2000s, despite the deplorable economies and hardship facing most nations, seem to points towards a political prospects and promises that may unfold in the Twenty-first Century.

REFERENCES

Ayittey, George B. N. 1991. Indigenous African Institutions. New York: Transnational Publishers, Inc.

_____ 1992. Africa Betrayed .New York. St. Martin's Press.

Chagan, Naomi. 1979. "Africa Voters at the Polls: A Re-examination of the Role of Elections in Africa." Journal of Commonwealth and Comparative Politics 17: 136-58.

Conteh-Morgan, Earl. 1997. Democratization in Africa: The Theory and Dynamics of Political Transitions. Westport: Praeger.

Curtin, Philip, Steven Feierman, Leonard Thompson, and Jan Vansina. 1994. African History from the Earliest Times to Independence. London: Longman.

Davidson, Basil. 1992. Black Man's Burden: Africa and the Curse of the Nation-State. New York: Times Books.

Decalo, Samuel. 1990. Coups and Army Rule in Africa. New Haven: Yale University Press

DuBois, W.E.B. 1990 (Reprint). The Soul of Black Folk. New York: Vintage.

Herskovits, Melville J. 1967. The Human Factor in Changing Africa. New York: Vintage Books.

Iliffe, John. 1995. Africans: The History of a Continent. New York: Cambridge University Press.

Isichei, Elizabeth. 1997. A History of African Societies to 1870. New York: Cambridge University Press.

Kenyatta, Jomo. 1938. Facing Mount Kenya. London: Secker and Warburg.

Khapoya, Vincent B. 1998. The African Experience: An Introduction. Upper Saddle River: Prentice Hall.

Mamdani, Mahmood. 1996. Citizen and Subject: Contemporary Africa and the Legacy of Late Colonialism. Princeton: Princeton University Press.

Mazrui, Ali. 1986. The Africans. London: BBC Publications.

Murdock, George P. 1959. Africa: Its Peoples and Their Culture History. New York: McGraw-Hill.

Nkrumah, Kwame. 1964. Consciencism: Philosophy and Ideology for De-Colonisation. London: Panaf Books.

Ramsay, Jeffress. 1999. Africa. Guilford: Dushkin/McGraw-Hill.

Rothchild, Donald and Victor A. Olorunsola. 1983 State Versus Ethnic Claims: African Policy Dilemmas. Boulder: Westview Press.

Shillington, Kevin. 1995. History of Africa. New York: St. Martin's Presss.

Tordoff, William. 1997. Government and Politics in Africa. Bloomington: Indiana University Press.

Chapter 3

Political Parties and National Integration in Nigeria

Robert Dibie and Ernest Uwazie

INTRODUCTION

Political parties are the major organizations other than the government itself through which people combine for collective political action. One of the crucial functions performed by political parties is that of national integration. The essential and defining feature of a political party is that it provides the label under which candidates seek election to governmental office. However, most parties do more than this bare-bones function. This is particularly the case in Nigeria. In Nigeria, the belief is that, political parties represent a platform whereby people of different ethnic and socio-economic backgrounds converge and relate with one another. In this platform people discuss national affairs. It is the assumption that party stalwarts can use their platform as a medium to discuss issues that can unite the entire country. Apart from this, the integrative aspect of party activities in Nigeria could reflect the following ways: mode of organization, mode of operation, and appointment of a national executive's cabinet by the party in government and so on.

During the pre-colonial political systems several political associations existed across the Niger delta area, what we call Nigeria today, yet, none of them can be associated with modern day political parties. Instead of saying that pre-colonial political parties aggregated people, some say that they aggregate interest. The two statements have approximately the same meaning, for an interest group, is a group of people who have a stake in what happens concerning a given matter. Parties help to keep government responsive and accountable by providing a two-way channel of communication between government and the people. Pre-colonial parties shared many things in common with "pressure groups." For instance, an association like the "Ogboni cult" (a religious/political association) in Yorubaland used to have inputs in the selection of Obas (Traditional rulers) in that area. With the official colonization of the country in 1900, a Western (modern) type of administration was imposed on the geo-political entity in Niger delta. The British government created three protectorates namely Lagos, Southern, and Northern between 1900-1906. It further divided the three protectorates into two Southern and Northern protectorates between 1906-1914. In 1914 the two protectorates were converted into Lagos Colony and the Protectorate of Nigeria.

After the amalgamation exercise of 1914, a Nigerian council was set up by the colonial administration in 1916. The composition of the council (especially as it affected African representation) generated national resentment on the part of educated Africans. Consequently, they began to press for an increased participation of Africans in the discussion of their own affairs. The National Congress for British West Africa (N.C.B.W.A.) formed by Casely Hayford in 1917 took this campaign to London in 1920. One of the eight-point demand of the association presented to the Secretary of State for the colonies was, the establishment in each territory in British West Africa of a legislative council one half of which would be elected while the other half would be nominated.

In the case of Nigeria, Sir Hugh Clifford gave the country a constitution in 1922. This was the first of its kind in British West Africa. One remarkable development in the constitution was the provision of the "elective principles" which was in line with the demand of the N.C.B.W.A. Since parties represent the platform whereby offices are contested for in democracies, a group of nationalists under the leadership of Herbert Macaulay founded the Nigerian National Democratic Party (N.N.D.P.) on June 24, 1923. The party won all four elective seats of the 1923 Nigerian Legislative council, and dominated the political scene in the country until 1938 when a more pragmatic party, the Nigerian Youth Movement (N.Y.M.) won election into the Nigerian Legislative Council.

In this study, we examine the extent to which Nigerian "colonial parties" and "post-independence parties" have performed the task of national integration, and explore the variety of ways in which Nigerians have participated in politics in the past century. Participation has involved voting, joining an interest group, protesting an issue, working in a candidate's campaign, and simply communicating political ideas in an effort to influence others. We also consider the different participation strategies used in recent years by individuals and groups opposed to military continuous rule in Nigeria. The major question we address is: Have political parties served as agents of national integration in Nigeria, since the history of the nation? In the concluding section, we offer some suggestions on how political parties in Nigeria can better perform the task of national integration.

PARTIES AND NATIONAL INTEGRATION

In their own explanation of the concept of 'a political party', Roberts and Edwards (1991:93) define a "political party as an organized group, which is made up of members who subscribe to some common set of values and policies. Such organization often has as its fundamental aim the attainment of political power and public office in order to implement its policies." On the other hand, Epstein (1967) defines a party as "any group however loosely organized, seeking to elect governmental office holders under a given label". This definition perceives a party from both organizational and functional perspectives and stresses the main aim of a party as capturing of political power. This factor is what distinguishes a political party from other political associations.

Harry Eckstein (1968) lists the usual functions of political parties as follows: They perform an aggregate function. That is, they draw people together to support or oppose something. They could oppose a candidate or slate of candidates, a legislative proposal, or some action, policy, or institution. Political parties aggregate people by formulating platforms and taking stands on issues (437-438). Political parties publicize what they do, calling attention to their causes in whatever ways they can. They publish newspapers and journals, hold meetings, have commercials on Radio, television, and so on. They also induce citizens to register and vote.

It is interesting to compare Eckstein's (1968) concept of political parties with observations made by Samuel Eldersveld (1982). Eldersveld speaks of three "images" of a party. The first image pictures a party as "a group seeking power by winning elections." The view of a political party focuses on all the activities associated with efforts to get candidates into public office. The second image pictures a party as "a group that processes interest-group demands." This view focuses on the clash of interests and the role of the party as a broker or mediator that works out a coalition among contending interests or factions; or one party may make compromises or an ideological competitor." It champions principles and policies, hoping thereby to win in competition with other parties that champion different principles and policies.

The view we are taking in this study is a common one. Thus, a government should be classified as democratic if it permits more than one party to operate. People should be free to organize and support a party that opposes the government, provided the party is committed to promoting human rights. In addition, if people form an opposition party, they should be free to vote it into office and thus oust the governing party. This is an essential condition of accountability.

Where the law allows people freedom to form political parties, the number of parties formed varies considerably. Scholars and others speak of one-party, two parties and multiparty systems, and various theories have been advanced to explain why different systems develop.

The theories of political parties tend to form around the interests of the people in a nation. If a country is deeply divided, for example along tribal, religious, or linguistic lines, the theory is that each community is likely to have its own party. This is what happened in Nigeria during the First, Second, Third and Fourth Republics. The greater the number and depth of the divisions, the greater the number of parties. The corresponding theory is that if a nation is ethnically homogeneous, the only serious division is along class lines, and a two party system is likely. One party represents the working class, and the other represents the owners and managers (the bourgeoisie).

Another theory is that party systems are largely creatures of their own histories (Eckstein 1968, 450). Once a system gets going, for whatever reason, it tends to keep going. Parties do not like to die any more than people do, and people find it more advantageous to work within established parties than to start new ones. This theory is advanced especially with respect to former colonies in which one dominant party developed about the struggle for independence. The tendency after independence is for people to continue to work within that party framework, which means that it continues to dominate.

Those who advance these theories can all cite cases supporting their views. Each theory seems to hold good somewhere. However, unhappily for those who seek simple explanations, none of these theories holds good everywhere, especially in Nigeria. The world is complex.

Political parties may help to either divide or unify a nation. This function is especially significant in pluralistic nations like Nigeria, in which the people are divided into different ethnic groups. If political parties are formed along such lines, they may accentuate divisions and threaten to break up the nation. However, political parties may play the opposite role, emphasizing the importance of attitudes and policies that integrate the nation or keep it integrated.

National integration as a political concept implies the presence of diversities in any geo-political setting. Diversities usually lead to conflict among the various sections of the country. For instance, there may be contest over the revenue sharing formula, sharing of political appointments, siting of industries and other governmental projects and so on. However, when these problems which serve as centripetal forces rear their heads, it becomes the responsibility of any "responsible government" to intervene in such a way that both sides will be fairly placated. This is the essence of integration (Elaine 1995:28).

Scholars perceive the concept of integration differently, because integration takes different forms. This explains why Jacobs and Teune (1964:3) posited that there is no single definition for integration; rather, scholars define it according to the form it takes. They regard this as one of the problems Social Scientists face in their understanding of integration. The other problems they identified are variables that have influence in producing integration or inhibiting it, and the difficult to measure the impact of each variable and all the variables in combination upon the political process.

Integration can take place at any level. This position is better exemplified by Jacob and Tuene (op. cit.: 9) who argue that integration is the unification or bringing together of diversified components either at international level, regional level, sub-regional level, national level, state or local community level. Our interest in this paper rests on integration at the "national level" which encompasses integration at "state or local community level". Integration at this level is so often necessitated by the different rivalries, which may be going on among the various ethnic groups that make up the country. Such rivalries may be in terms of the distribution of political power or the allocation of revenues (Awolowo 1947,115). In this type of situation, it becomes the responsibility of the political office holders to unite the diverse interests in such a way that the people of the political community can live together harmoniously. This was referred to as "political integration" which can be achieved via "coercion" or "compromise" (Roberts and Edwards 1991:103).

The foregoing explains why Duverger (1976) posited that "conflict naturally leads to integration, and antagonisms tend, by their development, to self-elimination and subsequently bringing about of social harmony". He finally explains integration as the process of unifying a society, which tends to make it a harmonious city, based upon an order its members regards as equitably harmonious (177).

In their own submission Coleman and Roseberg Jr. (Eds.) (1966:9) argue that National Integration is regarded as a broad subsuming process whose two major dimensions are "political integration" and "territorial integration". They explained political integration as the "progressive bridging of the elite-mass gap on the vertical plane." On the other hand, they define territorial integration as "the progressive reduction of cultural and regional tensions... in the process of creating a homogenous territorial political community".

The summary of all the different positions on integration reviewed in this study are shown in the fact that it serves as a mechanism of suppressing antagonistic tendencies that can inhibit the political stability of a state.

Nigeria is a polyglot state. Consequently, there are manifestations of certain cleavages, which often threaten the stability of the country. Some of them include: linguistic barriers, religious differences, uneven economic development, unbalanced educational growth, majority-minority issue, etc. The presence of any or a combination of two or more of the above listed mal-integrative forces calls for national integration.

Political theorists are divided over the issues of the desirability of parties in a political system. While a group considers parties as undesirable to political systems, the other view parties desirable to any political system. The position of the former is buttressed by the fact that, party activities often lead to divisions among the various sections of the country (Lapalombara and Weiner (eds.) 1966:22). On the other hand, the other school of thought considers parties as very relevant in view of the crucial roles they perform (especially that of national integration.) in any polity (Emerson 1966, 269).

Our interest in this study is to analyze the integrative function performed by parties in relation to Nigerian experience. Nevertheless, we shall analyze the activities of Nigerian political parties during the colonial and post-colonial periods and find out how they have performed in facilitating national integration. The following represent the major areas in which parties can unify the people of a state, especially in a plural nation like Nigeria; party organization, party ideology, party activities (e.g. campaign), party posts, policy statements, methodology adopted in the share of spoils of office, etc.

COLONIAL PARTIES AND NATIONAL INTEGRATION

By colonial parties, we mean those parties that operated in Nigeria before its independence in 1960. The origin of modern parties in Nigeria dates back to 1923 when the Clifford constitution of 1922 made provision for elective principle. The first political party to emerge in the political history of the country was the Nigerian National Democratic Party (NNDP). According to Theen and Wilson (1996) The NNDP was one of the first Nigerian political parties to advocate independence from Britain. By the mid-1930s, it was challenged by a new and more militant nationalist movement the Nigerian Youth Movement. Regional led by Nnamdi Azikiwe. Ethnic differences were soon evident in the various independence movements. Eventually, separate nationalist parties developed in each area: the Igbo-dominated National Council of Nigeria and the Cameroons (NCNC – known as the National Congress of Nigerian Citizens after independence) in the southeast; the Yoruba-led Action Group, and in the north the Northern Peoples' Congress among the Hausa-Fulani. Other major parties that were formed at different points in time during the colonial era are the Action Group (AG) and the Northern People's Congress (NPC). Apart from these giant parties, there were other minor parties like the Northern Elements Progressive Union (NEPU), the United Middle Belt Congress (UMBC) and the Dynamic Party (DP) which were formed to promote the interest of some minority groups in the country. These fall short of the group of parties we are discussing at the national level.

The new political parties found it difficult to unite their efforts to oppose the colonial administration. Aspiring leaders recognized that their best source of support was their own ethnic group. This belief heightened the ethnic rivalries and demands for independence. James Coleman (1986) contends that early electoral activities were a contest of tribalism. Competing parties appealed to people by trying to outdo each other in the use of nationalist slogans.

During the colonial administration in Nigeria, it was the better-educated and westernized southerners that filled most of the posts in public administration. Northerners became involved in national politics later than the others and were disadvantaged in competing for civil service and military jobs because they lacked European education. Northerners resented this and saw it as evidence of discrimination against them by the Igbos and Yorubas as well as the British (Theen an Wilson 1996)

The question we beg to ask at this point is: What efforts did the colonial political parties make in integrating the country? The colonial parties operated under an authoritarian political atmosphere. In fact, their political ideology negated that of the colonialists. The aim of the politicians at that time was to ensure increased participation of Nigerians in the determination of their own affairs and subsequently, achieve independence for the country. On the other hand, the colonialists were interested in how to perpetuate their rule and promote their economic interest. Furthermore, some policies put in place by the colonialists made it practically impossible for colonial parties to perform the crucial role of national integration. A good example is the elective principle of 1922 which was limited to the South, with the Northern part of the country not benefiting from the provision. Also, for some time, the Legislative Council instituted by the colonialists could only legislate for the Southern part of the country while the Government ruled the North by proclamation. This arrangement continued till 1946. All these help to explain why the colonial parties, which operated during that period restricted their activities to the South. Be that as it may, party operation, organization, offices and even programs could not reflect national character. Even, a party likes the Nigerian Youth Movement, which professed the unification of the tribes of Nigeria through encouragement of better understanding, and co-operation (Coleman 1986, 225) was politically handicapped.

At the end of the Second World War, the tempo of nationalist activities increased in the country. Parties that had pragmatic programs began to emerge in the country. However, the decentralization policy put in place by Sir Bernard Bourdillon in 1938 could be said to be the beginning of the emergence of federalism and conscious political awareness in the country. People began to realize the importance of self-government.

The National Council of Nigeria and Cameroon's (later National Council of Nigerian Citizens) which was formed in August 1914 is often regarded as the first national Nigerian party. This is because the party was the first to take campaign activities to the North. But on the other hand, the party failed to project national image in the composition of its executive. For instance, both posts of National President and National Secretary were held by Southerners (Herbert Macaulay and Nnamdi Azikiwe respectively). However, worthy of note here is the fact that other parties that emerged in the colonial period after the formation of the NCNC took a cue from its nationalistic posture. The Action Group party, which originally started as a Yoruba cultural association with a regional (West) outlook later, adopted a national outlook. The party took its campaign activities to every nook and cranny of the country, and went into coalition agreements with the UMBC. in the North and the Dynamic party in the East. NPC was an offshoot of a Hausa-Fulani cultural association -

Jamman Mutanen Arewa. Unlike the A.G. and N.C.N.C., for a long time, it limited its operational activities to the North. Furthermore, all its national officers were northerners. In defense of this, its first and only national chairman, Sir Ahmadu Bello, argued that, "It was because its founders wanted to unite the Northern people and that at that time, they were not looking much beyond their own borders" (Bello, 1986:85). But by the early 1960s, the party also dropped its conservative posture and adopted a national outlook, by entering into a governing coalition with the N.C.N.C. in 1960 at the federal level. The party also went into an accord with the Akintola's Nigerian National Democratic Party (NNDP) in 1963.

POST-INDEPENDENCE PARTIES AND NATIONAL INTEGRATION

First Republic

Post- independence electoral politics among Nigerian political parties in the First Republic (1960-1966) promoted instability and violence. Political campaigns heightened tensions between ethnic groups within and across regions as each party sought to maximize its turnout through extremist rhetoric. The last elections in the Western Region resulted in the near –total breakdown of public order and provided the pretext for the military's intervention into politics (Dibie 2001; Theen and Wilson 1996; Toyin and Ihonvbere 1985).

According to Lewis et al. (1998) the early years of the First Republic witnessed a complex series of battles over political formulas and alliances (see Table 3.1). "The northern NPC entered into a coalition with the mainly eastern NCNC, marginalizing the Action Group in the west. When the AG was rent by factionalism shortly after independence, the dominant alliance seized upon the opportunity to weaken the party's influence. The federal authorities cast their support behind Chief Samuel Akintola, the Western Region premier, who was Chief Awolowo's leading rival. A state of emergency was imposed in the west, and the legislature voted to create a separate Midwestern Region. The new region was quickly captured by the NCNC. The partition of the Western Region undermined Awolowo's power and provided Akintola's new party, the Nigerian National Democratic Party (NNDP), with the opportunity to secure election control" (Lewis et al. 1998, 30). Parties, which operated in Nigeria until January 15, 1966 when there was a military intervention in the country's political system, were inherited from the colonial period. Consequently, they did not deviate from their traditional mode of operation. What informs this position is that although their campaign activities widened, their organizations did not witness meaningful changes. In order to prevent a repeat occurrence, the constitutional engineers of the second republic defined in clear terms what were to be the constitutional obligations of parties in relation to national unity.

Table 3.1
Nigerian First Republic Political Parties 1960-1966

Abbreviation	Name	Leader	Description
NCNC	National Council of Nigeria and the Cameroons (later NationalConvention of Nigerian Citizens)	Nnamdi Azikikwe	Eastern Region?Igbo dominated political party
AG	Action Group	Obafemi Awolowo	Westrn Region/Yoruba dominated political party
NPC	Northern Peoples Congress	Ahmadu Bello	Northern Region/Hausa-Fulani dominated political party
NEPU	Northern Elements Progressive Union	Aminu Kano	Northern, populist political party, represented challenge to NPC
UPGA	United Progressive Grand Alliance		Alliance of Eastern NCNC, Western AG, and Northern NEPU
NNDP	Nigerian National Democratic Party	Samuel Akintola	Yoruba-based challenger to AG in Western Region
NNA	Nigerian National Alliance		Alliance of Northern NPC and NNDP

Source: Adopted from Richard, Sklar. 1964. Nigerian Political Parties. Princeton, N.J.: Princeton University Press. Peter Lewis et. al 1998. Stabilizing Nigeria. New York: The Century Foundation Press.

Second Republic

The activities of Nigerian parties were guided by constitutional provisions in the second republic as reflected in sections 201-208 of the 1979 constitution of the Federal Republic of Nigeria. What informed this was the experience of the past whereby parties were founded on ethnic chauvinism. Consequently, what determined the registration of a party in the second republic was its ability to meet the constitutional provisions. This explains why, out of about forty-five political associations seeking registration, only six assumed to have national outlook were registered by the Federal Electoral Commission (FEDECO), the National Party of Nigeria (NPN), the Unity Party of Nigeria (UPN), the Great Nigerian People's Party (GNPP), the People's Redemption Party (PRP), the Nigeria People's Party and Nigeria Advance party. The six political parties in the second republic blatantly avoided ethnic or regional appeal in both the 1979 and 1983 elections. Each party attempted to present ethnically balanced tickets for the positions at stake in the state and national elections. The ticket balancing referred to, as zoning by the Nigerians, was extensive and delicate. For example, the NPN reserved the presidential nomination for a northerner but stipulated that its vice presidential candidate would be an Igbo, its party chairperson a Yoruba, and its nominee for Senate president would be someone from a minority ethnic group. For a voter seeking to make a choice among rival party candidates, the party programs offered little variety despite the number of candidates. While their programs were basically

Table 3.2
Political Parties during the Second Republic

Abbreviation	Name	Leader	Description
UPN	Unity Party of Nigeria	Obafemi Awolowo	Western/Yoruba political party (similar to old AG
NPP	Nigerian Peoples's Party	Nnamdi Azikiwe	Eastern/igbo political party (similar to old NCNC)
PRP	People's Redemption Party	Aminu Kano	Northern, populist political party (similar to old NEPU)
GNPP	Great Nigerian Peoples's Party	Waziri Ibrahim	Northeastern, breakaway political party from NPP
NPN	National Party of Nigeria	Shehu Shagari/Akinloye	Northern, centralist political party (similar to old NPC)
NAP	Nigerian Advance Party	Tunji Braithwaite	Independent, radical political party

Source: Lewis, Peter, Pearl Robinson, and Bernett Rubin. 1998. Stabilizing Nigeria. New York: The Century Foundation Press.

similar in content, the parties nevertheless polarized ethnic fears. This polarization meant that, compromise and moderation were difficult to achieve. Table 3.3 shows the result of the 1979 and 1983 presidential elections and how the parties performed.

Table 3.3
Results of Nigerian Presidential Elections 1979 and 1983

Party	Percent of Votes Cast 1979	Percent of Votes Cast 1983
National Party of Nigeria	33.8	46.0
Unity Party of Nigeria	29.2	30.1
Nigeria Peoples Party	16.8	13.6
People's Redemption Party	10.3	6.8
Great Nigerian Peoples Party	10.0	2.5
National Alliance for Progress	0.0	1.1

Source: Oyeleye, Oyediran and Adigun Agbaje. 1999. Nigeria: Politics of Transition and Governance 1986-1996. CODDESRIA, Dakar, Senegal. Suberu, R. 1994. "The Democratic Recession in Nigeria," Current History, 3, 215-232.

Personal rivalries, such as the bitter personal enmity between UPN's Awolowo and the NPP's Azikiwe, reinforced the ethnic pattern (Ojo 1979;

Toyin and Ihonvbere, 1985). Therefore, the UPN headed by the Yoruba Awolowo won heavily in the west and took 80-90 percent of the Yoruba votes. The Igbo-led NPP with Azikiwe at its head won solid support in the Igbo areas. Even though parties avoided ethnic appeals, Nigerian voters still seemed determined to vote for they're own ethnic presidential candidates. Most of the activities of these parties reflected a national outlook. For instance, aside from the constitutional provision which made it mandatory for each party to open offices in at least two-thirds of the nineteen states of the federation at that time, each of them was guided by national principled in the following ways: campaign activities and appointment of executives. About party organization, all of the six registered political parties had national secretariats in Lagos, the then Federal Capital, and state secretariats in all the state capitals and offices in the entire nation's 304 Local Government Areas at the time. This development was a complete departure from the colonial days and First Republic when a party could rely solely on the support of a section of the country and make headway. Furthermore, party offices were filled in line with the provision in section 14 (3) of the 1979 constitution on reflection of federal character. For instance, the National chairman of the NPN, Chief Akinloye and the National Secretary of the party, Senator Uba Ahmed hailed from the southern and northern parts of the country respectively. Also, while the national chairman of the PRP, Mallam Aminu Kano hailed from the North, its national secretary, Mr. S.G. Ikoku was a Southerner.

In regard to campaign activities, all the parties regarded the entire country as their constituency. They took their campaigns to all the nooks and crannies of the country. Consequently, the Second Republic parties were detribalized in outlook and operation, unlike the practices in both the colonial era and First Republic when candidates (politicians) were denied campaign permits in some parts of the country (particularly the North) (Awolowo, 1978).

In making their appointments, the governing parties (both at the state and federal levels) were guided by federal principles earlier enunciated. While the nation's President, Alhaji Shehu Shagari hailed from the core north, his Vice-President, Dr. Alex Ekwume was an Easterner. The NPP, GNPP and PRP adopted the same policy. In fact, it was only the UPN, which failed in this regard by fielding Chiefs Obafemi Awolowo and Philip Umeadi (both southerners), as its presidential flag-bearers. This anomaly accounted for the poor performance of the party in the northern part of the country.

Third Republic

The military regime of General Banbagida introduced a transition program in 1991 and formed a National Election Council (NEC). NEC invited interested politicians to form new political parties. Thirteen political parties were formed in response to this invitation. The military felt that the number of political parties formed was too many, and their leaders had tainted reputations, ethnic and regional segregationist, as well as lacked discipline. General Banbagida's regime banned all the thirteen parties and created two new parties: the National Republican Convention (NRC) and the Social Democratic Party (SDP).

Table 3. 4
Political Parties and Organizations that participated in the June 12, 1993 Elections.

Acronym	Name	Leader	Description
SDP	Social Democratic Party	MKO Abiola	Center-left political party established by government
NRC	National Republican Convention	Bashir Tofa	Center-right political party established by government
ABN	Association for a Better Nigeria	Arthur Nzeribe	Movement in Favor of President Babangida
ING	Interim National Government	Ernest Shonekan	Appointed by Babangida as national government, August 1993
NADECO	National Democratic Coalition	-	Pro-Abiola movement, launched May 1994
MOSOP	Movement for the survival of the Ogoni People	–	Movement for Ogoni rights and environmental redress; included leader Ken Saro-Wiwa

Source: Adopted from Peter Lewis et. al. 1998. Stabilizing Nigeria. New York: The Century Foundation Press.

The two parties were entirely free of past associations with any earlier political organizations. Anyone who had participated in politics during the First and Second Republics was prohibited from joining or leading new political movements. Party leaders and active party members had to establish that they had no prior political tie and be cleared by the National Electoral Commission.

The resulting election was disastrous. It resulted in a complicated tangle of ethnic, religious, and regional loyalties and rivalries that were barely disguised at the beginning and openly expressed by the end (Suberu 1994; Theen and Wilson, 1996). For example, Moshood Abiola, was a Yoruba but Muslim. He found difficulty in winning the confidence of the north, which largely favored the NRC candidate and faced hostility in the south from Christians and Igbos who did not want to be ruled by a Yoruba. As Election Day neared, a disgruntled SDP Igbo, who was disqualified from running himself but who nevertheless enjoyed an insider position with the military regime, led the campaign to void the election.

The National Election Commission allowed the elections to take place under the cloud of the last-minute effort by General Banbagida to cancel the election. While Banbangida tried to stop the counting of ballots, independent and international sources showed Abiola with 58 percent of the vote and majority in 19 states and Abuja (Suberu 1994; Dibie et al. 2001). Moshood Abiola won majorities in 4 of 11 northern states (including Tofa's home state of Kano). He has 33 percent of the vote or more in twenty-eight states, well beyond the requirement that a successful candidate demonstrate cross-regional support and national integration by having a third of the vote in at least 20 states.

Wole Soyinka (1996), contend that on June 12, 1993, the Nigerian people not only voted overwhelmingly for a particular candidate, but in doing so affirmed "the nation as a single entity" (8). He consider the June 12, election that gave an unprecedented 58 percent majority to the Social Democratic Party led by Moshood Abiola, to be an event of extraordinary significance. Many Nigerians claimed that the vote was "a declaration of national unity," a nationalist political consciousness, and certainly a feat of historic dimensions of the Nigerian nation. In the absence of any formal accord on the part of the people to constitute a nation, Wole Soyinka (1996) asserts what action or events can be taken to represent such a commitment?

It is interesting to note that, although the military denounced the 1993 presidential elections results thereby obstructing a democratic political system in the nation, the imposed party system was still doomed to fail anyway. The experience of the 1993 elections suggests that Nigerian politicians and citizens have not yet found the basis for the kind of orderly and competitive party system that lies at the heart of representative democracy.

Fourth Republic

During the 1998/1999 transition process, the main political parties, People's democratic Party (PDP), All People's Party (APP) and Alliance for Democracy (AD) qualified after local government elections to participate in the gubernatorial and presidential elections because they were able to demonstrate a considerable amount of national integration. The Independent National Election Commission (INEC) headed by Justice Ephraim Akpata established that political parties must win electoral seats in at least ten states across the nation in order to qualify for the gubernatorial, state assembly, national assembly and the presidential elections. Such conditions were deemed necessary in order for political parties to promote national integration.

The 1999 Constitution of Nigeria also has provisions for a unity government. The clause contained in section 148 (6) of the constitution states that " any political party which has 10 percent or more of the total number of seats in the national assembly shall be entitled to representation in the national executive cabinet, proportionate to the number of seats won by the party in the national assembly." Both APP and AD were able to form alliance to produce

Olu Falae as their only presidential candidate for presidential elections. This type of collision was the first of its type in the history of the nation.

Table 3. 5

1999 Elections Result

Party	House of Rep. Seats	Senate Seats
People 's Democratic Party (PDP)	206	59
All People's Party (APP)	74	29
Alliance for Democracy (AD)	68	20
Others	12	1
Total	360	109
President Obasanjo (PDP) won 62.8% of the vote		
Olu Falae (AD/APP won 37.2 % of the vote		

Source: Independent National Election Commission. 1999. Abuja, Nigeria: Government Press.

This shows that the citizens of Nigeria are becoming more concerned for national integration than before. Appointment of ministers was also distributed among regions across the nation. While President Olusegun Obasanjo is from the West, the vice president is from the North. There is also the provision of rotating the presidency among the three major regions in the nation, North, East, and West. Table 2 shows that in the 1999 national legislative elections PDP won 206 seats in the House of Representatives and 59 seats in the Senate. This figure shows that PDP won majority of the seats in both national legislature, and the party constituted a broader basis for integration in Nigeria than APP and AD. APP won 74 seats in the House of Representative and 29 seats in the Senate. While the Alliance for Democracy, party won only 68 seats in the House of Representative and 20 seats in the Senate.

Finally, parties and elections often play an important role in Nigeria. Indeed, dominant parties in the Second Republic have used elections to strengthen their own rule. Dominant parties such as the NPN (1979-1983) maintained themselves by repressing rival parties or by allowing their existence but checking their ability to gain influence. In 1983, the National Party of Nigeria used elections to make itself appear more legitimate and mobilize the population to show support for the status quo. In 1999, the dominance of retired army generals in the membership of the People's Democratic Party has raised a lot of concern to Nigerian citizens who fear that the PDP might galvanize a new set of corrupt elected public officials. A good thing about the PDP, however, is that it is well represented across the nation, and thus promotes the ideal type of national integration.

CONCLUSION

This study focuses on pre-independent and post-independent political parties and their activities as a basis for national integration in Nigeria. As a rule, democracies, being responsive to the will of the people, permit people to organize parties as they please. Parties perform a number of functions. Formally, their main function is to nominate candidates for governmental office and to get them elected. However, we found that political parties in Nigeria have also performed a crucial function. This crucial function is the integration of the people of the nation.

This study evaluated election results from colonial regime elections, the First, Second, Third and Fourth Republics of Nigeria. The Third Republic is not given detail consideration because the period remains an inconclusive epoch in the nation's history. This study has given rise to certain observations about the activities of Nigerian political parties in relation to national integration. Foremost is the fact that, the colonial parties did not fair well in the task of national integration. Secondly, the origins of colonial parties served as an impediment to their task of national integration in the country. Thirdly, the colonial government was only concerned with how it could consolidate its position and achieved its economic interests at the expense of national unity. Fourthly, the activities of the Second, third and Fourth Republics political parties were guided by constitutional provisions which forced them to adhere to the principle of reflection of federal character. The motive of federal character has been to promote national integration in Nigeria.

In view of the above listed observations, our investigations have revealed that in as much as the task of national integration remains a core function of political parties Nigerian political parties should take to the following suggestions in their bid to integrate the country. Further, in order for Nigeria to truly achieve national integration we suggest that: (1) Future Nigerian political parties should be devoid of tribal sentiments. (2) Political Party activities should not be quarantined (or sectionalized). (3) Political Party offices should be distributed to reflect national character. (4) People should be free to organize and support a political party that opposes the government, provided the party is committed to promoting human rights. However, if people form an opposition party they should be free to vote it into office and thus to oust the governing party. This is an essential condition for accountability and respect of law, which is minimal in Nigeria.

On its part, the government should put in place certain regulatory policies aimed at mandating parties to stick to federal principle formula and laws. Also, policy makers and certain category of politicians should be given political education from time to time by research institutions like the Institute of Policy and Strategic Studies, Kuru Jos, Center for Democratic Studies and Administrative Staff College, Lagos, on the importance of national integration. This type of training will make political leaders pursue purposes that will satisfy the will of the people who they serve and not seek self-enrichment.

REFERNCES

Aborisade, O. and R. Mundt. 1998. Politics in Nigeria. New York: Longman.

Awolowo, O. 1946. Path To Nigerian Freedom. London: Faber and Faber Ltd.

Awolowo, O. 1987. Adventures in Power (Book Two): The Travails of Democracy and the Rule of Law. Ibadan: Evans Brothers (Nig. Pub.) Ltd.

Bello, A. 1962. My Life. Cambridge: The University Press.

Coleman, J. S. 1986. Nigeria: Background To Nationalism. Benin-City, Katrineholm: Broburg and Wistrom.

Coleman, J. S. and Roseberg, C. G. Jr. (eds.) (1966). Political Parties and national Integration in Tropical Africa. Berkeley and Los Angeles: University of California Press.

Crawford, Young. 1994. The African Colonial Sate in Comparative Perspective. New Haven: Yale University Press.

Diamond, L. 1988. Class, Ethnicity, and Democracy in Nigeria: The Failure of the First Republic. Syracuse: Syracuse University Press.

Duverger, M. 1959. Political Parties: Their Organization and Activity in the Modern State. London, Methuen and Co. Ltd.

Dibie, Robert. and Sharron Herron. 2001. Nigerian Public Administrators Perception of the Importance of Managerial Skills." International Journal of Public Administration (forthcoming).

Eckstein, H. 1968. "Parties, Political Party Systems," International Encyclopedia of Social Sciences, Vol. 11, pp. 436-453.

Eldersveld, S. 1982. Political Parties in American Society. New York: Basic Books.

Emerson, R. 1966. Parties and National Integration in Lapalombara, J. and Weiner, M. (eds.) Political Parties and Political Development. Princeton: Princeton University Press.

Epstein, L. D. 1967. Political Parties in Western Democracies. New York: Prager.

Epstein, L. D. 1975. "Political Parties," in Fred Green stein and Nelson Polsby, ed., The Handbook of Political Science. Vo. 4, Nongovernmental Politics. Reading. Mass.: Addison-Wesley.

Harris, P. B. 1979. Foundations of Political Science. London: Hutchinson and Co. (Publishers) Ltd.

Hodgkins, T. 1953. Political Parties in British and French West Africa. Information Digest, Africa Bureau, No. 10: London.

Ihonvbere, J. 1996. "Elections and Conflicts in Nigeria's Non-Transition to Democracy." Africa Demos 3 no.5, May: 8-11.

Jacobs, P. E. and Teune, H. 1964. The Integrative Process: Guidelines for Analysis of the Bases of Political Community in Jacob, P.E. and Toscano, J. V. (eds.) Integration of Political Communities. New York: J.P. Lippincott Company.

Luckham, Robin. 1994. "The Military Militarization and Democratization in Africa." A Survey of Literature and Issues." African Studies Review 37: 13-76.

Lewis, P., P. Robinson, and B. Rubin. 1998. Stabilizing Nigeria: Sanctions, Incentives and Support for Civil Society. New York: The Century Foundation Press.

Ojo, Olatunde. 1981. " The Impact of Personality and Ethnicity on the Nigerian Election of 1979," Africa Today, Vol.2, no. 3: 47-58.

Olaniyi, J. O. 1995. "Education as a Means of Achieving National Integration." Ilorin Journal of Education, Vol. 16.

Oyeleye, Oyediran and Adigun Agbaje. 1999. Nigeria: Politics of Transition and Governance 1986-1996. CODDESRIA, Dakar, Senegal.

Roberts, G. and Edwards, A. 1991. A New Dictionary of Political Analysis. London: Edward Arnold.

Theen, R., and F. Wilson. 1996. Comparative Politics. Upper Saddle River: NJ: Prentice Hall.

Toyin, F. and J. Ihonvbere. 1985. The Rise and Fall of Nigerian's Second Republic 1979-1984. London: Zed Books.

Van Dyke, V. 1996. Introduction to Politics. 3th ed. Chicago, IL: Nelson-Hall.

Shettima, K. Ahmed. 1994. "Engendering Nigeria's Third Republic." African Studies Review 38 no.3 (December), 61-98.

Sklar, R. 1964. Nigerian Political Parties. Princeton, N.J.: Princeton University Press.

Sklar, R. L. 1983. Nigerian Political Parties: Power in an Emergent African Nation. Enugu: NOK Publishers (Nig.) Ltd.

Soyinka, W. 1996. The Open Sore of a Continent: A Personal Narrative of the Nigerian Crisis. New York: Oxford University Press.

Suberu, R. 1994. "The Democratic Recession in Nigeria," Current History, 3, 215-232.

Chapter 4

Sub-Saharan Africa in the Post Cold War Era

Andrew Conteh

INTRODUCTION

The end of the Cold War was seen in many quarters as a reversion to the nation-state system. The Cold War had been a profoundly transnational struggle between two antithetical ways of life, whose champions felt justified in subverting and overthrowing governments of states run by those adhering to the opposite ideology. The end of the Cold War meant that the world no longer would be polarized into two supranationally organized coalitions and, presumably, could return to its "natural" political condition: a highly decentralized, virtually anarchic society of autonomous nation-states (Amin 1972; Betts 1994; Seyom).

This prognosis, however, confused the renaissance of national and ethnic self-assertiveness with the revival of the sovereign nation-state. To be sure, the collapse of the Soviet Union's totalitarian imperial domain in the late 1980s provided the basis for democratic national self-determination by the countries of Eastern Europe and allowed the ethnic republics of the USSR to secede from the Union (Chilcote 1982; Betts 1994; Gur 1994; Rothgells 1992). And in the Third World, following the demise of the Cold War coalition, states that were little more than pawns in the superpower contest for global dominance now achieved a considerable measure of "freedom" to develop their own international relationships.

Formal independence is not the same thing as actual sovereignty the power to determine the basic norms of behavior and conditions of life within the political entity. Nor does a country's internationally recognized legal status as a sovereign state necessarily reflect the ability of that country's government to provide the populations under its jurisdiction with the kind of civic order and justice they regard as legitimate or to control who and what enters or leaves the country (Smith 1974; Tordoff 1997).

Since the United States of America and the former Soviet Union ended a rivalry that shaped the politics of Sub-Saharan Africa through much of the 1960s to 1980s (Betts 1994; Hough 1986) the region has struggled to find a new basis for stability and development free of foreign tutelage. Progress has been made. But governments, economies and even whole countries artificially forged by European colonizers in the century, and propped up since achieving independence by the patronage of outsider powers, are beginning to fragment (Zolberg 1993).

Like most countries of the developing world, and in the former Communist Bloc of Eastern Europe, African states have tried to adopt the non-socialist world's formula for success. Most have pledged to open their economies and adopt free market policies, and many have begun talking about giving up autocracy or one party rule for democracy and pluralism. A few, most famously, South Africa - have succeeded.

Yet as much of the rest of the Third World appears poised to enter a new era of rapid economic growth and stability, Africa is still struggling to shake off the burdens of the past (Kilson and Cohen 1992), ranging from the borders drawn by the European powers to the corruption and economic mismanagement engendered by post-colonial dictators backed by Moscow, Washington, Paris or Beijing.

In many places, the old order is crumbling but nothing it seems is taking its place. There is too much talk about sustainable development, the environment and population growth and not enough talk about decay.

POLITICAL BREAKDOWN

1997 was a significant year in the history of political change in most parts of sub-Saharan Africa. Several sub-Saharan African states currently do not have working governments. This crisis reflects fundamental problems of statehood that have lingered on in African countries since they became independent in the 1960s. This raises profound questions about the nature of these governments. Let us examine a few examples from Sierra Leone, Zaire and Rwanda.

Sierra Leone is a nation-state in West Africa, which has been engulfed with throes of anarchy and confusion. The civilian government of Tegan Kabbah elected on March 29, 1996 was overthrown on May 25, 1997 by a dissident section of the army. This coup has since plunged the nation into chaos and a civil war. President Kabba now resides in Guinea taking refuge from that government. The Sierra Leone army has refused to hand over power to the civilian government despite pressure, albeit, a very weak one, from the Organization of African Unity (OAU), British Commonwealth of Nations, United Nations (UN), and the armed forces of the Economic Community of West African States (ECOWAS). The current Sierra Leone experience clearly demonstrates the weakness of institutional political structures in the face of some unruly and uncontrollable African military forces. In other words, the military in some African states still constitute a major threat to political stability in sub-Saharan Africa.

. **Liberia** has now found a political settlement to its conflict after the national elections held in August 1997. The polls resulted in the election of Charles Taylor as the president of Liberia. It is yet to be seen what influence the peace and settlement in Liberia will have on the refugee question among Liberia, Sierra Leone, Guinea and Cote d' Ivoire. Liberian refugees are now free to return from neighboring nations to their homeland but what about Sierra Leone refugees in Liberia? (Fleischman1994) Will Guinea support the Sierra Leone military as it did to the regime of Captain Stresser? Whatever happens will have important consequences for the relations among the states in West Africa.

Zaire (now Democratic Republic of Congo), a military revolution in 1997, has displaced the longtime president, Mobutu Sese Seko from leadership of the government. President Mobutu was popularly known as a protégé of the United States (West Africa 1997, 4179). Laurent Kabila, the new president of the Democratic Republic of Congo has yet to introduce any democratic reforms in the nation. His government, despite several promises to introduce democratic reforms, is still autocratic. President Kabila succeeded in reducing the excessive human rights abuse that was in the nation. Unfortunately President Kabila was killed in January of 2001. One of his bodyguards turned against him and shot President Laurent Kabila in January of 2001. Since his death, there has been a glimmer of hope among the people of the Democratic Republic of Congo, Uganda, and Rwanda. These people supported Kabila in his campaign to end the reign of Mobutu Sese Seko; however, they quickly backed the rebellion against Kabila after falling out with him. Angola, Namibia and Zimbabwe supported the late President Kabila in return for the promise of lucrative oil and mining concessions in Kinshasa. Western diplomats, however, think President Kabila's death may encourage the warring factions to seek peace. Much of the desire to seek peace will, however, depend on Kabila's eldest son, Major-General Joseph Kabila, who is just 31 years old, and the new leader of the Democratic Republic of Congo. In neighboring Congo Brazzaville, Denis Sasou Nguesso was able to come back to power in 1997 by defeating his predecessor Pascal Lissouba who is now in exile.

Political instability is still evident in Somalia and Rwanda. Somalia has not had a stable government since its United States backed dictator Muhammad Said Barre, was overthrown in January of 1991 (Tordoff 1997). A peace agreement that was signed by General Hussain Aideed and Uthman Hassan Ali Ato has had little effect. Unfortunately, General Aideed just before the agreement that was signed in Yemeni capital started to have gross effect in the Somalia.

After the collapse of the Rwanda government in 1994, following the unexplained death of President Juvenal Habyarimama, the Rwanda Patriotic Front

(RPF) established a new government in Kigali the nation's capital. This was just after a bloody civil war, which resulted between Hutus and Tutsi ethnic groups in Rwanda. More than a million people were killed in the civil war (Watson, 1994). It remains to be seen whether the RPF can consolidate its rule. Officials of Rwanda's new government have estimated that as many as 4,500 potential defendants may stand trial for war crimes and genocide. Observers, however, estimate that the international tribunal will prosecute only the top echelon of the defendants. This prosecution started in 1998 and the process is still going on. Other countries, from Uganda, Ethiopia and Mali are still waging small-scale wars against guerrillas, ethnic separatists or armed bandits that have made large chunks of territory impassable and lawless. Angola and Sudan seem hopelessly locked in civil wars that have effectively divided the nations along geographic lines. Thus, the scenario in some part of Sub-Saharan Africa is that of political turmoil and instability.

CAUSES OF POLITICAL TURMOIL

One key cause of this turmoil is Africa's loss of what was arguably its most important resource; its relevance. During the Cold War, the continent was a playground for the proxy conflicts (Klare and Kornblush 1988). The Americans, the Soviets, the Chinese, the Israelis, the Arabs, white South Africans, white Rhodesians, even the Taiwanese searched for allies and brought in aid, arms and advice. Much of the attention lavished on Africa proved destructive - fueling civil wars, as in Angola, or backing dictators, as in Somalia, Liberia and Zaire.

The outside attention also meant that highways were built, hospitals were kept supplied and a generation of Africa's elite was given access to education at home and abroad. African autocrats were able to play East against West, Arabs against Israelis, Chinese against Taiwanese in a bid for foreign largess. The game was always to find who would give the most aid, and some despots played it deftly. Another key cause of the conflict is the lack of good governance (Mamdani, 1996), which has led to the breakdown of civil order on the continent. This has been largely due to the stark reality that African governments are finding it extremely difficult to meet the expectation of their people in a rapidly changing global system. The reason why Africa has been finding it so hard to achieve good governance has been due to the flagrant disregard of the rule of law by some in authority (Dicey 1982). Indeed this is the root cause of bad governance that has eventually led to the widespread incidence on the continent of conflicts, poverty, environmental degradation, human rights violations, refugees, internally displaced persons and venal politicians. The arbitrariness of the actions of African politicians has often led to bad governance.

It was argued at the Kampala Sixth Annual Conference of the African Society of International and Comparative Law in September 1994 that attempting to rigidly copy the Western concept of democracy within an African context was not the answer to Africa's problem of bad governance. This may well be so. But it cannot be said of the concept of governance itself. This is universally acknowledged as a necessity for an ordered society - be it a democratic system in the Western or African mode. It is a system whereby individuals and institutions, both public and private, manage their common affairs.

In this sense, governance is a process through which diverse interests are accommodated and cooperative action is taken. Governance includes formal institutions and regimes empowered to enforce compliance, as well as more informed rules which people and institutions follow because they have committed themselves or else perceive it to be in their common interest to do so, notes the Geneva-based Commission on Global Governance. One institution in Africa that has a major role to play in ensuring good governance is the legal profession. It is universally acknowledged that the rule of law is essential for the well being of any society - the African one not excepted, despite what the continent's detractors may say. But the mere existence of rules is, of course, not enough to secure the rule of law, if they are not in fact observed in actual practice. The rule of law only becomes a living reality to the extent that these rules curb the arbitrariness of discretion and are in fact observed by the wielders of political power.

Making more Africans aware of the law - and of their rights, for that matter - is of utmost importance. Africans should no longer take it for granted that the authorities can ride roughshod over them without any complaint. They should not passively accept that when the police arrest them they automatically lose all their rights; that the same fate befalls them when they are imprisoned. African people should be made to understand that they are entitled to services provided by the government (Khapoya 1998). They do not have to bribe before they get what is rightly theirs. Africans have to speak out against a government that is not providing the goods and should not be afraid of being branded as subversive. Citizens in these sub-Saharan Africa nations should use elections a means of changing any corrupt president, minister or government that has not provided the goods and services they deserved. This, thought, does not mean that people should disobey the law. For the right of protection from the government, the people will have to obey the law, as do governments.

EFFECTS OF THE TURMOIL

Death and destruction are the obvious results of conflict. But this is just one side of the coin. These conflicts have led to more arms flowing into the war-weary countries. In 1993 and 1994 alone, the Angolan government bought more than $3.5 billion worth of arms and ammunition, easily making the country the largest weapons purchaser on the continent, excluding North Africa (Ramsey 1999). The situation still remains the same in 2000s. The government can afford to go on a shopping spree of weapons on the international market, knowing that Angola's oil resources will provide the money for such extravagant arms buying. A report in the U.S. edition of the Financial Times of September 2, 1994 stated that

Angola produced barrels of oil a day, worth some $2.75 billion a year but that 60 per cent of the earnings went on the defense budget. What is even more disturbing is a report by Human Rights Watch/Africa, which states that the government in Luanda, according to an international arms dealer, has been "issuing tenders for weapons on short-term loans, mortgaged against potential future oil production with short-term letters of credit (Ramsey 1999; Khapoya 1998). A United Nation source in Luanda told Human Rights watch that the next seven years of oil production has been mortgaged in this manner. Estimates based on Angola's current oil reserves indicate that production may last only 15 years (Tordoff, 1997).

The report, on Angola's Arms Trade and Violations of the Laws of War, since the 1992 elections has been published by Human Rights Watch, U.S.A. The Human Rights Watch has also noted that UNITA had been buying large quantities of weaponry from foreign sources, many of them private arms dealers. Pointing out that UNITA's arms procurement was in violation of a United Nations embargo, the report said the organization was financing its war effort, including its illegal arms import, with Angola's diamond wealth, mined in rebel-held territory in violation of Angola law.

This, though, is just part of the overall costs of conflict - the one that can easily be computed. But what about the hidden costs? The issue has been taken up by Safer-world, an independent United Kingdom based foreign affairs think tank. For the first time an attempt has been made to catalogue the full impact of conflict on the human race. In a new report, "The True Cost of Conflict," published by Earthscan, United Kingdom indicated that Saferworld has attempted to calculate the price of conflict using a cost-benefit analysis. The result has been that the costs far outweigh the benefits - even for Western countries which are the major suppliers of arms to war-torn nations in Africa (Ramsey 1999).

Lord Judd of Portsea, a former director of Oxfam, noted in his book that the true costs (of conflict) are often diffuse or unknown, and they are certainly taken to be secondary to the apparent economic benefits to Western countries of the arms trade. But a broader evaluation of the costs that result from the arms trade shows this easy assumption to be false (Tordoff 1997).

Nowhere is this clearer than in Somalia. The cost to the U.S. of Operation Restore Hope - one aspect of which involved rounding up all the weapons sold to Somalia - roughly equaled the value of the arms sold to the Siad Barre's regime. This is what Saferworld has attempted to achieve in the book; to encourage people in the West - who believe they are not affected - to look at conflict in a new light (Mamdani 1996). Apart from looking at what conflict costs to states bordering the country where fighting is taking place, it also assesses the impact of each war on the economies of the Western industrialized nations.

The book argues that if Westerners could be convinced that wars in foreign parts actually have costs for their nations and their citizens, as well as for the direct victims, then a new dimension of economic self interest might be added to the public's moral concern about conflict. "Policy makers and politicians would perhaps have more reason to re-appraise present policies. The interests of their own constituents would be at stake." The true cost of conflict looks at seven selected conflicts, including two in Africa - in Mozambique and Sudan. They were chosen to represent different kinds of conflict that occur, from wars between nations to guerrilla campaigns.

Mozambique's case has been quite disconcerting. At independence in 1975, the country had a greater potential development than most African nations, with its abundant agricultural and mineral wealth and its opportunities for tourism. For example, the country has the world's biggest deposits of tantalite, used in electronics and in specialist steels (Khapoya 1998). In the mid of the 1990s Western companies were awarded concessions to mine gold and rare minerals. Potential revenues from titanium were estimated at $44 million in 1987.

Soon after independence, the Frelimo government also introduced extensive health and education programs, to catch up on the legacy of Portuguese colonialism. All these potential social and economic benefits have been lost because of the civil war. In 1993, Mozambique came off worse against almost any indicator, when compared to other Southern Africa Development Community countries.

The Safer-world report shows how the West, as a result of the conflict in Mozambique, has had to pay for the sustenance of the country (Ramsey 1999; Tordoff 1997). Mozambique is the most aid-dependent nation in the world, with overseas assistance contributing some 70 per cent of its total, or $57 per capita in a country whose per capita was only $80 in 1991, the report says. The international community has also been responsible for bankrolling Mozambique's refugee programs; its transition; and the peace process, which was a huge $560 million between March 1993 and April 1994 (Mamdani 1996). The conflict has also affected member states that have been receiving increased international assistance to offset the adverse effect on their development programs as a result of the war.

Foreign investment in Mozambique has been negligible since independence, but after the signing of a Peace Treaty in 1992, there has been some $550 million of approved investment applications. Lonrho has by far the largest foreign investment in the country, with vast cotton estates valued at $80 million (Tordoff 1997). The company's investment has been at a huge price. The company's managing director in Mozambique, John Hewlett, was quoted in the book as saying that Lonrho's security outlays consumed 30 per cent of its local operating costs, which was about $1 million a year (Ramsey 1999). This did not include production losses due to sabotage.

For the West, it is further noted, the costs arising from the Mozambican conflict far outweigh any perceived benefits. The cost of providing aid to Mozambique has been immense. Billions of dollars have been spent helping to ensure the basic survival of the population, yet today, following the signing of the Peace Accord, billions more are required to assist in the rebuilding of its war-torn economy (Khapoya 1997; Tordoff 1997). The direct costs to private business interests have not been great, but the poor security situation had an impact on those already operating in the country. In addition costs have been imposed on international business interests operating in the southern Africa region. Perhaps the most important cost this group has suffered has been the loss of any potential investment opportunities.

The true cost of conflict in the mean time has tried to identify the economic costs of these conflicts to the West in order to make Westerners realize the consequences of their governments' lackluster approach to conflict prevention and management, as well as to their policies on arms exports. The book notes that if it can be demonstrated that conflicts fail an economic cost-benefit test, then the debate about conflict prevention might take on a new impetus.

For Africa itself, its development is at stake because a whole generation of children has been caught in a web of conflict that has left them traumatized. As war became increasingly indiscriminate - with nine out of 10 casualties being civilians - children are often targeted. At the height of the Rwandan holocaust, an extreme local radio station announced, "To destroy big rats you must kill the little rats" (Mazrui 1986).

As part of its 75th anniversary celebrations, Save the Children, a charity which is assisting children whose lives have been torn apart by conflict in some 20 countries, has produced a hard-hitting report about the effects of war on children. It was launched recently by Terry Waite who was held hostage by Islamic fundamentalists in Lebanon. He said that the gruesome statistics - 1.5million children killed in wars worldwide; 10 million traumatized; 12 million without homes; 1 million separated from their families; 5 million in refugee camps; 200,000 recruited as child soldiers - were a terrible legacy and a terrible indictment of 20th century civilization. "But one should not give up hope," he said, adding that he was not expecting to see change in Southern Africa in his lifetime.

The report has attempted to describe in graphic details the real nature of the suffering children are undergoing in the hope of relaying to the world the full horror of the situation. It also hopes to put across the message that unless the international community recognizes the need for development in the less privileged parts of the world, it would continue to manage crises. These are the true costs of conflict - to those directly affected and those providing the weapons of death and destruction.

THE MARGINALIZATION OF SUB-SAHARAN AFRICA

With the end of the cold war, Africa has become more marginalized than any time since Europeans first set foot on the continent 500 years ago. Zaire again tells the story. After years in which the United States, France and Belgium lavished aid on Mobutu, almost all-foreign assistance has been cut since 1990, and most expatriate workers have departed. In June 1994 Zaire was expelled from the IMF. Mobuto's exit and the change of leadership in Zaire has not resolved the nation's political, financial, and economic problems (Khapoya 1998). The lack of foreign interest and investment combined with the difficulty of implementing new economic and political models means that even outside war zones, Africans are struggling to come to terms with long-standing social and economic ailments.

According to the World Bank, the four poorest countries in the world, in terms of gross national product, are in Africa; seven of the world's 10 poorest countries are in Africa. From 1980 until 1991, African economies actually shrank an average of 1.2 percent each year, meaning Africans have gotten poorer over the last decade. The situation has not improved up till date.

African countries have the world's highest illiteracy rates, and they put the least public money per pupil into their education systems. Agricultural production has declined in most African countries over the last two decades, leaving Africa less able to feed itself and more dependent on foreign food aid. The World Bank estimates it will take 40 years for some African countries just to climb back to their pre-independence level. Africa is ravaged by disease, AIDS has become the most common cause of death for Africans, and in a dozen African cities, 20 percent to 30 percent of the adult population is infected with the virus that causes AIDS. More than 10 million of the world's 15 million people infected with the AIDS virus are in Africa. However, not all-African countries are in a downward spiral. Some countries, such as Ghana, are on the mend. Still, it is the absence of outright conflict in most African countries that makes their social and economic decline so remarkable. In state after state, public institutions have collapsed, health care has diminished, infrastructure has fallen into disrepair and poverty has deepened - not because of civil war, but simply because poorly supported, inefficient and sometimes corrupt governments have been unable to manage their countries daunting problems. Now marginalized, Africa's on-going hidden tragedies arouse only occasional interest outside the continent, when one of the waves of killings hit the television screen with brief images of horror illuminated by a western aid official handing out food (Tordoff 1997).

Africa is virtually excluded from the world economy, which revolves increasingly around the three dominant poles of Western Europe, North America, and the Pacific Rim. Earlier last year, in a move that symbolizes the increasing marginalization of the continent and the withering connection with the rest of the world, France devalued the West African currency, the CFA franc, setting off a chain of demonstrations, riots, and strikes among hundreds of thousands of West Africans whose standards of living took an immediate nose dive. It was a long-expected acknowledgment that the north now has little need for Africa's primary products. In addition, competition from Asia or Latin America, encouraged by the World Bank, brought the prices of African exports lower and lower.

RAW MATERIALS AND COMMODITIES

Raw materials and commodities, which account for 94 percent of Africa's export, have seen their prices crash on the world market (Cetron and Davies, 1991). Since 1973, the index of real non-oil commodities has fallen by 40 percent. In a decade, coffee and cocoa prizes have dropped by 34 and 46 percent respectively. Cote d' Ivoire, Tanzania, Ethiopia, Uganda, Kenya, Democratic Republic of Congo (former Zaire), Burundi, Rwanda, Cameroon and Madagascar have economies virtually dependent on these commodities. In Burundi, 80 percent of revenue comes from coffee alone (Khapoya 1998; Ramsey 1999).

Meanwhile, since 1960, the population of Africa has doubled, while food production has slipped back to a level 20 percent less than in 1970. This fall in food production stems partly from the agricultural policies, mainly suggested by northern experts and institutions, which gave priority to the export crops that have served them so badly; partly from the lack of investment in food crops, which has kept production methods at an archaic level of development; and partly from the disruption of agriculture by war or social disorder, which has driven people from the insecurity of the countryside to the towns.

In the countries of the Sahel - Mauritania, Chad, Niger, Mali, Burkina Faso, Senegal, Sudan, Somalia, Ethiopia - another factor in the vicious circle of instability is environmental degradation (Ramsey 1999; Tordoff 1997). Throughout the region, natural resources are diminishing, and the periodic droughts have pushed the fragile environment beyond its limits. The desert is encroaching on towns and villages, and the water resources that used to satisfy great herds of elephants, as well as the camels and goats of the nomads, have partially dried up. Centuries-old forms of land use are under impossible pressures and, like the Tuareg women who beg on the streets of Accra, or the former herdsmen who hustle in the markets of Dakar, hundreds of miles south of their traditional homes, a new generation is giving up the battle against a hostile environment. Among those who remain, the competition for scarce resources sparks ethnic tensions, such as expulsions of blacks from Mauritania and minor border wars between Burkina and Mali, or Togo and Ghana. It is a major factor in the more devastating wars of the Horn of Africa and Sudan.

The wholesale destruction of primary rainforest in Sierra Leone, Guinea and Cote d' Ivories is another strand of environmental degradation. In 30 years, Sierra Leone's rainforest has gone from covering 60 percent of the country to 6 percent. In Ivory Coast, it is down from 38 percent to 8 percent. The erosion that follows deforestation is visible from the east to the west of Africa as rivers run red-brown, carrying earth out to sea, and more peasants are forced off depleted land.

Uncounted thousands from the Sahel swell West Africa's urban slums, already filled with people from their own inland areas. Shantytowns surround all African cities and squatters from the countryside squeeze out a living on the margins of the formal economy, well outside the reach of government health and education. Their children's prospects of escaping are nil. The new scourge of HIV is spreading faster in urban Africa than anywhere else in the world, and AIDS is already threatening to decimate the most productive age group in society, with devastating effects on the economy.

In the next two decades, another 500 million people (about the size of the continent's present population) are expected to converge on these urban areas, swamping whatever services still exists (Mamdani 1996; Khapoya 1998). Latin American-style heavily protected ghettos, where the rich live, exist already. In a few years, they will need privatized armies to protect them.

INVESTMENT

Virtually no industrial investment comes into these urban centers today - there are no telecommunications, transport infrastructures or political and social stability to attract foreign business with the cheapness of African labor. In fact, it costs 50 percent more to run a business in Africa than in Asia, and the profits in Asia are nine times greater, according to a recent American ABC report. In the 1980s, three-quarters of all investment in developing countries went into just ten countries - none of them in Africa. The 2000s will experience the same trend if African leaders do not do something to stimulate investment in the continent.

King Moshoeshoe of Lesotho is one of the rare intellectuals to have held power in Africa, although briefly, as he was forced into exile by the South African government. Looking back recently to the independence struggle, the king, extremely critical of post-independence failures, pointed to the link in that period between intellectuals and the grassroots. Then, Kwame Nkrumah in Ghana, Julius Nyerere in Tanzania, Oginga Odinga in Kenya, he said, spoke for people's dreams (Brittain, 1994; Tordoff 1997).

The dream then was of freedom from colonialism. Today's dreams are more modest - personal ones born of the new mood of desperation: dreams of dignity, education, health, employment and land. Few of today's leaders articulate them for the grassroots. Thomas Sankara, the young president of the tiny, resourceless former French colony of Upper Volta in the mid-1980s, changed his country's name to Burkina Faso, meaning the Land of Honest Men, and went to war on behalf of the poorest peasants against the privileged urban middle class.

Sankara became a hero across the continent, because his every speech was an affirmation that change was possible, and that Africa was not condemned to a future as miserable as the present. More powerful than speeches were the symbolic shifts of power. Ministers saw their Mercedes replaced by small Renaults and, like the civil service, were obliged to don tracksuits and do compulsory sport weekly. The budget was publicly debated in the national stadium for days and nights and rich and powerful people went to prison. But Sankara was killed in a coup mounted by his long-time friend, the current president, and Burkina reverted to the backwoods that Upper Volta had been (Brittain, 1994; Ramsey 1999).

Even before the full economic disaster of the 1980s hit, somewhere around the mid-1970s, the wave of pride and confidence in post-independence politics failed at the most important point - the grassroots. The one-party states, including even Algeria and Tanzania, built into themselves a rigidity that prohibited democracy, a defensiveness that stifled debate, academic freedom, and the media, and increasingly, a divide between the elites in power and the people they had come to power to serve. After the death of Houari Boumedienne in Algeria, the FLN quietly changed its political philosophy and became mired in corruption; Tanzania's CCM began to change similarly in the years after Julius Nyerere stood down.

In reaction to years of political suffocation, an explosion of popular participation greeted the political opening to multi-partyism in 1989-90. Mass street protests culminated in national conferences in Benin, Madagascar, Mali, Democratic Republic of Congo (former Zaire), Cameroon and Congo that lasted for days, weeks or months, as years of frustration with an ossified system were vented by a civil society previously kept invisible by repression.

The changes of regime following these constitutional changes were far less dramatic than they promised. Some regimes, as in the Democratic Republic of Congo, Togo or Kenya, simply stayed in place; other countries, such as Nigeria and Algeria, saw elections canceled. In others where there was a change, as in Zambia, the incoming party was quickly bogged down in a crisis of disappointed expectations, because the new leaders have no more economic leeway than their predecessors do.

At another level, a more hopeful legacy of the political failures of the first post-independence years is emerging in a new civil society. From the six million or so peasants organized in the "naam" associations, which have spread from Burkina through Senegal, Togo, Guinea Bissau, Mali, Niger and Gambia, to the modest new non - governmental organizations grappling with the urban problems of street children, drug addiction and unemployment, a new generation is fighting local battles with old community structures, independently of their discredited governments or advisers from the rich north (Mazrui 1986; Ramsey 1999).

Battling to prevent what Robert Kaplan's apocalyptic article forecasts as, "The Coming Anarchy" in the third world, Africa needs a reversal of current education policies to produce a new generation of leaders with the vision and confidence to speak for their people's dreams of a different Africa.

THE IMF, THE WORLD BANK AND AFRICA

Since the debt crisis struck Africa in the early 1980s, the IMF and World Bank have dominated the economic policy of the continent. In fact that crisis was a godsend for both institutions. The IMF, which had lost its global currency management empire with the collapse of the Brettons Woods system of fixed exchange rates in the early 1970s, was given a new lease of life. Overnight the IMF emerged as the principal interlocutor between the Group of Seven industrial countries and the south, its seal of approval for budget policy becoming the condition of aid. The World Bank, hitherto mainly involved in product lending also altered its policy arena, with loans to promote export expansion.

The conditions attached to World Bank and IMF structural adjustment programs, through which their loans were disbursed, effectively transferred sovereignty from the African State to Washington. Edicts from the IMF required governments to reduce budget deficits through cuts on public expenditure and punitive interest rates (Khapoya 1998). These were backed by World Bank conditions linking loans to deregulation, import liberalization and the introduction of "flexible" labor practices - a euphemism for eroding trade-union rights. The aim was to set Africa on the road to export-led recovery. Fifteen years on, structural adjustment still reigns supreme, with more than 30 countries having embarked on World Bank-IMF "recovery" programs; and like a faithful Greek chorus, northern governments uncritically echo World Bank-IMF claims that their policies are hurting but working (World Bank 1998).

The facts tell a different story. Over the past ten years, living standards in sub-Saharan Africa have fallen by 2 percent annually and are now lower than in 1970. Unemployment has quadrupled to over 100 million and real wages have fallen by a third. Investment is lower in real terms than it was in the early 1980s, and a decade of "export-led recovery" has seen Africa's share of world trade fall from 4 percent to 2 percent. True, export volumes have increased. But this has contributed to a glut on the world commodity markets, driving prices down. The resulting deterioration in the terms of trade cost Africa around $12 billion a year during the eighties.

Nor has structural adjustment alleviated Africa's debt burden. Since 1980, the region's debt has tripled to $180 billion - and repayments represent a greater drain on resources than in Latin America at the peak of the debt crisis there. Each year, sub-Saharan Africa, the world's poorest region, repays its creditors $10 billion - four times as much as governments spend on the health and education of their citizens. Even this understates the problem, since it represents less than a third of what is due, so those arrears are building up at a frightening rate. For its part, the IMF's contribution to resolving Africa's debt problems has been to extract some $2 billion in interest payments than it has provided in new loans since 1987.

Unless the cycle of low growth and rising debt is broken, Africa's emergence as the third world within the third world will continue unabated. On current trends, some 300 million people - around half the region's population - will be living in poverty by the end of the 20th century. Behind these figures lies human wretchedness on a terrible scale. Africa is now the only part of the developing world in which poverty is increasing and health and education is worsening Khapoya 1998). One of the most chilling facts in the litany of grim statistics is that the region's children, who represent 10 percent of the world's total, account for a third of all under-five child deaths - and the proportion is rising.

This unfolding social holocaust has roots that go beyond structural adjustment. But it is no longer possible to ignore the profound failure of World Bank and IMF programs to create a framework for poverty reduction and economic recovery (Ramsey 1999). More evidence of this failure, if it were needed, was provided by the latest World Bank evaluation of its adjustment programs in Africa. After boldly asserting in the first sentence that "adjustment is working", 300 pages later the report's authors reach the conclusion that, after a decade of structural adjustment and net aid flows of $170 billion: "Current growth rates among the best African performers are still too low to reduce poverty much in the next two or three decades" (World Banl 1998). This staggering admission of failure is suitably decorated by eulogies to a small group of "successful" adjusters, with Ghana taking pride of place. But "success", in this context, is a growth rate that will leave the average Ghanaian below the poverty line for the next half century.

Critics of World Bank-IMF programs in Africa are swiftly introduced to their favorite economic model, Tina - or "there is no alternative" to adjustment. Up to a point, this argument carries real weight. Nobody in their right mind could deny the damage inflicted on African peasants by over-valued exchange rates, which act as a tax on exports and a subsidy on food imports; and there is little sense in governments running unsustainable and inflationary budget deficits, or in blanket protection to inefficient industries. But the fact remains that structural adjustment is not only failing to generate the economic recovery needed to reduce poverty, it is also imposing huge social costs on the poor.

Part of the problem can be traced to the preoccupation of the World Bank and IMF with monetary discipline, "stable prices" (for which read zero inflation) and market deregulation, to the exclusion of wider objectives, such as full employment and protecting public investment in social and economic infrastructure. This is despite World Bank President Lewis Preston's pledge to "make poverty reduction our yardstick" (World Bank 1998).

Consider the case of Zimbabwe, the flagship for the new model of "poverty oriented" adjustment, where the World Bank and the IMF claim to have made their loans conditional on a pledge by the government to maintain spending on health and education. In fact, per capita spending on health has fallen by a third and on education by a quarter since 1991, when the adjustment program came into effect. Even more onerous than these cuts has been the imposition of user-fees on basic health services. These fees have excluded some of the poorest people in the country from what was Africa's finest health system.

It is not only the human costs of deteriorating health and education services that present a cause for concern. The mindless pursuit of low inflation is destroying Africa's fragile manufacturing base, with cuts in public spending undermining the economic infrastructures on which efficient markets depend. In Zambia, a potentially competitive textile industry has collapsed under the weight of punitive interest rates, credit shortages and ruinous competition from imports.

Some 40,000 jobs have been lost, turning towns such as Livingstone into centers of unemployment and desperation. This did not prevent the IMF's deputy director for Africa, Edwin Bornemann, and recently describing Zambia as "a model for others to follow". The reason: in six months, inflation had fallen from 200 percent to minus 5 percent. (World Bank 1998)

Across Africa, the straitjacket of IMF policy has been accompanied by the destruction of small-scale, labor-intensive industries. This process has been accelerated by the deregulation of labor markets. This is supposed to pave the way for foreign investment and export-led recovery. In practice, the collapse of real wages has undermined the domestic market for manufacturing.

Ironically, monetarism in Africa has failed abysmally, even in its own narrow terms of lowering inflation. This is because, in many countries, the prime cause of inflation is no longer budget deficits or excessive money creation, but inadequate investment and the resulting shortage of goods. In a situation where, according to the Economic Commission for Africa, manufacturing production is operating at less than 50 percent of capacity, this is an absurdity (Ramsey 1999). Just how absurd is apparent in Mozambique, where the collapse of investment in small-scale grinding mills is pushing up prices for maize by forcing traders to transport it over longer distances.

So comprehensive is the failure of the World Bank and the IMF in Africa, that it is no longer possible for the industrialized countries to ignore the case for fundamental reform. What is needed is a return to the original spirit with fulfilling one of its central aims: namely, distributing the burden of adjustment between surplus and deficit countries. This would mean writing off a large proportion of Africa's debt in return for commitments from governments to expand investment in people. According to UNICEF, the total cost of meeting minimum human goals for health, nutrition, and education in Africa would be approximately $9 billion a year. Ending repayments on a debt that every expert agrees is unplayable (Khapoya 1998) could generate this.

Debt relief is a necessary, but not sufficient, condition for recovery. Equally vital is increased investment in health and education. The World Bank itself, in a recent review of the high-growth economies of south Asia concluded that investment in primary education is the single biggest factor behind their economic success, and sub-Saharan Africa's failure. The synergies between investment in health, economic growth and poverty reduction are equally well established. Stated simply, healthy people are more productive. Why, then, does the donor community allow the World Bank and the IMF to draw up adjustment programs that undermine Africa's fragile health and education systems, and deny its citizens their basic rights?

Fifty years ago President Roosevelt told the Bretton Woods conference that its task was to prevent "the great tragedy of our time" from happening again. He was referring to the great depression of the 1930s. Today, Africa's development disaster is the "great tragedy" of our age. That tragedy has been deepened by the indifference of northern government and the almost criminal imposition by the World Bank of a discredited ideology. It is time for a change.

Thus, the New World orders that is beginning to take shape is starting to look like a bad place to be a poor nation-state. As already stated the end of the cold war spelled relief for Washington, Moscow, Bonn and other cities at ground zero. But the view is less pleasant from other Third World capitals, particularly the capitals of African States.

Four decades after World War II, the two superpowers vied for the affections of poor nations. They showered the poor with military hardware, scholarships, and projects such as dams and steel mills, free air tickets and boatloads of subsidized food and other goods. Now, as the dust settles on the east-west struggle, the world is dividing into the industrialized north and underdeveloped south - and the poor nations are left to fend for themselves. Thus, the following observations can be made. (1) Ideology is out, and economic interests are paramount. Third World nations watch warily as North America, Japan and Europe lead emerging trading blocs, each dominated by one major currency. After years of being urged to lift themselves by their bootstraps, the poor fear that they and their products will be locked out of the new global trading patterns. (2) Slumping economies and the inward turning moods sweeping the industrialized world are drying up overseas investment capital. The U.S. is trying to step up its economic growth and deal with domestic ills. Germany has all that it can handle absorbing the former East Germany, and Japan is deeply shaken by the plunge of its stock market; (3) Much of the limited aid and private capital that are available for overseas purposes is going to the North's own poor - the former Soviet republics and Eastern Europe; and (4) Looking for levers to pry money out of the North, the South has turned to the environment.

DEMOCRACY AT RISK

As African nation-states fade from the radar screens of the affluent North, there is a growing risk that the widening divisions and bitter failures will bring profound disenchantment with democracy. All through the 1980s developing nation-states heard the rich West tout democracy and free markets. The collapse of the Soviet Union prodded them further. But if they are disappointed, authoritarianism and state-controlled economies could come back in full force. To meet the challenges of democracy it is necessary to promise the spirit of communal involvement in society. What we call the three "P's" - Program, Pragmatism and Participation - all in fact have one and the same aim: minimizing the danger of dispersion of energies. In this regard, democracy needs the following: (1) Democracy can only be based on the dual concern of setting up a government capable of ensuring social integration and therefore creating an awareness of citizenship, and of respecting the multiplicity of interests and opinions; (2) Democracy has to be representative, that is, its political officials must correspond to people in society, or at least to a sufficient extent for these people to be identified with political officials; (3) A well-functioning and transparent administrative system at the national, provincial and municipal level; (4) An independent and efficient judiciary catering directly for the people and above all ensuring the exercise of human rights (Mamdami 1996). Human rights are an essential element in democracy and democratization. Human rights call for pluralism and tolerance and broadmindedness and a balanced view of minorities. The struggle for human rights is inextricably bound up with the struggle for social justice, which cannot be won without a `minimum economic base'. Moreover, no economic situation and no amount of military and political pressure can justify subjecting people to torture, causing them to disappear or offending their human dignity. If democracy and freedom are to be viable, they must be founded on culture, education and economic efficiency. (5) It is indeed essential that each country should choose its own independent path towards democracy. The great powers must be dissuaded in this context from intervening in the affairs of developing countries since this tends to frustrate the democratic aspirations of its people. (6) It is necessary to strengthen the social component of democracy, to achieve a more equitable distribution of national income, and to ensure that the underprivileged sections of the community can play a bigger part in their country's government and economic management. (7) The military must become an instrument of the community through the state. The armed forces must no longer be the Praetorian Guard of the traditional candela in the interregnum between constitutional regimes.

OBSTACLES

The inequitable distribution of wealth in the world is a threat to democracy. Democracy cannot gain a permanent foothold in Latin America, Africa, the Caribbean and Pacific and Asia unless a balance of hopes replaces the balance of terror.

The obvious external obstacle to democracy is the debt burden. Debt are not in fact repaid, they are usually rescheduled. Increasingly, the crisis is becoming epidemic. The danger is that in the long run the economic situation will deteriorate so far as to trigger a popular reaction that could put an end to the present democratic process. Third, the rulers in several important countries refuse to give way to pressure for political rights and democratic practices. For example, the Kenyan President has been adamant to introduce changes in his country.

A fourth obstacle is the clear evidence of continuing and powerful resistance to any significant political changes and the continued use of political repression. Examples of this include Mali, Nigeria, Niger, Democratic Republic of Congo (former Zaire), Sierra Leone, Togo and Guinea (Khapoya 1998; Tordoff 1997).

Fifth, even if political liberty is reintroduced and opposition parties are permitted, ruling parties in former one-party states may retain their hegemony in society and state; this has occurred in Senegal since 1976.

CONCLUSION AND POLITICAL SOLUTIONS

A) At the international level:

1. Developed countries must recognize that a favorable external environment is essential for sustained growth.
2. Industrialized nation-states should recognize that certain conditions - like stability in international commodity markets, international support in terms of official Development Assistance, debt relief and free-access to world markets - are requirements for an international environment favorable for growth.
3. International action to combat the decline of developing nations must be pursued to enhance access to markets.
4. The developed countries need to make an effort to remove non-tariff barriers faced by the developing nations. Projectionist policies have been the most severe impediment to developing nations access to world markets.
5. The developed countries should also pursue policies that cushion the developing nations from major price fluctuations in the commodities markets and compensate them for large export earnings shortfalls because of these prize fluctuations. These compensatory measures could come in the form of grants or loans from individually developed countries or international organizations, and should be negotiated on a country-by-country basis.
6. The developed countries should actively attempt to reduce the burden of writing off some of the debt or converting it into grants. This should not be done without extracting promises for financial discipline in the form of reduction of defense expenditures and curbing of unproductive operations.
7. The developed countries should support the OAU mechanism for conflict prevention, management, and resolution by providing mediation and problem-solving training, organizational training and assistance, and logistics or support for specific missions.
8. United States diplomatic efforts should be coordinated to support, when desirable, OAU's conflict resolution initiatives.
9. The international community should be engaged, when appropriate, at each step of the conflict resolution process: pre-negotiation (bringing the parties to the table; the negotiation process itself, aimed at achieving a peace accord; and the peace-building or implementation phase.
10. The international community should provide continued support for

political liberalization and democratization in Africa to help mitigate conflicts there.

11. The United States of America should recognize that it doesn't have to go it alone; working with allies - particularly Britain and France - ought to continue to be a cornerstone of U.S. policy in Africa.
12. The United States should accept that it is unavoidably involved in Africa because of continuing national interests in the stability of the continent and to further other foreign policy objectives such as democratization. In sum, the international community must recognize that the problem of Africa is not a localized one but rather a source of general concern. Therefore, the development of Africa should not be thought of as a humanitarian issue either. The development of Africa will lead to a stronger world economy and gains for all nation-states. It will not suffice to say that Africans have the primary responsibility for their development. Themselves cannot tackle their problems alone.

B) The Domestic Side: The African Side:

1. The African governments need to place primary importance on the implementation of policies that stress continuity and consistence. Sectors like rural development, agriculture and training require priority.
2. The African governments should establish links between manufacturing and service sectors and try to harmonize all foreign-exchange-earning projects with the rest of the national economy.
3. They need to diversify exports and become more competitive internationally.
4. Socio-economic development requiring equitable redistribution of income and inclusion of the entire population in national activities must be stressed.
5. A strengthened partnership between the African states and other developing countries is essential for progress to occur in Africa.
6. African states need formidable diplomatic representation to the `industrialized countries' as well as to international organizations. Africa needs giant diplomats and not paid western lobbyists.

REFERNCES

Adelman, L. Kenneth. 1979. "Liberia: Hosting the O.A.U." Africa Report, (July-August). Africa News, (1980) April 21.

Allen, Susan. 1973. "President Tolbert: Exclusive Interview," Africa Development

8 (July).

Betts, Richard K. (ed.). 1994. Conflict after the Cold War: Arguments on Causes of War and Peace, New York, MacMillan Publishing Company.

Cetron, Marvin. And Oven Davis. 1991. Crystal Globe the Haves and have-nots of the New World Order. New York: St. Martin's, pp.185 - 205.

Chilcote, H. Ronald. ed. 1982. Dependency and Marxism: Toward a Resolution of the Debate, Boulder, Colorado: Westview Press.

Czempiel, Ernest-Otto. 1983. "America-Germany: A Particular Relations," German Foreign Affairs Review. Vol. 34. Ethnicity and Politics in Liberia,

Dicey, A. V. 1982. Introduction to the Study of Law of the Constitution. Indianapolis: Library Classic, pp. 107 – 179.

Howard, Lawrence (1988). Involvement in Africa South of Sahara, 1800-1860, New York: Garland Publishers.

Hough, Jerry. 1986. The Struggle for the Third World, Soviet Debates and American Option. Washington, D. C. The Brooking Institute.

Fleischman, Janet. 1994) Easy Prey: Child Soldiers in Liberia, New York: Human Rights Watch.

Gur, Robert and Barbara Harff. 1994. Ethnic Conflict in World Politics: Dilemmas in World Politics. Boulder, CO: Westview

Khapoya, Vincent. 1998. The Afican Experience: An Introduction. Upper Saddle River: Prentice Hall.

Kilson, Martin, and Mitchell Cohen. 1992. " Africa: Crisis and Change." Dissent summer, pp. 293 - 295.

Klare, Michael and Peter Kornblush eds. Low Intensity Warfare. New York: Pantheon Press.

Lawyers Committee for Human Rights, (1991) First Steps: Rebuilding the Justice System in Liberia. New York, N.Y.: Lawyers Committee for Human Rights.

Lumumba-Kasongo, Tukumbi. 1992 "Clinton and Africa" Africa Notes

(December).

Mamdani, Mohmood, 1996. Citizen and Subject: Contemporary Africa and the Legacy of Late Colonialism. Princeton, NJ: Princeton University Press.

Mazrui, Ali. 1986. The Africans. London: BBC Publications.

Ramsay, Feffress 1999. Africa. Guiford: Dusdkim Mcgraw-Hill.

Rothgells, John. 1992. Defining Power: Influence and Force in the Contemporary International System. New York: St. Martin's.

Seyom, Brown. 1995. New Forces Old Forces and the Future of World Politics: Post-Cold War Edition. New York: Harper Collin.

Smith, Stewart. 1974. U.S. Neo-colonialism in Africa, New York: International Publishers. Survey of Current Business, August 1963, October 1968 and 1971.

Tarr, Byron. 1993 "The ECOMOG Initiative in Liberia: A Liberian Perspective," Issue: A Journal of Opinion, Volume XXI/1-2.

Tordoff, William. 1997. Government and Politics in Africa. Blomington, IN: Idiana University Press.

United States Congress, House Committee on Foreign Affairs Sub-Committee on Africa. 1994. U.S. Policy in Liberia: Hearing before the Sub-Committee on Africa of the Committee on Foreign Affairs, House of Representatives, One hundred Third Congress, Second Session, Washington, D.C.: GPO.

West Africa. 1997. "Africa in the Changing World" No. 4179 (April 15).

World Bank. 1998. Annual Report. New York: Oxford University Press.

Zolberg, Aristide. 1993. "The Specter of Anarchy: Africa States Verging on Dissolution." Dissent, Summer, pp 303 - 311.

Chapter 5

United States' Legacy in Liberia

Tukumbi Lumumba-Kasongo

INTRODUCTION

What kind of claims has the United States made historically vis-à-vis the political development in Liberia? What have the dynamic relations between them produced in the history of state formation and various mechanisms and processes of power and class struggles in Liberia?

In this chapter, I intend to specifically examine the past and current trends of economic and political relations between Liberia and the United States and their impact and/or implications during and after the Cold War on the Liberian state and society at large. The dialectics of these relations, that is to say, their conflicting and/or contradictory philosophical base and policy implications, will help us comprehend the nature of politics and class relations in Liberia, especially as they have related to various processes of the global capitalist economy. Using guidelines based on a historical-structural analysis, I will discuss economic and political relations from the view of their "historical causation" and significance locally and internationally.

It is difficult to literally define what Cold War was because of the complexity surrounding its origin and its evolution. It meant many things to different people depending on one's school of thought and one's location in geo-politics and political economy of the world system. However, in the context of this chapter, I will identify its dominant characteristics and its manifestations. Between 1945 and 1989, the Cold War was reflected by polarization of the world politics, ideological and military contests, struggle for influence, containment and the balance of power between the capitalists in the West and the socialists in the East and their alliances. During this period there was no conventional war between the United States and the former Soviet Union on their own territories. However, their confrontational policies engendered hot wars in many parts of the world, including Africa. These two powers were expansionists, and intolerant. The Soviet Union supported revolutionary movements and/or self-proclaimed revolutionary leaders while the U.S. articulated the status quo in supporting the reactionary movements and/or self-proclaimed capitalist leaders. Another characteristic is the struggle between the world commercial centers and raw material providers. There are some scholars who believe that the destruction of the Berlin Wall in late 1989 is the symbol of the beginning of the end of the Cold War (Hogan, 1992) and that the collapse of the former Soviet Union and the formation of the commonwealth of the independent states marked the end of what is conventionally known as Cold War. This polarization had an impact on the ways their peripheral allies related to one another. It also penetrated the African institutions and political economy in weakening the policy base of the African states. What is the meaning of the Cold War and its end in Liberia? It should be noted that when we talk about Liberia, we refer to the state, its institutions, and the ruling power. An analysis of the Liberia-United States relations will clarify many dimensions of the above definitional elements concerning the Cold War politics.

The ruling class in Liberia has had an eclectic view vis-à-vis its own politics, culture and the U.S. Liberia was not forced to be permanently part of the U.S. and its economic system that the Black settlers "hated" and "admired" very much at the same time. However, from 1847 to the end of the 1970s, their politics, arts and religious practices and behaviors, one finds some systematic efforts to be emancipated from American ways and political history, and at the same time, one finds a systematic effort to maintain strong cultural and symbolic identification with the U.S. values and institutions as a way to rule and to diffuse tensions or conflict. During the Cold War, when the world became divided between the socialist East and capitalist West, Liberia's alliance with the U.S. took the form of neo-colonial relations. That is to say that the Liberian State became a peripheral state in relationship to foreign investments, foreign policy, and development of the strategic interests of the global capitalism. Identification with the political philosophy and social values that the settlers hated is one of the characteristics of Liberian uniqueness. It should be emphasized that the decision of the ruling class in Liberia to have closer economic and political relations with the U.S. was neither absolutely fixed in history nor deliberately random. The settlers could have decided to de-link themselves from the cultural and economic domination of the U.S. and look for other options. Why were other options not systematically explored? What implications did the dynamics of their relations have on socio-political and economic conditions in Liberia during the Cold War and after? What are the prospects for the future?

Between 1944 and 1980, many important political and social changes occurred in the state formation process in Liberia and in its relations with the

U.S. The coming-to-power of Tubman shortly before the end of World War II, as an imperial president, with his "integrationist" and open door policies, he consolidated the incorporation process of Liberia into the peripheral capitalist world. He was fully influenced by the Cold War politics and he also used it to advance his own political objectives. The 1980 military coup *d'état* in Liberia, though it did not seem to seriously question the sense and direction of history, brought a new social category into the power system.

STATE VERSUS ETHNIC INTERESTS

For more than a century, as a peripheral capitalist state, the local allies, mostly members of the True Whig (With Hope in God) party and their families, consolidated their power and disassociated themselves from the masses. As Wallerstein stated: "In peripheral areas of the world economy, however, the primary contradiction is not between two groups within a state each trying to gain control of that state-structure, or to bend it. The primary contradiction is between the interests organized and located in the core countries and their local allies on the one hand, and the majority of the population on the other. In point of fact, then, an "imperialist" national struggle is in fact a mode of expression of class interest (1973, p.377).

This contradiction in Liberia took the form of ethnic, class and power struggle. Before 1944 the Liberian State was in transition toward a "complete" neo-colonial state where the dominant interests of the U.S. became well articulated and clearly protected by the legal system of a client state. Clientism is "the process of building up functional support on the basis of material pay-off to clients" (Sandbrook, 1993, p.28). As Western powers began to consolidate their powers and interests through investments and financial assistance schemes, after the Second World War, Liberia gradually became a *veritable* peripheral state. Its social formation, which at the beginning reflected a combination of slavery and "primitive" capitalism, ensured that the elements of a dominant mode of production survived through the imposition of high taxes, slave-like labor and wages, and financial support from foreign corporations. Only by the processes of gradual internal change, alliances of power between the ruling class and the Congo's (the assimilated Africans), power struggles and the conflicts of families did the interests of this state become well-defined and its role of appropriating surplus labor and products for its own benefit and those of the metropolis become clearly articulated.

The emergence of Liberia, during the Cold War, as a fully peripheral capitalist state with strong and elaborated state apparatuses, an expanded export-import oriented economy, development of a bureaucratic and petty bourgeoisie in commerce, agriculture and public sectors and educated elite, created infrastructures for the development of peripheral capitalism. By and large, it can be said that although objective conditions may be manipulated and promoted by ruling classes and their allies for specific interests and ends, those conditions are important for determining the nature of the actions/policies of the states. Within a framework of historical-structural perspective, individuals, social classes or states relate to each other from where they are, who they are and what they have. This is what I mean by objective conditions.

The analysis of political and economic relations is not a technical inquiry. It deals with power configurations and their social impact. They can be strategic and instrumental in promoting various objectives; they can also be developmental and intended to essentially pursue social objectives. Thus, political and economic relations during the Cold War era must be analyzed within specific historical parameters. The degree and the nature of the impact of those relations in a given milieu depend on the specificity of local conditions, the nature of the actors/actresses involved, and the historical configurations in which the relations have evolved. Despite the dynamism that those relations are capable of engendering from their own embodied agenda and energies, and their underlying ideologies and policy implications, they cannot comprehensively be approached as autonomous phenomena unto themselves. The "non-objective" factors also influence the relations of exchange, of production, of management and of consumption.

It is important to distinguish between primary/ dominant relations in a given context (for example, those associated with class/state) and those which are predominantly peripheral to production, reproduction and the maintenance of a given social system. To better understand any social system of interactions, its major actors and the structures in which they function, it is necessary to identify how those actors have historically and socially produced and reproduced themselves. Mechanisms they use locally, regionally and internationally to enter the world system and consolidate their power, must also be examined.

It is argued that the relations of politics and the economy are more complex than just the mechanisms of capital inflow or outflow, technological dependency or transfer, distribution and surplus accumulation that are regulated and monopolized by the dominant classes. Social and cultural interests also contribute in shaping center-periphery relations. Relations in the periphery are not just passive all the time, even in the most reactionary political situation. A peripheral state can manipulate international economic relations or resources for its own political survival.

Within the dominant paradigms (realist and positivist typologies in Western scholarship), studies of the interactions or linkages in political economy include state-state agenda, state policies, economic ideas/ideals embodied in those policies, the availability of the necessary resources to implement them, and the political climate of the social milieu. Within this state-centric approach, many scholars tend to neglect the value of the primordial/cultural factors and their impact on state-state relations. Though it is difficult to quantify them, cultural elements also influence political and economic relations among nation-states.

Assumptions in conventional international relations stipulate that all sovereign states can have, in principle and legality, equal access to the same international resources regardless of their past political history: their location, national resources, and identities, are utopian and historical. However, the view that these states can exercise their rights equally in the international political economy and collective security systems if they respect existing agreements, conventions, laws and norms of international for and institutions, and if they do behave accordingly, is politically unfounded. Although politics of the Cold War had tendencies of being rigid, it took into account the geo-political arguments, history and the nature of the local ruling class and its relationship with people at large.

Could the Cold War conditions: search for alliances, regional military building, aggressive economic assistance, etc., produce in Liberia an "internal capitalism," comparable to the developments of the newly industrialized countries in Asia? The objective conditions and the dynamism of the world capitalism, along with ethnic/ruling-class interests have determined and influenced the nature of state formation and its policies in Liberia. In the long run, the nature of its relationship in diplomatic, economic and military areas with the U.S. contradicts the black settlers' philosophical base, which is: "The Love of Liberty brought us here." Since the early 1990s, with the collapse of both state and society as a result of a bloody power struggle, Liberia entered into a "dark" period, unprecedented in its history. How the state and people will be able to rebuild their political community depends much on their understanding of the nature of forces that had been involved in the foundation of Liberia as a contemporary state and country, and the dialectics of economic and political interactions between Liberia and the U.S. that shaped that foundation.

Since its foundation in 1821 by the American Colonization Society[1] (ACS), Liberia was considered by many as an "abnormal" or a strange political animal in Africa, because it was not formally colonized by the Western powers. However, this "abnormality" did not help the Liberian people and their state to avoid colonization in their effort to construct a nation. With consequences of the dynamics of the world system, it became a de facto neo-colonial state *par excellence*. Its history has been the object of much criticism on the basis of both the behaviors of the founders of the state and their sponsor. It did not completely fit into the paradigms of conventional Western scholarship in its way of defining Africa. From the perspective of state formation and control of resources, which includes the process of its incorporation into the world system and the internal consolidation of power in the post-colonial era, Liberia was the land of political extremism. It had a high dosage of cultural exclusivity in its political formation and discourses. Although it shared many characteristics with neo-colonial Africa, it also kept its own unique history. "The Love of Liberty brought us here," a slogan found in the preamble of all Liberian constitutions, shaped the behavior of this state and its relations with other states. But the "Love of Liberty" was applied mainly to protect the interests of the Americo-Liberian settlers.

For many years, as an emigrate political class, the Liberian political elite developed expansionist tendencies with a strong assimilationist policy. Its relationship with the local Africans was that of conquest and rivalry rather than dialogue and compromise. A permanent struggle and distrust characterized it until Tubman came to power with a strong assimilationalist and integrationalist policy. Although in the history of its formation, the Liberian State and its politics did not completely follow the rules usually applied to a classical colonial situation, the structures of its political economy were not much different from that of other colonial situations.

The violent collapse of the Liberian state and society simultaneously in the early 1990s, the ambiguity of this state, and the "passive" attitude of the U.S. vis-à-vis the vicious power struggle in Liberia, motivated me to critically re-think the economic and political relations between Liberia and the U.S. during and after the Cold War. As Liberians are struggling to reconstruct their society and state, a political analysis of the past, especially its relationship with the U.S., is a *sine qua non* toward the understanding of the forces that have shaped Liberia. This past should help us understand the present with intention of projecting the future. What were the roots of this political violence? What went wrong in Liberia? Is the collapse of the Liberian society the result of or a product of its "abnormality" or the negative implications of the end of the Cold War? Some ways to look at these questions are to analyze the nature of Liberia's political economy, the dynamics of its culture, and the nature of relations among civil society, the state and different classes. The nature of Liberia-U.S. economic and political relations will give us information and insight needed to examine the nature of this state and its policies and their impact on the Liberian people. As Byron Tarr stated: "The Liberian civil war suggests the failure of a grand illusion, the idea of Liberia as an African outpost of Western civilization. Unsolved cleavages between settlers and indigenes, and among indigenes, ensure poor governance that sustains failed policies" (1993, p. 74).

Since the formation of the League of Nations, Liberia has maintained a high profile and level of international visibility in defending the political interests of Africa, especially concerning its right for independence. It aggressively searched for political alliances in Africa based on the notion of mutual respect of liberty and self-determination. It is interesting to note that on the day of the celebration of Ghana's independence in 1957, Kwame Nkrumah stated in his inaugural speech that "once upon a time one could look around the world but not find a free Black Country. Marcus Garvey sought to create one, but he did not succeed. He cited the efforts of other people who tried but did not succeed. Then he went on to say that today the spirit of all those who fought to found a free black state has become a reality in this day with the independence of Ghana" as the first country in sub-Saharan Africa to earn its independence from the colonial powers. He did not mention Liberia as a free black state that had had its independence from the ACS since 1847. One could imagine the reactions of the Liberian delegates who were most likely present at this ceremony. This omission is an important reflection of the ambiguity the nature of the Liberian State represented among people in Africa. Some of the questions raised included: Was Liberia in Africa? Was it part of the U.S.? What has been the basis of the loyalty of the state/ruling class in Liberia? Since 1821, economic conditions in Liberia have been unstable. The struggle to survive in a new environment without sufficient human and natural resources resulted in welcoming foreign investments from the U.S. and other Western countries even if this meant, virtually, the colonization of Liberia. Who benefited from this decision? What kind of benefits are we discussing? And at what cost?

The premises and principles that motivated the Americo-Liberians to rule Liberia absolutely for more than one hundred years and to engage themselves in "contradictory" relations with the United States should be viewed within the context of the international division of labor, world economy, and the Cold War politics. What role has Liberia played in the structures of world politics and economy? This question can help us understand the nature of the Liberian State in terms of its economic interests, its political ideology, its reproduction system, its performance and its current internal crisis.

LIBERIAN-AMERICAN GENERAL RELATIONS

A General Political Perspective:

A short historical perspective is needed to be able to locate the U.S.-Liberia's relations. Liberia is a product of peculiar relations and efforts of the U.S. As a product of the movement of the epoch, its progress and the laws that dominated its history have depended on the development of American social formation and the global capitalist world. George Plekhanov stated that "Human history is a process conforming to laws, but does not proceed independently of humankind; history is made by men (sic) who set the problems of progress and solve them in conformity with historical conditions of the epoch"(1940, p.7). Though Liberia was not founded as even a weak semi-modern state, but through the mechanisms of capital formation, accumulation, the expansion of capitalism and its production processes, which directly affected the Liberian settlers' conditions, it was gradually incorporated into the backyard of international capitalism, where it has been playing the classical role of mainly securing the development of the metropolitan capitalist economy (or the center). The ruling class in Liberia opted, in conformity with the historical conditions of the epoch, for capitalist ways of solving its socio-economic difficulties. The impact of this choice on social formation and the Liberian economy, especially beginning in the 1940s, is one of the most important causes of the Liberian malady.

As stated earlier Liberia experienced an internal colonial situation as a result of interactions between immigrants (mostly free black people who came to settle in this part of West Africa), the native Africans (previous inhabitants of this land) and the U.S. As a "modern" political community with some territorial boundaries, Liberia was founded in 1821 by the ACS and the U.S. government following the passage of the March 3, 1819 anti-slave trade law (Dunn, 1979). Three philosophical tendencies seem to have motivated this Society to found

Liberia:

1. A humanitarian and charitable one based on the "civilizing" and "Christianizing" mission.
2. A commercial motivation; this concerns the possibilities of establishing a colony in the West Coast of Africa. As with any colony, trade should be established to promote change in the colony for the benefits of the metropolis.
3. Social and psychological pressures among the ruling class and old slave masters to get rid of second-class citizens (Lowenkopf, 1976, p.13). Stephen Hlophe also shows that free blacks and manumitted slaves saw no future within the United States (1979, p.82).

Liberia is, in reality, a result of the combination of many philosophical tendencies and purposes. It was historically and economically difficult for capitalist modes of production to actively reproduce them in Liberia earlier. As a colleague of mine (a Liberian sociology professor) jokingly told me: "How can you expect anyone who has not had any vision of freedom, a vision of a true Christianity or a vision of sovereignty to come and reproduce the true visions of these phenomena in this different social context?" What did the new immigrants reproduce? If the spirit of the epoch means anything, the motive of the establishment of Liberia as a commercial alliance would have been in perfect accordance with the movements in Europe. Liberia behaved as a formal colony of the U. S. as a result of the movement of capitalism and legacy of Cold War. The U.S. has historically been the principal source of foreign economic assistance to Liberia and has continued to hold this paramount position despite a great expansion of the flow of aid from other governments and United Nations Agencies (McLaughlin, 1966) until the collapse of the state in 1990. But, their relations have not only been economic ones.

Although Liberia was founded without an established structure of governance on which to articulate consistently societal interests, it gradually became a Commonwealth with essential political power in the hands of the ACS. Between 1839-1847, this Commonwealth had some expansionist objectives and behavior. The representatives of the Society governed it. The first governor of the Commonwealth of Liberia was Thomas Buchanan, the cousin of the President of the U.S., James Buchanan. The constitution of the Commonwealth was drawn up with the help and guidance of Greenleaf, professor of law at Harvard College.

On July 26, 1847, Liberia was granted its political independence from the Society. The constitution resembled that of the U.S., though Liberia was not a Federal Republic. The behavior and organization of the various counties resembled that of the states in the U.S. The flag and individualist philosophy that shaped the behavior of the political community reflected many dimensions of the U.S. Although Liberia became an independent state, the Society continued to work as an agency that served as a channel through which aids, donations and grants could be made to Liberia; it continued to play the role of persuading other blacks in the U.S. to join other Liberian settlers (Lowenkopf, op.cit. p.18), and behaving like an "advisory bureau" for Liberia's affairs, it represented Liberia's interests in the U.S.

What was "strange" and philosophically contradictory is the U.S. attitude toward Liberia after the declaration of its independence. The U.S. government did not legally and diplomatically recognize the independence of the newly established Republic until 1862, well after England and France. This would be understandable if Liberia had won its independence with the rejection of the capitalist culture and ideology.

It is possible that the U.S. government had its own internal problems inherited from colonialism and slavery; and so domestic policies were probably considered more important than foreign relations were. Recognition would also imply the acceptance that free black people could have political success; former slave masters could not likely envision that. They may have had the attitude of "let a new Republic struggle for its own bread and wine." And, at the time, Liberia did not yet represent any important market for its own raw materials, labor, and ideologies or for foreign commodities.

The argument developed by Lowenkopf that the U. S. was not interested in exploiting raw material in Liberia and in making it a consumer society does not appear to be consistent with the trends of Liberian-American economic relations during the Cold War era. It could also be that the U.S. government might have adopted a wait-and-see attitude because it did not have, then, enough capital and other resources to throw into what they conceived as a "dark" continent. This view can be supported by another assumption that U.S. capitalism was not yet strong enough to create and sustain the outside market. The competitive elements of the capitalist economy were not well developed at that time to accommodate adventuresome and a high level of risk taking.

From the Commonwealth to the Republic of Liberia, the infrastructures of dependency were created: schools, churches, a bureaucratic structure, and the formal and informal economic sectors, most of which had financial and cultural supports from the U.S. The first period that political and cultural dependency started was when political power was in the hands of the ACS; the second phase was after independence, when the Republic was proclaimed with a constitution, virtually American. But Liberal democracy, an American model, was not instituted as a political machine of the state formation. The ideal of "Love of Liberty brought us here" was restricted to the Americo-Liberian ethnic group and its ruling class. But even within the Americo-Liberian community there was a serious internal power struggle.

The third phase of dependency, which developed during the Cold War era, within the development of the peripheral capitalist state coincides with the "Liberian economic take-off." The meaning of this phase is that most instruments of "economic transformation" were controlled by about forty major foreign concerns. Though the average GNP per capita then was one of the highest in the world (Clower, op.cit.), the domestic economy was highly fragile due to the dominance of foreign investments and one rubber commodity. The later development of the mining sector contributed to an increase in the Gross Domestic Product (GDP) as well as fostering an export economy. The last phase of dependency coincided with socioeconomic problems engendered by the decline in commodity price, including rubber and iron ore and competition among their producers and consumers.

The United States government and its agencies took responsibility for economic assistance without positively changing the structure of the economy. The International Monetary Fund and the World Bank, with the guarantee of the U.S., assisted Liberia with many specific projects as well as fiscal stabilization for a short period of time between 1983-86. Another element which played an important role in determining the nature of Liberian-American economic relations is the choice made by the Liberian state in January 1944, to change its currency from the pound sterling to the U.S. dollar (Ibid. p.145).

ECONOMIC RELATIONS

The Point of View of the Private Sector

The role of American private investments in the productive system in Liberia has been quite complex in that it incorporated Liberia into the capitalist world the hard way and at the same time, it pacified the misery of the Liberian people by creating unrealizable expectations. The motto was that everyone could have his/her own business to make money and succeed. Although my specific goals in this section are not to discuss in detail the nature of American private investments, a brief and constructive analysis is helpful to understand Liberian-American economic relations and their political implications.

In general, Liberia has a rich resource base: ore deposits, large portions of land suitable for rice cultivation, cassava, maize and a variety of food crops that can also provide a basis for agricultural expansion. One of the important multinational corporations that monopolized economic activities in Liberia was the U.S. base corporation, Freestone Rubber and Tire Company.

With the support of the U.S. government, in 1926 the Firestone Corporation introduced the rubber industry to Liberia. For the government, this was going to increase its national income through taxes and royalties; for Liberians, both unskilled and skilled labors were needed. In this year, the firm released one million acres of land for $ 5 million (African News, 1980, pp. 2-3). Starting in 1934, in every year (when it opened its first trees for tapping) until 1958, rubber accounted for an average of well over 50 percent of the total dollar volume of Liberian exports (Clower, et al., 1966, p.145). This is an example of an enclave enterprise that produced primary products essentially for exports. It had a limited link with other sectors of the economy, if any. This is a typical case of a disarticulated economy.

From the time of its establishment up to the 1970s, the Liberian government, people of Liberia and the company's owner considered the corporation as the hope for "development." Robertsfield International Airport was constructed to transport rubber to the U.S. Firestone expanded its rubber plantations from 34,000 to 56,000, increasing its production two and a half time.

The export of rubber from Liberia in 1945, for example, was 10.3 thousand tons (World Trade Information Service, 1958, pp.1-5).

Rubber exports were increasing yearly 66.7 million pounds in 1950; 95.4 million pounds in 1960; and 182.9 million pounds in 1972. Wage employment also increased from about 30,000 workers in 1950 (practically all engaged in rubber estates, principally the Firestone plantations) to an estimated 125,000 workers in 1970 (Mehmet, 1978, pp.127-129). In the past, more than 40 percent of the total money labor forces were employed on rubber plantations of foreign concessions.

To be efficient, the company developed a relatively stable scheme of benefits for the workers. Housing, medical and schooling facilities were provided "free." It provided an "impressive" welfare system compared to what the Liberian government was able to give. In addition, roads leading to the plantations were paved as a necessity for evacuation of the commodity, although the total percentage of paved roads in Liberia as of 1985 was less than 10 percent.

Before the war and the vicious power struggle of the 1990s, Firestone had, as the largest private concession in the country, a monopoly on wage labor. The daily wage rate (minimum wage) was $.25 in 1950; $.30 in 1955; and about $2.00 in 1984.[3] Liberian employees, especially those who were working for Firestone Rubber and Tire Company, were the lowest paid in the World Rubber Industry (Africa News, 1980, pp. 2-3). Although their conditions seemed to be "better" compared to the poverty-stricken people and lumpen-proletarians in Monrovia and in other urban centers, they far from reflected the development of society at large.

To understand its relationship with the political and economic machinery of the ruling class, one must discuss general characteristics of the concessionaire agreements. The company was granted extensive "reserve areas" within which it selected its development area; the concession covered one million acres; land rental fee of $.06 per acre per year (for 99 years) was payable on land. Firestone's original agreement called for royalty on gross production; stipulation of workers' compensation which included medical, educational and other fringe benefits to employees; entitled concession to import, duty free, all equipment and supplies required for the development of the enterprise; and assistance from the government to secure an adequate labor force (recruitment).

These characteristics reflect a high degree of operational autonomy for the corporations. They seemed not to depend on governmental resources and rules. Their relations were those of partners. As many members of the ruling class had their own private rubber companies, their relationship to Firestone was business-like. Firestone provided technological and financial support to the ruling class' own firms and the state helped the enterprise to maximize its profits, as Mehmet noted: "Foreign firms are only able to transform profits, dividends and other remittances abroad freely; they are also assured of government help in keeping wages down and trade unions in check (p.129). Although the situation of concessions started to be threatened by political instability, Firestone was still considered the most significant source of state revenue until recently.

THE TUBMAN ERA (1944-71)

Tubman believed that the personal building up of power and the establishment of a strong state were pre-requisites for the construction of a nation. He took seriously the rhetorics of Cold War. On the 28th of February 1951, he declared:

> "Since the incipiency of this nation, first as a colony and later as an independent state, relationships between the United States of America and her have been cordial. As a matter of fact and history, the founding of the Republic of Liberia was sponsored by the most eminent of the U.S. statesmen and citizens; men such as Judge Bushrod Washington, Henry Clay, Judge Simon Greenleaf and scores of others. After one hundred and twenty-eight years of the establishment of this Republic on the western shores of the African homeland as a colony by the pioneers with the moral sponsorship and benevolent assistance of the U.S. government. Concrete spiritual and material evidence of the growing intensity of friendly intercourse, cooperation and assistance between our Great Best Friend of the Western Hemisphere, the U.S. and our Republic have become manifest by signing in Washington, D.C. an agreement of assistance and co-operation" (Richardson, 1959, pp.229-230).

This statement speaks for itself. Tubman chose closer economic relations with the United States. His policies made him popular and spiritually "immortal." His foreign policy was aimed at maintaining international sovereignty, preservation of Liberia's independence and determination of the further internal development of national human resources (Dunn, op.cit. p.51).

Liberia had serious economic problems due to the consequences of the Second World War and disturbances of its trading by that war. Thus, Tubman committed himself to "save the liberal democratic ideology." To do this, he formulated and enforced some policy affinities with democracy's torchbearers (Townsend, 1955, p.168). He re-enforced his anti-socialist sentiments. This political choice had an impact on state behavior and internal power consolidation. To be able to maintain his position, he promoted a unification and integration policy. He divided the country into nine counties, five coastal counties and four in the interior (Dunn, op. cit., and p.51). He opted for an "open-door policy."

The policy was designed to encourage foreign investments, grants, loans and trade in the country from the capitalist world. The government's goal was to collect money for the expenses of the state in the absence of any strong productive industry. Although foreign investments were not totally unfamiliar to Liberia's foreign policy, during the Tubman leadership, all this was intensified. As a result, the picture of Liberia's growth became higher than any other new states. Robert Clower describes this situation in these terms:

"Growth domestic money income more than quadrupled. Government receipts increased more than eightfold, tonnage of goods imported nearly quadrupled, rubber exports increased from nothing to nearly three million long tons per year, the money sector labor force nearly tripled, net money income of tribal households more than quadrupled, and mileage of all-weather roads quadrupled " (p.91).

If growth means development, Liberia could be then considered a newly developed economy. The sector of the economy that provided jobs and brought infrastructures was an enclave within the total economy of the country and the foreign corporations also controlled it. American economic assistance contributed to the "economic stability" that was well known in Liberia during Tubman's era. With a high gross national product and various forms of assistance, the government was confident about implementing its integration policy.

During the period 1946-1980 (including Tolbert's era), the United States provided more than $450 million to Liberia[4] to help the majority of poor

Table 5.1
Indices of Growth Real National Product in Selected Countries 1954-1960 (1954=100)

Nations	Real Gross National Product 1960	Real Gross National Product Per Capita 1960
Liberia	175	170
United Kingdom	116	112
United States	121	109
Japan	180	150
West Germany	150	140
Ireland	104	108
Switzerland	131	122
Congo	110	105
Nigeria	150	140
Ghana	160	155
Uganda	125	120

Source: Robert W. Clower, et al., *Growth without Development* (Evanston: Northwestern University Press), p. 24.

work and develop projects in various areas. In this period, many projects were funded and sponsored by the United States; to cite only a few: J.F. Kennedy Hospital ($16.8 million); public utilities ($41.5 million); Monrovia sewer system ($7.0 million); rural roads ($25 million); Mount Coffee Hydro-electric Dam ($25 million); the White Plains water supply ($7.2 million); telecommunication ($10.3 million); agriculture and rural development ($30 million); Lofa and Bong counties agriculture projects ($11 million) (ibid.).

Besides the development of some specific projects, the U.S. economic assistance increased yearly: between 1946-48, $7.5 million was given to Liberia, and between 1949-52, $2.3 million was given (it did decline here); between 1953-61 Liberia received about $29.2 million and from 1962 to 79, about $259.3 million was provided by the United States government. Loans and grants for economic assistance also show the same trends: loans between 1946-48 were about $7.5 million, 1948-52 it was $.2 million, 1953-61, it was about $3.2 million and between 1962-79 the Liberian government received a loan of $102.4 million. These economic assistance's consolidated the U.S. position in Liberia as a "good friend."

TOLBERT'S ERA (1971-80)

Tolbert attempted to move toward the "modernization" of Liberia. Although an "open-door" policy was still the foundation for foreign policy and relations, Tolbert also came to be known for his "non-alignment" statements. Some U.S. political circle as unpredictable perceived him. From 1971 to 1980, he ruled as a centralist ruler and with a monopoly on the domestic economy, using state apparatus as channels to promote his own economic interests.

Liberia became a member of the Economic Community of West African States (ECOWAS) and of the Mano River Union as well. The gap between the haves and have-nots became sharper. The forces and elements of social struggle also became more visible than ever before and political protests began to appear among various social classes in Liberia.

In Liberia, ruling class interests have been strongly and highly mixed with those of the state. The state apparatus and its bureaucratic organizations have promoted the private interests of this class. Although the bureaucratic bourgeoisie has enlarged itself within the machinery of the state, its power to change things qualitatively through "normal" bureaucratic channels has been minimal and inefficient, not having autonomy of itself. It has historically played the role of securing the interests of the ruling class, on which it depended economically. Though not unique to this period, this situation became even worse during Tolbert's presidency.

Tolbert was not an "imperial president" like Tubman, although he wanted to become one. The project of transforming himself into an imperial president characterized his political behavior and the nature of his policies during his tenure. During his first four-year term in office he made some efforts to align the government with "politics of efficiency and total commitment" for the advancement of public service and economic development (Adelman, 1979). In the interview with Africa development, his position toward modernization can be summarized in his own words:

> "Efforts are being made to fully mobilize our domestic resources. We are initiating programs for reducing illiteracy and increasing

> knowledge through quality education for our people. Development of human resources is an essential component of our self-reliance policy. My administration's priorities for this year include development of agriculture, increased rice production, development of all-weather roads and communications, development of education"(Allen, 1973).

In the middle of the Cold War, his determination to modernize Liberia led him to diversify his relationships. He maintained diplomatic relations with East Germany, the Soviet Union and China. He was committed to improving relations with international and multinational financing institutions in order to secure grants, loans and other various types of economic assistance. His relations with the group of countries characterized as "friends" of Liberia (United States, Japan, Saudi-Arabia, West Germany, etc.) were cordial. He gave the impression of maintaining a "neutral" Cold War position.

As Tubman's vice-president for nineteen years, he was well acquainted with the "open-door policy." He inherited it and prompted it as a means of maintaining himself in the office, expanding the basis of his power and enlarging his constituency. Though he seemed to believe in non-alignment as a means of diversifying sources of economic support, his main concern was to maintain a free enterprise system as an economic approach to development. As a prominent businessman himself, free enterprise was the principle used to advance his economic interests, including those of his family and his cronies. American economic interests were not threatened by Tolbert's domestic policies. However, his monopoly on the domestic economy and his diversification orientation did not seem to be fully supported by the United States by the end of the 1970s.

American behavior vis-à-vis Liberia was to continue to maintain the status quo. In this regard, the relations between them were not to be unique. The United States was also interested in "discovering" other parts of Africa. Liberia could have been used as a bridge for that purpose. President Carter's journey to Lagos (Nigeria) and stopping only at Robertsfield International Airport was not a good sign of friendly relations between the United States and Liberia. But Tolbert's government convinced him that it was a good idea if he could visit Monrovia.

By and large, Tolbert's nine years as president were marked by deteriorating economic conditions caused partly by falling world prices for Liberian exports and diminishing interest on the part of the donors. The international market of rubber and iron ore was no longer promising. Synthetic rubber was starting to compete with natural rubber. While Liberia has maintained a yearly growth rate of 4% between 1967 and 1976, per capita income averages a paltry $500, an income distribution badly skewed, while illiteracy still afflicts three-fourths of the citizenry (Adelman, op.cit.). In short, the disparity between the ruling class, mostly living in an urban setting, workers living in the semi-urban areas, and the so-called aborigines (natives/indigenes) living mostly in isolated villages, reached an explosive stage during Tolbert.

Direct economic assistance from the United States was still firm. In the 1970s decade, the United States gave Liberia some $300 million in aid. The U.S. investment there had soared sixfold from the past decade. From 1962-1979, the United States provided Liberia with about $259.3 million in economic assistance without counting specific supportive projects; in the same period, $102.4 million was given as loans and $156.9 million in grants.

After the World War II, specifically from 1946-1980, the United States provided more than $450 million to Liberia in the development area. Although government revenue increased, from $3.9 million in 1950, to $32.4 million in 1960 and $78.1 million in 1972 (Mehemet, p.127). U.S. assistance even within a ten-year period has been far beyond that of government revenue. In that regard, U.S. economic assistance was a very important source of support for the domestic policies of the governing elite and dominant class. Liberia remained the strongest ally of the U.S.A in Africa. But the internal economic and social conditions in Liberia worsened.

DOE'S REGIME (1980-1990)

The Cold war reached its peak in the early 1980s with Ronald Reagan, challenging militarily the former Soviet Union's regime and its allies in many parts of the world and high level of power struggle in the former Soviet Union. In Africa, the U.S. continued to support the military regimes with the exception of the socialist inspired ones. The self-declared African Marxist regimes in Benin, Congo, Ethiopia, to cite only a few were still committed to the revolutionary or class struggle approaches. The economic conditions in many countries were worsening.

On April 12, 1980, Africa's oldest Republic began a new regime: army rule. The then late Master Sergeant Samuel Kanyon Doe who was assassinated on September 9 1990 by elements of Prince Johnson's militia led the new regime. Although Liberia did not practice "democracy" *à l'Américaine* with the previous ruling class, members of the True Whig Party, the political system was recognized by its apparent institutional stability like Côte d'Ivoire under Félix Houphouët-Boigny or Kenya under Mze Jomo Kenyatta. But the social conditions created by the previous governments and domestic policies of the True Whig Party precipitated the violent removal of Tolbert from power along with his collaborators. Tolbert was killed and most of his team, including his relatives, was executed eleven days after the coup by firing squad. The People's Redemption Council (PRC) took power with enthusiasm to "change" history, though this does not seem to have happened.

The coming to power of the military regime was massively welcomed in Liberia. It came at the time, when Liberians were fed up with the social conditions created by the True Whig Party. They were looking for a hero, a new leader, someone who could make a difference. For many this is a symbol for change. And for others, this regime could be used as an instrument toward reaching higher societal objectives in the future. It was conceived as the symbol of a break from the past. The new regime was actively supported by most progressive forces, such as the Movement for Justice in Africa (MOJA), Progressive People's Party (PPP), and so on. Thus, within Doe's government a strong team of Liberian progressive intelligentsia such as Togba Nah Tipoteh, Boimah Fannbuleh, Bacchus Matthew, etc., accepted some cabinet posts, even if they later resigned from their posts because of the reactionary tendencies of the regime.

Why capture power? In the early hours of April 12, 1980, when Doe announced the formation of the PRC he said: "Mr. Tolbert and his collaborators were guilty of rampant corruption conflict of interest, misuse of power, and total disregard to the civil human, and constitutional rights of the Liberians," (West Africa, 1985, p. 731). In another speech, Doe repeated that "soldiers came to power to find answers to the sufferings, oppression and exploitation of the poor farmers, *yanna* boys, school children and all citizens whose rights were being overlooked, (ibid.). The classic position was that the military came to power to restore discipline needed for an effective and efficient functioning of the state apparatuses. For many, this was the beginning of the struggle for the cause of the people and for others, this was the end of the tyranny of the Americo-Liberian oligarchy.

Toward this goal, Doe appointed a Constitutional Commission chaired by Dr. Amos Sawyer. Between 1984 and 1985, as Does decided to become the first native civilian President, the democratic process to return the power to civilian rule had many difficulties, unpredictable and dangerous. Ruling by decrees, Doe terrorized the leaders of the opposition parties and manipulated the democratic process by not allowing political competition.

According to William Swing, the former United States ambassador to Liberia (in 1984), Doe's government was satisfied at the state of relations between the two countries. The aim of the United States was to avoid shortages and political instability.[5] Since the coup d'état, U.S. economic assistance increased tremendously. For the U.S. government, assistance programs were an integral part of a carefully balanced approach aimed at promoting economic recovery and "political stability." It has been consistent in its assistance to Liberia though it hardly produced any political stability in the country.

Liberia's foreign policy under Doe was also based on "open-door" and laissez-faire principles. This is reflected in a statement made by Ernest Eastman, then Foreign Minister, in Washington, D.C.:

> "Moreover, if Liberia is to be expected to play a significant role at all in African and World affairs, the economic well being of the Liberian people must be assured. With its traditional enthusiasm for the free enterprise system based on its heroic love of liberty, Liberia possesses incalculable potential for becoming a model nation for private enterprise in Africa. Indeed, Liberia is one of the few countries in the

> World with the least non-economic controls and policy constraints that make it an ideal place for the embrace of the private investor" (1983, p. 1).

This statement characterizes Doe's objectives in international relations. Although Liberia had diplomatic relations with a few eastern bloc countries, its foreign policy principle and behavior have, generally, been anti-socialism and/or anti-communism. Socialist and/or communist dogmas were considered threats to the development and stability of Liberia. They were called "foreign ideologies," in comparison to capitalism, which was considered "the indigenous or local ideology."

The general picture of Liberia's economy was not bright in the 1980s. The growth in its export-import economy was seriously constrained by the weak world market for its iron ore, rubber and timber. As a result, in 1980, the value of Liberian imports fell 6.1. and 5.2 percent respectively. The situation worsened with the internal instability caused by the struggle for power.

In 1982, Head of State Samuel K. Doe made an official visit to the United States and was received by President Ronald Reagan. As a result of this trip, for the next two years the United States provided Liberia with the highest per capita levels of U.S. economic/security assistance ever extended to any sub-Saharan African country.[6] The combat against socialism began.

Total economic assistance (without counting food for peace, aid, Peace Corp, narcotics, and so on) was increasing yearly: $55.1 million in 1981; $65.5 million in 1982, and $62.8 million in 1983 (a slight decline). Loans given under economic assistance have also been increasing. For example, in 1981 it was about $15.0 million and in 1982 it was the same, while in 1983 it reached $16.7 million. Grants for the same years were $40.1 million, $50.5 million and $46.1 million respectively. Of the over $78 million in U.S. assistance in 1984, $13 million was for development grants, and $15.8 million for military assistance. The Economic Support Fund, known also as security support, was increased tremendously. Between 1962-79 the total amount was $5.2 million, while in 1980 it was $5.2 million; in 1981 it was about $32.0 million, in 1982 it was increased to $35.0 million; in 1983 it was $32.0 million and in fiscal year 1984, the security support fund increased to $34.15 million.

The over-all proposed aid for 1986 was $93 million, of which $48 million was for economic support and $13 million for military aid (Seyon, 1985, p. 856). The United States Congress stated that the $93 million would only be given if the elections were considered fair and meeting the liberal systems' standard. Despite the fact that the elections were far from being without fraud, the $ 93 million was delivered.

Additionally, the United States has had various programs for Liberia, such as PL-480, which supplied funds for the import of essential foodstuffs, mostly rice. Another program called DA provided some infrastructure assistance in "key development" areas such as education, health, sanitation, medical care, agriculture and training; ESF was disbursed in close cooperation with the IMF. It was used for debt service and to assist the government meets tough IMF performance criteria and conditionalities. Some specific programs were used to improve military conditions, such as housing, equipment, and so on, and to train Liberian soldiers. In 1979, military aid was $1.5 million. By 1983, it was $12.7 million, an increase of 846 percent (Ibid.).

Between 1980-1985, economic assistance had been directed toward one main objective: to allow the Liberian military government to make good progress toward its goal of returning the country to a civilian constitutional government by January 1986. The U.S. government had contributed at various stages of the government's effort to respect its promise. Yet the military regime did not allow free elections to occur, though two other parties were symbolically allowed to compete with the Doe Party (the National Democratic Party of Liberia).

Table 5.2
Some Key Economic Indicators of Liberia (in millions)

	1980	1981
Total Exports to the U.S.	125.6	23.5
U.S. Share of Exports	20.9	23.3
Imports for U.S.A.	22.8	30.7
Budget Revenue	222.4	223.7
Recurrent Expenditures	196.8	241.0
Development Budget (Govt.)	57.59	57.01
Debt Service Payment	47.5	25.1
Debt as % of Revenues	21.7	11.2
Balance of Payments	104.4	65.4
Population	1.80	1.86

Source: Economic Survey of Liberia, 1981.

Liberia has had an outstanding debt, which was estimated in 1986 to have been approximately $900 million. The IMF, with the support of the United States, committed itself to provide loans on a year-by-year basis. The U.S. served as the guarantor for Liberian loans from commercial banks as well.

SOCIAL AND POLITICAL IMPLICATION FOR LIBERIAN SOCIETY

During the cold war, Liberia was fully integrated into the periphery of international capitalism with the blessing and support of the U.S. At the end of the Cold War, consequence of this integration, among other factors, engendered the bloody power struggle that led to the collapse of the Liberian State and society. What are the implications of this integration and total marginalization (or what some call abandonment) on the Liberian people and society as a whole?

Where did the U.S dollar go and who did benefit from it? Before the formation of an oligarchic state, Liberian-American relations were basically maintained at cultural and historical levels. That is to say, cultural domination in Liberia did not go along with economic or financial domination, as was the case in most parts of Africa. Liberian settlements served like some kind of American cultural reservoir, to be used as a means of "civilizing" Africa. It is debatable whether this "civilizing mission" was based on humanitarian principles or it had only a hidden economic agenda. However, economic motivation began to surface with the formation of the Liberian State.

Pressures from the French and the British colonial powers, internal power struggles among Americo-Liberians and hostilities from the hinterland are among the factors which contributed to the development of different forms of unifying fragmented nationalist sentiments. The threats to the survival of black settlers did play a vital role in their solidarity and awareness that were reflected in some aspects of the formation of the state and its policies. Tubman understood this well when he pursued "unity," solidarity, assimilation, and open-door policies as prerequisites for nation building. Though there were some short periods of power struggle among various political parties in Liberia, the True Whig Party was the dominant political organization until 1980, though Liberia was never constitutionally a one-party state.

Liberia, as an oligarchic state, conducted its business like "family affairs." The True Whig Party and caste-like web of family-lodge-church cliques maintained this tradition as such. As Elliot Berg, quoted by Mehmet, said:

> "For more than 100 years the Liberian government operated like a kind of private club--without budgets, records, accounts, filing systems and procedures for making public decisions and executing them once made. It was a system in which expenditure control resided in the presidential power to sign all checks over $25, and in which formal budgeting was unknown, it was something dealt with in conversation with the president. That things worked this way didn't matter much before the 1950s, since governments had only a few million dollars to spend anyway, most of it for salaries" (Ibid.).

The state meant the ruling class and national interests represented those of this class. Economic assistance was used in the areas that helped to strengthen its power. American economic assistance began consolidation in Liberia when Liberia was almost about to become a British colony by defaulted because of its' numerous loans taken from British banks. The intent of U.S. and Firestone rubber venture was "to rescue" Liberia from its financial difficulties and to shift the dependence of the Liberian state from the European-centered capitalist-world economy to the American dominated capitalism.

The first thing that occurred in terms of the impact of U.S. relations during the Cold War is state privatization and development of both the bureaucratic and commercial bourgeoisie. Firestone encouraged the development of the commercial bourgeoisie, which could then depend on its technology and its capital. In the areas of trade and exploitation of rubber, this bourgeoisie would not threaten the interest of the United States and Firestone.

Generally, the bureaucratic bourgeoisie is comprised mainly of those members of society who want to secure social mobility through normal socialization processes: having University diplomas or having a good connection within the state apparatuses or prominent families. Most have been associated with the dominant values of the Americo-Liberian elite. One important feature of bureaucratic bourgeoisie is its 'nationalistic' outlook. Being in possession of state, it sees itself as the savior of the nation and identifies what are objectively its own or interests of the petty bourgeoisie or even the interests of other classes, as the interests of the whole nation.

Privatization of state operations meant the control of the state's affairs by very few members of the ruling class. Most of the members of this class were involved in joint ventures with multinational firms. Their own firms were often financed out of government subsidies. One example of this is the late Stephen Tolbert's Mesurado group of companies. Tolbert was the former minister of finance, and brother of the late President Tolbert, who himself was one of the largest private rubber producers in the country.

The state, in reality, was a private committee for managing the common affairs of the Liberian peripheral bourgeoisie. Its interests were sponsored and promoted both by multinational corporations and U.S. economic assistance. The ruling class interests and those of foreign corporations have not been philosophically in contradiction. This class has used its power to gain more wealth by exploiting natural resources with the managerial skills and technology of multinational corporations like U.S. Firestone. The government that kept wages down, controlled potential labor disputes and allowed transfer profits and dividends outside the country without much difficulty had also assured the multinational corporations.

AMERICAN ECONOMIC INTERVENTION

American economic assistance and private companies intensified Liberia's integration into the capitalist orbit. Without a strong national bourgeoisie, this whole process created a peripheral capitalist economy characterized by its low degree of development of the capitalist mode of production and articulation inside the country and also by its weak domestic policy for the distribution of public services.

In this peripheral formation, production was mainly for profit and not for the development of productive forces or the national economy. This profit was obtained through the creation of surplus-value consequent to the exploitation of labor-power in capitalist production and international trade. The result of this process divided Liberian society into that which Kenneth Adelman referred to in these words: "The disparity between the urbanized settlers and the rural natives once resembled that described by a Medieval priest: First, there's king, then nobility, then the gentry, then the merchants and laborers. Then there's nothing, and again nothing, and once more nothing. Then there's the peasant"(p. 11).

U.S. economic assistance supported existing political structures, and in that regard, it has been used to maintain and perpetuate the power of the ruling class. That is to say the U.S. dollar has also been utilized for political purposes. With this dollar, Tubman, Tolbert and Doe succeeded in reproducing themselves and maintaining their power.

American support became even more visible in the military regime as the U.S. financially sponsored the democratic processes that were destroyed by Doe. In October 1985, Samuel Doe "won" the presidential election with 50.9% while his party (the National Democratic Party) garnered 21 of 26 Senate seats and 51 of 64 positions in the House of Representatives. The Liberian election was considered by the majority of Liberians and foreign observers and journalists in Monrovia as a fiasco due to massive fraud and political manipulations organized by Doe's party. Though the United States considered using penalties against Doe if the elections were not fair and just, $86 million allocated by the Congress for the fiscal year 1986 was delivered in its entirety.

In addition, for many years the descendants of the Americo-Liberians received over 60 percent of the national income. In 1970, for instance, the average income of Liberians was $70 per annum while a top income group (mostly Americo-Liberians) was about $3, 272. The U.S. dollar went into the various sectors--balance of payments, to pay loans, to alleviate deficits and for political campaign funds. It was even used for monthly payments to government employees.

At the societal level, the impact of American economic intervention in national/domestic policies accelerated the development of internal contradictions. Three main social phenomena were engendered as a result of this economic assistance: consolidation of the ruling class' power as a *compradorial* class, manifestation of social and political movements, and development of the culture of poverty, or underdevelopment.

The dependent bourgeoisie that controlled the business of the state owed its position to the patronage of the metropolitan bourgeoisie and multi-national corporations. Though the Liberian ruling class had its share and interests in the national and private economic sectors, it was not capable of or even intended to compete with the U.S. and other foreign corporations. The Metropolitan U.S. continued to provide economic and military aid used by this class to maintain the status quo until the war. Economic assistance increased during the military regime even as Doe and his regime constantly violated human rights and democratic principles. Constitutionally, Liberia has never been a one-party state. But the ruling class utilized its political resources to make it function as a one-party state. Even with very little internal support, the military regime managed to change its uniforms to a civilian dress. In this process, terror and the economic and political instabilities that were created reached a level incomparable in previous Liberian regimes. Militarily and economically, American assistance was greater by the 1980s than in the previous decade. Yet Liberia became less "developed" than in the ten preceding years. The ruling class was too pacified by the illusion of capitalist success to introduce real innovations in production and appropriate social policy reforms.

Economic assistance supported the weak domestic policies of the ruling class, which appropriated surpluses, exploited labor, lived in comfort, exercised power and enjoyed their inflated social status. As a result of the unequal distribution of resources and access to power, manifestations of conflicts, contradictions and underdevelopment became part of Liberian society.

Starting in the 1970s, Liberia experienced both serious economic problems and political pressures from the progressive intellectuals who advocated more power-sharing and equal distribution of resources. The series of strikes in the private and public sectors in the 1970s, the Rice-Riot of 1979 and Amos Sawyer's (former President of the interim government and one of the founding fathers of the Movement for Social Justice [MOJA] in Africa) running for the Monrovian mayor's office against the True Whig party's candidate, led Liberia to a piece of history *sans retour*.

The origin of most social movements in Liberia can be found in the monopoly of power structures of the U.S.- sponsored ruling class, including the military regime. Most of the movements, like the Progressive Alliance of Liberia (PAL), believed "in sharing the pie in equitable ways and more political participation for all Liberians." All those opposition movements were born to challenge the ruling class.

Operating in Liberia since 1973, five years longer than PAL, MOJA has focused on grassroots work in rural development projects. Its support came from a wide range of social areas: rural peasants, students, and Liberian intelligentsia and business communities, to name a few. During the time of political struggle between the late president Doe and progressive forces, he characterized the University of Liberia as being "all MOJA people." From July 1984, following the lift on political bans as a step toward a return to civilian rule intended for January 1986, Liberia was a *théatre* of about ten political parties. Some of the most important include: Doe's National Democratic Party of Liberia (NDPL), the United People's Party led by Bacchus Matthew, the Liberian People's Party with Amos Sawyer as its leader, and the Liberian Action Party (led by the late Jackson F. Doe).

The United States encouraged and sponsored the processes which engendered "multi-partyism" in 1985, but despite the rough road it took, Doe did not lose his U.S. financial support. The United States could not trust and support any other party for fear of not being able to predict the political ideology and behavior of "an outsider." They feared the emergence of progressive movements among the youth and their leaders at the Universities. The development of events forced them to support the compromised leaders in the Philippines and Haiti, but why not in Liberia?

Though the democratic process had not worked in Liberia in the past, it would seem difficult to destroy its moral basis among various progressive forces in Liberian society. The University of Liberia was slowly producing anti-American sentiments among its student body. Though this does not mean the complete rejection of the American culture, it is a spirit of protest against the United States past policy vis-à-vis South Africa and its almost unconditional support of the Liberian ruling class. As internal contradictions continued to be rooted in the country, the role students played for the advancement of history was more important than the expected role of the small size of the urban working people (proletariat) and their potential allies, peasants. Although they were not armed and did not have means to take over state power, students in Liberia had a greater influence over the direction of political events in Liberia than the organized labor movement or any trade union.

The culture of poverty fostered the psychology of dependency historically connected with ruling class tactics, who used to distribute money and other commodities on the streets during carnivals and other occasions of festivity, much like Duvallier's style in Haiti. At the individual level, many people, especially the lower social strata, lost confidence in working or any other activities of self-reproduction. These people were virtually waiting for "manna" to come from heaven. The effects of the culture of poverty on Liberian society have been numerous: laziness, corruption, speculation and the loss of any nationalist sentiments. As a direct product of the peripheralization of Liberia, the culture of poverty has been, by its nature, an inherited dominant political culture in which the ruling class was perceived as God and therefore should not be challenged. Democracy from the top was not a political model that could be used to find solutions to this social crisis. In short, U.S. economic assistance directly divided society by supporting a *compradorial* bourgeoisie that was incapable of controlling the reproduction of the labor force, of collecting efficiently surplus and its allocation, and of controlling the market and technology.

I discussed the impact of U.S. relations with Liberia in terms of the Liberian state in crisis: crisis of legitimacy, crisis of mobilizing scarce resources for the development of the Liberian nation and cultural crisis. The Liberian State was in a serious crisis of legitimacy at the end of Cold War. The personification of the state was one of the symptoms of this crisis. The capitalist mode of production was considered a natural and not a foreign ideology. Yet the state was not capable of effectively and efficiently promoting the laissez-faire principle. The crisis of world capitalism was felt more seriously here than in Angola for instance. That is so because in Liberia, the state gave the impression that every one could make it and that capitalism with the U.S support could bring miracles quicker. Yet in reality only a few people participated in and benefited from the activities of the former sector of the economy.

The crisis of legitimacy was reflected in the incapacity of the ruling class to deliver services and satisfy the majority of people's needs. Being unable to influence the behavior and norms of the international market for the production and marketing of its commodities, the state counted mainly on "donations," "charity," the IMF and the World Bank, and the United States and taxes for its survival. Because the Liberian state did not have any legitimacy from either Liberian history and culture or its performance, the only tools it had to manipulate were the "legal system," "security of the state argument," coercion and co-optation. A common and/or national culture: vision, belief and worldview, etc. was almost absent in Liberia. Christianity, Islam and/or African religions did not very much provide the ground for the legitimacy of the state as in northern Africa, where Islam plays the role of unifying force.

Many people could not understand why the United States stood by and watched Liberia being torn down by an internal war. It is only through an historical analysis that one could be able to make relevant comments on U.S. behavior and its implications in the Liberian-American relations at the end of the war. There is no simple answer to this question. The United States watched the development of the events in Liberia carefully after the assassination of Doe. What happened was not very strange. It was predictable. Maybe the magnitude of what took place was unpredictable. In the early 1980s, it was clear to me that Liberia was about to enter a dark and tragic period. Doe was too rigid to consider debates and compromises. The distributive mechanisms were fundamentally biased against the majority of the population, because they were rooted in the dominant political philosophy of the ruling class.

Liberia is a land of political extremism. The U.S. embassy in Mamba Point, Monrovia was still functioning at the beginning of the carnage. It sent the marines to evacuate the U.S. citizens. Many foreigners and Liberians who could afford (who could pay) were evacuated as well. Not necessarily using the escape-goat argument, the United States is not innocent in what has happened in Liberia. It strongly supported all of the last three Liberian presidents before the collapse of the state in 1991.

TRENDS AND PROSPECT AFTER THE COLD WAR

One cannot say with a high level of precision what direction Liberian-American political and economic relations will take in the 21st century and beyond, how they will be operationalized or what forms they may take and which packages they might be put in. This is due to the fact that the world is in a major transition of uncertainty and ambiguity. Many factors are still undefined. People around the world, including Liberians and Americans, are in the process of redefining themselves in order to articulate, for better or for worse, what they consider to be their interests. However, we can identify certain patterns in these relations that can be generalized for policy and scholarship purposes.

One of the most important characteristics of world politics today is the search for new re-alignments in power relationships. Within the logic of multipolarity, every state is looking for a new identity, be it cultural or political. Another characteristic, which is specific to Africa, is further marginalization of the continent. The assumption that the end of East-West confrontational policies and politics will engender more relationships between the north and south is misleading. Africa came out of this political, ideological and military battle extremely weak in economic and social progress, institutional building and political terms. One of the consequences of the end of the Cold War is the fact that through regional or sub-regional movements, states are prepared to promote their interests collectively. ECOMOG in Liberia has its appreciation within this regional framework. Capitalist America has also some internal and external pressures to re-adjust itself to the demands and forces of a polycentric world. Despite the fact that it did not formally have any colony in Africa, today the United States has a wider political leverage, that is to say, a larger political space to operate from. In addition, it is attempting to resume its post-war position: the police of the world in a truncated world capitalism of which it is the primary creator. What can it offer to Liberia or gain from it in the 21st century and what can Liberia offer to or gain from the United States?

During the Cold War, the conflict between the state and aspirations of the majority of the Liberian people exploded. The privatization of the state accelerated the process of monopolization of business by the ruling class. The hegemony that this class established in the total control of domestic politics and economics was sponsored and supported by American economic assistance and private investments.

Tubman, Tolbert and Doe believed, as the leaders of the client regimes of the U.S., that they could acquire all the necessary inputs for the development of Liberia. The result was different. Liberia was incorporated into the backyard of capitalism where it had no power to change the mechanisms of its intercourse in international relations. These regimes reproduced themselves with the blessing of American assistance, but they were too weak to foster any qualitative internal change for providing more jobs, for allowing any real political participation to occur, or for appropriating surpluses.

American economic assistance and private investments increased before the war. Between the 1970s and the middle of the 1980s, the performance on the national economy was degraded as shown in budget deficits, a decline in national revenues and in the international price of rubber, iron and timber. The American dollar has had a strong economic and political role to play here as it went to pay salaries and debts, and sponsored political campaigns. But American direct economic assistance, either as grants or loans, was not invested on a long-term basis. It was used mainly to support existing political institutions. This created social disequilibrium between political leaders and people rather than creating "socio-political stability." In addition, the structure of Liberian social formation: a peripheral capitalist state with client regimes organized by the *compradorial* class was authoritarian instead of liberal (U.S. model). The Americo-Liberians had been incapable of forming an internal capitalist state.

The hegemonic political position of the previous regimes, including Doe's ambitions to be like Tubman and/or an Americo-Liberian elite (or the Congoes), and their U.S. support accelerated the process of power struggle. As social and political conditions deteriorated daily, the progressive forces voiced their claims, supported by the poor masses. The ideological battle between Doe's regime and some groups among the progressive forces could be predicted. The privatization of the state's agencies increased the unemployment rate and also promoted high taxation policies that provoked social dislocation in both urban and rural sectors.

For many years, the United States' interests in Liberia covered a whole range of areas: economic, geo-political, military and strategic. The actualization of these interests and their maintenance were the undertakings of a dependent state that had no clear vision of national interests. This weak domestic policy could not survive without the direct intervention of the United States. That is to say, the United States' economic relations with Liberia have been more than economic. The U.S. identified priorities for Liberia and provided services and human resources in many sectors.

All previous trends of U.S. foreign policy show that it continued to intensify its economic assistance to Liberia in order to impede and/or to counteract the struggle of leftist groups, even after the collapse of Marxism. This assistance is likely to be small compared to the real needs for eliminating the crisis Liberia has experienced. Before the collapse of the state, Liberia was not in a transitional phase toward any kind of democratic society. It has to be re-constructed first. Though one would not predict with precision in what direction the forces of change may lead the country, it must not be mistaken that anti-Americanism is likely to emerge among social groupings of suffering Liberians. The humiliation many Liberians are experiencing from American embassies in West African capital cities will also contribute to the emergence of a nationalist consciousness.

At the end of the Cold War, the political equation changed. Liberia's geo-political role is dead at this point. Iron ore and rubber are not as attractive as they used to be in international markets. Ideologically, Liberia did not present any threat to the "stability" of the West African sub-region. Doe did not have any strong relations with America's potential or real enemies in the world. He was in the process of transforming himself into becoming either a Mobutu or an Eyadema. It should also be added that for some reason, the United States has always had some ambiguous attitudes toward Liberia. Many questions are still unanswered, especially on how Charles Taylor emerged from the Boston prison in Massachusetts where he was indicted for embezzling money from the general service office when he was its general manager (it had the privileges of a ministerial position in Doe's government). Although he used mostly the U. S made weapons, the U.S. did not officially support Taylor's invasion. It did not strongly support the interim government of Amos Sawyer either.

An armed power struggle in Liberia continues to destroy lives, culture and values. Almost every Liberian has lost a relative or a friend in the war. The trauma of this war will last for many years among the Liberian people. What is likely to happen after this tragic episode is over? The process of re-construction will be difficult and slow because of the lack of initial capital, material resources and philosophical guidance. But this war has produced several phenomena. For example, loyalty to ethnicity and the spirit of class struggle are simultaneously emerging. It should be said that both the Americo-Liberians/Congoes and other ethnic groups have proportionally suffered from the war. Yet the non Americo-Liberians/Congoes tend to consider themselves as victims of the system that was created and supported by the United States. Thus, re-construction will be shaped by strong feelings of nationalism. This nationalism is likely to be generally ethnic and anti-American. Even Charles Taylor has used nationalist slogans against what he calls the "imperialist intervention of the ECOMOG operation" initiated by Ibrahim Babangida, the former President of Nigeria. The new leaders of the future Liberia will attempt to diversify their economic relations.

A generalized common sense assumption that derives from the logic at the end of the Cold War is that the new era may stimulate and/or encourage more understanding among states and peoples, creating a new comprehensive basis for a worldwide cooperation that is needed for global change (Betts, 1994). This idealistic view has to be critically analyzed and understood in light of specific historical and political configurations. Could this idealist assumption be applicable to the asymmetric Liberian-American relations? Realist scholarship, based on the centricity of the state, may suggest a different perspective; that is, the end of visible ideological and militaristic conflicts between the Americo-Liberians/Congoes and other ethnic groups has not altered the possible confrontation about security and interests of the state east and West.

The claims embodied in the current movements of changes are reflected by the rise of national and popular movements in most parts of the world, the intensive degradation of the ecosystem by overuse of chemical products and high technology in the systems of production and manufacturing, the improvement in long distance communication technologies and computer science, rapid mechanisms in the transfer of capital, the globalization of capital and the internationalization of poverty. Although the Cold War unexpectedly ended without the incidence of a major war between the United States and the former Soviet Union on their own soil, the legacy they created between 1917 and 1989 is still strongly with us. That is to say, the world remains dangerously militarized. Liberia is a case in point. An access to weaponry of various sophistication, including nuclear capability, is much easier today than what it was yesterday. In addition to worldwide poverty, polarization between the north and south will be intensified as we continue in the 21st century, a century of unprecedented competition. Resources will be scarcer and world population will disproportionally continue to increase.

The effects of the Cold War have been more devastating in Africa than in other parts of the south because for more than three decades Africa was partially transformed into the battle zones between the communist Soviets, and capitalists America and Western Europe. The U.S. sponsored regimes in Liberia suppressed, oppressed and killed thousands of people and displaced almost million of Liberians. In the new Liberia, the hot war will be inherited with all its implications. Ad hoc peace arrangements will not produce stable conditions for implementing liberal democracy and policies that can articulate the agenda of sustainable development.

The United States tried to maintain its hegemonic power between 1945 and 1970. During this period, its visibility in world affairs, including Africa was intensified. Strategically, it needed Liberia to be used as a preparatory ground/space or information center to move to other parts of Africa and Asia. The Voice of America was also playing such a role in Liberia. Suddenly, the equation changed. A different ball game with its own rules has replaced the old one. After much destruction in Liberia, which is one of the consequences of the policies of U.S.-supported dictators and the Americo-Liberian elite, the United States has neither political will/interest/moral commitment nor the financial interest to reconstruct Liberia. The United States is working through its dominant institutions: the International Monetary Fund (IMF) and the World Bank, to impose its dominant ideology and economic programs throughout the world. After peace is totally restored and political and social institutions are established in Liberia, the United States may intervene through those institutions to give loans to Liberians. It may do so in order to ensure that U.S-manufactured goods are revitalized in Liberia, although this constitutes a miniscule market, indeed. However, this is not likely to be the major objective in U.S. policy. The U.S. private sector may return to make speculations again. But the United States will not play the role of guarantor of Liberia's foreign loans and grants, as was the case in the past.

Since 1997, when he was elected as the president of Liberia, Charles Taylor, the former rebel, has not developed clearly predictable relations between his government and Liberia. Two years after his election, the relations between United States and Liberia have not been "normalized." He is being accused of supporting the rebel movement in Sierra Leone. As it is reported by Human Rights Watch:

> "A rift in U.S.-Liberia relations followed the September 1998 outbreak of violence in Monrovia when Liberian security forces were responsible for wounding two Americans in a shooting incident outside the U.S. Embassy, and the war in Sierra Leone further strained relations. The U.S. and other international donors made it clear that there would be no resumption of non-humanitarian assistance to Liberia until an investigation into the September events had been conducted" (1999, p. 55).

The United States government is still suspicious of Taylor's dictatorship political tendencies. In addition to the fact that the Liberian State is far from being defined even as a semi-democratic society, human rights abuses have not decreased. Many Liberians were angry when "July 1999, the U.S. announced that it was ending the Temporary Protected Status (TPS) program for Liberians on September 1999, which allowed some 10,000 Liberians in the U.S. since 1991 to remain and work in the U.S. However, in September, the

President granted Deferred Enforced Departure (DED) for Liberians, which will provided temporary relief for one year (1999, p. 55).

African states in general are deeply weakened by multinationals and multilateral financial institutions. If a liberal approach is what Liberians would opt to use in order to re-organize their system of production and social relations, their chance to have access to foreign capital, investments and technologies in the north is not with the United States alone but rather with multilateral financial and economic institutions and multinationals. Liberians would have to be able to compete with others. Liberian-American economic relations may move in the area of trade, but this will not be done at the level of U.S. bilateral economic relations specifically with Liberia, but within a framework of sub-Sahara Africa in general. Chance and hope for Liberia lie not with the United States, but with Africa, its sub-regional organizations, and countries in the south.

Liberia must re-organize its priorities in order to prepare itself to enter the century 21st century with a relatively high level of confidence. Its policies must be autocentric and pan-African. The end of the Cold War gives Liberia a chance to change from being a passive actor in world politics. Its policies need to be more nationalistic and democratic within the framework of strong cooperation with African states, countries and people. Policies inspired by determined popular needs and national interests might provide the ground for changes of economic and political relations between Liberia and the U.S. It is only when the criteria and conditions of relations are set up in Liberia and by Liberians for their own interests that economic and political relations between Liberia and the U.S. will be productive and beneficial for Liberians. This requires a structural change in the Liberian political economy, its social systems, and a new leadership that is linked to the people and which also gets its power and legitimacy from them. Only that can make a difference. Popular needs and national economic development trends that are fully democratic are likely to create such a leadership.

CONCLUSION

Between 1945 and 1989, Liberia-U.S. relations were neo-colonial. The U.S. intervened in most aspects of the state apparatuses, including in policy formation and implementation. The intervention weakened the compradorial bourgeoisie to invent and compete with the metropolitan bourgeoisie. With the U.S. financial and military support, the Liberian ruling class monopolized the local economy without necessarily controlling its marketing processes in the international environment. The contradictions of Cold War politics and political philosophy helped the Liberian ruling class to consolidate its power. This consolidation allowed Tubman, Tolbert and Doe to rule absolutely, but it did not destroy completely the dynamics of civil society. Those contradictions were responsible for the emergence of the popular movements that forced the state to accept the multiparty politics. As the geo-politics of the world changes, the U.S. interest for Liberia declined to almost zero by 1990.

The end of the Cold War cannot be viewed only as the end of some negative perception of history characterized by domination and exploitation of superpowers, and the so-called triumph of capitalism. The end of a bipolar world can also articulate new possibilities on the multipolar base. It can advance new ways of thinking and possibilities for Africans and their elites to concretely think about themselves as being in the center of the world politics. As a result of further marginalization of Africa in the world market and politics by the Western capitalists, strong nationalists are likely to emerge in Africa in the 21st century. That is to say, Africans are being forced to invent new means for their survival. At the end of the Cold War politics, Liberia was not rescued by the U.S. but by the ECOMOG (Economic Community of the West African States Peace Monitoring Group). The contradictions of the Cold War in Liberia have contributed toward the re-creation of Liberia. Liberia has become an integrative part of Africa. If peace is established in Liberia, the U.S. will try to renegotiate its position with various elite in Liberia. Despite the fact that the U.S has an eye on Liberia, it has not started this re-negotiation yet. Since 1997, the United States political elite has had an ambiguous position toward Liberia. As it is stated in Human Watch:

> "The U.S. sought to provide approximately (U.S.) $ 27 million in assistance to Liberian during financial year 1999, the bulk being some $10 million in development assistance aimed at capacity-building and democratization and $ 13.1 million in food aid. However, Congress put a hold on $1.2 million of aid designated for strengthening civil society and supporting the legislature, and for protecting human rights" (1999, p. 55).

However, the remaining important questions are: What will be the new basis for this re-negotiation? And can/should the U.S be trusted after its indifference regarding the Liberian tragedy?

The legacy of extreme poverty combined with a high level of political instability and serious elements of political struggle challenge any claims the United States has had toward the Liberian state and the Liberian people. Liberians should explore options for a selective de-linking approach from the structures of the U.S. dominated zone of influence and they should try also to promote diversification. This is one of the best options that is objective and would also make sense politically, socially, and economically.

Notes

1. This was a philanthropic organization established in the United States in 1816 for the purpose of repatriating slaves and free blacks from the United States. Many abolitionists supported it both blacks and whites.

2. The Americo-Liberians, known also as settlers, refer here to a small ethnic group of the descendants of the free black people who came from the U.S. and

settled in the West Coast of Africa starting in 1821. Today, though the expression is not popularly used in Liberia, it includes both assimilated natives and the Congoes.

3. The author's interview with some workers in Harber, Liberia, 1996-1999.

4. A Document from the United States Embassy in Monrovia, "Decline in Economic Growth, U.S. Trade Opportunity, Monrovia A-17.

5. From a private conversation with the author in early 1984 at a reception with Mr. William Swing, then U.S. ambassador to Liberia.

6. Unclassified Document from the United States Embassy in Monrovia, 1984.

7. Human Rights Watch, *World Report 2000: Africa Section*, New York, New York: Human Watch, December 1999.

REFERENCES

Adelman, L. Kenneth. 1979. Liberia: "Hosting the O.A.U." Africa Report, (July-August). Africa News, (1980) April 21.

Allen, Susan. 1973. "President Tolbert: Exclusive Interview," Africa Development 8 (July).

Betts, Richard K. (ed.). 1994. Conflict After The Cold War: Arguments on Causes of War and Peace, New York, Macmillan Publishing Company.

Cardoso, F. and E. Faletto. 1979. Dependency and Underdevelopment in Latin America, Berkeley, Los Angeles, University of California Press.

Chilcote, H. Ronald. ed. 1982. Dependency and Marxism: Toward a Resolution of the Debate, Boulder, Colorado: Westview Press.

Clower, Robert et al. 1966. Growth Without Development: An Economic Survey of Liberia, Evanston: Northwestern University Press.

Czempiel, Ernest-Otto. 1983. "America-Germany: A Particular Relations," German Foreign Affairs Review. Vol. 34, 78 - 101.

Eastman, Ernest. 1983. The Speech on "Liberia's new role in Africa." Georgetown University, November 29. Washington, D.C.

Dunn, D. Elwood. 1979. The Foreign Policy of Liberia During Tubman Era: 1944 -1971, Benham, Hutchinson Pub. Group.

Hlophe, Stephen. 1979. Class, Ethnicity and Politics in Liberia, Washington, D.C.

Howard, Lawrence 1988. Involvement in Africa South of Sahara, 1800-1860, New York: Garland Publishers.

Gifford, Paul. 1994. Christianity and Politics in Does' Liberia, Cambridge, New York: Cambridge University Press.

Fleischman, Janet. 1994. Easy Prey: Child Soldiers in Liberia, New York: Human Rights Watch.

Lawyers Committee for Human Rights, 1991. First Steps: Rebuilding the Justice System in Liberia. New York, N.Y.: Lawyers Committee for Human Rights.

Lumumba-Kasongo, Tukumbi. 1992. "Clinton and Africa." Africa Notes (December), 18 – 31..

Lowenkopf, Martin. 1976. Politics in Liberia: The Conservative Road to Development. Stanford, California: Hoover Institution Press.

McLaughlin, V. Russe. 196l. Foreign Investment and Development in Liberia, New York and London: Frederick A. Praeger, Publishers.

Mehmet, Ofay. 1978. Economic Planning and Social Justice in Developing Countries, New York: St. Martin's Press.

MPEA, 1973. Indicative Manpower Plan of Liberia for the Period 1972-1982, (Monrovia, June).

Nkrumah, Kwame. 1971. Neo-Colonialism: Last Stage of Imperialism. New York: International Publishers.

Nimley, Anthony J. 1991. Government and Politics in Liberia, Nashville, Tenn., Nashville, Academic Publishers International.

Packenham, A. Robert. 1976. Liberal America and the Third World: Political Development Ideas in Foreign Aids and Social Sciences, Princeton, N.J.: Princeton University Press.

Plekhanov, George. 1940. The Materialist Concept of History, New York: International Publishers.

Ruiz, Hiram A. 1992. Uprooted Liberians: Casualties of A Brutal War, Washingrton, D.C.: U.S. Committee for Refugees

Richardson, R. Nathaniel. 1959. Liberia's Past and Present, London: The Diplomatic Press and Publishing Co.

Saha, Santosh C. 1990. A History of Agriculture in Liberia, 1882-1970: Transference of American Valuea, Lewiston, New York: Edwin Mellen Press.

Sawyer, Amos, 1992. The Emergence of Autocracy in Liberia: Tragedy and Challenge, Francisco, California, Institute for Cotemporary Studies.

Schlesinger, A. 1967. A Thousand Days, New York: Fawcett World Library.

Seyon, Patrick. 1985. "Liberis: Threat to Democracy," West Africa, No. 3528 (8 April).

Smith, Stewart. 1974. U.S. Neo-colonialism in Africa, New York: International Publishers. Survey of Current Business, August 1963, October 1968 and 1971.

Tarr, Byron. 1993 "The ECOMOG Initiative in Liberia: A Liberian Perspective," Issue: A Journal of Opinion, Volume XXI/1-2.

Townsend, E. R. (ed.) 1955. President Tubman of Liberia, (London: Consolidated Publications, Co., Ltd.

U. S. AID Report on a brief history of development assistance to Liberia by the United States government (1946-1980).

United States Congress, House Committee on Foreign Affairs Sub-Committee on Africa. 1994. U.S. Policy in Liberia: Hearing before the Sub-Committee on Africa of the Committee on Foreign Affairs, House of Representatives, One hundred Third Congress, Second Session, Washington, D.C.: GPO.

Wallerstein, Immanuel. 1973. "Class and Class Conflict in Contemporary Africa." Canadian Journal of African Studies,Vol. 7, No. 3. 34 - 55.

West Africa. 1985. No. 3529 (April 15), 457 - 469.

World Trade Information Service. 1951. Part 1, No. 58, 45-58.

Chapter 6

The Illusion of Governance in Kenya

Shadrack Wanjala Nasong'o

INTRODUCTION

At the turn of the nineteenth century, missionary evangelists represented an exemplification of a mind convinced that it has a monopoly of truth. They left their Western world to carry the gospel to the 'heathens' of Africa with a supposedly honest and genuine desire to save their souls from eternal damnation, from fire and brimstone. They were deeply hurt and frustrated when the 'obstinate heathen' would not 'see the light' and persisted in worshipping his own ancient gods or, at best, adapted the teachings of the new religion to his own traditional forms of worship and continued to worship within the context of the religion of his forebearers as illustrated by the emergence of Elijah Masinde's *Dini Ya Msambwa* in Western Kenya in the 1940s (Were 1971). The most ardent of the missionaries could not understand why.

Since the 'death of God' in the Western world, as Nehru (1980: 126) points out, the mantle of the missionary has fallen on the evangelists of democracy who are equally convinced that they are in possession of the universal and only truth. They regard it as their divine duty to propagate the new gospel to the rest of the world and are as deeply hurt and frustrated as their missionary evangelist forerunners were, at the stubborn refusal of the Third World to accept it. Nonetheless, as we come to the threshold of the third millenium, the question of democracy has assumed a hitherto unheralded importance "...partly because every other category has experienced intellectual exhaustion or the exhaustion of intellectuals, and partly because the issue of democracy, whatever we mean by it, has been linked to human rights concerns in general" (Harowitz 1981:37). The issue of democracy has thus become so compelling a force that in respect of Kenya, a myriad of civil organizations sprang up to help push forward the democratic agenda. The main preoccupation of these groups is with how to bring about a people's government; a transparent and accountable government; or simply, democratic governance.

This chapter discusses the meaning and dimensions of democracy and evaluates the democratic experience in Kenya vis-à-vis the ideals of representative government and liberal democracy. The paper analyses these issues both in Kenya's first and second republics under Jomo Kenyatta and Daniel arap Moi respectively. The paper's main thesis is that whether one looks at it from the standpoint of the democratic activists in Kenya; from the vantage point of the merchants of political pluralism; or from the fervent argumentations of the powers-that-be, the idea of democratic governance in Kenya within the rubric of existing socio-economic, political, and constitutional structures is, in fact, an illusion of the epoch.

THE AGE OF DEMOCRATIC CONFUSION

Democracy is the most often used and invariably the most widely misused concept in political parlance. The concept of democracy has become increasingly honorific especially in the twentieth century so much that governments of all shades and orientations claim to be democracies. Hence the idea of 'progressive democracy', 'popular democracy', 'Liberal democracy', ' Christian democracy', and 'non-party democracy' among others, are advanced to describe all manner of political systems. Against this background, Sartori (1965:9) quotes Bertrand de Jouvenal who asserts that discussions about democracy, arguments for and against it, are intellectually worthless because we do not know what we are talking about. He argues that democracy is "... a highflown name for something which does not exist, a misleading term for what it claims to designate".

According to Abraham Lincoln, United States President in the mid nineteenth century, democracy is 'government of the people by the people for the people'. Literally therefore, democracy is assumed to mean 'power of the people', hence the popular slogan of ' let the people decide' in contemporary Kenyan politics. However, Dahl has it that what are labeled, as democracies are actually polyarchies (Sartori 1965:4). There thus is no agreed definition for 'democracy' and any attempt to make one is resisted by all since"...defenders of any kind of regime claim that it is a democracy, and fear that they might have to stop using the word if it were tied down to one clear meaning" (Sartori, 1965:3). In this regard, Sartori contends that we are living in an age of democratic confusion for, as Eliot points out (in Sartori 1965:8), "When a term has become so universally sanctified as democracy, I begin to wonder whether it means anything in meaning too many things."

Trite though it may seem to say, the term 'democracy' has its origins in the Greek lexicals '*demo*' meaning people, and '*kratia*' meaning power. Hence the etymological idea that democracy is power of the people. Within this understanding of the concept of democracy, the ancient Greek City States are presented as democratic ideal models where all the people met in a kind of town square and deliberated over the affairs of state in a political system of direct participation in matters of government. This position is however fallacious and therefore entirely incorrect. It is fallacious and wrong because, even within the Greek City States, significant sections of society were excluded from participation in matters of governance. These included the propertyless, slaves, women, and needless to say, children. It is in respect of this, one is wont to surmise, that Plato once said: " I thank God that I was born Greek, not barbarian; freeman, not slave; man, not woman; (and above all, that I was born in the days of Socrates)" (Durant 1927:19).

Democracy has thus never been realized in absolute terms across time and space. The idea of representation is therefore central to the whole essence of democracy. In this regard, democracy is government by the will of the governed and in their interests and aspirations. Towards this end, the people must have the right to choose their representatives, to elect those to constitute the government in free, fair and just elections; and to review the mandate they bestow on their representatives at regular intervals.

The above position notwithstanding, a problem emerges at this level as to what is meant by 'people'. As Sartori (1965) points out, even in Greek the term *demos* is ambiguous. In the fifth century B.C., it meant the Athenian community gathered in the *ekklesia*; in which case *demos* could be assumed to mean *plenum* – the entire body; or *polloi* – the many; or *pleiones* – the majority; or *ochlos* – the mob. Such ambiguities proliferate with translation into modern languages. For instance, Italian *popolo*, French *peuple*, and German *volk* are said to convey the idea of a singular entity denoting an organic whole that may be expressed by an indivisible general will. The English word *people* on the hand indicate a plural. In this respect, to say 'democracy' is tantamount to saying 'polycracy' meaning a separable multiplicity, just a great many; or an integral plurality meaning everybody; or an entity, meaning an organic whole. Alternatively, we may have 'people' as a plurality expressed by an absolute majority principle as well as a majority expressed by a limited majority principle.

For all practical purposes, the usage of the term 'people' insofar as democratic governance is concerned refers to many individuals and not to a quasi-monolithic and transcendental being possessed of its own independent existence. This usage refers to 'the many' – the majority as opposed to ' the few' – the minority. This however, is not to say that democracy is a dictatorship of the majority. It is, indeed, a system in which the will of the majority reigns supreme; but in so reigning, it takes cognizance of minority views and protects minority rights.

THE THREE DIMENSIONS OF DEMOCRACY

On the whole, democracy exists at three levels. In its abstract form; in its practical sense, and lastly in its concrete moment. As an abstract concept, democracy is a hypothetical reality or state of affairs conceived of and existing in the minds of individuals. "It is an intellectual creation, a mentally visualized reality postulated or proposed as a model of the possible, the desirable in matters of social co-existence, social intercourse and the governance of men and women in society" (Gitonga 1987:7). In its abstract dimension therefore, democracy is a dream, a vision that represents an ideal and envisages a world of perfection, a utopia. It is because of this that many argue that democracy is impossible to attain hence assertions to the effect that democracy is forever impossible.

In its practical sense, democracy consists of the ways and means of translating the democratic ideal into a concrete reality. It comprises the technicalities or the `how' of implementing a democratic program or strategy. According to Gitonga (1987:12), this poses the question "How should the people organize themselves to exercise their rules?" or, "What institutional arrangements or mechanisms ensure that in its concrete effects or results, the government manifests the attributes of a good, fair and just government?"

Lastly, the concrete dimension of democracy comprises the balance sheet of the past and present experiments of mankind to install a democratic order, and hence realize the ideal of democracy. This raises a number of questions according to Gitonga; What, for instance, has come out of the immeasurable sacrifices of blood, sweat, and tears that have been shed at the alter of democracy? In terms of the democratic ideal, where does the world stand today? What is the gap between the ideal and the real? These questions relate to the determination of the distance that has been covered and what remains to be covered before humanity finally reaches the `Democratic Promised Land'.

Generally, what is aspired to in the African quest for democratic governance is actualization of the ideals of liberal democracy. The main features of liberal democracy are free competition among political parties, free and fair periodic elections, and respect for the fundamental freedoms of thought, expression, and assembly. According to Makinda (1996:556), plenty of evidence exists which illustrate that such a system of government has the potential to encourage political stability and accountability, and to help consolidate public institutions.

DEMOCRACY UNDER KENYATTA: 1963 – 1978

The record of democratic practice in post-independence Kenya is very poor. Whereas the fight for independence was intended, *inter alia,* to afford the Africans an opportunity to fully participate in their own government, once political independence was attained in 1963, the political elite set about creating structures that undermined this objective. The independence constitution, a product of the Lancaster House compromise was intended to facilitate democratic practice in independent Kenya. It provided for a multiparty political system, a quasi-federal (Majimbo) form of government with six Regions each with a Regional Assembly responsible for agricultural land, primary and intermediate education, local government, and public health. The Regional Assemblies drew their very existence and powers from the constitution not from the Central Government. On its part, the Central Government was responsible to the central parliament for external affairs, defense, international trade, customs, major economic development, and sourcing of foreign economic assistance. At the center was instituted a bicameral parliament with a Lower House (House of Representatives) and an upper House (Senate). The Lower House consisted of elected representatives from Single member constituencies while Senate was made up of one member from each district. Senate was constituted to guard the constitution from arbitrary amendment, as such amendments would require a 75% majority in the Lower House and a 90% majority in Senate. In effect, Senate was given powers to delay bills except those relating to finance (Chweya, et al. 1996).

Unfortunately however, this independence constitution was never intended to be implemented. The Lancaster compromise was a mere political gimmick by the victorious Kenya African National Union (Kanu) party to hasten the granting of independence. Within one year of independence, the opposition Kenya African Democratic Union (KADU) was compelled through intrigue and manipulation to disband itself and by 1966, the two Houses were merged effectively reversing the independence constitutional arrangement. The occasion of KANU's 'self dissolution' in 1964 saw Kenyatta declare that "...opposition for opposition's sake has died for ever and ever, Amen" (Mutoro *et al*, 1996:13). Indeed, Kenyatta was very uneasy about opposition to his rule and dissenting political views within the ruling party, KANU. He moved to stem the tide of ideological polarization within the party under the aegis of the Limuru KANU delegates' conference of March 11-13, 1966 where the left wing under Oginga Odinga was marginalized from the center of power. This led to the emergence of Kenya People's Union (KPU), a formidable opposition party but which Kenyatta banned in early 1969 following a verbal exchange between Odinga and himself at Kisumu followed by a riot by Odinga's supporters (see Mutoro *et al*, 1996).

Kenyatta went further and barred ex-KPU members from contesting in the general election held later in 1969. Essentially therefore, by forcing the dissolution of KADU and banning KPU, Kenyata effectively derailed the institutionalization of liberal democracy in Kenya. As Chepkwony (1987) argues, political developments in the country saw an active people's participation in national politics decrease with elections remaining a mere formality, a political ritual devoid of any meaning. In spite of the fact that elections were held periodically during Kenyatta's rule, in 1969 and 1974, therefore, these were not democratic elections as they involved only one political party, KANU, competing against it. Without alternative forms of government, competing political values, programs and platforms in the form of political parties vying for governance, such elections remained basically a contest between personalities and therefore irrelevant in respect of the ideals of liberal democracy.

Kenyatta's move against democracy was supported and bolstered by a number of constitutional amendments, which increasingly vested power in his office. Between independence in 1963 and 1969, there were ten such amendments, which necessitated a rewriting of the entire constitution to incorporate them. The tenth amendment of 1969 for instance, empowered the president to appoint members of the electoral commission whose role is to determine the number and boundaries of constituencies, among others. "The executive is thus entrusted with discretionary powers in the manner of constituting the very instrumentality which organizes the representational basis of the legislature" (Oloo 1996:18). The amendment further replaced the twelve specially elected members (elected by parliament) with twelve nominated members (nominated by the president), thereby changing parliament's composition to the advantage of the sitting government, and to the detriment of representational variety. Hence the argument that "...institutional authoritarianism marked the advent of the decade of the 1970s" (Chepkwony 1987:108).

Kenyatta can thus be said to have closed the door to democracy and successfully established what has come to be called personal rule in the history of continental African politics. Kenyatta felt so comfortably powerful that once he used KANU to marginalize Odinga and his fellow radicals in 1966, he had no more use for the party and left it into abeyance with neither meeting of its top organs nor national party elections between 1966 and 1978 when he eternally left the political scene. He even went further o create a power base disguised as a welfare association known as Gikuyu Embu Meru Association (GEMA) which, by mid 1970s, acted informally as parliament, cabinet, and quite often, as judiciary in the country, prompting the late popular member of Parliament for Nyandarua North, Josiah Mwangi Kariuki to remark thus:

> "I tell you the cabinet is not running the country. It is no use having ministers who do take decisions, who have no control over their ministries" (Chepkwony 1987:169)?

Martin (Joseph Olukhanya) Shikuku, Member for Butere was later to complain in parliament that the Kenyatta government was intent on killing parliament the same way it had killed KANU; a remark that elicited demands for substantiation or withdrawal to which the presiding Deputy Speaker and Member for Tinderet, the nationalist Jean Marie Seroney loudly wondered how Shikiku could substantiate the obvious! Both Shikuku and Seroney were arrested within the precincts of parliament soon thereafter and shuttled to detention without trial with Kenyatta metaphorically warning, "the hawk in the sky is ready to swoop on the chickens" (Chepkwony 1987:167).

Essentially, from 1969 to the end of his tenure in August 1978 when he met his demise, Kenyatta reigned supreme, like a monarch, unchallenged. His ideology of nation building tended to justify and emphasize bureaucratic centralization of power rather than its dispersion to other organs of state. It was thus anathema to the fundamental ideals of democracy.

DEMOCRATIC SEESAW UNDER MOI: 1978-1992

Daniel arap Moi took over the presidency in 1978 after a decade as Jomo Kenyatta's vice president. Despite the precarious nature of his ascension to the highest office, with attempts having been made to thwart his assumption of the presidency by Kenyatta's Kiambu caucus, Moi consolidated himself in power soon enough and vowed that he would follow in his predecessor's *nyayo* (footsteps). Thus was born the era of *Nyaoism* in Kenya's political history. Moi remained popular among the Kenyan people for about five year's upto the attempted coup of August 1, 1982. From then on, he over-reached himself in respect of clamping down on competitive politics, which he saw as sedition and treason. The clampdown on political dissenters was so intensive that many people, especially 'radical' lawyers, university lecturers and students were arrested and locked up. Some of them were truly anti-establishment and political activists. While others were jailed simply for reason of sporting a beard, interpreted as Marxist and hence communism which, in the eyes of the Moi regime, was a 'threat to state security'.

Moi increasingly became intolerant of the freedom of the press, expression, and assembly so much so that in 1982 he rushed through parliament legislation making Kenya a *de jure* one party state thereby facilitating the beginning of KANU's supremacy over parliament as the supreme decision-making body in the country (Maren 1987:210). The introduction of section 2(A) to the constitution through this legislation was ostensibly meant to forestall the eventuality of an opposition political party which Jaramogi (Adonija Obadiah Ajuma) Oginga Odinga and George (Moseti Matandiko) Anyona were then contemplating to register. Under the crackdown on political dissenters that followed, advocates of political competition either fled to exile or were forced to operate underground leading to such clandestine organizations as *Mwakenya* (Patriotic Front for the Liberation of Kenya) with their underground publication *Mpatanishi* (The Arbiter) whose existence became public knowledge in March 1986.

Moi crowned all this by officially declaring that KANU superseded the authority of parliament and thus in effect relegating parliament to an advisory role; he further removed the security of tenure of the constitutional offices of the Attorney General and Controller and Auditor General, as well as that of members of the Bench making the posts political appointments under his personal control. The climax of Moi's onslaught on democracy came when the secret ballot process of voting was replaced, in 1986, by the infamous *mlolongo* or queue voting which was put to effect in the 1988 general elections. To the diehard KANU supporters, queue voting was meant to counteract vote fraud and shady dealings by instituting 'open air democracy'. The system however, "...guaranteed complete top-down control over elections, since no Kenyan would dare contravene the stated will of the party" (Maren 1987:212). In this event, the 1988 elections went down in the annals of Kenya's political history as the most rigged elections and the sixth parliament derived therefrom as the most ineffectual; without a voice of its own, it remained a mere rubber-stamp to the whims and capricious decisions of the executive. In essence therefore, whereas Kenyatta simply closed the door to political competition, Moi effectively locked up the same and consigned dissenting political values into political limbo.

The aftermath of the 1988 general elections generated a lot of discontent and disaffection among democratic forces that forcefully came up to champion the cause for multi-party democracy. These advocates found favor within the international political environment especially after 1989 following the collapse of the communist empire, the disintegration of the Soviet Union, and the consequent democratization of the hitherto hard-line communist states of Eastern Europe. The emergent international political environment was one that was hostile to Third World dictators and thus facilitated calls and struggles for change towards political pluralism. Political developments in Kenya within this framework saw the Saba Saba riots of July 1990, called for political changes similar to the ones put in place in Eastern Europe. This also led to Odinga's declaration that 1991 would be the year of the repeal of Section 2(A) of Kenya's constitution and the establishment of multiparty democracy, which he followed up by launching the National Democratic Party.

Anyona who, charged with others for sedition, said in mitigation in July 1991 captured the political mood of the moment in Kenya at this particular juncture:

> ...We, the accused, are imbued with the knowledge that a new dawn is breaking on the eastern horizon of our political panorama. Liberty will come, and with it, the advent of (political) pluralism ... (Weekly Review 12.7.91:4).

These internal forces of democratization were supplemented and reinforced by external pressure in the form of an aid crunch against Kenya by both the bilateral and multilateral aid donors as well as diplomatic pressure premised on the contention that the days of the African dictator were long gone, to force the Moi regime to scrap Section 2(A) of the constitution in 1991 and pave way for a multiparty political system. This was followed by multi-party general elections in December 1992, the first in about 25 years.

It can thus be said that under Moi, Kenya went through a democratic seesaw between 1978 and 1992. From a *de facto* one party system in 1978, the country became a one party *de jure* in 1982, before finally going full circle to multi-partyism in late 1991. Under political pluralism, the country is now back to where it all started, at independence in 1963.

MULTI-PARTYISM AND THE ILLUSION OF DEMOCRACY: THE 1990s

The repeal of Section 2(A) of Kenya's constitution in 1991 opened the floodgates of opposition to government hitherto closed by Kenyatta and effectively locked by Moi. Quite a number of political parties emerged to compete for the control of the state apparatus with KANU. These include the Forum for Restoration of Democracy in Kenya (FORD-K), Forum for Restoration of Democracy Asili (FORD-A), Democratic Party of Kenya (DP), Kenya National Congress (KNC), Kenya Social Congress (KSC), Kenya National Democratic Alliance (KENDA), Party of Independent Candidates of Kenya (PICK), Social Democratic Party (SDP) and National Development Party of Kenya (NDP). The emergence of these political parties in Kenya's political arena is a point to the widening political space in the country, which is a process of democratization. In spite of this however, democratic governance in Kenya remains an illusion due to a number of factors.

One of these factors is the way the state has been used over time to serve the self-aggrandizing activities of incumbent political elites and their supporters, sycophants and political hangers-on. Because of this, the state is seen as the source of all manner of largesse and hence competition for political office in Kenya is not premised on a calling to serve, to provide alternative leadership, but on the greedy urge to control the state apparatus so as to have limitless access to state resources, the so-called 'fruits of independence'. It is against this background that existing political parties have taken on an ethnic angle with each ethnic community supporting a party led by one of its own. In this kind of scenario, political divisions tend to be vertical as opposed to the situation in Western liberal democracies where representation and political competition is often shaped by class interests and organized groups hence political divisions tend to assume a horizontal dimension (Makinda 1996:557).

Consequently, the quest for State House by existing parties in Kenya is not carried out by these parties as political parties *per se*, but as conglomerates of ethnic interests intent on capturing the state for its own sake. For instance, former Cabinet Minister Elijah Wasike Mwagale argued that Kikuyus should keep off the contest for the presidency in the 1997 polls because the community had its share of leadership during Kenyatta's time and others have to get a chance. Mwangale contends that the Kalenjins from whom president Moi hails will complete their term in the year 2002 and usher in the Luhya's turn to rule, and quips: "...when we talk of the presidency, the Luhya community should not be underrated since we have political heavyweights like me" (Daily Nation 14.10.96:4).

The second major factor is the lack of ideology in the existing political parties in Kenya. The concept 'ideology' denotes an explicit, rigid, and closed set of rules; an inflexible image of political life. It is a system closed to conflicting information, a specific explanation and code of political conduct for most situations. According to Starr (1973) an ideology includes within it three images or models of society. The first is a counter model, an explanation of what is wrong with society. The second is a utopian model, which describes how society ought to be reconstituted. And third is an action-oriented model, which explains the means of restructuring the existing society and realizing the ideal. Such an ideology is, in its origins, the product of artifice, a creation, rather than the result of spontaneous evolution (Starr 1973:21).

The importance of ideology in the politics of a society is reflected in the fact that it is impossible to grasp the essence of the political life of a people without first understanding the patterns of thought which perceives that life by the people themselves. In the absence of such patterns of thought crystallized in an ideology, as is the case in Kenya, politics become devoid of any essence and profundity. In any case, it is party ideology that creates the party myth depicting the emergence and development of a party and its place and mission in society in ways that coincide with the self-image of its founders and leaders and galvanizes the commitment of its followers to its ideals. In the absence of party ideology in Kenya, politicians have come to perfect the art of the politics of opportunism where they are in one party today, tomorrow they announce their defection to another depending on their own changing political fortunes. Immediately after the 1992 multi-party elections for instance, protus Momanyi, DP MP for Bonchari defected to KANU and retained his seat on his new party ticket in the ensuing by-election.

Momanyi's success facilitated further defections by Opposition MPs to KANU. The entire group of FORD-Asili MPs in Kakamega district defected and recaptured their seats in the ensuing by-elections. These included Apili Wawire of Lugari, Nicodemus Khaniri of Hamisi, Japheth Shamalla of Shinyalu, Benjamin Magwaga of Ikolomani, and Javan Ommani of Lurambi. However, similar defectors like Kiruhi Kimondo of Ford-Asili, Starehe; Julius Njoroge of Ford-Asili, Makuyu; and Tom Obondo, FORD Kenya, Ndhiwa; lost their seats to candidates of Parties from which they had defected. Nonetheless, Ireri Ndwiga, KNC Siakago, and Agnes Ndetei, DP, Kibwezi, defected from their parties to KANU and recaptured their seats on their new party mandate. This illustrates with particular clarity the fact that without an ideology, party allegiance is determined by rational self-interest. Hence if you fail to get nominated to contest a parliamentary seat or the presidency by one party, you simply move to the next and try your luck there. Under such circumstances, even the very basic and rudimentary tenets of democracy can never take root.

Equally important is the constitutional framework factor. Only one section of the constitution (2A) was repealed to facilitate a return to multipartyism. The rest of the one-party structures remained intact. As Murungi (1997) observes, the constitutional roots of parliament remain weak and precarious. Sections 58 and 59 of the Kenya Constitution empower the president to summon, prorogue, and dissolve parliament at will. In effect, the institution of parliament has no clear calendar of its own and operates at the mercy of the president who has absolute powers, like the thirteenth century European monarchs, to summon and disband parliament at will. Democratic governance under such a constitutional framework is, one would say, a total mirage.

Interestingly, the Inter-Parties Parliamentary Group (IPPG) compromise on constitutional reforms before the 1997 elections ended up further consolidating more powers in the office of the president instead of facilitating conditions for democratic governance. In the first place, the IPPG recognized that the Electoral Commission as constituted could not carry out its duties impartially as it is not independent, having been appointed by president Moi. It was thus resolved that ten more commissioners, whose names shall be proposed by opposition parties be appointed to the Commission, yet the IPPG had the audacity to recommend that the final approval of appointment rests with the president, the same person who appointed the existing commission! Even more badly is the recommendation in the proposed constitutional reforms to the effect that the winning president be empowered to constitute the cabinet from all parliamentary parties. This would have the effect of nipping in the bud the nascent democracy in the country because the incumbent president would have the leeway to even appoint leaders of opposition parties to his cabinet thereby killing such parties. It would be back to a single-party system all over again.

An appropriate amendment would have provided for at least a government of national unity if not a coalition one. In the former, it would be provided that a certain percentage of cabinet positions would go to a party that secures a certain percentage of seats in parliament. The ultimate appointment would rest with leaders of such parties and not with the triumphant president. It would seem therefore, that in recommending for cabinet appointments across the political spectrum, participants in the IPPG compromise were motivated by selfish interests and regarded themselves as possible beneficiaries of this kind of provision.

The fourth factor is the issue of control of information flow. As Almond (1978:156) argues, the sustaining myth of democracy is popular control over political leaders. He points out that the claim of a democratic system is that the people can make their wishes known to office-holders and can, at regular intervals, "throw out the rascals" if the job is not being done properly. Towards this end, availability of a variety of autonomous mass media communication structures is crucial in ensuring that the will of the people is continuously communicated to the leaders as well as the leaders' programs and political agendas to the people. The situation in Kenya however, is such that Government controls the major channels of political communication namely Television and Radio, and monopolizes usage of the same to the exclusion of opposition parties and other civil society organizations vying for space in the political arena. For though a number of independent print media Houses and privately owned Television and Radio stations do exist, the print media is limited in its circulation while the private Radio and Television channels have been licensed to operate purely on an entertainment and commercial advertisement basis. The key channels of political communication in Kenya thus remain the Kenya Broadcasting Corporation Television and Radio which have a nation-wide reach, and the Kenya Television Network; all of which are controlled by Government and have thus remained largely public relations organs for Government.

Without accurate knowledge of the actions of leaders and without an understanding of the relationship between those actions and popular goals, a meaningful articulation of interests and exercise of political influence by the masses is impossible. Similarly, without access to the all-important channels of political communication, the activism for democratic governance by opposition political parties and civil society organizations remains the proverbial cry in the wilderness (see chweya, *et al,* 1996:30), as the ruling elite engage in a downward information flow which they manipulate to facilitate public cooperation and support.

Lastly, but of great significance is the hypocrisy of evangelists of democracy embodied in the diplomatic representations of Western embassies and High Commissions. From the independence decade of the 1960s to the thawing of the cold war at the end of the 1980s, Western powers, through their diplomatic representatives supported financially, materially, and even philosophically, the most megalomaniac dictators on the African continent. This facilitated what has come to be known in political science parlance, as personal rule in Africa, on the threshold of the twenty-first century, the self centered forces are calling for democratization and observance of human rights arguing that the days of the dictator are long past. The question becomes are these Western forces genuine or are they merely advancing their own selfish interests in changed circumstances? In any case it took more than a millenium, many civil wars, bloody revolutions, and an unparalleled intellectual and philosophical ferment in the native soils of these democratic evangelists for the ideas of democracy and human rights to evolve into their present form of liberal democracy. Therefore to expect an African State of three decades political independence, with its own peculiar socio-economic, political and cultural nuances to fully embrace the principles of liberal democracy is a pure exercise in political fantastication.

Indeed, as Nehru (1980:126) observes, the application of this Western end product of liberal democracy to societies whose social and economic conditions are entirely different does not make sense today. Nehru quotes Brandt who argues further that;

> "Our brand of (Western liberal) democracy is not for export. All previous experience suggests that it is associated with a certain level of economic and educational development." (Nehru 1980: 130).

This position very much buttresses arguments of fervent American nationalists of two or so centuries ago that posited that history shows no instance of a tropical people who have demonstrated a capacity for maintaining an enduring form of republican government. To them, neither the Anglo-Saxon (Germanic) race, nor democratic institutions could survive in a tropical climate. The most ardent nationalist Senators of that time argued that civilization is, as it were, suffocated in the tropics, a part of the would that lies in the torrid zone, 'Nature's asylum for degenerates'. For descendants of these avowed Americo-centrics to turn around and press the case for wholesale adoption of the American political model in Africa is the height of hypocrisy. On this score, one is wont to argue that given the uniqueness of Africa's situational context, what is required is not wholesale democratization of the continent on the basis of the Western political model but, rather the Africanization of this democratic model taking cognizance of the aforesaid African socio-economic peculiarities so as to adapt it to the unique African context for it to take root and flourish.

Nonetheless, that it should take external actors to push the case for good governance in Africa constitutes a shame to African statesmen. Indeed, the propensity of African political leaders to hang onto power even at a time when it is evidently clear that the populace no longer wants one is something of a mystery. It would seem that once the African assumes political power, he swears a covenant, much in the same way as the exchange of nuptials between bride and groom, to stick to power till death does him part. Arguments and demands for democratization and activism for constitutional reforms to facilitate political pluralism and genuine political competition such as the pro-reform struggle that culminated in the death of about thirteen people in the second 'Saba Saba' riots of Monday 7th July, 1997 in Kenya are, in the eyes of such personal rulers as Moi, the work of 'disgruntled' political elements working in tandem with their 'foreign masters' to destabilize popularly elected governments.

CONCLUSION

This chapter has examined the various postindependence democracy processes in Kenya. From the foregoing exposition, coupled with the situational circumstance of the Kenyan socio-economic context, democratic governance in Kenya remains an illusion of the epoch. Illusion of the epoch constitutes the pseudo-ideology of the dominant classes in society in a particular epoch and comprises the essence of what has to be emphasized as the reality and natural order of things (see Nabudere 1979:68). For instance, according to the incumbent regime under Moi, given that elections have been regularly held in the country since independence, democracy has been the hallmark of Kenya' political process notwithstanding the fact that the country has vacillated from multipartyism at independence, to *de facto* single-partyism, to *de jure* single party politics and back to multipartyism.

To Kenneth (Stanley Njindo) Matiba and his cohorts, he was robbed of presidential victory in the 1992 general election through `rigging'; democracy was thus subverted and therefore `Moi must go'! While to such civic society organizations as the National Convention Executive Council, no other group except itself has the `mandate' and requisite commitment to push forward the democratic program. Yet to others, no meaningful democratic reforms can be attained in collaboration with the Moi government.

It is noteworthy therefore, that right from the defenders of the *status quo* in Kenya, to advocates of political pluralism, civil society organizations, evangelists of democracy, and all manner of political activist groups, democratic governance is interpreted in a myriad of ways. All these interpretations are viewed by each group as the democratic *sine qua non* to be believed in, advocated for, and maintained; positions that are as confusing and fallacious as any can be. This however, is not to say that one is anti-democracy. Indeed, the interest of the people must be served by any political system that aspires to endure and persist in governance, for there is no political principle as sacrosanct as one that says the voice of the governed must be heard and acted upon by the governors because, as political philosophers of yonder have argued, their voice, when they speak as `we the people', is the natural voice of God in politics. There thus is no gain saying the imperious necessity for democratic governance in Kenya. What form or model this should take however, is for now, more than I can tell.

REFERENCES:

Almond, G. A. 1978. Comparative Politics (2nd edition) New York: Little, Brown & Co.

Chepkwony, A.1987. The Role of NGOs in Development: A study of the NCCK 1963-78 Uppsala: Scandinavian Institute of Africa Studies.

Chweya, L. et al. 1996. "Political Communication: Its Role in State-Civil Society contest in Kenya", in African Council for Communication Education Biennial Conference, Cape Town, Cape Town, South Africa, November, 1996.

Daily Nation, October 14, 1996.

Durant, W. J. 1924. The Story of Philosophy: The Lives and Opinions of the Greater Philosophers. Garden City: Garden City Publishing Co.

Gitonga, A. K. 1987. "The Meaning and Foundations of Democracy" in Oyugi, W.O. et al, (eds) Democratic Theory and Practice in Africa. Nairobi: Heinemann.

Harowitz, I. L. 1981. "Military Origins of Third World Dictatorship and Democracy" in Third World Quarterly Vol.3, 1981 pp. 37-47.

Makinda, S.M. 1996. "Democracy and Multi-party Politics in Africa". In The Journal of Modern Africa Studies Vol.34 No. 4, Cambridge University presses pp. 555-573.

Maren, M.P. 1987. "Kenya: The Dissolution of Democracy" in Current History. Africa Report, May 1987 pp. 209-212.

Murungi, K. (1997. "Parliament Need Not be so Toothless" in Sunday Nation, April 20, 1997 p.9.

Mutoro, H. et al. 1996."Political Leadership and the Crisis of Development in Africa: Lessons From Kenya" in International Conference on 'Good Governance as a Precondition for Sustainable Development', Center for Development Studies, The University of Western Australia, Perth, Australia, October 1996.

Nabudere, D. W. 1979.Essays on the Theory and Practice of Imperialism. London: Onyx Press.

Nehru, B.K. 1980. "Western Democracy and the Third World: A Further Comment", in Third Word Quarterly Vol. II pp. 126-130.

Oloo, A.G. R. 1996. "The Doctrine of Mutual Control and Accountability: The Case of the Legislature and Executive in Kenya", in African Association of Political Science (Kenya Chapter) Conference on `Democracy and the Constitutional Process in Kenya', Nairobi, July 1996.

Sartori, G. 1965. Democratic Theory. New York: Praeger.

Starr, J. B. 1973 Ideology and Culture. New York: Harper and Row.

Weekly Review, (Nairobi) July 12, 1991.

Were, G. S. 1971."Politics, Religion, and Nationalism in Western Kenya, 1942 1962: Dini Ya Msambwa Revisited", in Historical Association of Kenya Annual Conference.

Chapter 7

Political Parties and Ruling Governments in Sub-Saharan Africa

Tukumbi Lumumba-Kasongo

INTRODUCTION

How are the opposition parties functioning in a hegemonic party system that tends to characterize most African party politics despite the efforts toward multiparty democracy? Although in most countries in Africa it is not clear whether or not the basis of their conflicts are ideologically, culturally, or personally defined, opposition parties and the ruling powers are serious political enemies in the struggle for power. One of the common characteristics of various forms of liberal democracy is the existence of one or several opposition political parties known in the Western democracies in a form of a loyal opposition. In Great Britain, for instance, which produced the oldest liberal democracy in the world, the opposition is defined as: The official opposition, the largest nongovernmental party in the Parliament, is a vital part of the British system. Its leaders are seen inside and outside Parliament, as an alternative government. Its function is both to subject government to criticism and to seek to replace it, as well as to participate in the working of the system. The opposition acts as a responsible group in criticism of the government. It proposes alternative policies and tries to change government policies, get concessions on government bills and defeat the government (Ammendola, et. al, 1997, p. 80).

The opposition expresses itself differently in depending on the nature of political culture and the dynamics of the state formation in a given country, and its place in the global economy. Is there any functional necessity to have a conscious and legal opposition in Africa that can perhaps, in challenging the ruling party, contribute to the improvement in policy formulation and implementation?

Since the early 1990s, multipartyism has once again become one of the most identifiably debated and appreciated characteristics of current political reforms and power struggles in Africa. It is popularly perceived as the most "legitimate and legal" channel to transfer or share power and/or to participate in the African political process, especially by the middle class, the working class, and university students. Political parties have mushroomed all over Africa, especially in urban areas. The quest for a basis of new development or social progress is also being carried out. This idea is articulated mainly by coalitions of various class interests and popular movements.

Despite the rise of hundreds of parties and the progress that some have made in contributing to create the culture of democratic discourse in terms of elections, researchers continue to ask whether or not there are genuine opposition parties with clear ideological foundation, materials resources, and organization capabilities in African politics, as compared to those of other developing countries like South America. Within the framework of power struggles, how do the opposition parties interact among themselves? How do they link with the people? And how do they deal with ruling parties? What kind of institutions do they set up to pursue their quest for power?

This chapter critically examined the nature of the discourses of some select African opposition parties, to identify their objectives and their ideological foundations and to project what kind of role they are likely to play in the 21st century and beyond toward the needed de-construction and/or reconstruction of African Society. Although many examples are derived from many parts of the continent, allowing a comprehensive view of the nature of opposition parties in Africa, I will pay particular attention to Côte d'Ivoire and the Democratic Republic of Congo for the reasons that: (1) after the death of Felix Houphouët-Boigny on December 7, 1993, the transition was relatively and unexpectedly smoother than that of many other countries (with respect to the existing constitution - even by the opposition from the left); However, the nature of this situation changed drastically when the power struggle between the President Henry Konan Bédié in the exile in Paris, France and Alassane Ouattara, former Premier Minister of Felix Houphouët-Boigny and Deputy Director of the International Monetary Fund (IMF) took the direction that directly or indirectly contributed to the military coup d'état en December 24, 1999. (2) For more than three decades, Felix Houphouët-Boigny did not allow or tolerate any serious opposition to emerge in the country. And (3) In Democratic Republic of Congo (former Zaire), Mobutu, by resisting real political reforms for several years, between the end of the 1980s and 1997, paralyzed the state and the country. This resistance and Mobutu's military arrogance led to the collapse of political institutions and virtually the disappearance of the state and the economy. I will examine the situation of the opposition during Mobutu's era up to May 17, 1997, the date a new regime was established by Laurent Désiré Kabila in Kinshasa, the capital city of the Democratic Republic of Congo. In the DRC, the political opposition was deeply divided and also radicalized.

I will analyze the opposition party theories as they have emerged within African conditions and examine what kind of societies they have proposed, if any. The inquiry is part of a search for a theory of political opposition within the dogmas and claims of political *pluralism à l'Africaine.*

My main objective is to discuss some of these political parties' functional and ideological dimensions, particularly what they say or do and how their statements or actions either do or do not relate to the much needed democratic discourse. This exercise is an attempt to depict nuances in the claims of some selected political formations and to point out their ideological and policy basis.

Some questions guiding this analysis include: What is the ideological foundation of the opposition parties within existing multiparty politics in Africa? What are the policy implications of such a foundation? A comparative-historical analysis on what the opposition parties say and/or do, and how they conduct themselves in political arenas will help us identify what they have or do not have in common in terms of behavioral trends and ideological bases. This is important for further identifying the characteristics of African democracy and the kind of society the African parties' leaders would like to create. In multiparty democratic systems adopted in Africa, the role of opposition parties has apparently become vital or central to political discourse.

In the media, parties, clubs, soccer fields, and on the streets in Africa, the degree of democracy in most countries, has been measured by the activism of what opposition parties do or can do and by the nature of the political space given to them by the ruling party, the government, or this obtained by themselves. In fact in some cases, the perception of politics has been reduced to being politically involved in political development, means being in the opposition party. That is to say that political development has been equated to some large extend to the dynamics of the opposition party.

A GENERAL HISTORICAL PERSPECTIVE

After the failures of the nationalist agenda and militaristic based policies of the African petty bourgeoisie and the African Marxist regimes of the 1960s and 1970s to formulate and implement relevant policies that could positively transform living conditions and the political economies of most people, the majority of Africans, especially farmers, peasants, working classes, women and the lumpen-proletarians, are once again attempting to rise up to organize themselves in an extremely difficult global and national socioeconomic and political environment. For many, multiparty democracy is associated with a search for the means and the mechanisms to improve their social and economic conditions, despite skepticism based on past experiences. In spite of problematic raised by scholars concerning the assumption of linking development to democracy and the lack of substantial empirical evidence to support such an assumption in Africa, what generally has been agreed upon by most students of politics is that there cannot be any broad social progress or social transformation in any society until its people fully and consciously either participate or become involved in the processes of that societal project; that is to say, until the people of that country become consciously engaged in building ideologies and institutions. Recently, in Africa, many people have come to believe that the time for their participation has come. The demands for popular participation can be taken as an important step for realizing democracy. As Jacques Mariel Nzounakeu stated:

> "The demands for multiparty systems that are being made today are therefore an attempt by the African countries to claim democracy through other means...But aside from this argument, most African countries see the multiparty system as a way of stimulating ideological debate, improving human rights, increasing democracy and finally, as a means of accelerating economic and social development" (1992, p.44).

Popular movements and multiparty politics, both of which demand openness in the political process, power sharing and the fair distribution of resources, are challenging the power of the African state, its policies and its legitimacy. The antinomy (Wallerstein, 1984, p.175) between state and society has become sharper than ever before in the post colonial era because, as a result of state inefficiency, corruption, malpractice in the process of surplus accumulation and structural world inequality, the majority of the African people have become poorer in absolute and relative terms. Yet these are just the symptoms that reflect the existence of a larger structural malaise. In 1993, it was estimated that there were about 300 million poor people in Africa. Two thirds of that number were classified as extremely poor. They live under the estimated a dollar a day. These figures did not include displaced people, refugees and many others who were not counted due to logistics problems and political instability.

In this context, poverty is defined in terms of the lack of access to basic resources, of a productive and creative life, and of the necessary means to have the kind of decent life to which every human being aspires. It cannot be narrowly measured by per capita income or by calorie intake only or by personal savings. And it is not a natural product of an evolution of a people or society. Thus, the state and its apparatuses have alienated the majority of the African people, especially the poor. In some countries like Democratic Republic of Congo, several observers have described the masses of people (in relationship to state) as being in state of nature or being "resigned" poverty. But in reality, people do not resign themselves to poverty. Nevertheless, resources are becoming less available and renewable and the state has become more authoritarian in its management of them. In addition, political instability does not allow the development of individual initiatives for the majority. Animosity toward the state is the function of the relationship between people's expectations of what the state should do (duty and obligation), and the state's actual performance in its irrational/rational and irresponsible/responsible behavior. The state's reactions to the demand of political change vary from partial resistance to accommodation and/or the reluctant acceptance of the legalization of multipartyism.

Although it is obvious that opposition parties in Africa wanted to capture state power, it is simplistic, however, to conclude with certainty that capturing power is philosophically an end in itself. To understand where some of them are coming from, one must also ask some other important questions such as: Why do they want to take power in a period where most African economies have been completely unproductive or with little growth and strong marginalized from the world system? And what would they do with the power or with the conditions they may inherit? Do the opposition parties come with social and/or ideological projects? In short, what do they want to accomplish? It is difficult to generalize and quantify the objectives and agendas of these opposing political parties in Africa. However, general trends can be identified.

The history of the origins and the formation of opposition parties, the political culture of societies, and the role of the country and state in the international political economy are neither similar nor identical. International division of labor and globalization of capital and productive forces have attempted to create the homogenization of demands and behavior on these political institutions. However, the parties' objectives and behavior depend a great deal on their origins, the nature and history of social classes, the socioeconomic and political conditions in the milieu in which they have emerged and operated, the influence and legacy of the colonial powers, and the level of their communication technology, among others.

Different political parties have had different *raisons d'être* and different agenda. For instance, the African National Congress (ANC), now the ruling party in South Africa and the South West African People's Organization (SWAPO) differed from the Democratic Party of Mwai Kibaki in Kenya, the *Mouvement Populaire de la Révolution* of Mobutu in Democratic Republic of Congo, *Parti Démocratique de* Côte d' Ivoire (PDCI), the Islamic Salvation Front (FIS) in Algeria or the National Democratic Alliance in the Sudan (NDA), to cite only few, in terms of the nature of their political culture, their strategies to acquire power, their objectives and their targets. In the Sudan, the main objective of the NDA has been to overthrow the Islamic Fundamentalist military regime in Khartoum (Sudan Democratic Gazette, 1992, p.5). The adoption of Islam as a state religion, its underlying political philosophy and the civil war with some racial and ideological tendencies are the major issues here. In South Africa, for more than three centuries their struggle was based on the right of the African people (especially blacks) to exist and live as citizens and the opportunity to politically exercise that right. In a country like Côte d'Ivoire, the struggle has been based on how to maintaining and sharing power or participating in the political process and the claim to equal distribution of revenues. In Southern Africa, the element of race has always been one of the most important factors in both the political and ideological formations of the state and public policy formation and implementation. In countries like Côte d'Ivoire, Burkina Faso, Ghana, Kenya, Liberia, Mali, Morocco, Togo, DRC, etc., the class origin of the ruling power and its relations to the international capitalist economy has played a more determining role in the policy process of allocation and the distribution of resources.

Mobilized for non-ethnic objectives as well, the complicated ethnic factor is also an important tangible force in the way liberal democracy is practically conceived, organized, and promoted. In addition, the cultural inheritance of colonial administration makes a difference in the way people have been socialized. The elements of African culture or primordial attachments are still strongly present in the way people choose their party affiliations as well as the way they behave vis-à-vis their leaders. However, from the institutional and behavioral point of views, theoretically, some generalizations can be made concerning the parties' objectives.

THEORIZING OPPOSITION POLITICAL PARTIES

First of all, it should be said that in the writings of theorists like Aristotle, Amilcar Cabral, Machiavelli, Kwame Nkrumah, Nelson Mandela, Karl Marx, Ibn Khaldun, Plato, Oginga Odinga, Julius Nyerere, and Max Weber, regardless of their ideological, intellectual and racial differences, there is a consensus that a positive societal change cannot occur as a natural phenomenon. Political community can change either by class struggle, power struggle or gradual accommodations change or revolts. Political power changes if state power is either penetrated with concrete purposes of making reforms (new inputs) or taken over by people with revolutionary or nationalistic agendas. State power does not change by its own will. Aristotle talks about the immortality of *polis*. Kwame Nkrumah believed that the search for "political immortality was the solution for eternal life." He also advocated class struggle as means of radically transforming power systems. Within this logic, the opposition parties as legally and legitimate political formations in a given social context, should be concerned about either how to obtain state power, to influence it and/or to associate with or change it.

Second of all, it should be added that institutional opposition movements/parties since the 1980s in Africa were born out of the worsening social and economic conditions at the national level, the generalized crisis of peripheral capitalism, the collapse of Marxist African regimes, and the excess in the process of power consolidation of the personalized and centralized states. All these factors had a direct impact on the nature of the *conjoncture Africaine*, which provoked social dissatisfactions and anger. Third of all, in many cases, the opposition movements/parties started with intelligentsia at universities (state owned schools), in the existing ruling parties, within the trade unions, and outside the continent among exiled Africans (some organic intellectuals and former members of the ruling parties).

In theorizing about the ideological tendencies of the opposition parties, their social base and their intended objectives, I am interested in discussing the deontology of being in the opposition parties in Africa. As already indicated, this is not a case-by-case analysis. The generalization concerns what it means to be in opposition parties against the dominant or ruling party. One of my working assumptions is that: a situation that has a longer history of political struggle both inside and outside the country against the ruling party or the state before the emergence of multipartyism, is more likely to produce the opposition parties that have clearer agendas than those of newcomers. Having an opposition party with a clear ideology and political agenda creates a new ground for political debates and prospects of political stability.

OPOSITION PARTIES IN KENYA

The question of what opposition parties want, in Kenya for example, was clearly articulated in the major opposition parties before the Kenya December 1992 general elections. It was clear that Kibaki, Matiba and the late Odinga wanted to challenge the Kenya African National Union (KANU), the ruling party since the country earned its independence from the British. Jomo Kenyatta had been its leader in the early 1960s. But what were not clear was how to make this challenge operationally effective and what strategies should be used to reach the intended objective. Kibaki and the late Odinga had been vice presidents of KANU at different times, therefore, they were insiders. In this case, most of the opposition parties had one thing in common: they all were against totalitarianism or the power monopoly of KANU and its leader Daniel Arap Moi. Each leader of the opposition party, especially within the Forum for the Restoration of Democracy (FORD), wanted to become party president. That is to say, each wanted to present his candidacy for the presidential elections. They forgot that the bigger picture was how to capture state power and defeat Moi and his party in both presidential and legislative elections? Based on gauging people's moods and level of enthusiasm in various constituencies, the leaders of the opposition believed that all social and political conditions were met for this challenge, despite massive resistance from the ruling party and state against accepting the normal functioning of multipartyism and the excessive use of force by KANU and the state to stop the multiparty democratic process. The leaders of the FORD did not split because of some ideological differences. As Michael Chege stated:

> "The opposition's road on this destiny of grief began with the bickering within the unified FORD about the primary elections to determine the party leadership. It was not essentially a battle of "tribes" for power as Kenya's ruling party and most of the media have portrayed it. If Kenyan ethnic groups detested each other so much, there would not have been a FORD in the first place. The party had genuine trans-ethnic

> representation and its rank and file remained united in their hostility to KANU. On the issue of leadership however, their leaders would not agree. Odinga wanted indirect primary elections in contrast to Motiba and Martin Shikuku who preferred to let the people decide in nation-wide primaries. .... And as if one major split in the opposition was not enough, Mwal Kibaki jumped ship from KANU in December 1991 and founded the Democratic Party" (1993, p.10).

Although the opposition in Kenya had a long history of struggle against Moi, especially Mwa Kenya, an underground movement, the opposition leaders had poor judgement to have believed that despite division among them and internal struggle for power, they could still defeat Moi. As reflected in the 1992 elections, the competitive politics in Kenya were very much personalized and disorganized, leaving the interests of people aside. The traditions of opposition were not combined with new strategies related to the dynamic of the milieu. The parliament was the only political space for the opposition parties to defeat Moi or challenge the proposed policies of the KANU.

Upon the "victory" of the 1997 election, President Daniel arap Moi's political party, KANU, is still the majority party in the parliament. The opposition has had enormous difficulties to break down the almost absolute power that the executive branch is enjoying. Despite pressures from the international donors and Western powers to persuade Moi to produce greater democratization and make political reforms as a requirement (conditionality) for having access to foreign investments, the reform crisis remained unsolved (Human Rights Watch, 1999, p. 48). In relationship with the opposition, "cosmetic" reforms such as the creation of a Law Reform Coordinating Committee, cut government ministries from 27 to 15, and appointment of a new head of the Civil Service, have produced less consultative constitutional review in the parliament. As it is reported by Human Rights Watch:

> "The government selected ruling party and opposition politicians to serve on an Inter-Parties Parliamentary Group (IPPG) with responsibility for constitutional change, while excluding the broad-based National Convention Executive Council (NCEC), a pro-democracy coalition of opposition parties, human rights, religious, and nongovernmental groups, from participation in the reform process (1999, p. 48).

It is not clear that in since the 1990s the opposition in Kenya has learned lessons in changing its strategies from its failures to prepare itself to capture the parliament in the next elections. A coalition among the leaders of the opposition means restructuring their party platforms and main objectives to reflect the need for institutionalizing the opposition.

OPOSITION PARTIES IN THE DEMOCRATIC REPUBLIC OF CONGO

What have been the dominant strategies of the opposition political parties in the DRC? It should be said that from the time Mobutu came to power on November 24, 1965 through a military coup d'état to May 1997, he was confronted with three major opposition movements, which can ideologically be grouped into:

1. The Lumumbaists or those associated with the ideology of the progressive government of Stanleyville (Kisangani) in the 1960s, both before and after the assassination of Prime Minister Patrice Lumumba in January 1961.

2. The secessionists, or those associated with the ideology of separatism; and

3. The accommodationists, or those who fought to either integrate Mobutuism or to replace it with a similar political agenda. This categorization is far from perfect. However, for the sake of clarity, it represents current major ideological tendencies needed for understanding the nature of the origins of Congolese opposition parties and any underlying philosophical bases.

Lumumbaists attempted by either ideological convictions or sentiments of opportunism to raise issues concerning nation building in Zaire. They believed that an ideology of unity or radical/progressive nationalism could advance social progress in the country, with respect to the goals of Patrice Lumumba. How could this happen?

In the early 1960s, Lumumbaists succeeded in advancing two important points: the consolidation of a strong alliance with the then Eastern European bloc during the Cold War and the organization and promotion of a second independence movement (Nzongola-Ntalaja, 1987). Starting from Kwilu and rapidly reaching over almost all the Congo with Lumumbaism as its ideological base, the struggle, starting in 1964 as a second independence movement (known as mulelism), was crushed by the intervention of the West by 1967, notably France, the United States, Belgium and a few African countries. But this military crush did not succeed in dismantling Lumumbaism as an ideology. Even Mobutu once used this ideology to enhance his own power, to popularize his policies, to expand his political base, and to consolidate his power. Although there has not been a single political agenda grouping all Lumumbaïsts on how to promote an ideology of a "united country and/or nation," many of them believed that the change in Democratic Republic of Congo should occur at the levels of both ideology and personality politics. Mobutu and mobutuism had to leave state power. That is not to say that all those who called themselves Lumumbaïsts were absolutely against Mobutu. In fact, many worked with him and continued to work for him in different capacities even after his death in

Morocco in 1997. However, the dominant political position among Lumumbaïsts has always been that Mobutu was ruining the country and should not have continued to rule, for ideological and social reasons. From this point of view, theoretically, the courses these opposition parties have been advocating are those of structural change.

The secessionists believed (and some still believe) in the political independence of each major sub-region of the country. As argued elsewhere, especially in the case of the Katangan secessionist movement, this ideology had its roots in colonial policies and the structures of the colonial state and its peripheral economy (Lumumba-Kasongo, 1988/89).

In October 1996, however, Laurent Désiré Kabila was able to build a strong opposition coalition force against Mobutu. Using combined national and popular liberation strategies; Kabila's army invaded the country and finally reached Kinshasa, the capital city on May 17, 1997. Thus, Mobutu was forced out of the country with disgrace. In the process of starting to clean the mess created by Mobutu, Kabila changed the name of the country back from Zaire to Democratic Republic of Congo. His opposition to Mobutu and mobutuism for more than 30 years was solidly ideological. But the coalition of Bana Mulenge and Bana Masisi, Rwandese Tutsis, Uganda, etc., that he created in the name of the Alliance of Democratic Forces for the Liberation of Congo-Zaïre, which put him in power, was not. It was dissolved on January 22, 1999 and was replaced by Popular Committees.

It is not necessarily the internal weaknesses or deficiencies of African culture and ethnicity that forced Tshombe and Munongo to actualize the secessionism. That is to say, secessionism was a political instrument that was used by the Katangan and South Kasaian elite (notably Albert Kalonji) to promote particular class interests. Despite the authoritarian and totalitarian systems imposed in the country by Joseph-Désiré Mobutu between November 25, 1965 and May 1997, he did not succeed in eliminating the strength of this ideology. Secessionism can succeed because from the point of view of some natives, its dynamism is still based on emotional and cultural argument and beliefs. Mobutu's policies of favoritism and "quota," for instance, in the education system at certain periods, further contributed to the evolution of secessionist tendencies. He reinforced it by developing clientist politics. Using the well-known old premise of *diviser pour reigner*, he disoriented his clients by giving them an impression of sharing wealth but not power with them through co-option, random promotion, and political appointments and dismissals. This client-petty bourgeoisie did not have a strong class base. That is to say, the clientist bourgeoisie had neither power nor wealth. From a class perspective there are always dynamic relations between power and wealth, in a capitalist sense. One can produce the other and vice-versa. To better understand the above ideological categorizations and the nature of the opposition's discourses, a brief discussion on how the opposition parties emerged becomes essential.

With strong internal social pressures caused by deteriorating economic conditions, the weakening of highly centralized state apparatuses, and political turmoil in the former eastern bloc, Mobutu reluctantly announced on April 24, 1990 the birth of multipartyism for the purpose of avoiding massive uprisings and a violent end to his regime. He then proposed establishing a "limited" democratic system with two other parties. The *Union Pour la Démocratie et Le Progrès Social* (UDPS) led by Etienne Tshisekedi Mulamba, co-founder of the MPR and a former Minister of Interior in Mobutu's regime was among the first parties that accepted this option. Although Tshisekedi had seriously opposed Mobutu for more than a decade, his party did not, at the beginning, clearly articulate any viable alternative nationalist ideology and agenda with a vision of a newly created society. That is to say, in this case, there was a lack of a clear political project. UDPS could therefore be characterized as a product of the power struggle rather than the ideological struggle. In addition, UDPS had previously experienced a division between radicals and moderates. Until recently, its constituency was dominated by an ethnic alliance, though this did not discredit Tshisekedi's political ambition and populism. On the basis of centralized and monopolized power in the party as well as strategies the party had used in the past, Tshisekedi gave the impression that he was interested more in power than in establishing a democratic process. Despite change in political configurations and political game in the DRC, Tshisekedi perceives himself as the only person who should replace Mobutu because he opposed an authoritarian and totalitarian Mobutu at the time when only a few people would have dared to do so. *Ileo-Nzango Amba, a former Mobutu's bras droit, led Parti Démocratique et Social Chrétien (PDSC) whose members were dominated by Christians and Kimbanguists (African Independent Church)* for many years and President of the National Assembly under Mobutu's regime. He shared ethnic affinity with Mobutu. Ideologically, this party is not dissociated from mobutuism though its program of actions are based on the premises of peace, justice, and charity. Inspired and supported by the European Christian Democratic parties, it has not been able to mobilize the non-Christian masses in rural areas. Parties such as the *Front Commun des Nationalistes* (FCN) of Bula Nyati or Kamanda, whose leaders were active members of the MPR and often-cabinet ministers of Mobutu, had tendencies of political opportunism. Only a few parties, like the *Movement National Congolais/L* (MNC), the socialist party, and *Parti Lumumba Unifié* (PALU) had apparently not had systematic ideological relations to the MPR. *Le Rassemblement Démocratique de la République* (RDR) of Mungul Diaka articulated anti-Mobutu slogans. However, it should be noted that Mungul Diaka worked for Mobutu in several ministerial capacities in the past. Highly elitist, the FCN did not have any strong roots in the social, economic and political conditions of the poor, who comprise the majority of the people. The FCN was composed of intellectuals who did not seem to be comfortable with the MPR. Their aspiration was to acquire power. Nguza Karl-I-Bond's party was essentially the most opportunistic of all, based on his acrobatic political history. He counted mostly on his ethnic affiliation in Shaba Province. He had always been close to Mobutu and accepted permanent positions in Mobutu government.

As social protests intensified, the regime was threatened with losing its support, even among the coalition of various members of the old political school. Thus, Mobutu attempted to impose a new constitution on the people. Between April and July 1990, there were more than seventy (70) political formations in the country. In March 1991, nineteen (19) "legally recognized" parties prepared to contest the legislative and presidential elections originally planned for April 1991. Twenty-three opposition parties grouped in the *Front Uni* ("United Front") were interested more in setting up a democratic process than in replacing Mobutu. In April 1991 Mobutu accepted the idea of a national conference with a clear agenda of hijacking it, but the opposition parties insisted that Mobutu should resign before the conference. In June 1991, more than one hundred (100) parties, many of which did not fulfill Mobutu's requirements were organized. He attempted to sabotage the process by offering cabinet posts and other ministerial positions to members of the opposition parties in various dysfunctional transitional governments. The conflict between the popular movements' objectives and those of the political parties' essentially elitist groupings slowed down the process of democratic struggle. Democracy, as perceived in this context, had mainly become a process of élite political maneuvering to acquire power.

There were three dominant positions within the democratic opposition in the DRC. There were those who tended to think that it were impossible to achieve democratic objectives in popular movements without forming coalitions with Mobutu. These groups tended to see themselves as realists. They worked for power sharing with the regime and opportunistically accepted the cosmetic proposal changes that it offered. Then there were those who believed in embarking on a strategy of advocating and using violence. For them, the language that Mobutu better understood was militarism, regardless of cost. There was also a small group of idealists who saw popular movements as opportunities to debate on the nature of the society that the majority of the people in the DRC would like to create. With or without Mobutu the discourse should engender new ideas about where the society should go.

Between 1993 and 1997 over 200 political formations in DRC were created, many had as their bases: class, ethnicity, regionalism and religion. They had clearly articulated the position that Mobutu should have left his position and let people put their homes in order according to their tastes and their local social and political realities. This logic is based on the idea that no one from outside any locality or region can better understand and appreciate the needs of the local people. Mobutu's public policies reinforced this kind of position. Whether one agrees with this logic or not, further deterioration of social and economic conditions in many regions provided the basis and justification for secessionist discourses within the then existing political parties. What is interesting is that no region in DRC was economically better off, including Mobutu's own, with perhaps the exception of his constructed village (Gbadolite) or *fief à la* Yamoussokro. Economically, the region of Bandaka/Equateur was no better off as far as social progress is concerned than any other regions. This secessionist tendency seems to have appealed to many people as a natural political choice for those who did not have any other means to survive. For them, democracy has to promote a highly decentralized society and power structure with each region having complete autonomy. Some people, in this categorization, envision DRC either as a confederation or having loose political regions. Ethnicity is an important element upon which discourses within this ideological tendency are articulated.

Accommodationist tendencies in the opposition parties implied the acceptance and incorporation of mobutuism into general political discourse in the DRC. One may define this as a "class ideological choice" or as already indicated, clientism. This tendency transcended ethnicity or regionalism. It was strongly based on opportunism. Most of its advocates were intellectuals, especially professors or university graduates.

The *Union Sacrée* was the biggest political forum in DRC. It is composed of several major parties, each with its own ideological orientation. Its main objective was to explore how to construct strategies to be rid of Mobutu, legally or constitutionally. This coalition was not ideologically based; rather, it was a strategic instrument used by the opposition parties to fight Mobutu. It called for the national conference and the establishment of a transitional government. To them, getting rid of Mobutu was the pre-requisite for the democratic struggle. Did this guarantee the establishment of democracy? Is the idea of a union government necessarily democratic? My position is that a union government is not necessarily democratic as long as the process for its establishment is undemocratic. What does the opposition want? To attempt to answer these questions, one must identify who the leaders of opposition are or to what social class they belong. It is difficult to provide quantitative answers because democracy is an ongoing process in Africa, especially in Democratic Republic of Congo.

Tshisekedi, Mungul Diak, Ileo, Nguz Karl I Bond, Kamitatu, Kazadi, etc., (all of whom are considered as the old Binza's petty bourgeois and their young associates) wanted some political change in the country. But what kind of change did they pursue? First, it should be said that many of those opposition leaders wanted to replace Mobutu. For many of them, as Tshisekedi said in August 1991, when he was nominated Prime Minister he refused to take oath in front of him, "Mobutu is a monster." Second, their concept of struggle was more of a power struggle until recently, rather than that of a class or an ideological struggle. What does this mean? It means that their target was Mobutu. As with any power struggle strategies, they concentrate on the personal/individual weaknesses of the target.

Unlike the opposition parties in Côte d'Ivoire, where the university community was mobilized as the center for political formations, in DRC the public universities were often decentralized, demobilized and closed at the beginning of multipartyism. Consequently, they played an insignificant role in the formation of larger political parties. Private universities seem to have little interest in national politics. There were parties of intelligentsia like the one of

Kamanda wa Kamanda, but they did not have their base at the universities. That is to say, political discourses in DRC were not necessarily similar to those associated with Professor Francis Wodié's political discourses, for example, which are basically intellectualistic, highly philosophical, and abstract.[1]

It should be noted that the power struggle orientation of the opposition parties in Democratic Republic of Congo has gradually been transforming itself into an ideological struggle through popular pressures and struggles which have been accelerated and consolidated because of the arrogance of Mobutu and his ruling party (MPR). The opposition parties in DRC have not been, as static as many people seemed to have believed earlier. But the social and economic conditions in which they have been operating are extremely difficult. They have radicalized themselves by popular actions. The resistance of the ruling party/state against any serious democratic discourse is an important factor that contributes to the consciousness raising of the opposition and the people at large. Despite all these political transformation initiated by Kabila, he was killed by one his bodyguards in January 2001. Kabila's son Major-General Joseph Kabila was sworn in as the new president of DRC.

Though it may be the case in other countries, in Côte Ivoire, for example, as it will be discussed further, radicalism here has been part of some parties' ideological choices from the beginning. There are no social indicators that show that even after the death of president Felix Houphouët-Boigny, parties are radicalizing themselves as in Democratic Republic of Congo and consequently radicalizing the masses because of the inflexibility or the arrogance of the *Parti Démocratique Ivoirien-Rassemblement Démocratique Africain* (PDI-RDA). I do not think that the actions of the *Front Populaire Ivoirien (FPI-"Ivorian Popular Front"),* a popular party, are further radicalizing the people's ideology either. On the contrary, the actions of the FPI seem to alienate many. There are about eight functioning leftist parties there whose leaders opted for radical leftist ideologies from the time they were formed to guide their discourses and actions. Although they do not proclaim to be Marxist or Socialist, as will be discussed further, they combine leftist nationalism, populism and socialism in their public discourse.

Besides the *Union Sacrée* in Democratic Republic of Congo, which was purely a strategically functioning, not an ideological political coalition, there were minority leftist groups and *Partis alimentaires*. Many of these *parti alimentaires* were formed with strong and special relations with the ruling party, the MPR of Mobutu. Ideologically, they were not qualitatively different from mobutuism though they also talked about democratic struggle as a means to save Democratic Republic of Congo from its current social, economic and political *marasme*. They tend to be antagonistic to Lumumbaism and less to secessionism. Their discourses are power centered, rather than democracy centered. Given the level of resistance to change from Mobutu and his party to articulate any compromise and the harsh social and economic conditions in the country, the only remaining option, as articulated in April 1994 by some members of the *Union Sacrée* in Democratic Republic of Congo, is the use of armed struggle to overthrow Mobutu and establish some form of democracy. Mobutu himself has not been neutral as far as the massacre of Kasai people in the Shaba and Bukavu provinces between 1992-1994 goes. The conflicts orchestrated and organized by Mobutu continue to discredit the opposition's work.

OPPOSITION PARTIES IN NIGERIA

In Nigeria, the military regime thought that it was possible to militarily control the behavior of the two imposed opposition parties and the outcome of their performance in nominating the pro-Babangida in various posts of the constitutional commission and government, thereby polarizing the parties. Babangida's behavior contributed to a certain level of radicalizing the Social Democratic Party (SDP) whose candidate seemingly won the presidential elections of June 1993. Babangida's government cancelled the results. It should also be said that the leaders of both political parties were close to the military regime. In December 1993, General Abacha, the Nigerian Head of State, engaged in organizing debates on the constitution, an activity which became expected as routine in many African countries, especially in those with military regimes. Many Nigerians saw this call for the constitutional debate as another maneuver set up by Abacha and his click to remain in power for many years. Was this a phenomenon of *déjà vue*?

Babangida's behavior and actions estranged many Nigerians from forming political oppositions, though he did not destroy their basis. True opposition to the military regime was coming from various professional organizations and people although the Social Democratic Party with Abiola continued to mobilize voices. But these organizations were also centered by strong regionalist sentiments. These sentiments tended to weaken the strength of the organizations in terms of the sense of common objectives to be pursued. However, it should be noted that as General Abacha started to resemble like Babangida in terms of behavior and policy, the elements of opposition associated with human rights organization increased the level of their protests. At the time of his mysterious death in June 1998, Sani Abacha was able to consolidate his "rule in jailing the elected president and launching the greatest wave of political repression in the country's history—because the majority democratic powers divided among themselves. And sadly, those divisions paralleled the fractures within Nigeria's political class, over access to contracts, commerce, and the source of virtually all Nigeria's wealth, oil" (Diamond, 1999, p. 480).

The interim government of General Abdulsalami Abubakar, who replaced general Abacha, set up the motion for the return to the civilian elected government. Finally, under the regime of General Abubakar, between December 1998 and February 1999, Nigeria held local, state, and federal elections, leading to the inauguration of General Olusegun Obasanjo as president on May 29,

1999.

General Obasanjo has started to make massive reforms. Within the frameworks of these reforms, combined with the dynamics of a strong civil society, and independent media, the opposition in Nigeria is likely to consolidate itself and become a more forceful democratic instrument of change in the 21st century.

OPPOSITION PARTIES IN COTE d' IVOIRE

As indicated earlier, Côte d' Ivoire and Democratic Republic of Congo, as independent and contemporary states, came to the scene of international power struggle through different strategies. They chose different paths of organizing, advancing and maintaining state interests. That is to say the history of political formations and state building in these two countries differs from one another.

What have the ideological and intellectual orientations in the discourses or actions of the opposition in Côte d'Ivoire been? In comparison to political situations in many other countries in sub-Sahara Africa, Côte d'Ivoire under late Felix Houphouët-Boigny enjoyed a considerable political stability, in relative terms, for many years. Debates and consensus were done, to a certain extent, within the one party-state, like TANU in Tanzania. In Côte d'Ivoire, one might even have gotten an impression that there was a consensus of ideologies and values. With a stable state (patrician or elite), a growing middle class, flourishing cocoa and coffee production and marketing reflected by the increase in the Gross National Product (GNP) and the dominance of the foreign investments, especially those of France, Côte d'Ivoire was considered in the 1970s by many as being ready to take off. Why is it that Rostow's theory did not succeed here as the Ivorian people had expected, especially the middle class? What went wrong in Ivorian policy formation and implementation? A brief analysis of the history of political conditions is needed to help understand how the state related to society and how opposition parties later emerged.

Samir Amin has indicated that the big challenge for Côte d'Ivoire then was the state's ability or political determination to mobilize its resources for the use of the agricultural sector to support manufacturing and industrialization projects (Amin, 1967). In other words, the challenge was how to transform the agricultural sector through capital and intensive labor into an industrial one and how to create a strong local capital and investment base. If this challenge could have been taken seriously and effectively, in my point of view, probably Côte d'Ivoire would have transcended the characteristics of the peripheral capitalist economy and joined the orbit of capitalism with its internal dynamics and contradictions, as was the case of the semi-peripheral status of the Gang of Four in Asia (the newly industrialized countries). But without a consistent policy of large-scale agricultural production, that is to say, massive mechanization, which would lead to the transformation of productive forces, Côte d'Ivoire, could not take off without creating a national industrial base. What has taken place in some sectors of the Ivorian public sector is an effort towards modernization without industrialization.

From the mid 1970s, Ivorians talked about *la conjoncture or la fin du miracle mirage ("the end of the miracle")* as part of daily conversations that reflected their high living standards in the country and national indebtedness. But unlike Democratic Republic of Congo or Ghana after Kwame Nkrumah, Côte d'Ivoire had a single political party that succeeded in managing the affairs of state for many years, so they maintained a stable state, a routine bureaucratic performance and a prosperous middle class. As a main goal, this state gave itself the creation of the Ivorian nation. Seven Ivorian plantation owners formed the Syndicat Agricole Africain (SAA- "African Agricultural Union" in 1944. At the time of its formation, the main objective of its members was neither necessarily to challenge existing colonial power structures nor to struggle for power sharing. Their interest was mainly economic; the SAA members wanted to sell their cocoa and other agricultural products at the same price granted to French farmers (Assié-Lumumba and Lumumba-Kasongo, 1991).

Gradually, as the dynamics of the colonial economy and state intensified, this economic grouping, having attracted unexpected popular support, was transformed into a political organization in 1946: *Le Rassemblement Démocratique Africain* with its branch *Parti Démocratique de Côte d'Ivoire* (PDCI-RDA). Felix Houphouët-Boigny, cofounder of the SAA, and first chairman of the RDA, was the President of Côte d'Ivoire from 1960 when France granted the country until his death in December 1993.

PDCI-RDA, the state-party for more than three decades, was a hierarchical, elitist party, but with a strong social base in the rural areas. It took advantage of its historical origins *(parti des paysans-planteurs)* to claim its legitimacy. Despite some internal power struggles within the party in the 1950s and 1960s, the state-party ruled the country with apparently traditional consensus *à la Baoulé*, that is to say, in a manner very close to the Baoulé system of governance. There were no major political and legal "challenges" until April 30 1990, the date the late President Houphouët-Boigny approved the legalization of opposition parties along with the intent to hold multi-party elections in Côte d'Ivoire.

The end of the 1980's intensified la conjoncture intensified by the collapse of the international cocoa market, one of the major export products in Côte d'Ivoire. This economic crisis greatly contributed to the events that led to the emergence of multipartyism, with its social implications. The PDCI-RDA was, as were other ruling parties in Africa, reluctant to accept the establishment of multipartyism. Finally, through tremendous national and international pressures, and to avoid a generalized social crisis that could lead to a political crisis, Konan Henri Bédié now the President of Côte d'Ivoire, who was then President of the National Assembly, announced the birth of multipartyism.

Before April 1990 the *Front Populaire Ivoirien* (FPI), party general secretary Mr. Laurent Gbagbo, who had been in prison between February and July 1992, led the first major leftist political organization. He acted almost alone as an organizer of a populist power struggle movement challenging the ruling party without having a strong national social and political base. The movement was popularized and publicized in the 1970s by international media, especially those from France where Gbagbo put himself in exile. While in France, he developed an alliance with the French socialists. In Côte d'Ivoire many people called him such names as "betrayer," "power hunger," "adventor," etc. The French Socialist Party was involved in supporting the FPI, at least at the beginning. Its actions were then based on the massive critique of the "immortality" claimed of President Felix Houphouët-Boigny. The power struggle approach could not bear any positive fruits without organizing a national democratic struggle because the leader of the FPI was an outsider to the political machinery of the Ivorian State. About forty parties were formed after April of 1990, of which only twenty are still actually functioning. The most important of those with leftist ideological tendencies include *Parti Ivoirien du Travail* (PIT), *Union Sociale Démocratique* (USD), *Parti Socialiste Ivoirien* (PSI), *Mouvement Démocratique et Social* (MDC), etc., to cite only a few examples.

What are the social bases of some of these parties and what do they wish to accomplish? I do not intend to make an inventory of the behavior and actions of all those parties in this section. However, identification of some of their major behavioral and ideological tendencies may give us a comprehensive picture of the nature of the oppositions' discourse in Côte d'Ivoire. It should be stressed that unlike Democratic Republic of Congo, where the major opposition parties emerged from within the ruling party, MPR of Mobutu, in Côte d'Ivoire the major opposition parties came from outside of state apparata or the PDCI-RDA. They originated as university based organizations with teachers and students as the major actors. Most of party leaders were strongly associated with the SYNARES, which is the *syndicat* or the Union of teachers of higher education. That is to say, parties were formed with the spirit and basis of *revendications* with rights as the most important characteristics of their *raison d'être*. Until recently, the FPI has been organizationally broader and more publicized among the more advanced opposition parties in political recruitment. The FPI had its Constitutive Congress between February 19 and 20, 1988 (*MDS Info*, 1991, p. 1).

Its activism influenced many other social and political groups and individuals. It is the only party that fulfilled all requirements for presenting a candidacy in the November 199Os' presidential elections. Laurent Gbagbo was the only leader of the opposition parties who dared to openly challenge the regime of Felix Houphouët-Boigny. How should I characterize the nature of its political discourses with brevity?

From its activism as a populist movement to its "transformation" as a legal political party, the FPI has been consistent in articulating its objectives. Moïse Koumoué in the FPI's statement of March 3, 1990 repeatedly stated prior to the event of February 18, 1992, in which the party was accused of acts of vandalism and breaking the law, that the FPI was ready to take over state power to govern and to apply its own social, economic and cultural programmes.

It was prepared to govern and change economic relations, especially by increasing the price of cocoa for the small producers/small householders. Its activities and its meetings were focussed on how to capture state power by all means possible. This objective, which is a normal political objective for any party, dominated the party agenda. But it also contributed toward isolating the party from an effort for unity with other leftist parties until recently. It also refused to accept the concept of the *national conference* as a phenomenon that has been *dépassé*. Although democracy does not necessary mean capturing state power for the FPI, it is believed that this process may give the party an opportunity to penetrate the government and change policies from within the system. That is to say, this party has refused to behave and act as a political pressure group *à l'Américaine*. Whether or not its means to reach its objectives are legally or "morally" acceptable by the people and state is entirely another story. In short, it is a power centered party with ethnicity as its base, even though there are members from ethnic groups other than the Bété. At the beginning of the movement, ethnicity was used as an easier means to manipulate and mobilize people based on their geographical and linguistic affiliations--emotional and cultural factors that do not require social and national consciousness in its performance.

In Côte d'Ivoire, one of the major issues of discussion among many people before the death of Felix Houphouët-Boigny, was on the nature of violence associated with the actions of some political formations, especially the FPI. Many Ivorians tend to perceive the Bétés who dominate the FPI as essentially physical or violent. Thus, they perceive this party as developing and/or encouraging cultural antagonisms against other ethnic groups, especially the Baoulé. However, sociologically, it is difficult to conclude that the Bétés or other ethnic groups they associate with are naturally more violent than any other Ivorian ethnic groups. They have different traditions in the way their society is organized and social relations are appreciated. Historically, they have cooperated and worked with other ethnic groups, especially the Baoulé, concerning the use of the forest for plantations, for instance. Until recently, *Les Baoulés* have been welcome in the Bété geographical areas without many difficulties. The confrontation that has occurred among them in the past originated in a political struggle rather than a cultural one, as suggested by most members of the ruling party, PDC-RDA.

What is the origin of the violence associated with political discourse in the FPI? Four explanations can be articulated. Violence could be:

1. A product or consequence of the frustration of a popular movement which does not seem to have a concretely convincing political agenda;

2. A product or result of lack of dialogical relations between the party and other parties, civil society and state. A deadlock on the issues of how to share power can also provoke violence;

3. An outcome of the misinterpretation of what democracy is or ought to be; and

4. A product or consequence of the dynamics of the culture of the dominant ethnic group within the party. Many people, especially members of the PDCI-RDA take this explanation more seriously than any other possibilities.

In any case, can violence advance democracy in an African context? An appropriate question should be what kind of violence can or cannot promote democracy? What are its objectives and who is advancing the violence? Spontaneous violence in itself cannot advance any form of democracy. However, many historical political struggles in world politics testify that some organized political violence with concrete political objectives has been used as a means of advancing national revolutions in different regions and countries. Cabral, Fanon, Machel, Mandela, Memmi, to cite only a few, have rightly indicated in their writings and political actions that the only way to dislodge colonialists/imperialists was by using a combination of means similar to what they themselves used. Political violence can be an instrument of either class or power struggle. But it should not be the basis for illegal activities of any populist movement. Even Machiavelli's discourse does not see violence as a permanent instrument of power struggle or maintenance of power. It can be used for specific objectives, but cannot become a permanent instrument for advancing the immortality of the state. In short, political violence as an element or instrument of political discourse should be, in principle, a conscious activity, socially disruptive, but politically constructive. As Henry Bienen believes:

> "Angola and Mozambique, ex-Portuguese colonies, were held out as examples of what would support Frantz Fanon's propositions that individuals and peoples would become whole again and would have a political rebirth by participating in violent politics...Violence was instrumental in creating new societies also because individuals would forge new ties expressed through revolutionary organizations" (1993, p. 280).

Political violence as used in this context is not the equivalent of the indiscriminate breaks similar to those that occurred on what is known in Abidjan as "black" Tuesday – February 18, 1992. One should note that society and politics do not change naturally by themselves. It is their internal contradictions that can provoke desirable or undesirable changes. But how society and politics effectively change, who changes them and for what objectives depend much on the nature of social and productive relations in a given society, of its ruling class and of its political culture. How does one deal with the energies that lead to the material destruction of properties, for example?

First, disruption is a consequence of social and political battles. Second of all, it is not an end in itself. To deal with it adequately, all social forces in a given society and state must enter into serious national dialogue. The issue of the identity of the people involved in the disputation in Côte d'Ivoire, for instance, was irrelevant in a situation of sharp political struggles and where movements among the parties were fluid and not based on any specific ideology. It should also be emphasized that every political party that has means could, in theory, penetrate other parties for the sake of *espionage*. This is an old story in world politics. Although I do not support violence, I disagree with Bienen who thinks that violence has not settled issues in Africa beyond the period of the anti-colonial struggle (Ibid, p. 280). The empirical facts lead me to believe differently. Several political regimes in Africa came to power either violently or have been removed to power through violent means. As I explained below, the main issue is about the nature of violence and its origin.

Not all forms of violence are aberrant or pathological in Africa. This depends on what one means by violence and who the actors/actresses or institutions are that are involved in violent actions. Recent democratic movements came with a high dose of organized violence. In my view, violence should not necessarily target the elimination of the individual member of the dominant class or the whole community, a Stalinist approach, but it should set up a different political motion of restructuring society, that is, creating new power relations and new mechanisms to distribute power and participation.

Another leftist political formation called *Le Parti Ivoirien du Travail* (PIT-Ivorian Labor Party) whose leader is Francis Wodié, a representative from Cocody[2] who has also been active in Ivorian politics should be briefly discussed. In principle, the social base of this party should be the working class, which resembles the leftist working class party in Europe. In reality, however, it is a party of intellectuals. Some people call it an "intellectualistic party." How can we characterize PIT?

I should start in saying that the PIT has two major characteristics, legalism and philosophy/intellectualism. In the reasoning of the PIT leader, decolonization was born out of the contradictions of colonization, therefore democracy has to engender itself out of the contradictions of the non-democratic systems (Wodié, 1992).

The rupture between the search for democracy and the non-democratic culture that exists cannot happen through an evolutionary process or a natural order of things. In the case of Côte d'Ivoire, the contradictions of a one party-state engendered debates on multiparty politics through *Le Conseil National* ("National Council") in which the *journées de dialogue* ("days of dialogue") were state-organized. Multipartysm is defined as an anti-thesis within the Ivorian social formation. That is to say, multipartyism, as a transitional political force, has to be qualitatively different in its behavior and form from the thesis of the one party-state and its behavior and policies. Democracy is considered a synthetic discourse within this logic. The PIT perceives the discourse of multipartyism as a necessity toward democracy. As

Francis Wodié said: "The need for multipartyism is this of diversity of interests and opinions which goes across every free society, necessarily opened on the tensions more or less sharp, it leads to freedom of choice and belonging, expression of free and equal participation in political game (Ibid, p.16)."

For a discourse to be considered democratic, two principles can be derived from the above definition. The principles of liberty and equality, with respect for diversity of interests, opinions and choices. The elements of this discourse cannot be fully expressed by a one-party state because that party is not a product of social contract. For Wodié, in a transitional Africa, it is only the sovereign national conference that personifies the will of the state and clearly expresses it. It is believed that out of the activities of this conference, a new social contract may emerge. This assembly that should be constituted of national fractions (the people), becomes, on the basis of national consensus, sovereign and representative (Ibid. p.13). As expressed in its ideology, the PIT's discourses do not seem to have any consolidated proletarian base in reality. Wodié has intellectualized and theorized politics and democracy, but he has not yet given them strong social forms. It is still interesting to look at the PIT's relationship with the trade unions.

Another party that is worth mentioning among leftist political parties is the *Mouvement Démocratique et Social* (MDS). This one also has its base at University of Cocody in Abidjan. Its first president was Professor Lanciné Sylla, specialist in political sociology at the *Institut-d'Ethno-Sociologie*. Born in July 1990, MDC, as in other leftist parties, was formed by intellectuals. It defines itself as a movement, a laboratory of moving ideas and ideals. It is a movement with the promotion of people's aspirations to social justice, freedom and respect for fundamental human rights as its major objectives.[3]

In the 1990s, the party defined itself as a movement of reflection on democracy. In terms of membership or affiliation, it was open to all people regardless of individual religious, ethnic or ideological origin. It put more emphasis on the agenda of socializing people with democratic ideas and promoting the spirit of democracy with the objective of creating a democratic process and consequently a democratic nation. It competed and failed in the presidential and legislative elections in 1995. As Kouamé Nguessan, a sociologist who was in charge of the party's external affairs, told me: "its success will depend on its ability to mobilize members, to advertise its programs and to finance its actions." The party was considered as an educator and it defined Côte d'Ivoire as being in a non-democratic transition. Its objective is to contribute toward the establishment of the values and norms of a democratic transition.

Between 1990 and early in 1994, the political situation in Côte d'Ivoire was characterized by the behavior of a regime in a difficult transition, a *régime de désequilibre* towards democracy. Every transitional situation is fragile, therefore, unstable. It can shift to either a dictatorship or some form of democracy. Democratization could be pursued in the forms of renovations or reforms. For Wodié, this pursuit must be pluralistic and diverse. It is open to sovereign people to opt for any strategy that fits a given social context. Pluralism and diversity are two factors that must be promoted to create conditions in which democratic discourses can occur.

In short, the transition toward either democracy or dictatorship is a complex phenomenon. For any democratic system to succeed there is a need for a high level of tolerance among African people of different political parties, the promotion of respect for differences and laws, and of the ideal of consensus. Are parties in the Cameroon, Côte d'Ivoire, Ghana, Kenya, Nigeria, South Africa, Democratic Republic of Congo, etc., capable of accepting and tolerating differences and promoting the ideal of a nation? In my view, the objective of the parties should be first to articulate and advance the culture of democracy and second to actualize this ideal in the policies and processes of production and distribution of resources. They also must be self-corrective organizations. President Konan Henri Bédié, then President of the National Assembly, perceived this objective in these terms. As he stated during the opening of the parliamentary session: "We have to count on ourselves, on our will to live together in tolerance, the mutual respect and respect to laws. The pursuit together of a minimum common objective imposes itself on all political parties. The multypartyism is not an end in itself; it has to be a means to expand the well being to which all citizens convincingly aspire to (1992, p.14).

OPPOSITION PARTIES IN BURKINA FASO

What have the opposition parties been realizing in Burkina Faso? Two factors tend to characterize the behavior of the current transition toward democracy in Burkina Faso: spirit and the willingness to work hard or the sense of responsibility and the tight military security in Ouagadougou. Here, militarism and nationalism seem to function closely. The important question is what characteristic or tendency will dominate in the process of democratization as the state and society at large is struggling to progress?

Strong urban social explosions as I have indicated earlier accompanied the emergence of multiparty democracy in many parts of Africa on the streets in many parts of Africa. The cases of Cameroon, Nigeria, and Togo, are more telling. Confrontations took the forms of physical struggle and massacres and assassinations. The nature of explosion varies with social conditions and the political culture of each milieu and its governance. It is those explosions that exposed and publicized the general state of affairs in Africa and in international politics/relations. The general process embodied two major forces through which change was supposed to occur: a national conference and the referendum on the question of a constitution.

In Burkina Faso, the national conference or national forum did not complete its course, as was the case, for instance, in Bénin, the Congo, Niger or Togo. This makes it different from other dominant political trends in the Francophone countries in sub-Sahara Africa. Côte d'Ivoire also did not have a national conference. But one could easily predict this situation in Côte d'Ivoire.

It also produced a non-elected Prime Minister Alassane Ouattara and his technocrats. In Burkina, it was not possible to predict that their national conference would be sabotaged given the nature of the political history of struggle of Burkina. With the exception of the brutal physical elimination of Sankara and his associates in 1987 and other executions that followed, Burkina Faso did not produce other strong social explosions like in Mali and uprisings that could lead to a coup d'état or social disruption like in DRC. And Burkina Faso is in a transition, as are other examples that I have considered and discussed earlier in this chapter.

Two schools of thought can be considered here. Some Burkinabè believe that the process of democratization as it has taken place in Burkina will lead to the establishment of a political culture needed for fostering a genuine democratic society. As social and economic conditions improve with an ethic of hard work and the people's determination and the introduction of more discipline in the performance of the state apparatuses and public administration, people will eventually support the democratic ideal. This ideal has been a reflection of people's social conditions. It is a strong cooperation between the state and people that may make democracy a reality. And there are those who are skeptical. For them, the behavior of the state is still strongly militaristic, especially when it comes to the actions and policies related to the question of its security. The state, especially its executive agency, the government, has not separated itself from the traditions of a military regime: tight control and suspicion. It does not seem to have built enough confidence yet in its actions to allow the political philosophy of multiparty democracy to make its way through and be reflected on the free flow of ideas (debates), and the free movement of goods and people.

It is appropriate to make a general observation that there is a systematic effort or societal determination by the people and state through its privatization policies to improve the living conditions of the majority of people through structural adjustment programs (SAPs). However, facts show that the SAPs have not yet qualitatively improved the conditions of the majority of the African people even in the so-called success stories. What do the opposition parties in Burkina Faso wish to promote and establish? How did these opposition parties emerge? From the time multipartyism was legally instituted to the time of presidential and legislative elections, there were little more than sixty (60) political parties and about four thousand (4, 000) political associations. But only twenty-seven (27) political parties participated in the elections. I will not to discuss the political philosophies of all those parties and associations which claimed to be in the opposition to the former military regime, which was accused of being dictatorial. Rather, I am interested in the categorization of tendencies.

It should be stated that in this case, democratic process, if simply defined and characterized by the preparation of both legislative and presidential elections, was said to be quick and "efficient" in Burkina Faso. It produced its intended objectives in a short period of time: an elected president in December

1991 and elected national assembly members in May 1992. It should be indicated that in Burkina, unlike in many other countries in Africa that produced multipartyism, the presidential election took place before the legislative elections. The president-elect could influence the course of the legislative elections. But will this process produce a democratic culture that is needed for creating a democratic society? What have been objectives of opposition parties and their vision of society, if any? It should be noted that the outcome of this process has been different compared to Côte d'Ivoire because of the differences in their political culture, their social milieus, the political economy of each country, and the nature of the legitimacy of the ruling parties, among other factors. Is it fair to hypothesize that Blaise Compaoré, the president of Burkina, his party and regime have only changed their uniform in order to legitimize them in power? The answer cannot be that simple. It should be said however, that as of early 1993 about three fourths of the members of the ministerial cabinet were from opposition parties in the Compaoré's civilian government. Seventeen parties out of twenty-seven had seats in the parliament. Three out of five declared Sankarist parties that participated into the legislative elections had no seats in the parliament. Has Sankara been completely rejected in Burkina? What does that mean in an analysis on the nature of democratic processes and discourses in Africa?

Burkina Faso has come to the current problematic on democratic process from a background of the populism and spirit of the Sankarist-Compaorist revolution that begun in 1983. In addition, it had a history of having one of the strongest unionist movements and organizations in West Africa. The major political parties in Burkina Faso include *l'Union Nationale pour la Défense de la Démocratie* (UNDD), which was inspired by the ideological tendencies of the *Rassemblement Démocratique Africain* (RDA), the grand old party of the first generation of the Francophone West African élite, *l'Alliance pour la Démocratie et la Fédération* (ADF), and *le Mouvement des Démocrates et Patriotes* (MDP), *Rassemblement Social Démoctatique Independent* of the well-known historian Ki-Zerbo. All the leaders of the parties seem to agree that the struggle for democracy has to be part of a struggle to improve people's material and social conditions. Despite the fact that Burkina has a long history of trade unionism, the current major political parties do not seem to emphasize the working class ideological differences among the parties.

Many parties joined the government to make internal policy reforms possible. For others the opposition has been silent since it joined the government because many of them do not have a clear ideological conviction or basis. Non-conventional opposition parties, that is to say, those that operate outside of the legal national jurisdiction, continue to see this transition of Burkina Faso as undemocratic. However, in the 1990s, many believed that Compaoré was the only one among the leaders of the various parties who could reconcile the country. The fact is that the opposition is divisive on the ground of personal and individual ambitions, ethnic and, to a lesser extent, ideological affiliations.

CONCLUSION

Democratic discourses in Africa have started on a slippery slope. Economic crises cannot and will not advance democratic discourses. In addition, they are articulated, manipulated and dangerously linked with primary nationalist elements like ethnicity, religion and/or local cultural elements in such a way that if those forces are not critically questioned, they may become the dominant ones in political discourse. Their absolutism can also be detrimental to any real democratic discourse. I say that the above elements must be understood and given a different, more proper role in a democratic struggle.

Ethnic or local nationalism is a phenomenon that can easily destroy any democracy because its philosophy is closer to religious absolutism than secular politics. For democracy to have social meaning, political parties must socialize people and advance the concepts of human and social rights including the right to *logos* and life, freedom of expression and religion, respect for the law and tolerance, and appreciation of differences. All these rights must advance and protect human values individually and collectively. Democratic discourses that are separated from economic development projects and industrialization programs are socially meaningless. That is to say, the struggle to have food, shelter, education, etc. has to be part of the struggle for democracy. Its does not make any sense to have the right to *logos* without a right to life. In short, our democratic discourses must have as a main objective the improvement of the social and economic conditions for individuals and society at large.

Another problem the struggle for democracy faces is the lack of a respectful and lawful democratic political culture within existing political parties. In Africa, personal or individual political choice is still conceived as family, clan, or even as a whole ethnic group matter. Government opposition and differences in political views are not easily tolerated. That is to say, democratic discourses have yet not been conceived and practiced as objective and rational discourses. One function of the political parties, both ruling parties and the opposition parties, is to promote political culture through debates and collective actions with respect to law and "constructive African humanism."

Democratic discourses must be guided with an agenda and an ideal for nation building: building a political community, rather than building a country or state. Many parties still behave as if they desire to create a country or reorganize ethnic interests against those of nations. Many are not performing from the collective consciousness perspective. Collective interest, that is to say, the interest of the nation, must be the priority in democratic discourses. And the notion of a social contract based on African consciousness and social realities must also be articulated within these discourses.

It must be said, however, that African people are not necessarily or ontologically allergic to contemporary democratic discourses, whether they are procedural and/or substantive. To illustrate a few cases, legislative elections took place in the Congo in 1965 without producing any incidence of violence in the country that had just emerged from the Congo crisis, despite massive communication problems. In 1991, in Zambia, Benin, etc., the electoral process was realized without any serious violence. The same held true in Mali in April 1992, in Burkina Faso between January and May 1992 and in Congo/Brazzaville in July 1992. The local, legislative and presidential elections in Ghana did not produce the violence that had been anticipated. In Malawi, the massive people's participation in the legislative and presidential elections between April 25th and 29th of 1994 in South Africa show also legitimatized multiparty democracy. On May 1994, Malawi's multiparty elections were held unexpectedly without much violence and disturbances. In short, despite intrigue and violent actions perpetrated by some internal political forces and parties, with discipline and determination, the African people are firmly deciding to choose their leaders democratically. The political parties have the responsibility to advance African societies toward the creation of democratic rules and institutions. The democratic society must be conceived as an ideal society, superior to other forms of governance.

The targets for the opposition parties must be the state's public policies, its mechanisms of allocation and distribution of its values and its ideologies, not necessarily individuals or personalities (though it may be difficult to dissociate personal actions from the institutions in which they function). They must act lawfully to give a good example as a new leadership, highly needed for the promotion of democracy. Political parties like the national institutions should be separated from the state. They should be equipped with the necessary tools for policy analysis and political evaluation. Their actions must be predictable.

I must emphasize the fact that political reforms, that is to say, the introduction of multipartyism without serious economic reforms, will lead to the failure of any effort towards democracy. This may paralyze the democratic process, which is as important as their outcomes.

Finally, many attempts at democracy have already occurred in Africa, but they did not succeed due to a multiplicity of factors, among which the most important are: lack of a democratic political culture in many cases, the confusion between democracy and multipartyism, an alien form of democracy that did not fit the African culture but was imposed de facto or forced in some cases, and the fact that economic reforms preceded political reforms. Political reforms should have been made before economic reforms. The outcomes of political reforms can be much better at the national level than economic reforms that are usually linked to the rules and the dynamism of the international economic system.

Africa's greatest hope is the establishment of real social democracy and decentralized power systems to give people chance to think about themselves, to reorganize their systems of production and consumption, to promote their culture and their history and to think internationally, yet act locally. However, democracy *à l'Européenne* has a tendency of being exclusive. This exclusivity is well reflected in the behavior and structures of political opposition groups. Popular participation in both state affairs and nation building is, in my view, the sine-qua-non for progress in Africa. A true democracy is one where conditions can be set for the promotion of a viable and progressive nation through individual and collective actions. This democracy is a democracy of the people.

To avoid unwanted and unnecessary civil wars, unpredictable military interventions (or their return to power) and secessionist movements, all political forces in African countries, including the states, must advance and incorporate democratic discourses into public policies and development projects. This can be done in multiparty systems as well as in one party-systems. Africans should not restrict themselves in their choices of democratic discourses. Political parties should not function as religious organizations with their members having "irrational" convictions in them. Their actions must be verifiable and testable in public domains and social policies. The rationality of political parties is made up of their ability to bargain based on their platforms, their vision of society to be realized and their consistency in political behavior and actions. A political party that will not bargain becomes a religious organization, incapable of entering into a broader social discourse. Absolutism of any religion does not allow for the creation of a common social base for growth. The search for some forms of social contract or general transformational paradigms or objectives is one of *raisons d'être* of political parties. Social contract or consensus, as used here, has to emerge from the bottom up.

Given the nature of current philosophical and ideological contradictions within African institutions and development models and the seriousness of the African economic crisis, democratic discourses that come with different options and choices must deal with the poverty elimination scheme and political realism rather than poverty alleviation and individualistic development approaches. It is only through massive coalitions of social and political forces with continental transformational objectives that poverty can be dealt with effectively and globally. The need for the vanguard party, movement or state is still vital. The coalition of progressive people and parties/movements can advance the causes of real democracy in Africa. They should play the role of political educators.

At the end of the Cold War, with the weakening of European leftist parties that have morally and financially supported leftist parties in Africa, the African leftists have opportunities to form genuine broader coalitions with other elements of the society in order to create common grounds for building stronger oppositions with populist and Pan-African visions of the society to be created. As long as opposition parties lack clear political ideology, they will continue to articulate incoherent and self-interested policies that will not collectively mobilize people's views. The petty bourgeois opposition has been essentially exclusive and anti-peasant/farmers. Yet they are composed of more than fifty of the population in sub-Saharan Africa. Imitating European opposition parties, but not functioning under European infrastructures and political institutions, petty bourgeois opposition parties seem to be dysfunctional, irrelevant and powerless to challenge the ruling parties and link themselves with people. Opposition party without any vision and/or a clear ideological base is likely, if it succeeds to capture power, to fail to address people's demand with confidence. The current African conditions require that the opposition parties be philosophically revolutionaries and culturally African in order to challenge the undemocratic practices of the ruling parties and states. Accommodationism and political reforms, which are essentially European oriented without a clear philosophy of the kind of society to be created or without a political passion, are likely to continue to produce the politics and policies of excessive dependency on the West and economic *marasme*. For the Africa's opposition parties to work properly and have the support of the people, they have to be a political educator rather being only protesting agencies. They must present policy alternative to the society. They have to be in the parliament. They also must socialize the people. Given the fact that the African democracies are either partially stable or unstable, the opposition parties must first create the institutions and the culture of the opposition within the civil society. They must depersonalize their organizations and claims. The opposition has to transform itself into an institutional machine with clear rules and rewards systems for its memberships. Why not searching for the Africa's own theory of opposition party that may be relevant and appropriate to the African objective conditions and grand agenda for social progress?

Notes

1. Professor Francis Wodié is the General Secretary of *Le Parti Ivoirien du Travail* (PIT). He is the only representative of his party in the national Assembly (Parliament). He is the former dean of the school of law at the National University of Abidjan. He has *deux agrégations* and is well-known scholar.

2. Cocody is one of the luxurious *communes* (districts) of Abidjan. The active and productive members who inhabit it are mostly middle class and university students.

3. Faites connaissance avec le MDS, a document of the MDS 1992 for advertising.

REFERENCES

Amin, Samir. 1967. Développement du capitalisme en Côte d'Ivoire, Paris.

Ammendola, Curtris, Blonddish, and Kommers Lancaster, Western European Government and Politics, New York: Longman, 1997.

Barkan, Joel D. ed. 1994. Beyond Capitalism vs. Socialism in Kenya and Tanzania, Boulder, Lynne Rienner Publishers.

Bédié, Henri Konan. 1992. "The Speech of the first ordinary opening session of the

Parliament" in Abidjan, Côte d'Ivoire, on April 29.

CODESRIA Bulletin .1993. No. 1.

Construire l'"Afrique: le Magazine panafricain de la politique et de l'enterprise 1994. No-21-Aôut-Novembre

Diamond, Larry, Juan J. Linz, and Martin Lipset (Eds.) Politics of Developing Countries: Comparing Experiences with Democracy, Boulder, COLO: Lynne Rienner, 1995.

Ginsburg, Mark B. Ed. 1992. Understanding Educational Reform in Global Context :Economy. State and Ideology, New York: Garland Publishing, Inc.

Human Rights Watch, World Report 2000: Africa Section, New York, New York: Human Watch, December 1999.

Ihonvbere. J. and O. Vaughan. 1995. Nigeria: Democracy and Civil Society. The Nigerian Transition Program, 1985-1993 in J.A. Wiseman (ed), Democracy and Political Change in Sub-Saharan Africa. London: Routledge, pp. 132 - 153.

Lumumba-Kasongo, Tukumbi. 1991. Nationalistic Ideologies, Their Policy Implications and The Struggle for Democracy in African Politics, New York: Edwin Mellen Press.

Lumumba-Kasongo, T. 1995. "Towards A Political Re-definition of Africa." (SAPEM) Volume 8, No.6 March: 33-36.

Lumumba-Kasongo, T. 1998. The Rise of Multipartyism and Democracy in the Context of Global Change: The Case of Africa, Westport, CONN: Praeger.

Nzongola-Ntalaja, Georges. 1987. Revolution and Counter-Revolution in Africa :Essays in Contemporary Politics. London and New Jersey, Zed books.

Sklar, R. 1979. The Nature of Class Domination in Africa. Journal of Modern Afica Studies, Vol, 17, no. 4, pp. 560- 571.

Wallerstein, Immanuel. 1984. The World Politics of the World Economy: The States, The Movements and the Civilizations, New York, Cambridge University Press.

Wodié, Francis. 1992. . "Problématique de la transition démocratique en Afrique," paper presented at Seventh General Assembly of CODESRIA, Dakar, Senegal, 10-14 February.

Zolberg.A. R.1966. Creating Political Order: The Party States of West Africa. Chicago: Rand McNally

Chapter 8

The Politics in Uganda

Robert Dibie and Samory Rashid

INTRODUCTION

Two recent political trends in East Africa pose particular dilemmas for the Western World. First is the emergence of a new model of governing that is different from both the old style African autocracy and the Western liberal democracy that has been heavily promoted by the United States and Britain in Africa since the end of the Cold War. The second is the growing tendency of African nations to intervene militarily in the affairs of their neighbors.

Uganda's new economic promise lies in a change in its political systems and the way its government now does business. Uganda was one of the most advanced nations in East Africa at independence in 1962 (Mazrui 1986; Richard 1997; Tordoff 1997). Unfortunately, this legacy was wasted when Idi Amin ousted Uganda's elected civilian leaders in a military coup in 1971. Amin overthrew Obote's government while President Milton Obote was attending the 1971 Commonwealth Conference in Singapore. Tanzania granted political refuge to Milton Obote and refused to recognize the legitimacy of Idi Amin's regime.

During Idi Amin's reign (1971-1979) over 100,000 Ugandans were murdered and the economy collapsed due to the social disruption caused by his government Jackson and Rosberg 1986; Mutibwa 1992). Amin's tyranny adversely affected both the civil and the socioeconomic conditions of the country. The coup was soon followed by repressive and exclusionary mandates, at the policy level. Senior officials became vulnerable to Amin's suspicion, jealousy, and many were removed arbitrarily from their posts (Jackson and Rosberg 1986). The disappearance and murder of Chief Justice Benedicto Kiwanuka in 1972 and the decrees that place the military above the law effectively terrorized judges, magistrates, lawyers and even the police, with the result that the legal system ceased to function in any meaningful sense. In short during Idi Amin's regime Uganda was reduced to something resembling what Hobbes called "the state of nature."(Legum 1983; Sandbrook 1975). In 1978, Amin's army crossed the border into Tanzania in pursuit of soldiers who had carried out an unsuccessful mutiny. The Ugandans stole property and destroyed the livelihood of many Tanzania's. President Nyerere called on the Organization of African Unity (OAU) to censure Amin for his act of aggression, and, when the OAU failed to do so, Nyerere ordered his troops to support the forces of anti-Amin exiles in the invasion of Uganda. Amin's forces were defeated and his regime destroyed. Amin sought exile first in Libya and later on in Saudi Arabia.

In 1986 the military led by Yoweri Museveni took over control of Uganda. Since Museveni's leadership in Uganda the era of misrule, ethnic conflict and civil war has reduced drastically. Museveni's government has been primarily concerned with ensuring peace and stability and promoting economic development. Many scholars as a dramatic turnaround in Uganda's political and economic fortune (Rothchild 1997; Kasfir 1998; Udogu 1999) have described his reign. In 1995 the United Nations ranked Uganda as the 13th fastest growing economy in the world.

After 14 years of rule by President Yoweri Museveni and "The Movement" formerly known as the National Resistance Movement (NRM), Uganda has become a mountain of relative political and economic stability in an increasingly turbulent Great Lakes Region. Uganda stands out because it is symbolic of the new "African Renaissance."(Rothchild, 1997). But Museveni's rule has not been without controversy, and Uganda does not fit exactly into the model of what Western government likes to see in developing nations. Rather than laying the foundation for an open, democratic society upon which to build an open advanced market economy, Museveni has kept a rein on political dissent in Uganda, by instituting what he terms no party rule. President Museveni believes that his no party models in which individuals are allowed to participate politics but political parties are not allowed is essential to keeping the peace in Uganda. Museveni contends that most African nations are not ready for Western style multiparty democracy, which he believes requires a society that has thriving economy and a stable middle class that can form parties around the ideas rather than ethnic identity.

The number of African regimes that have made a transition to multiparty democracy in the 1990s is quite impressive. In 1989, 39 out of 45 sub-Saharan African countries had authoritarian forms of rule, while in 1995, 31 out of 45 held democratic or presidential elections (Kasfir 1998; World Bank 1997). But increasingly, scholars are realizing that the hoped for "quick fixes" of democracy in Africa have not transpired. The norm has become a "workshop of democracy as deception" not the anticipated African "workshop of democracy"

(Joseph 1998:56; Udogu 1999; Zakari 1997). There have been multiparty elections in Kenya, and Zambia for example, but President Daniel Arap Moi as well as President Fredrick Chiluba have manipulated the political area to re-politicize ethnicity as well as prevent a viable opposition from developing. Political and economic instability has become unfortunate consequences of these political survival techniques. It is thus difficult to ignore the persuasive successes of the Movement regime under Museveni. The Movement regime has led Uganda from its horrifying and bloody past to a new envied and glorified position in the African continent, so much that even U.S. Secretary of State, Madeline Albright referred to Uganda as a "beacon of hope" (Houston Chronicle 22 March 1998).

Museveni's Movement regime is appealing to most donors because Museveni has been able to bring Uganda from the brink of chaos to a semblance of order and stability while vigorously embracing economic liberalization. Yet, Uganda is not a multi-party democracy. Political parties are allowed to exist in Uganda, but elections are held on a "no-party" basis, with candidacy based on individual merit rather than political party affiliation. Museveni and the Movement thus represent a "no-party democracy" based not on multi-party electoral competition, but a broad-based, inclusionary model of governance. Although the Museveni regime has implemented only limited political liberalization, it has pursued more substantial economic liberalization. There are four key variables that form the characteristics of the Museveni's regime: (1) limited political liberalization; (2) extensive economic liberalization; (3) substantial external aid and international legitimacy; and (4) a visionary political leadership. The key to Uganda's "success" lies in economic liberalization policies that won it substantial external aid and international support. This support was absolutely crucial to maintaining the levels of growth and recovery that Uganda experienced in the late 1980s and the 1990s. At the same time, Museveni's regime allowed for limited political liberalization by controlling consensus from above using strategies of incorporation and exclusion where necessary. While this was going on Museveni maintained that he was opening up political participation to all Ugandans via the Local Council (LC) system. Hence, his regime was able to control the pace of political and economic liberalization while stabilizing the political arena. The capstone to this successful equation was Museveni's visionary political leadership and charisma. Museveni was able to convince his internal and external constituency that he was the only man capable of leading Uganda out of its dismal past to its current glorified position. Adopting a position similar to Julius Nyerere as the "teacher," Museveni placed himself above the political fray and presented himself as committed to leading Ugandans toward the "right path to development and democracy."

This chapter examines the Ugandan model of no-party democracy and the stability and economic growth that might form a prerequisite for long-term development and democracy. The study attempts to provide answer to the following questions: Are there African alternatives to the Western concept of multiparty democracy? The fact that Uganda has experienced more political stability and substantial economic growth under a no-party system, than many other African countries that have adopted multiparty regimes, warrants a critical examination of its politics. What are the fundamental characteristics of Museveni's no-party system and how viable and appropriate is it in Uganda and other post-conflict states? Can post-conflict countries like Rwanda and the Democratic Republic of Congo adopt such a model? This chapter caution readers that we must look at the democratizing movement in Uganda in terms of a process rather than a sharp break from authoritarianism to more open political systems.

THEORETICAL OVERVIEW OF DEMOCRACY

Many political scientists have been struggling with the theoretical problems stemming from the definition of democracy. For instance, in defining democracy, Schumpeter (1960) visualized it in terms of methods rather than goals. According to Schumpeter democracy is an arrangement for arriving at political decisions in which individuals acquire power to decide by means of competitive struggle for the people's vote (269). Lasswell, Lener and Rothwell, 1952) contends that a system could be termed a democracy even if power is exercised by a few elites and situated the onus on accountability. In the Africa case, Ali Mazrui (1986) contents that a system in which the elders (or Chiefs) of a community met and debated societal problems until a consensus was reached (an oath taken to abide by the decision) represented a form of African democracy and accountability.

Other scholars assert that the elites, not the masses, are the true custodians of democracy and human rights. In this respect, Key (1961) notes that, "the critical element for the health of the democratic order consists in beliefs, standards, and competence of those who constitute the influential, the opinion leaders and the political activists (p558). A more contemporary traditional democratic theory is grounded on a number of axioms. For example, Robert Dahl (1989) suggests five pillars on which democracy could be sustained. These are the equality of voting, effective participation, enlightened understanding, final control (of a body or group of citizens) over the agenda, and inclusion.

Given the record of authoritarianism in Uganda since its independence, the initial assumption that could be made is that the current push towards democratization entails the establishment of political rights usually associated with bourgeois liberalism which Robert Dahl called polyarchy (1971). Dahl's notion of polyarchy has three principal elements: competition for government power, political participation in the selection of leaders and policies and civil and political liberties (Nyang'oro 1994). In Uganda many of these conditions have been absent. Indeed part of the rationale for President Museveni's present no political party system is the introduction of these rights within the nation. The authors of this chapter caution that we must look at the democratizing movement in Uganda in terms of a process rather than a sharp break from authoritarianism to more open political systems. The process also has to be discussed within the context of political economy. Richard Sandbrook (1988) who represents an important strand in African politics studies contends that despite democracy's limitations in Africa, liberal democracy represent a step forward from one party or military authoritarianism to multiparty political systems. Thus, the value of liberal democracy can be demonstrated by an example from Uganda under President Museveni.

These foregoing analyses were intended to illuminate some of the characteristics of democracy and to provide a backdrop against which ethnic groups in a nation might be examined and perhaps better understood. It is given that one of the central elements of a democratic nation is competition for vote or support from the electorates. It is such support that helps legitimize the system, but systems in which support are sought after on the basis of ethnicity tend to suffer from the problem of legitimacy and instability. This in turn hampers democratic development. Indeed the competing for ethnic hegemony in the governance of various polities in Africa has rendered the state problem and interethnic relations conflict. The centrifugal tendencies of ethnic rivalries, therefore, tend to render the state "irrelevant" (Ihonvbere 1994) to a majority of the ethnic minority groups, especially those marginalized because they were on the losing end in ethnically-oriented political contests (Udogu 1994). This has, in some nations led to military coups and the abortion of democracy. Uganda is a classic case in point. There are several other examples around Africa that are related to ethnic dissatisfaction with the distribution of power and the nation's resources. Such an unstable political situation tends to render the flowering of democracy extremely problematic in practice. One of the ways to avert such problems is the no-party rule system that Museveni has introduced in Uganda. The extent to which no-party rule can foster economic development and political stability is still too earlier for us to know, but Uganda has successfully practiced it for almost 15 years.

POST- INDEPENDCENCE

Uganda had a multiparty democracy from Independence in 1962 until 1966, thereafter, the nation suffered through three decades of brutal rule, alternating between differing degrees of repression with Milton Obote's two periods of rule; Obote I (1962-1970) and Obote II (1980-1985). Obote's parliamentary position was strengthened following independence when members of opposition parties crossed the floor of the National Assembly to the government side. As a result, Obote was able to dissolve his alliance with the Kabaka Yekka (KY or King Alone). In a reaction to criticism of his conduct and the conduct of some of his ministers, Obote carried out a coup; he arrested his critics, suspended the constitution, and assumed full state powers. Subsequently, he introduce a new constitutional immunity, fused the head of state and head of government positions into a single presidential office, and gave himself authority over the entire country. Obote used the national army under the command of General Idi Amin to suppress the Kebaka and all his critics (Jackson and Rosberg 1986).

While Obote was attending the 1971 Commonwealth Conference in Singapore, General Idi Dada Amin overthrew his government. Amin's regime was initially well received by the Ugandan people and by foreign governments, especially Britain. Amin proclaimed an 18-point charter for a free and prosperous Uganda and rescinded Obote's decision to give the state a majority holding in major private enterprises. That action pleased not only the international business community but also the Ugandan commercial elite, including the vital Asian community. Political detainees were release, most of them enemies of Obote, and Idi Amin vowed to restore civilian rule within five years (Jackson and Rosberg 1986).

According to Jackson and Rosberg (1986) and Phares Mutibwa (1992). The period of post-coup optimism was relatively brief. Amin faced his enemies and Obote supporters among the population and even the within the army. Amin's regime issued decrees that granted extensive powers of arrest and confinement and other deprivations of civil rights. The regime used threats and acts of violence to deter and, if necessary, to eliminate anyone believed to be an enemy. Suspected members of the population, army, and police were detained and often-murdered Major political disappearance occurred during Amin's regime and people who avoided arrest had to flee for their lives. The dictatorial rule of Idi Amin Dada (1971-1979) followed by equally corrupt and repressive military-controlled transition regimes in 1979-1980 and 1985-1986. Ugandan citizens have consequently associated the nation's government with repression, manipulation, corruption and exploitation. Ethnicity, regionalism and religion were manipulated by those in power, and by those seeking power thereby undermining the viable functioning of the state and the society in Uganda during this period. The Northerners were pitted against Southerners, Protestants against Catholics and Muslims, and ethnic group against other ethnic group. The state was significantly weakened by bad political leadership and weak political parties that relied on politicized ethnicity, regionalism, and religion to keep civil society divided and suppressed (Mutibwa, 1992).

When the Uganda People's Defense Forces (UPDF), formerly named the National Resistance Army (NRM) took over Kampala in 1986, it inherited a legacy of division, destruction and despair. The UPDF was able to quickly establish legitimacy in Uganda because of its highly disciplined nature and the guerrilla component of its warfare. The Movement, the political wing of the UPDF, was able to secure legitimacy from engineering a "revolution from above" promoting economic growth and political stability, although rebellions continued to rage in the Northern regions. The "Movement" regime led by Museveni has been able to rebuild the state as well as the state's accountability and legitimacy. How successful has Museveni's regime been in building this accountability and legitimacy?

By the time Museveni took over the leadership of Uganda, the nation was plagued with low literacy rates, weak infrastructure, weak political parties without appropriate policy agendas and ideologies, and extreme poverty. Museveni and the Movement make the argument that given Uganda's bloody past; it is not yet ready for full-fledged (multi-party) democracy (Kasfir 1998). President Museveni argues that, "...eighty-two percent of Ugandans are peasants, pre-capitalists, living a tribal form of life. When you in the west insist arrogantly that all societies, in the world must be organized in exactly the same form as you, you are wrong. Multi-party system is not a healthy basis for Uganda to build its democracy. Political parties in Uganda are inevitably based on tribe or ethnicity, and they intensify friction. In some cases, they result in disaster" (Hansen and Twaddle 1996). Thus, Museveni cites the desire for stability and the need to rebuild the Uganda State to justify his anti-multi politics position.

EXCLUSIONARY POLITICS

Museveni's regime claims to legitimacy rest on two main components: (1) economic growth; and (2) political participation via the LC system. The first priority of the new regime was to implement its "Ten-Point" program which summarized the basic ideology of the Movement including: (1) the notion of popular democracy; (2) the restoration of security; (3) the consolidation of national unity; (4) defending national independence; (5) building a national economy; (6) the restoration and rehabilitation of social services; (7) the elimination of corruption and misuse of power; (8) the resettlement of displaced people; (9) regional co-operation and human rights and (10) a mixed economy (Oloka-Onyango 1991). Museveni insists that a multi-party democracy is not a necessary or desirable component of this revival. In fact, since storming into power in 1986, the NRM has been able to rule through what it calls a "no-party" system of governance. Museveni declared that political parties were the culprits of past instability and bloodshed, claiming that "no-party" competition was crucial to avoid the "sectarianism" that dominated politics in pre-Movement Uganda. Museveni's regime cites that politicized ethnicity, encouraged by the old political parties; the Uganda Peoples' Congress (UPC), the Democratic Party (DP) and the Conservative Party (CP) as the key culprit to political and economic instability in the 1970s and 1980s. The Movement does not consider itself a political party, but a broad based, inclusionary "movement" which operates on a non-ethnic, non-regional and non-religious basis.

One of the main claims of Museveni's regime is that "no-party democracy" is providing an alternative form of "democratization" for Uganda—one that is indigenous to Ugandan culture and political history. According to Museveni, the Local Council (LC) system (previously named Resistance Councils (RCA) prior to 1995) is a consensual, participatory, grassroots alternative to multi-partyism. Museveni has state that Uganda does not need multi-party politics, but what it needs is greater participation; "Pressure for change is coming from exclusion. So many people have been excluded from the political process. It is a struggle for participation.

Museveni's regime consists of five level Local Council/Committee (LC) systems, LC1-LC5 consisting of; LC1 (village level), LC2 (parish level), LC3 (sub-county level), LC4 (county level) and LC5 (District level). Parliament (the National Resistance Council) with the National Executive Committee (NEC) (cabinet) are at the apex of the system (see Dicklitch, 1998, pp. 76-78). The Ugandan system consists of a combination of direct participatory democracy (at LC1) and electoral colleges (LC 2-5). The LC committee is composed of nine executive members. Every Uganda citizen is a member of a village level Local Council (LC1). Individuals are allowed to run for office, but based on personal merit rather than political party affiliation (Kasfir 1998).

In addition to the LC council, every district has a Central Government Representative (CGR), formerly called the District Administrator, who is appointed by the president. The CGR is concerned with political and administrative issues in the district, including "...providing political direction, supervising and ensuring the implementation of Government plans and policies, and chairing the security and development committee" (Okoka-Onyango 1991:136).

Museveni's regime practices a policy of both political inclusion and co-optation of significant opposition members. This is part of the broad based, no-party approach of the regime. The actual degree of the broad based inclusionary representation, especially in the cabinet for example, significantly decreased after the constituent Assembly elections and the 1996 parliamentary and presidential elections (Kasfirl 1998). In fact, Museveni has used cabinet reshuffles every year since 1986 (except for 1987 and 1997) as a way to punish disloyal ministers and promote loyal "Movementalists". Political participation is thus encouraged, but only within the formal structures of the system (Reuter June 22, 1995), and without much criticism of the Movement system.

Several elections have been held during the Movement's 14 years of rule. All the elections were held on a "no-party" basis, with parliamentary elections held in 1989, 1992, and 1996 with Constituent Assembly elections to debate the draft constitution held in 1994. Elections for the Constituent Assembly were generally considered free and fair, with an estimated 118 out of the 214 directly elected Constituent Assembly members in favor of the no-party system with continued suspension of political party activities, while 86 elected delegates supported an immediate return to a multi-party system (Kasfir 1994:2). Approximately 150 seats were won by "NRM candidates" (Watson 1994:25).

One of the outcomes of the Constituent Assembly deliberations was the 1996 Presidential and parliamentary elections. These elections like the proceeding 1989 and 1992 elections were held on a no-party basis, but this was the first time that the President actually ran for office. Thus, individuals could campaign for positions within the LC system, but they could not campaign as a representative of a political party campaigning on the basis of "no change",

Museveni was able to win the Presidential elections of May 1996 with 74.2% of the votes, Paul Ssemogerere the Inter-Political Forces Cooperation (IPFC) candidate came second with 23.7% of the votes, and the third-runner, Mohammed Mayanja won only 2.2% of the overall votes (Watson 1994; Washington Post 1996). Although international election observers suggested that the elections were mostly free and fair, there were several pre-election inconsistencies and irregularities. Many diplomats and opposition leaders maintained that the restriction to only one month to campaign, and the ban on political party activity, gave Museveni such a heavy advantage that he could not lose (The New York Times March 31, 1996).

Museveni traveled throughout the country before elections "...ostensibly top promote an anti-poverty program" but instead seemed to promote his candidacy by handing out bicycles, and the like (New York Times 31 March 1996). More disturbing however, was Museveni use of scare tactics to intimidate voters, like advertisements in the New Vision newspaper which suggested that if Ssemogerere won the election, because of the Uganda People's Congress (UPC) and Democratic Party (DP) coalition in the IPFC, Ssemogerere was going to bring back Obote (leader of the UPC) and the slaughter associated with his rule, especially in the Lower Triangle. In addition, Museveni's supporters have harassed, stoned, and stampeded, kidnapped and beat Ssemogerere and Mayanga supporters at numerous political rallies. At another political rally, Museveni said that he was not ready to "give up the army that we have struggled to build" (Kasfir 1998). The UPDF is closely associated with Movement rule. After decade of civil strife, it is perhaps little wonder that Ugandas chose the "safe" option of continued Movement rule. As a consequence of the misconduct that occurred during the presidential elections, the IPFC resolved to boycott the parliamentary and Local council poll in June 1996, stating that "...the IPFC has completely lost confidence in the electoral process, adding that "any Ugandan wishing to participate in the forthcoming parliamentary and Local council elections may do so well knowing that the rigging machinery is still in place and will adversely affect the results" (McGreal 1996). One of the negative side effects of the elections was to turn the LCs into "partisan political organs of the state" (The Monitor June 6, 1999).

But viable alternatives to Movement government do not presently exist. Current political directives of the Movement compounded with the legacies of the past continue to undermine the development of a viable alternative to Museveni's rule. Political parties are still widely associated with "nepotism and human rights abuses" and are considered "poison" by half the population (Christian Science Monitor June 19, 1997: 8). The Movement regime helps to promote these imagines by labeling political parties "sectarian" and interested only in obtaining power. The main political parties, UPC and DP, fronted a united presidential candidate, Paul Ssemogerere, in the IPFC, but like the Kebaka Yekka-UPC alliance of the sixties, this alliance was unstable and based on convince (a united desire to get rid of Museveni as President and bring in multipartyism) rather than a united attempt to "democratize" the political arena (see Dicklitch 1998:35-38). Ssemogerere allied himself with the UPC, "...the party that he had always charged with cheating the DP of its victory by threatening to use the army" (Kasfir 1998). In fact, these political parties do not display "democratic compromise", trust or willingness to play by the rule of law. The political parties are united against their commonly perceived enemy, Museveni, but beyond that, they can agree on little else.

These parties are also internally divided, with radical splinter wings developing in most of the main political parties; Democratic Party (Democratic mobilizer's group), UPC (those preferring to have Obote, who is still in exile in Zambia, lead the party and those wanting someone else) and the CP (those under Mayanga who want to join the IPFC and those under Secretary General Ken Lukayaka who want to push for a more federalist position). These divisions are compounded by the fact that political parties remain fundamentally undemocratic because they have not been able to hold intra-party leadership conventions, due to the constitutionally enshrined government ban on political party activities.

Non state actors in general are thus tolerated by the regime as long as they continue to function in an apolitical and non-confrontational manner. The degree of autonomy and power that non-state actors have outside of the LC system is therefore significantly limited. Furthermore, with the promulgation of the new Constitution of Uganda in November 1995, independent, autonomous political activity was further marginalized in Uganda politics. Article 269 effectively banned political party activities and multi-partyism until the year 2000.

The most important political question here is the need to limit the possibilities of authoritarianism gaining more ground in Uganda than it already has. In Museveni's idea, the assumption is made that the military cannot be kept out of governance, and, therefore, the compromise that must be reached is for the civilians and the military to govern together. This presumably would be the only way to maintain political stability in Uganda.

DYNAMICS OF MANAGING CONSESUS

According to Naomi Chazan (1992, 281), a genuine civil society is one that has connection to the state in terms of recognizing the state's proper role while advocating particularistic interests which the state must respond to if it is to remain legitimate. Most important, however, is that groups within civil society must not aspire to destroy or become part of the state. Once the mission of organized groups becomes the replacement of the state, then they cease to be part of the civil society. This approach to civil society is still missing in Uganda. Although Museveni has instituted some politically liberalizing changes, there are significant counteracting non-liberal tendencies of the regime. For example, Museveni's government still continues the kyankwazi schools, or "politicization" school, locally known as "chaka muchaka" (or jogging in Swahili). After considerable foreign pressure, Museveni suspended the politicization schools in 1995, but reinstated them shortly after the Presidential and parliamentary elections (U.S Dept. of State 1998). President Museveni claims that these schools have been established to "demystify the gun", unify the country and ensure that another dictator like Idi Amin cannot hold hostage an entire country. Cadres are sent to these schools to learn about Uganda and the Movement philosophy. Increasingly, it seems that the government is cracking down on any political dissent or alternative to Movement rule. In 1999, Museveni's government began to require that "...civil service employees in selected ministries and offices, including the Ministry of Information and the President's office, register in writing their political affiliation" (U.S Dept. of State, 1999). The arrest, harassment and imprisonment of non-Movementalists, or anyone critical of the Movement or Museveni has also increased. The latest Referendum and Provisions Bill, 1999 introduced to Parliament calls for a canvassing during polls to be on an individual basis, which essentially undermines political parties' ability to compete with the Movementalists and essentially creates an unequal playing field. The Movement, making the opposition politicians takes heed of Movement warnings (The New Monitor June 6, 1999 has suppressed several peaceful political rallies).

Journalists too, have learned to practice self-censorship, since the regime has made it clear that it will not tolerate too much criticism. Regime response has included resorting to outdated laws on sedition and criminal libel, framing and general harassment, including imprisonment (U.S Dept. of State 1998). Critical journalists have also been threatened and pursued by army vehicles (The Monitor June 6, 1999). High-ranking members of the Movement regime have been labeled the media as one of the five main enemies of Uganda (The Monitor June 6, 1999).

Although human rights have significantly improved under the Movement regime there remain some serious problems related to the insurrections in the North and the West. For example, Local Defense Units (LDUs), the police and military sometimes tend to use extreme forms of punishment often surpassing legal limits to secure confessions and the like (see U.S Dept. of State 1998). With the rise in urban terrorism in Kampala and the spillover effects from the war in the Democratic Republic of Congo (DRC) and Sudan, the government of Uganda has introduced a "safe houses", or "ungazetted detention policy. This policy gives the police and the military the authority to arrest treason suspects and other imaginary 'enemies' of the state. When suspects are arrested they are illegally manhandled and tortured." (Kasfir, 1998). President Museveni has increasingly been used this method to quell dissents. Twenty terrorist bombs in Kampala since 1997 have left 46 people dead and hundreds injured (The Monitor June 6, 1999). Insecurity has increased dramatically with a daring daylight robbery involving some 30-50 bandits closing a busy downtown street for one and half-hours while innocent bystanders were robbed (The Monitor, 3 April 1999). This rise in insecurity and repression has severely tarnished Uganda's image of stability and peace, so much so, that even the U.S. Peace Corps has fled Uganda (The Monitor June 6, 1999).

Instability in the North and West continues to plague the regime. The Lord's Resistance Army (LRA) led by Joseph Kony has escalated its attacks on civilians and the UPDF in the North. Hundreds of thousands of people have been displaced by the fighting in the North and thousands have been killed (see Dicklitch 1998: 72-74). The LRA is fighting for the establishment of a regime based on the Biblical Ten Commandments. Joseph Kony apparently wants his "...own nation in the country's north" –the "Nile Republic" (Kasfir 1998). The major difficulty Museveni and the UPDF have in fighting the LRA is the fact that they are supported and funded by the Sudanese government, introducing greater geo-political consequences.

Another rebel group, the West Nile Bank Front (WNBF), led by Juma Oris, a former colonel in Idi Amin's army, has been working with the LRA to destabilize the North. With over a third of Ugandans living in the region and with strong support for the UPC and DP, this creates a major legitimacy problem for Museveni (Reuters, 17 March 1996). A third major rebel group, the Allied Democratic Forces (ADF) has stepped up attacks in Western Uganda. The ADF, representing a "...coalition of an Islamic sect (Tabliqs) and fighters from a previously defunct Ruwenzori-based group, the national army for the Liberation of Uganda (NALU)", have been fighting to overthrow Museveni since 1986" (Kasfir 1998). In total, the ADF have killed over 400 people and the LRA 200 in 1998 (The New Vision March 11, 1999).

In general Museveni's regime has engaged in only limited political liberalization. Political parties are still not allowed to function; election are restricted to a "no-party" basis; a biased politicization still occurs with the chaka muchaka schools; and the separation of powers is not clearly delineated. Although the Movement regime has engaged in far less human right abuse than previous regimes, there is still a disturbing degree of repression and control from above. Museveni and the Movement's continued legitimacy is thus closely linked to the maintenance of stability and economic growth in post-conflict Uganda. The regime's prioritization of rebuilding the state and economy in addition to fear of the past (ethnic conflict, civil war) expressed by many Ugandans gives the regime even more justification for its actions. The limited accountability that is secured through presidential and parliamentary elections as well as the Constituent Assembly elections debating the new Ugandan constitution of 1995, also gives legitimacy to the regime. At best, Uganda is still a "guided democracy", characteristic of a soft-authoritarian and rather paternalistic system. However, Uganda is still very much perceived as an emerging "success story", especially by Western donors and the IMF and World Bank.

ECONOMIC RECOVERY PROGRAMS

The practical reality of Uganda's political economy is against the possibilities of bourgeois democracy being introduced in the near future, as well as due to the objective limitation of its political economy. But there is much more to the concept of civil society and its relationship to the political economy of a nation, than the current discourse on democracy in Uganda has allowed. One of the key successes of Museveni's regime is the impressive rehabilitation of the economy, through the introduction of the Ugandan Economic Recovery Programs (EPR) in 1987 and the implementation of IMF (International Monetary Fund) and World Bank structural adjustment programs (SAPS). Uganda has been praised by the IMF and Western donors as a "role model" for Africa for its "success in implementing reforms which have helped produce economic growth averaging six percent since 1988" (Reuters 21 February 1996). Uganda's growth rate for 1998 was a stunning 7.8 percent.

Uganda has also been labeled a role model in encouraging a positive investment climate. In fact, with the introduction of the 1991 Ugandan investment code, Uganda has been rated as the best country to invest in because of easily repatriated profits. It is estimated that countries investing in Uganda are able to triple their investment (World Bank 1997).

By lifting exchange control, disbanding state-run marketing boards, slating Inefficient companies for privatization, offering tax incentives and establishing a healthy dialogue between state and private sector, President Museveni has created one of Africa's most encouraging investment climates (Reuter February 21, 1996). Part of the privatization program included the return of Asian property confiscated during Idi Amin's rule in the 1970s. In 1990, President Museveni completed an Investment Code to protect foreign investers, in particular, dispossessed Asian Uganda's (Van Buren 1994:935). Before 1971, some 70,000 Asians owned 90 percent of the country's businesses. With the NRM-formed Departed Asians Property Custodian Board, some 8000 cases were on the list but only 7000 Asians re-based in Uganda (Financial Times 5 February 1996). The return of the confiscated Asian properties resulted in some 524 properties being returned to their original owners by January 1993 (Van Buren 1994:935). Asians have invested some US$500 million in Uganda, which accounts for Uganda's foreign investments (Kasfir 1998). Complementing the development of a positive investment climate, the NRM's privatization program, started in 1993 under World Bank pressure has resulted in the selling off of 40 enterprises for a total of approximately $100 million (Reuters 21 May 1996).

Inflation has dropped from 65.7 percent in 1985-95 to 8.6 percent in 1995, and has remained steadily under ten percent for the last few years (Kasfir1998). Government employment has been slashed by half, ministries have been reduced by a third and the armed forces by 30 percent (Kasfir 1998). In addition, price liberalization on producer prices, including a 182 percent rise in the coffee price paid to farmers have been introduced (Sharer et al 1995:5).

However, these positive economic growth indicators hide the negative side of the growth equation. Uganda may have one of the fastest growing economies, but it also is one of the most indebted countries in Africa owing approximately $3.6 billion (1995) in total external debt (Kasfir 1998). The national debt ratio outstrips the national income by 110 percent (Washington Post May 9, 1996). Uganda's debt situation is so bad, and its adherence to structural reform so good, that it has been given the first World Bank Heavily Indebted Poor Countries (HIPC) Debt Initiative grant, amounting to $338 million in Net Present Value (NPV) terms (World Bank 1997). Poverty is nation-wide, but particularly endemic in the rural areas and in the North (Dicklitch 1995-6:103-125). The government spends $3 per person on health as compared to $17 on debt repayments, yet one in five children die before their fifth birthday because of preventable diseases (Sarer et al. 1994). Cholera and even famine have become serious problems in parts of Uganda (see Dicklitch 1998:69-70). Since December 1997, cholera has killed an estimated 2,000 people (Hansen and Twaddle 1996). With continued insurgency in the North and West, peasants have been displaced into UPDF "protected villages" where they cannot farm their land, putting an even more serious stress on food production in those regions.

The Uganda economy may have benefited from tremendous economic growth since the Movement government came into power, but Ugandan's still remains among the poorest people in the world. For example, the gross domestic product (GDP) per capita is only US$320 (1997) (World Bank 1998:191), While approximately 55 percent of the population lives below the national poverty line (1989-94) (World Bank, 1997). Chronic malnutrition is seventeen times higher than accepted levels with infant mortality at 97 out of 1,000 live births. But the Movement regime is attempting to curb some of these disturbing social indicators. By launching the Poverty Eradication Action Plan of 1997, the Movement aims to increase primary health care spending, primary education spending and rural road maintenance. Meanwhile, defense spending has increased by 20 percent in 1998 due to incursions into the DRC and continued LRA insurrection in the North.

The no-party system is different from the old, authoritarian one-party states of the past in several ways, but the crucial difference between Museveni's no-party democracy and the old "one-party states" rests on the embrace of economic liberalization and the subsequent attempt to separate economic and political power. The Uganda State is divesting in parastatal organizations, and overall states control over the economy. In other words, through economic liberalization and stringent anti-corruption campaigns, Museveni has tried to wean Ugandan's from perceiving political office as a tool for economic gain. Economic liberalization is still occurring at a considerable place, but corruption has increased, so much so that the Movement's legitimacy is also being affected. In fact, Transparency International ranked Uganda twelfth among the most corrupt countries in 1998 (Kasfir 1998).

Consequently, the health of the economy and the legitimacy of the regime are increasingly eroding due to the growing rates of corruption. For example, a 1998 World Bank study report disclosed that corruption caused the government a financial loss of 350 billion Shillings (approximately $3.5 million US) (The Monitor, 28 December 1998), while other aid donors estimated that corruption scandal cost Uganda US $200 million a year (Financial Times February 5, 1996). Corruption has become so bad that one reporter likened it to AIDS (Acquired Immune Deficiency Syndrome) and called it ASIDS (Acquired Socio-Immuno-Deficiency Syndrome), claiming that some government departments and ministries like Police, Judiciary, Privatization Unit, State House, Ministry of Agriculture, Animal Industry and Fisheries already have full-blown ASIDS (Reuter May 21, 1996).

The enthusiasm in which the Uganda regime is pushing forth economic liberalization has won the regime considerable external support. Museveni has clearly secured a Western consensus on the basis of his willingness to implement IMF and World Bank austerity programs. Because he has been so successful, and perhaps because the IMF and World Bank are in such need of an African economic "miracle", Museveni's regime has been able to backslide on political conditionalities. There is also a hesitation on the part of Western donors to pressure for multi-party politics in Uganda, given Uganda's bloody past and the chaos that has developed in countries surrounding Uganda.

FOREIGN AID TO UGANDA

The last two decades of economic decline in Uganda have taken their toll in terms of poor facilities in social services, education, health and communications. It is correct to argue that part of the impetus for political space comes from the inability of previous Ugandan regimes to deliver on the question of economic development. Uganda's recent impressive economic growth is the consistent and omnipresent foreign aid to Uganda since Museveni adopted its aggressive economic liberalization position in 1987. Uganda has become the "darling of the West". Heralded by the IMF and the World Bank as "an economic success story", Uganda has eagerly applied structural adjustment programs (SAPs) and other IMF and World Bank directives. Thus, a key element in President Museveni's achievements and legitimacy, especially with regard to the growth and restructuring comes from outside the country. External donors are happy with Museveni's "enlightened authoritarianism" and justify Uganda's lack of democracy by its economic successes. One United State Government official claimed, "it's not that we have a double standard…it's that we have varying standards based on historical context" (New York Times 25 March 1998:14).

With the threat of Islamic fundamentalism growing in East Africa, particularly in the Sudan, and the continued political instability in the Great Lake Region, Uganda has become a major power broker and partner particularly in U.S. initiatives to stabilize the region. For example, in November 1996,

Uganda received US$20 million in military equipment to defend itself against the Sudan. But the United States is not alone in supporting Uganda's economic liberalization and limited political liberalization. Most Western donors have supported Uganda's limited reforms, funding Constituent Assembly elections, parliamentary and Presidential elections (see Dicklitch 1998:95; Hauser 1997:105). In fact, Uganda receives US$800 million in foreign aid annually (The New York Times 29 January 1995). Uganda would not have experienced the economic success that it has without the amount of foreign aid that it has received. President Clinton's trip to Uganda and the new United States, Partnership for Growth and Opportunity in Africa focusing on trade and investment rather than aid gives further support and legitimacy to the Museveni regime. The persistence of Western aid further strengthens the Movement's claims of legitimacy. As long as the West continues to give Uganda aid and support Museveni's limited political liberalization and more substantial economic liberalization, Uganda is given external legitimization. Because political party alternatives remain weak, neighboring countries remain unstable, and Uganda continues along a line of economic and political success, Ugandan's tolerate, if not embrace the Ugandan model of "no-party" democracy. But the increasing insecurity in Kampala and elsewhere has consistently eroded the legitimacy of Museveni's regime.

DYNAMICS OF POLITICAL LEADERSHIP

How a nation's leader perceive the constraints it face and the costs, benefits and risks attached to alternative courses of action affects the outcomes of his polices. Tactical and strategic choices of leaders are partly a function of the incentive structures political and economic institutions offered by a pragmatic leader. Further electoral rules, the amount of central control over important electoral resources such as the media, participation in regional monetary agreements – all of these institutions shape the options available for building coalitions. The success of president Museveni's government could be tied to the charismatic and visionary leadership that he has displayed for almost two decades. Most Ugandans and foreigners would concede that President Museveni has done a lot for Uganda and for Ugandans. He is considered a "man of vision" – a dedicated and charismatic leader. Even though corruption is still endemic in Uganda, people do not usually question Museveni's character. In fact, in the earlier years of his regime, Ugandans, as well as many analysts of Uganda, shuddered to think what would happen to Uganda without Museveni. President Museveni has carefully formulated a populist image of himself as the liberator of Uganda, as the only one capable of ruling Uganda peacefully. Museveni and his Movement regime offer Ugandans an alternative to the civil strife and violence of the past. But, as Kasfir argues, "...what is the NRM now? Without institutions, without an ideology, and, finally, without a rational that can justify its no-party democracy, it no longer has any existence apart from its leader" (Kasfir, 1998, p. 62)

Museveni represent a new generation of African leadership, which is savvy, cosmopolitan, risk-taking, pragmatic, and willing to engage the West and International Financial Institutions (IFFIs) in dialogue, even if often one-sided. This group has been characterized as a "...disciplined, incorruptible if authoritarian group that acts aggressively to promote their national and shared regional security interests" (Booker 1998). Men like Museveni, Isaias Afwerki, Meles Zenawi, Paul Kagame and Jerry Rawlings are the new "big men", the "veranda boys" that are supposed to make everything better. These men, like Museveni, are the new "enlightened despots" of Africa, taking the place of Nyereres, Nkrumahs, and Kenyattas. But like their predecessors, they are not perfect and they alone cannot bring Africa out of its current crisis. They are an important start, but they cannot be the African messiahs as so hoped for by the donor community as well as the African people.

The most recent focus on effective political leadership as the panacea for African woes is very dangerous. It is not the equivalent of political institutionalization and the supremacy of the rule of law, which is fundamental for establishing long-term political and economic success (Zakari 1997:42-43). Ultimately, the establishment of the rule of law, peaceful transitions, political competition and effective political participation may be the ideal form of rule for Uganda, but given the current stage of development, effective political leadership combined with concerns for political and economic stabilization must be acknowledged as very important steps toward short term and long term growth and stabilization.

Increasingly, a polarization between good political leadership and long-term political institutionalization is occurring. Museveni and his contemporaries are deriving legitimacy from the International arena rather than by securing it internally through genuine political competition and participation. Sophisticated manipulation of the political arena ensures a certain degree of compliance and stability. For example, Museveni has also developed a broad-based inclusionary system, bringing political leaders from all the political parties, regions and ethnic groups into the government by using both the "carrot and the stick". Increasingly however, Museveni and the army have become less tolerant of criticism from members of parliament (MP) and the cabinet. Cabinet shuffles have become and effective way of silencing dissenting MPs and promoting loyal "movementalists" and "Musevenists".

CONCLUSION

This chapter has examined the Ugandan model of no-party democracy and the stability and economic growth that might form a prerequisite for long-term development and democracy. The study argues that Uganda's no-party political system might be an African alternative to the Western conception of multiparty democracy? The fact that Uganda has experienced more political stability and substantial economic growth under a no-party system, than many other African nations makes the nation's model worthy of critical study. Several factors come together to provide the conditions for Uganda's current economic and political success. Is this "success", however, simply short-term, or will be around for the long haul? Museveni and his NRM government have secured power until at least the year 2000. Uganda has achieved impressive economic growth and relative political stability (with the major exception of the instabilities in the North, the West and increased terrorism in Kampala). The LC system has allowed for limited participation and community self-help, but there are clear limits to popular participation. Economic liberalization is occurring at an accelerated pace, while political liberalization has encountered clear roadblocks. It seems as if Museveni still believes that he is the only one that can lead Uganda out of its difficult past. He has clear control over the military and clear support from the West, but decreasing control over the country.

It is, however, questionable how long he will be able to control the political process from above. Although political parties are divided, they are united in their resolve to bring back freedom of association, political pluralism and to rid Uganda of Museveni. The population may wish to avoid the turbulence of the past, but undermining the development of a viable opposition will only create more extrajudicial movements like the WNBF, the LRA and NALU. Although one could argue that Museveni's "no-party democracy" has allowed for significant economic and political stability, the degree of freedom in Uganda, measured by such indicators as freedom of association, elections, political participation, separation of power, respect for human rights and the rule of law indicates that Uganda is far from a transition to or consolidation of democracy.

Political participation is present in Uganda, in fact actively encouraged, but through the LC system. In other words, political participation is controlled and channeled through state establishment structures. Political parties are allowed to exist, but not to effectively participate in the political process. Multi-party democracy is not allowed (at least until the year 2000), yet Uganda is considered on the right path to democratization. Unfortunately for the NRM regime, however, its consensus from above cannot be successfully imposed throughout Uganda. The North, Northeast and Western portions of Uganda have been in a state of virtual civil war since 1986, although relatively speaking; Uganda is still considered one of the more stable countries in the Great Lakes Region.

President Museveni has successfully implemented its ERP, receiving considerable accolades from the West and the IMF. A positive investment climate has been encouraged and substantial economic growth has occurred in Uganda, even though the gaps between the rich and the poor, the urban and the rural have been increasing rather than decreasing. All in all, Uganda is still considered a relative "success" story, mainly because it is on the road to economic recovery. The key to Museveni and the Movement's success in ensuring economic restructuring and limited political liberalization while securing Western support rests on their ability to control consensus from above. Similarly, Museveni's success and popularity are contingent to economic success, which is based on the whims of export prices, international aid and recognition, which are for the most part, beyond his control.

While making some real changes with regard to holding elections, especially presidential elections in 1996, the regime still ensured its continued position of power by limiting the election to a no-party basis, using intimidation when necessary and overall controlling the speed and timing of political liberalization. The whole issue of whether the Movement has been "successful" and whether it is a "durable" success story revisits the classic debate over whether strong-man rule is necessary in developing societies, and whether economic growth must precede competitive, political participation. Exclusive Movement rule from 1986-1996 may have been necessary to stabilize the political and economic arena, but Museveni and the Movement have missed their window of opportunity to make Uganda a truly democratic nation. The most recent controversy over referendum 2000 and the attempt by the Movement regime to ban political party campaigning does not bode well for the democratic or stable future of Uganda. In other words, Uganda under Museveni can be characterized as a "soft authoritarian" system which is increasingly resorting to not so soft methods of holding onto power.

Too much rests on one man as the messiah of Uganda. International donors and institutions may currently perceive Uganda as a successful story, but the long-term sustainability of Uganda as a success story to perhaps emulate, will depend on the institutionalization of power, the opening up of political competition, and the move away from glorifying one man as the savior or in contrast, the enemy of Uganda. Ultimately, there are no "quick fixes" for democracy and development in Africa. Uganda may well be stuck with an imperfect but reasonably effective and functioning alternative that is a compromise between dictatorship and democracy.

REFERENCES

Booker, Salih. 1998. "Thinking Regionally: Priorities for U.S. Policy Toward Africa" (http://www/africapolicy.org/bp/region.htlm). Background paper (Internet source).

Bratton, Michael 1998. "Second Elections in Africa", Journal of Democracy, Vol. 9, No 3, July, pp. 51-66.

Burkey, Ingvild (1991) "People's Power in Theory and Practice: the Resistance Council System in Uganda". Unpublished paper, Yale University.

Chazan, Naomi. 1992. "Africa's Democratic Challenge." World Policy Journal. 9/2 (spring) 279 – 305.

Christian Science Monitor (The), 1 April 1998, "Africa's Dreams Begin to Take Root", (Kate Dunn), p. 1.

Christian Science Monitor (The) 19 June 1997 "New Rulers, U.S. Plan Give Africa a Future", (Judith Matloff).

Daily Telegraph (The), 9 May 1996 "Ugandan President seeks Poll Approval after 10 Years in Power", (Louise Tunbridge) p. 15.

Dahl, Robert. 1971. Polyarchy: Participation and Opposition. New haven, CT: Yale University Press.

Dahl, Robert. 1983. Dilemmas of Pluralist Democracy. New Haven, CT: Yale University Press.

Dahl, Robert. 1989. Democracy and its Critics. New Haven, CT: Yale University Press.

Dicklitch, Susan (1995) "Indigenous Non-governmental Organizations, Civil Society and Democratic Transition in Uganda: 1986-1994". Ph.D. Dissertation, University of Toronto.

Dicklitch, Susan (1998) The Elusive Promise of NGOs in Africa: Lessons from Uganda. London and New York: Macmillan and st. Martin's.

Dicklitch, Susan (1995-96) "Uganda: a microcosm of crises and hope in sub-Saharan Africa", International Journal, Vol. LI, winter, pp. 103-125.

Duignan, P. and Robert Jackson. 1986. Politics and Government in African States 1960-1985. Stanford, CA: Hover Institute Press.

Financial Times (The), 5 February 1996, "Uganda Asians start up again: An Enterprising Community Six Years after it was Allowed to Return", (Michael Wrong), p. 7.

Gertzel, Cherry (1990) "Uganda's Continuing Search for Peace", Current History, Vol. 89, No. 547, May, pp. 205-208, 231-232.

Gitonga, Afrifa K (1988) in Walter Oygui O., A tieno Odhiambo, Michael Chege and Afrifa K. Gitonga (eds). Democratic Theory and Practice in Africa.

Guardian (The) (London). 22 June 1998, "Guerrillas Intensify Uganda Terror Raids", (Anna Borzello), p.14.

Hansen. H. B. and M. Twaddle. 1996. "Uganda: The Adent of No-Party Democracy in The New Struggle for Democracy in Africa, edited by J. Wiseman. Avebury, England: Aldershot.

Hauser, Ellen (1997) "Donors and Democracy in Uganda: An Analysis of the Role of Western Donors in Democratization Efforts in Uganda", Ph.D., Dissertation, University of Wisconsin-Madison.

Houston Chronicle (The), 22 March 1998, "Ugandan Leader's vast Popularity Marred by 'No-Party' Democracy," (Scott Staus), p. 9.

Ihonvbere, Julius. 1994. "The Irrelevant State: Ethnicity and the Quest for Nation-hood. Africa Ethnic and Racial Studies 17 (1), pp.42-40.

Independent (The) (London), 10 June 1993, "Museveni takes Measured Route to Democracy: Uganda President Explains why he Resists West's Pressure for Change", (Richard Dowden) p. 13.

Jackson, Robert, and Carl Rosberg. 1986. "The United States of East Africa: Tanzania, Uganda and Kenya," in Politics and Government in African States 1960-1985, (eds.) by Peter Duignan and Robert Jackson. Stanford, CA: Hover Institute Press.

Joseph, Richard. 1998. "Africa, 1990-1997: From Abertura to Closure", Journal of Democracy, Vol. 9, No. 2, pp. 3-17.

Joseph, Richard. 1997. "Democratization in Africa after 1989: Comparative and Theoretical Perspectives", Comparative Politics, April, pp. 363-382.

Kasfir, Nelson (1998) "No-Party Democracy" in Uganda", Journal of Democracy, Vol. 9, No. 2, pp. 49-63.

Kasfir, Nelson (1994) "Uganda Politics and the Constituent Assembly Elections of March 1994", Paper presented at the Workshop on "Developing Uganda", Lyngby Lungbrosskole, Denmark, 2-5 June.

Key, V. O. 1961. Public Opinion and American Democracy, New York: Alfred A. Knopf.

Lasswell, H., Lerner D. and Rothwell, C. E. 1952. The Comparative Study of Elites. Stanford, CA: Stanford University Press.

Los Angeles Times, 12 July 1998, "Horn of Africa: A Blow to Africa's Renaissance", (Chris Landsberg), p. 2.

Los Angeles Times, 11 July 1995, "Ambition and Dread in Uganda: The Nation is Struggling to Escape its Bloody Past and Become the Pride of Africa", (John Balzar), p. 3.

Makinda, Samuel M (1996) "Democracy and Multi-party Politics in Africa", The Journal of Modern African Studies, Vol. 34, No. 4, pp. 555-573.

Mazrui, Ali. 1986. Legacy of Lifestyle: The African Triple Heritage, Washington D.C. Broadcasting Service.

McGreal, C. 1996. "Museveni Swear by his No-Party Panacea." The Observer (May12), p. 19.

Monitor (The), 6 June 1999, "Parties, Referendum Bills Split Parliament" (Kampala), p.1-3.

Mutibwa, Phares (1992) Uganda Since Independence: A Story of Unfulfilled Hopes. London and Kampala: Fountain Publisher Ltd., and C. Hurst and Co., Publishers Ltd.

New York Times (The), 25 March 1998, "A New Model for Africa: Good Leaders Above All," (James C. McKinley Jr.), p.14.

New York Times (The), 15 June 1997, "Uganda Leaders Stand Tall in New Africa Order," (James C. McKinley Jr.), p. 3.

New York Times (The), 31 March 1996, "In Uganda, An Election Where Parties are Silenced" (James C. McKinley Jr.). p. 9.

New York Times (The), 29 January 1995, "Uganda Strongman a Favorite of World Leaders," p. 3, (Donatella Lorch).

New Vision (The), 11 May 1999, "Museveni pardons Kony, offers LRA Boss Ministry" (Kampala). p. 7

Newsweek, 29 January 1996, "Uganda: Special Advertising Section".p. 27-30.

Nyang'oro, Julius. 1994. "Reform Politics and the Democratization Process in Africa." African Studies Review, 37, no.1, (April) 133 – 149.

Ofcansky, Thomas. 1997. The Tarnished Pearl of Africa. Boulder: Westview Press.

Oloka-Onyango, Joe. 1993. "Popular Justice, Resistance Committee Courts and the Judicial Process in Uganda: 1988-1992", Beyond Law, (Legal Pluralism), Vol. 3, No. 7, and July.

Oloka-Onyango, Joe. 1991. "The National Resistance Movement, "Grassroots Democracy" and Dictatorship in Uganda" in Robin Cohen and Harry Goulbourne (eds). Democracy and Socialism in Africa. Boulder: Westview Press, pp. 125-141.

Pittsburgh Post-Gazette, 22 July 1998, "Uganda Olive Branch", p.9.

Ranney, A. and Kendal, W. 1969. Basic Principle for a Modern Democracy. In C. Crnudde and D. E. Neubauer (eds.) Empirical Democratic Theory. Chicago: Markham. pp.41-63.

Reuters, 21 May 1996. "Uganda Steps up Publicity Drive for Privatization" (Edmond Kizito). P. 1-2.

Reuters, 17 March 1996, "Ugandan Leader Faces Dilemma over Rebel Challenge" (Edmond Kizito). P.3.

Reuters, 12 May 1996, "Uganda's Triumphant Museveni to be Sworn in." (Peter Smerdon).

Reuters, 1995. "Ugandans Reject Party System." Financial Times (London), 22 June. p. 7-9.

Reuters, 21 February 1996, "IMF Praises Uganda's Economic Reforms." P.3-4.

Reuters, 19 February 1996, "Ugandan Groups Lobbies Donors on Debt Reduction." p.1-2.

Sandbrook, Robert, 1988. "Liberal Democracy in Africa: A Socialist-Revisionist Perspective." Canadian Journal of African Studies, Vol. 22, no.2, 240 - 267.

Schumpetter, J. 1960. Capitalism Socialism and Democracy. New York: Harper and Brothers.

Sharer, R., C. Schiller and M. Ahmad (1994) IMF Survey, 24 January, pp. 21-24.

Sklar, Robert. 1979. "The Nature of Class Domination in Africa." Journal of Modern African Studies, vol. 17, no. 4, 540 - 552.

Smock, David. 1976. The Search for National Integration in Africa. New York: The Free Press.

Tordoff, William. 1997. Government and Politics in Africa. 3rd ed. Bloomington, IN: Indiana University Press.

Udogu, Ike. 1997. (Ed.) Democracy and Democratization in Africa: Toward the 21st Century. Leiden, The Netherlands: E. J. Brill.

Udogu, Ike. 1999. "The Issue of Ethnicity and Democracy in Africa: Toward the Millennium." Journal of Black Studies. Vol. 29, (6), 790-808.

U.S. Department of State. 1999. Uganda Country Report on Human Rights Practices for 1998. Washington: D.C.: U.S. Dept. of State.

U.S. Department of State. 1998. Uganda Country Report on Human Rights Practices for 1997. Washington: D.C: U.S. Dept. of State.

Uzodike, U. O. 1996. "Democracy and Economic Reforms: Developing Underdeveloped Economies." Journal of Asian and African Studies, 31 (1-2), 21-38.

Van Buren, L. 1994 "Uganda: Economy", Africa South of the Sahara 1994. (21st Edition). London: Europa Publication.

Washington Post. 9 May 1996, "Ugandan Vote to Test 'No-Party' System: Fears of Violence Precede Presidential Poll", (Stephen Buckley), p. 31.

Washington Post. 15 March 1995 "Uganda, in Comeback, Attracts Investors; Aid Donors", (Stephen Buckley).

Watson , Catherine. 1994. "No to Multi-Party", Africa Report, May-June: 24-26.

Wiseman, J.A. 1996. The New Struggle for Democracy in Africa. Avebury, England: Aldershot.

World Bank 1997. "World Bank Approves Debt Relief Package for Uganda", News Release No. 97/1324-s, 23 April.

Zakaria, Fareed 1997 "The Rise of Illiberal Democracy", Foreign Affairs, November/December, pp. 22-43.

Chapter 9

Ethnic Conflict and the Dilemma of Dual Citizenship in Rwanda, Nigeria and South Africa

Robert Dibie and Sharron Herron

INTRODUCTION

Some social scientists have linked cultural and psychological processes with the politics of ethnicity in Africa. Marc Ross (1993) made a comparative analysis of ninety cultures and the factors that cause conflict within them. He concludes those "psychocultural" factors, i.e., assumptions, perceptions, and images about the world that are widely shared with others and not idiosyncratic are crucial. The notion of culture of conflict draws attention to how people in communities in Africa develop and share interpretations rooted in psychocultural dispositions. Dahrendorf (1968) has suggested that the first questions asked by sociology were these: "Why is their inequality among men? Where do its causes lie? Can it be reduced, or even abolished altogether? Or do we have to accept it as a necessary element in the structure of human society?" (Marger 1997; Esman 1994; Dahrendorf 1968: 152). These questions also fit well into the situation in Rwanda, Nigeria and South Africa and many other African nations. These nations have several ethnic groups and a diverse and rich cultural heritage. The different ethnic groups differ in physical features, reasoning capacities, talents, strength, musical aptitude, and so on. All these inequalities are a product of colonial legacy, social learning and cultural inheritance though, the significance of each of these factors is not always clear. Perhaps more important, however, the ethnic groups are also unequal in their access to social rewards; that is, various forms of wealth, power, economic development, and prestige. These differences, all primarily of social origin, are of greatest consequence in accounting for the crisis among these various ethnic groups that constitute members of one nation-state.

In Nigeria, Rwanda and South Africa no problem has more fiercely challenged political order and state cohesion than ethnic conflict. The recent debate on dual citizenship and the relevance of ethnicity to democratic politics has focused on which institutions are appropriate to govern a multi-ethnic nation-state (Ndegwa 1997; Lemarchand 1995; Esman 1994; Diamond and Plattner 1994). The intrusion of the military (1966 in Nigeria and 1973 in Rwanda) into civil politics is the ultimate factor in the wake of ethnic conflict and political violence in these countries. It would therefore appear that the incident was indeed one that was not only inevitable but also desirable. In the 1990s, it has become quite clear that such move by the military was not a blessing in disguise. For as was the case with ethnic conflict and political violence in the past, military incursion into politics could be said to be related to the status quo of inter-ethnic rivalry and chauvinism, intra-class struggle for power, the oppression of minorities, as well as the institutional decay of the armed forces. The ethnic concerns of urban working class tend to be heavily symbolic, and the retention of strong ties to rural areas of origin, represent strong impediments to inter-ethnic competition in Rwanda and Nigeria. Similarly, under the apartheid regime that started in 1948 in South Africa, a system was created which assured white supremacy over Blacks, Colored and Asians. In this light, the political mobilization and manipulation of ethnicity by rising ethnic elites appeared as a form of class action, both to appropriate to themselves a disproportionate share of the material rewards of political control, and to preclude political mobilization on the basis of conflicting class interest.

Conflict is an important aspect of ethnicity. This is inevitable under conditions of inter-ethnic competition for inequality is accepted as natural, and wealth is esteemed. The fear of inequality generates divisive and destructive socioeconomic competition, which has anti-social effects. Conflict makes it possible for the "in-group" to accept the expression of hostility toward the "out-group". For instance the Biafra secession (civil war) of Nigeria 1966-1970 by the Igbos was a result of hostility towards them by the Hausa-Fulani groups. The Hutu slaughter of over a million rivals Tutsis within a few weeks is also evidence of hostility against them by the Tutsi. One ethnic group against the other to limit competition in favor of the in group therefore used aggressive behavior. Demonstration, rioting and various forms of violent agitation become instruments in ethno-political conflict.

In political terms, coming to grips with the Nigerian, South African, and Rwandan systems is complicated by the lack of settled and predictable political patterns. Independent Nigeria has had two civilian governments (one based on the Westminster model, one on the American presidential model), five successful and several attempted military coups, a costly civil war, and ethnic and religious strife that has taken thousands of lives. The various ethnic groups in Nigeria have suffered both economic and political marginalization. Rwanda like Nigeria has passed through democratic as well as military regimes. Under apartheid, South Africa political system was characterized with separation and duplication of institutions among the society's various ethnic groups, extreme politicization between dominant and subordinate groups, high levels of prejudice and discrimination, and a vastly inequitable distribution of wealth. Therefore, through structural realignment, these nations might become economically more efficient, politically more stable and socially more integrated. Thus, democracy is viewed as a broad balance of power among contending classes, ethnic and state forces formed by representatives of the present structure.

This chapter demonstrates how dual citizenship can lead to ethnic politics, and how ethnic loyalties have undermined national stability in Nigeria, Rwanda and South Africa. This comparative approach provides a discourse of what the rights and obligations as well as opportunity and constraints of the citizens are in the societies of a nation-state. Second, it argues that inter-ethnic tension may be related to how the concept of dual citizenship has been conceived differently in post-independence Nigeria, Rwanda and South Africa's ethnic communities and regions. The chapter concludes with a discussion of how consociational and federalism mechanism can be used to bridge the gap between ethnic groups in these nations.

CONFLICT AND MULTIEHNIC THEORIES

Judging from news accounts of violence and general hostilities in multiethnic societies, it would seem that ethnic relations are as a rule conflictual. Indeed, almost all theorists have viewed conflict as a fundamental, if not permanent, feature of relations between ethnic groups. Conflict theory and ethnic competition constitutes radical approaches to social and political problems (Gurr 1993; Esman 1994). They put the call for change high on the public agenda, and suggest that custom, practice, and tradition, instead of being useful to an orderly society, may create its problems. They start with the assumption that individual needs and potential should be fulfilled. Any situation that interferes with the desired fulfillment is therefore seen as a social problem, which should be examined. According to Peter Ekeh (1974), Richard Sklar (1993), (Martin Marger (1997) Milton Esman (1994) and Saxton and Kaufman (1971), the emphasis in conflict theory is upon restructuring society so that it can better fulfill the needs of its members, rather than upon adapting the individual or groups to the existing order.

The literature on ethnic identity and solidarity defines these terms in two perspectives: (1) narrow perspective and: (2) broader perspective. The narrower perspective denotes a community that claims common origin, often including common descent or kinship; that posses distinctive and valued cultural markers in the form of customs, dress, and especially language; that traces a common history and expects to share a common destiny. Persons born into such a community generally share a collective identity and constitute a distinct people (Harowitz 1985; Nyangoro 1994; Esman 1994; Halisi 1997).

The broader characterization of ethnicity incorporates other ascriptive solidarity groups such as race, religion, and nationality. In this study, the broader definition is used, and it includes a collective identity and solidarity based on inherited culture, racial differences, belief systems or sentiments of common nationality. In Canada for example, the main cleavage is defined as cultural-linguistic - Anglophone versus Francophone - though in the twentieth century it contained an important religious element, Catholic versus Protestant. Today, the claims of Canada's aboriginal people introduce racial as well as cultural differences. In Malaysia, the differences between Malays and Chinese include racial and religious as well as cultural dimensions. In Northern Ireland, the dispute between Catholic and Protestants do not in fact concern theological issues but the relative power, status, and resources available to each community (van den Berghe 1975; Crawford 1976; Horowitz 1985; Richard 1987; Malcolm 1989; Esman 1994). Although the parties in Southern Africa have been defined by race, the majority Black society encompasses highly mobilized peoples differentiated by distinctive cultures and institutions. The ultimate consideration in this study is ethnic pluralism, that is two or more ascriptive solidarity groups, "us and them" coexisting under a single political national government.

Liberal theory on ethnicity regards the individual as the main unit of social value and predicts that progress will inevitably break down artificial barriers based on parochial, ascriptive allegiances. In the emergent society, free of ascriptive or communal constraints, people would participate and compete as self-determining individuals valued and rewarded according to their individual contributions and performance (Esman 1994; Crawford 1976; Parson 1975; Glazer and Moynihan 1975; Deutsch 1953). No preferences, no discrimination a level playing field for every individual. Ethnicity would survive only as nostalgic vestiges of an earlier and less enlightened stage of historical development

The influential modernization variant of classical liberalism argues that voluntary associations based on occupational and other "rational" interests would supplant status groups based on particularistic and parochial solidarities. In the wake of economic development and nation building ascriptive loyalties would lose their social function and gradually wither away (Esman 1994; Parsons 1975; Glazer and Moynihan 1975).

Ethnicity as politics is meaningful only in a relational framework. As a collective identity ethnicity is shaped not only by self-definition but also by constraints imposed by outsiders. Thus the internal "we" must be distinguished from the external "they." Where no relevant others exist, the need for solidarity disappear and society fragments on the basis of internal differences (Ndegwa 1997; Esman 1994; Rothchild 1981; Crawford 1976). The need for ethnic solidarity arises only when strange, threatening, competitive outsiders must be confronted. Only then is distinction between "us" and "them" arising. Consequently, this would lead to the need for internal solidarity and discipline. Thus, ethnicity is shaped by environment, by the threats and the opportunities it affords.

Different levels of ethnic inequality can be combined with the processes of assimilation and pluralism to shape a topology of multi-ethnic societies. Milton Yinger (1981) defines assimilation as a process of boundary reduction that can occur when members of two or more societies or smaller cultural groups meet. Robert Park (1920), Donald Horowitz (1990) and Milton Esman (1994) in their theory of assimilation explain that groups first come into contact through migration and subsequently, engage in competition, often characterized by conflict. Out of such competition eventually emerges some form of accommodation among the groups, leading finally to assimilation. Like Robert Park (1920), Milton Gordon (1964) and Milton Esman (1994) explains assimilation as a series of stages, or steps through which various groups pass. But rather than following a straight line leading from contact to eventual absorption, groups may remain indefinitely at one or another of these stages. Out of the seven stages that Gordon (1964) outlined, cultural assimilation and civic assimilation are the most complete. The first two, cultural and structural assimilation are, however, the most important. Cultural assimilation or acculturation according to Martin Marger (1997), Ekeh Peters (1974) and Donald Horowitz (1985; 1990) denotes the adoption by a minority ethnic group of the dominant group's cultural patterns, language, political beliefs and so on. But acculturation, though a prerequisite, does not assure movement to the next phase. Gordon explains that groups become very much like the dominant group in behavior and values but still remain structurally segregated. Structural assimilation, the second stage, is seen essentially as what we can refer to as primary or informal structural assimilation. This stage is the most critical because it is the key to all subsequent stages. Gordon asserts that once structural assimilation has occurred, either simultaneously with or subsequent to acculturation, all of the other types of assimilation will naturally follow.

Pluralism according to Glickman (1995), Ottaway (1994), Martin Marger (1997) and Peter Ekeh (1974) is a set of social processes and conditions that encourage group diversity and the maintenance of group boundaries. Pluralism must be understood as a variable for groups and societies. Ethnic pluralism never entails an absolute separation of groups. Ethnic groups in this chapter refer to a distinguishable group within a lager society. In a pluralistic society we assume that there will always be some common political or economic system that binds various ethnic groups together.

There are two forms of ethnic pluralism in modern multiethnic societies. The first group is referred to as equalitarian pluralism. In this pluralism, groups maintain cultural and structural autonomy but remain relatively equal in political and economic powers. The separation of groups under this pluralism is voluntary. The second pluralism is called inequalitarian pluralism. Under this pluralism, groups maintain structural segregation and perhaps cultural distinctness as well as unequal political and economic powers. Group separation in inequalitarian pluralism is involuntary. Inequalitarian pluralism is the chief feature of the Nigerian, Rwandan and South African societies or any other society that has experienced colonialism. In the Nigerian, Rwandan, and South African cases, one group exerts maximum political and economic powers, which enables it to shape the nature of the military, as well as inter-ethnic relations in such a way as to sustain its interests.

In the societies of nations such as Belgium, Canada, Malaysia and Switzerland structural and cultural differences among ethnic groups are protected by the state and institutional provisions are made to encourage an ethnically proportionate distribution of societal rewards. This type of pluralism is referred to as corporate pluralism. In corporate pluralistic system, the government formally recognizes ethnic units, and political and economic powers are allocated on the basis of an ethnic formula. Such systems are sometimes referred to as consociational federalism (Rothchild 1964; Bates 1974; Lijphart 1977; van Berghe 1981; Horowitz 1990). In corporate pluralistic societies, the groups are relatively balanced in political and economic power, and no single one is able to exert its will on all vital society issues. Moreover, group segregation is mainly voluntary. As Hunt and Walker (1974), Peter Ekeh (1974), Horowitz (1990), Richard Sklar (1993) and Milton Esman (1994) describe it, group relationships are so ordered that the extremes of inequality found in segregation are avoided and each group feels that it is gaining some benefit from association in the common society.

Conflicts therefore rests on four premises: (1) that contention and disputation can be a useful way of forcing problems to the attention of those in position to solve them; (2) that change and disequilibrium are not to be shunned or avoided; (3) that the causes of social and political problems often reside within social and political institutions; and (4) that changes in institutional behaviors will, therefore result in resolving social and political problems. In the Nigerian, Rwandan, and South African context ethnic conflict begins with the idea that social institutions are not beset with problems, but are, in fact, the source of the problems.

Studies on ethnic relations have developed a view that ethnicity is an inherent aspect of social change in all culturally heterogeneous societies. This view argues that neither the disappearance nor a significant amelioration of ethnic conflict is possible. It sees the stability of these societies as threatened not by communalism, but by the failure of national institutions to explicitly recognize and accommodate existing ethnic divisions and interests. It recommends political arrangements which accord to all communal groups a meaningful role in national life and which are able to keep communal conflicts within manageable bounds (Melsen and Wolpe, 1970). This view partially explains the inevitability of political instability in Rwanda, Nigeria, and South Africa.

The theory of relative deprivation began in the early 1960s with the publication of James Davies' book "Toward a Theory of Revolution." The theory states that revolutionary events are likely when a prolonged period of rising expectations and increasing gratification is followed by a short period of sharp reversal. During this time, the gap between expectation and gratification quickly widens and becomes intolerable. This is what is also known as Davies' "J-curve" theory. One of the shortcomings of this study is the typical conclusion reached when transition to majoritarian democracy fails. In these failed transitions where ethnicity is evidently a factor in mobilizing for political change or for anticipated electoral politics, a more vivid explanation for the conflict can be found by applying the dual citizenship theory.

In Gurr's work, Why Men Rebel, he argues that "the primary causal sequence in political violence is first the development of discontent, second the politicization of that discontent, and finally its actualization in violent action against political objects and actors." Discontent is the product of relative deprivation, which is defined as a perceived discrepancy between men's values, expectations and their value capabilities (Gurr 1970, 12-13). Thus, relative deprivation from Gurr's perspective leads only to the potential for political conflict. The translation of this potential in Nigeria requires structural and cultural facilitation, organizational mobilization, and careful evaluations of the risk involved in confronting the military government.

The most dominant theme of the modernization perspective is that increased urbanization, commercialization, schooling, communication and professionalization on ethnicity will lead to the integration of diverse ethnic groups (Morrison and Stevenson, 1972). Although economic factors are usually mentioned, most modernization analysts tend to deal with them briefly and then go on to emphasize bicultural factors such as the degree of inter-ethnic racial and cultural differences, ethnocentrism, differences in institutions, the absence of value consensus, and the clarity and rigidity of group definition, or to synthesize subsets of these.

According to Sanda (1976), one major theoretical issue in many of the recent studies of ethnic conflict in Africa is the extent to which ethnic units and cultural entities coincide, or the extent to which ethnic affiliations can be said to be predictive of socio-cultural attitude and beliefs.

Richard Sklar's (1976; 1993) position on the same controversy agrees with those of Sanda, that tribalism is an instrument in the hands of political elites. According to Richard Sklar (1993), tribalism is widely supposed to be the most formidable barrier to national unity in Africa. It is less frequently recognized that tribal movements may be created and instigated to action by the new men of power in furtherance of their own special interests which time and again constitute the interests of emerging social classes. Tribalism then becomes a mark for class privilege. Donald Horowitz (1987) argues that the social psychological perspective may explain incidents of ethnic conflict and violence that are otherwise intelligible only in terms of some hypothesis - inadequate, in his view - of elite manipulation and deception. Re-interpreting the account of conflict between the Itsekeri and Urhobo ethnic groups in Nigeria, that erupted into mob violence, he writes: "A more fruitful explanation . . . lies in the disparaging evaluations of group worth to which Itsekiri and comparable groups were subject, evaluations that led them to want to do something to retrieve their self-esteem". This threat to ethnic groups is sufficient motive for mass involvement in any ethnic conflict in Nigeria, Rwanda, and South Africa. The contest for group legitimacy, for political inclusion and exclusion, merges with the quest for group worth to form a politics of ethnic entitlement (Diamond 1987; Lemarchand 1995). This constitutes the major engine of mass ethnic conflict in the three nations. Thus, as ethnic consciousness increases in scope and intensity, the socioeconomic and political atmosphere becomes charged with tension. Under these circumstances, the ethnic factor assumes a self fulfilling and self-sustaining dynamics of its own. Ethnic hostility, loyalty and identification are passed on to successive generations through the process of socialization. The family, press, private and public conservation and other agencies of socialization are infected by ethnicity. Therefore, even when the original basis of ethnicity, socio-economic competition among classes and individuals is eliminated, there remains the problem posed by the internalized dimension.

In recent times, ethnic groups have formed two types of nationalism. Geertz (1994) called this civic nationalism and ethnic nationalism. According to Michael Ignatief (1993), and Milton Esman (1994) civic nationalism is when a nation is composed of its entire people regardless of race, color, creed, gender, language, or ethnicity. Here, people possess equal political and social rights and choose to be members of a nation, along with others, regardless of ethnicity, who share broadly similar beliefs and values. Ethnic nationalism, by contrast, holds that people's allegiance is to an ethnic group or nationality into which they have been assigned, not to a larger political entity encompassing many different ethnic groups or nationalities. Here, an individual's deepest attachments are inherited, not chosen.

The dual citizenship theory provides a precise way of analyzing the relationship between ethnic identity, authority and legitimacy. On one hand, ethnic citizenship, legitimacy and authority rest on cultural practice, family, clan, extended kin, and to a community. On the other hand, individual claim to nation-state citizenship is vested in the public realm by passports, voting cards, bureaucratic and legal instruments. Ethnic legitimacy in post-colonial Rwanda, Nigeria, and South Africa begins at the clan level that provides the basic unit of solidarity and public discourse outside the family. According to Stephen Ndegwa (1997), Stewart (1995), Frost (1994), Peled (1992), ethnic identity rests on a socially, as opposed to a legally constructed definition of belonging. Belonging in the Nigerian, Rwanda, and South African societies or ethnic communities is established by birth, marriage or adoption into a family and kin that believe in shared history and values. Therefore, duality of citizenship is complicated by the fact that it is conceived differently in the nation-state of these nations and their ethnic communities. The recognition of ethnic groups as a basis of citizen formulation and the strong loyalty attached provides a powerful instrument to explain why ethnic groups are more committed to their communities than their nation-state. In the past four decades Rwanda, Nigeria, and South Africa have witnessed cases of intense ethnic conflict based on dual citizenship and ethnic nationalism - the Biafra civil war in Nigeria, genocide in Rwanda and several riots in South Africa due to white supremacy regime are examples.

FORMS OF DUAL CITIZENSHIP IN RWANDA

The origin of dual citizenship in Rwanda can be traced to evidence of history, identity, authority, and legitimacy of members of two ethnic groups - the Hutus and the Tutsis. The Hutu tribal groups were the first ethnic group in Rwanda, and like other African ethnic groups, established their citizenship and sense of national consciousness. They were farmers and mostly above six feet in height. History tells us that the Tutsi warrior tribe from the northern part of present day Rwanda invaded the Hutu ethnic group and defeated them in a tribal war four centuries ago (Destexhe, 1995). As a result of this defeat the Tutsi who were of a different ethnic citizenship became tribal lords in Hutu land, and the Hutus had to work for their new lords in order to be protected from harassment from other Tutsis warriors. This unfortunate situation made the Tutsi to dominate the political and economic power structure of Rwanda before the inauguration of a German East African colonial regime in 1899. The formalization of colonial rule was accomplished at the Berlin Conference of 1884-85 when the European nations met and petitioned Africa, recognizing each other's share of the continent.

Following World War I, Germany - as a defeated nation - was deprived of all her colonial possessions, which were parceled out to the victorious allies as trust territories under the League of Nations Mandate system. Belgium took over the colonial regime of Rwanda 1916, under the Mandate of the League of Nations, but did not see anything wrong with the relationship between the Hutu and Tutsi for several years (Khapoya 1994, Pruntier 1995, Uvin 1997). As a matter of fact, the colonial government recognized the Tutsi's dominance of the Hutus.

Towards the close of the colonial period the restless Hutu citizens revolted in 1959-1960 calling for equality for all ethnic groups in Rwanda. During this period the Rwanda social order was such that the Tutsis which constituted nine percent of the population were the aristocrats. The Hutus that made up 90 percent of the population were cattle rearers and performed various other services for the Tutsis. The Twa or pygmies who were about one percent of the population were regarded as the outcast (Lemmarchand, 1994). A Tutsi with the title "Mwami" or King was the head of the political hierarchy in Rwanda (Uvin, 1997).

Towards the ending of the 19th century the Germans (Bazungu - term used for white Europeans) conquered Rwanda by means of force and diplomacy. They delegated political role to the Mwani (king) and the Tutsi rulers, and established an indirect rule, which consisted of native authorities. Mamdani (1996) and Grosse (1994) assert that with the Germans help, the control by the central

Tutsi aristocracy over the territory of Rwanda greatly increased. Some small Hutu kingdoms in the Northwest were annexed and their land tenure systems brought under monarchic control, while the other peripheral regions of the nation were brought more forcefully under centralized command.

Under the colonial rule by Germans, new sources of power and privileges emerged, and the exclusive beneficiaries of these new authority were people of Tutsi descent (Willame 1995; Urvin 1997). During most of the colonial period, the Germans were convinced that the Tutsi were more intelligent, reliable and hardworking than the Hutu. For many Rwandans, the origins of ethnic conflict and racism in Rwanda lie in this ideology cum practice of the German and later Belgian colonial regimes. It is therefore sufficient to say that the German and Belgian Bazungu (white) instituted a system of rigid ethnic classification, involving things such as measurement of nose and skull sizes, and the attribution of obligatory identity papers stating one's ethnicity. The colonial regimes in Rwanda also reversed education, as well as jobs in the administration and the army, largely for the Tutsi.

According to Peter Urvin (1997) and Funga (1991), in 1950s, 31 of the 33 members of the "coseil superieur du pays" were Tutsi, as well all 45 "chefs de chefferies" and 544 out of 559" sous-chefs. With the military backing of the Germans and later Belgians, the Tutsi power holders saw their strengths greatly increased. Note, however, that not all Tutsi benefited from this policy. There were a few hundreds of thousand Tutsi in Rwanda, and they did not all have positions in the government or church. Prunier (1995) documented that "it is mainly two (Tutsi) clans that monopolize the advantages: thus 31 out of 45 "chefs des chefferies" were in the hands of the Abanyiginya clan and five with the Abega clan". Prunier (1995) also quoted data that show that the average income of 287 Tutsi families in the mid-1950s, excluding holders of political office, was only four percent higher than the average income of 914 Hutu families. Hence, under indirect rule, social relationships in Rwanda changed greatly: they became more uniform, rigid, unequal and exploitative, with a clear hierarchy from white Germans or Belgians to Tutsi to Hutu to Twa, with persons at each higher level having privilages denied to those at lower levels and disdaining those below them. While formally the old political structure of Rwanda, revolving around the monarchy was still intact, its nature had changed proudly.

On the death of the Mwami in 1959, the Hutus staged a bloody revolt against the Tusti aristocracy because they wanted equality in the sharing of political and economic powers in their nation-state. The United Nations intervened and put pressure on Belgium to hold pre-independence elections in 1961. The Hutus won the elections because they were larger in population, and political parties were formed on the basis of ethnic citizenship. Thus, the social revolution led to the overthrow of the monarchy, and its replacement with a presidential Republic.

Renewed conflict between the Hutus and the Tutsis occurred in 1963, 1973, and 1994 due to inter-ethnic competition for power and social rewards. This exploded ethnic violence resulted in the flight of hundreds of thousands of Tutsi ethnic group to Burundi, Tanzania, Zaire and Uganda (Destexhe 1995; Prunier 1995; Urvin 1997). This refugee population was about one million between 1992-94 and successive Rwanda governments headed by Hutus questioned their citizenship when they planned to return to their homeland. When General Juvenal Habyarimana, a Hutu, seized power in a military coup in 1973, he institutionalized a one-party state in an attempt to overcome ethnic divisions. Yet the Hutus and Tutsis were more loyal to their ethnic citizenship than their national citizenship. This ethnic loyalty resulted in further hostility when fighting erupted between both ethnic groups in late 1993 in Burundi. This warfare eventually spilled over to Rwanda in 1994, when a plane carrying General Juvenal Habyarimana crashed at the Kigali airport, killing him and other top personnel of his government. Unleashed by a lack of central leader, the Hutu dominated national army ensued in genocide in which more than 1.5 million people mostly Tutsis were killed. The Tutsi patriotic front attacked and captured Kigali, the headquarters of Rwanda and proclaimed themselves the new leaders of the nation. They also announced the formation of a coalition government, and named Pasteur Bizimungu, a Tutsi, President, and Faustin Twagiramungu, a Hutu, as the Prime Minister.

Ethnic prejudice in Rwanda is derived from two means. One emanates from government, and the other from the needs or competition among the major ethnic groups. Anti-Tutsi conflict serves as a deliberately maintained strategy of legitimization of the powers that was kept alive in Rwanda through a systematic public structure of discrimination and education, in which the different and problematic identity of all Tutsi was constantly being referred to. At the same time ethnic prejudice was a means for small people, squeezed from all sides, to make sense of their predicament and scapegoating. Favoritism of one ethnic group against another fulfilled a crucial social function; seeds planted from above fell on fertile ground. Hence, Peter Uvin (1997), and Simpson and Yinger (1953, 83) contend that the designation of inferior groups comes from those on top, an expression of their right to rule, as well as from frustrated persons often near the bottom, and as an expression of their need for security.

Despite the present political arrangement in the nation, social and economic activities are still viewed from the Hutu/Tutsi or dual citizenship perspective. This in turn determines how national rewards are distributed in Rwanda. There have also been several reports of Tutsi soldiers invading refugee camps and killing members of the Hutu ethnic group in the Democratic Republic of Congo (formally Zaire).

ETHNIC POLTICIZATION IN NIGERIA

As shown in history and geography, Nigeria is united by a common destiny and under one political system, called a federation. This indicates that Nigerians do not have another country, therefore the citizens should salvage their nation together. However, with the present political, military and ethnic conflict, is the nation being salvaged or damaged?

Before the Berlin Conference of 1885, the River Niger valley had different ethnic citizens (Hausa, Fulani, Yoruba, Igbo, Tiv, Edo, Ijaw, Isoko, Ibibio, Urhobo, Nupe, Idoma and so on) which later came to be tagged Nigeria. These different ethnic citizens were autonomous political units, each one rich in culture, with sophisticated socio-political systems and viable economies. Nigeria had different traditional leaders to head its respective governments. These different kingdoms or ethnic citizens came under the British imperial colonial rule separately through conquest. Separate treaties were entered into by the indigenous rulership and the British gave legal backing to the new colonial dispensation. British rule in Nigeria enlarged ethnic allegiances, centralizing administration, bringing ethnic groups into a wider field of interaction, and exposing them in varying degrees to the resources of modernization. The British also actively promoted differential treatment of ethnic groups as a matter of policy. For instance, they protected the northern conservatism against the direct rule system that they established in the southern part of the country.

In 1914, Lord Lugard amalgamated the Northern and Southern provinces, which had sophisticated indigenous citizenship into one unit, called Nigeria. This integration was made for administrative convenience for the colonial administration. Lugard became the first governor-general of Nigeria. According to Dokun Jagun (1993), the genesis of today's discord over the fate of Nigeria was sown in the 1914 arbitrary amalgamation, as well as the error of block independence granted in 1960 to a geographical entity called Nigeria. Thus, the tissue culture for the propagation of the virus of conflict was prepared in 1914. The politicization of ethnicity and regionalization of politics was encouraged by the colonialist. The Richard's constitution of 1946 led to a political and budgetary regionalization of the country. Designed in part to preserve the authoritarian system of indirect rule, it established a legislature in each of the three regions, the North, East, and West, was based on elections from the undemocratic native administrations. The regional legislatures in turn sent representatives to the central legislature (Nnoli 1980). The constitution was premised on the assumption that regional political integration will foster tribal differences. Thereafter, the colonial administration made every effort to encourage regional thinking, thereby fostering ethnic loyalty in disguise. The MacPherson Constitution of 1951 not only preserved the regions but also increased their powers. It manifested some characteristics of federal concept, and provided for a central legislature, called the House of Representatives, comprised of indirectly elected member's -i.e., governors, president and six ex-officio members. According to Robert Ola (1994) the dissatisfaction with the 1951 constitution which was accentuated by the Eastern Regional government crisis of 1953 and the Kano riots of the same year, led the constitution to be rewritten to provide for greater regional autonomy.

In conformity with the relative deprivation and modernization theories, ethnic conflict started with the concern over the allocation of particular resources, such as jobs, public funds, foreign aid, and via the population census, voters and constituencies. Secondly, parties disputed more general questions regarding the constitutional framework within which competition takes place, such as revenue allocation, the creation of new states, and the proper relations between regional or ethnic citizenship and national citizenship. Although such issues were often argued in terms of general principles, disputes turned on the consequences that their application would have for particular groups, defined in regional or ethnic terms.

In another development Obafemi Awolowo (1947) stated in his book that Nigeria is not a nation. It is a mere geographical expression. There are no Nigerians in the same sense as there are English, Welsh, or French. The word Nigeria is merely a distinctive appellation to distinguish those who live within the boundaries of Nigeria from those who do not.

During the 1950s, the British government remained the arbiter in the constitutional conflict and electoral competition among the various ethnic groups. It directed developments by playing ethnic citizens who were politicians against one another, and by protecting the institutional base of northern conservatism in the Northern Region government and the Native Authorities (Williams and Turner, 1978). Therefore, ethnic and sectional incompatibility tended to grow in size as those concerned became more educated and civilized. The conflict over economic and professional interest also helped to set the stage for events that propelled the country irretrievably into the politicization of ethnicity. Abubakar Tafawa Balewa, the first Prime Minister of Nigeria was quoted to say: "Since the amalgamation of the southern and northern provinces in 1914, Nigeria has existed as one country on paper. It is still far from being united" (David-West 1994; Dibie 2000).

In another instance, Ahmadu Bello said to Nnamdi Azikiwe during the Constitutional Conference on Independence in 1959 that: "Let us understand our differences. I am a Muslim and a northerner. You are a Christian and a southerner. By understanding our differences, we could build unity in our country ... Nigeria is so large and the people are so varied that no person with a real intellectual integrity would be so foolish as to pretend he speaks for the country as a whole ... Lugard's amalgamation of 1914 is the mistake of 1914" (Bello 1962, 67 & 133).

Between 1947 and 1951 politicians sought office as spokesmen for ethnic groups, within their regions. This opened the way for them to accept compromise as the price of access to state office, and to the revenue of state. Politics thus came to be the process of gaining control of public resources for the pursuit of private ends. The Action Group and Northern Peoples' Congress were formed as regional parties in the West and North respectively, in response to the nationalist challenge of the National Council of Nigeria and the Cameroon, and Northern Elements Progressive Union, and to the threat of Igbo and southern competition. This kind of ethnic competition and conflict continued in Nigeria until 1966 when the military took over control of government.

The ethnic conflict of the era of politicians was not resolved when the military assumed power in January 1966. Instead the army itself became the focus and source of such conflicts. During the military regimes socially enacted relationships between ethnic identity, authority, and legitimacy competed with the legally sanctioned membership and legitimacy of the nation. The first military coup brought General Ironsi, an Igbo, to power. It destroyed the old political system and killed the north's leading politicians, as well as a number of southerners. But no Igbo leader died. Although Igbos masterminded the coup, their ardent supporters included Yorubas and some Hausas. The majority of Hausa-Fulani ethnic groups, however, saw the coup as part of an imagined Igbo strategy to dominate the country. In July that same year, the Hausa-Fulani ethnic groups brought their vengeance (counter coup), killing General Ironsi and putting a northerner, Colonel (later) General Gowon who was not a Muslim in place. The second coup had sparked off a massacre of Igbos in the north. This led the Igbos to finally give up everything and return home to the eastern region. They lost confidence in a federated Nigeria and had no illusion left about the chances of wedding Nigeria into a single nation. In a similar vein Odumegu Ojukwu at a meeting of the National Conciliation Committee led by Obafemi Awolowo, at State House, Enugu on May 16 1967, reflected as follows: "The question which seems to bother us is the question of Nigerian unity. Can there be unity in Nigeria? Has there been unity in Nigeria? To these two questions my answer is "No"... The north has made it abundantly clear that no association which they are not controlling the center machinery is acceptable to them" (Awolowo 1981, 28). During the military regime 1966-1997, the dynamics of resource allocation generated divisive ethnic conflicts. Military and bureaucratic officials were in competition to control the allocation of revenue, jobs and contracts. Middlemen competed for access to state officials. Foreign corporations competed by proxy through their ethnic agents. The operations of commercial triangles perpetuated nepotism, tribalism and statism. The triangular form of commercial relations created a closed government system in the country. This led the public to resent the increasing corruption and incompetence of the military government. Thus, politicians, businessmen, and academics resent the appropriation of opportunities by small cliques of ethnic minded military rulers and their ministries' directors general. They see themselves as qualified and competent to help the Nigeria improves economically, technologically and politically rather than hold on to ethnic status quo.

The annulment of the June 12 1993, presidential election by a northern military Generals do justify the above Ojukwu's prognostication or apocalypse made over two decades ago. Moshood Abiola, a Yoruba, was said to have won a presidential election in 1993, neat and square against a representative of the Hausa-Fulani tribes, but it was annulled. Northern dominance in Nigeria has meant nothing more than power for the Hausa-Fulani ethnic group, via the use of some upstart civilian, politicians and military officers. Under the able scheming of the Sokoto Caliphate, northern power alternates between its civilian and military minions in an unabashedly rabid power play that reduces the entire south to glorified second class ethnic groups.

The implications of the Hausa-Fulani grip of political power in Nigeria are what Geertz (1994) refers to as ethnic nationalism. The right to political control is seen as an allegiance to an ethnic group into which they have been born. An adequate solution to the ethnic problem must therefore tackle the question of dual citizenship and competition among citizens, come to grips with individual insecurity and the internalized dimension of their ethnic sentiments. It must, however be preceded by a detailed examination of how ethnicity has emerged, persisted and grown in a concrete case such as Nigeria.

In 1997 the Federal Military Government headed by General Abacha decided to place a new local government headquarters in the domain of Ijaw ethnic group in Warri, Delta State of the country. The government however, decided to move the headquarters within one month to the domain of another ethnic group (the Itsekiris). This precarious decision of the federal government galvanized inter-ethnic violence between the Ijaws and the Itsekiris, which resulted in the death of several hundred citizens in the region.

It is true that the rivalry between the Ijaws, the Itsekiris, and the Urhobos ethnic groups of the Warri region goes a long way. However, we may argue that these people do not have a genetic agent that encouraged mutual distrust and even hatred. On the contrary, co-existence and inter-marriage is a common feature of the ethnic groups of that region. The problem, like in most parts of Nigeria, started with the arbitrary drawing of administrative boundaries, initiated by the British and left to continue by the Nigerian government after independence. What is peculiar about the ethnic conflict in the Warri region is that, the ethnic groups in the region watched oil companies drilling away for about 40 years, and they do not have the political clout like the Hausa-Fulani groups to re-direct resources back into their communities. The only commercial city (Warri) in the region continues to suffer from neglect from the federal government.

The ethnic conflict in the Warri region is really a microcosm of the broader dual and competing citizenship, as well as political and economic problems facing Nigeria. The Warri ethnic problem is a case of transferred aggression. The ethnic groups are really sending out a cry for help and a plea for political and economic rewards or progress. Riots, hijacking oil company equipment and personnel are symptomatic of the deeper issues raised above. If given real political and economic rewards, ethnic groups attitude, tolerance and patience will build up and whatever administrative mechanisms that exist to resolve boundary and local government headquarters problems will stand a better chance of resolving these issues. It is therefore clear from the foregoing that ethnic groups draw legitimacy and loyalty from their ability to provide for their members in the time of need.

ETHNIC AND RACIAL NATIONALISM IN SOUTH AFRICA

The principal motivating force of the former apartheid regime in South Africa was economic and political power. Because of the drive for natural resources - gold and diamonds - the white settlers of South Africa aspired to reduce and keep down the African. This motive in turn led to dual and competing citizenship that resulted in the loss of several thousand of lives. As part of South African ethnic hierarchy, the African population is by far the largest, constituting over 75 percent of the population in the nation. Though until 1994 Africans shared a common societal powerlessness, they are not a single ethnic group. Rather, they derive their original citizenship from several Bantu tribes, the largest among them are the Zulu, Xhosa, Sotho, Tswana, Ndebele, Venda and Tsonga (Khapoya, 1994). The whites constituted less than 15 percent of the population but, until 1994, completely dominated government and the economic powers of the nation. The whites comprise two major elements, Afrikaners and the English-speaking. The Afrikaners were of Dutch origin, while most of the English-speaking whites were of British origin. Out of the sexual and sometimes marital unions of whites and blacks during the early settlement in South Africa an intermediate racial group called Coloreds was created. The Colored are about 3 million or 8.5 percent of the population (Marger, 1997). The Asians constitute about 2.5 percent of the population of South Africa. The Asians are made up of Indians, most of who are traders, shopkeepers, and worker at various skill levels.

As soon as a transfer of power was effected from Britain to South Africa in 1910, the white government, dominated by English-speaking whites, set out to devise a system in which they would exercise complete political control. The first major legislation was the Native Land Act, introduced in 1912 and enacted in 1913, which divided the nation into African and European areas. Africans were given only 13 percent of the land (Beinart, 1994). Under this law, certain areas - called reserves - were established for African people. Africans could not acquire land outside these areas. A further refinement to the law was made in 1936, when the Bantu trust and Land Act was passed.

The Prohibition of Mixed Marriage Act was passed in 1949, to prevent the blurring of racial lines, forbidding marriage between whites and non-whites (Lelyveld 1985). Although interracial marriage was outlawed, sexual liaisons between persons in different racial categories continued to occur. So another law, the Immorality Act of 1957, was enacted, making sexual intercourse between whites and blacks a criminal offense. The political dominance of whites was firmly established with the victory of the National Party in 1948. According to Leonard Thompson (1990) and Martin Marger (1997) political policies designed to create and sustain inequality among South Africa's four ethnic citizens was grounded in two overriding principles: (1) the maximum physical and social separation of the four groups, particularly the two major groups, whites and Africans and (2) the subordination of nonwhites in all areas of social, political, and economic life.

Restaurants, hotels, buses, trains, public toilets, waiting rooms, hospitals, schools, parks, beaches, theaters, and the like, were for the most part, segregated. Moreover, these separate facilities were invariably unequal in quality and quantity. These principles were justified by the premise that peace and order could be ensured only if people of the various colors mix as little as possible (Beinart, 1994). So great was the incompatibility of blacks and white ethnic groups, it was felt, that contact between them could lead only to conflict, hence, minimizing contact would be the logical solution to this perceived problem.

In the process of forcing the South African government to end its apartheid regime, the international communities placed sanctions against South Africa in 1986. The sanctions terminated landing rights for South African Airways and prevented many nations' aircraft from flying to South Africa. Commercial transactions such as new investments in South Africa; loans to South African government; importation of any mineral, metal, defense equipment and agricultural commodities were prohibited. Multinational corporations were called to divest their interests in South Africa. As a desperate effort to preserve white rule, a new constitution was adopted in 1993, creating a tripartite parliamentary body, representing whites, Colored and Asians. This new governing system however assured the continued dominance of whites and, most important, made no provision at all for the representation of Africans. This exclusion of Africans from the constitution further precipitated civil unrest in the nation.

In 1990, President de Klerk's government restored the legality of various black political organizations. This includes the African National Congress (ANC), Pan-Africanist Congress (PAC) and Inkatha Freedom Party. Nelson Mandela was released from prison in the same year, after serving twenty-seven years for anti-regime political activity. In October 1992, de Klerk basically declared an official end to the apartheid system. Despite overwhelming support among the black population for a change in the apartheid system, serious rifts existed between the ANC and, the Inkatha Freedom party, a political movement of mainly Zulus. This major political division lies between Nelson Mandela leader of ANC and Chief Mangosuthu Buthelezi the leader of Inkatha Freedom Party. Before elections were called for 1994, Inkatha and the ANC had engaged in a bitter and bloody conflict in many black townships.

The historic elections held in 1994, in which all South Africans, blacks and whites, voted for the first time, were won by the ANC, bringing Nelson Mandela to power as the nation's first African (black) president. Although the initial stages of transformation have been relatively peaceful, there is no certainty that violent ethnic conflict may not erupt in the future. The key issues facing South Africa today, therefore, concern the course the society will follow in the movement toward greater ethnic equality. The impatience with the pace of change so far in South Africa is natural and appropriate. If South Africans cease to be impatient, the urgency of transformative efforts will dissipate. The new leader of South Africa, President Mbeki is now challenged with the struggle to dismantle the structural arrangement that created black poverty and white wealth. President Mbeki will have to enact policies that will compensate for the cumulative disadvantages borne by too many, and encourage deepened democratic values, as well as promote sustainable development and a better quality of life for all, especially those who have been so long devalued and marginalized.

ANALYSIS AND PROSPECT FOR RESOLVING CONFLICT

The general analysis of Rwanda, Nigeria and South Africa's political history provides a systematic support for the point made by situationalists that "politicized communal contention over economic distribution issues is the prevalent form of political relevant ethnicity" (Ekeh 1976; Gurr 1993; Sklar 1993). While the above analysis suggests a clear dichotomy in citizenship and in the form it takes, the reality is less clear-cut. In Nigeria, Rwanda and South Africa, individuals hold multiple and shifting identities and change roles depending on the situation in which they find themselves. Ethnic groups also experience liberal citizenship demands at the national level that they may not find consistent with ethnic community demands. Faced with this situation ethnic community demands will be met, and national liberal citizenship demands undermined. Ethnic conflict in Rwanda and Nigeria demonstrate to a great extent how dual and competitive citizenship among indigenous ethnic groups could lead to explosive, bitter and bloody confrontations. A common ground among the three nations, however, was the fact that ethnic conflict resulted due to unequal access to political and economic rewards. One important factor that comes up in this analysis is that the relative frequency of conflicts among the various ethnic groups reflects the super-imposition of colonial divide-and-rule politics, and postcolonial political competition on the primordial ethnic map of pre-colonial Africa.

Table 9.1 shows the different ethnic groups in Nigeria, Rwanda, and (racial groups) in South Africa. Under this multi-ethnic structure co-existence in these nations is not the same as in single political community of most modern nation-states.

South African ethnic conflict is unique in the sense that it was the only nation in the world where racial supremacy had a constitutional sanction. Moreover, South African blacks - be they Zulu, Sothos, Xhosa or Tswana - did not have to cross any seas to set foot in South Africa. The differences in citizenship in the nation-state and ethnic communities has implications in these three nations under study, especially those in which there are great size disparity among groups - Hausa-Fulani in Nigeria, Hutus in Rwanda, and the Blacks in South Africa. Members of large ethnic groups, exercising their ethnic duty to vote for their community, propel their group to electoral dominance and therefore benefits from liberal democracy with majoritarian institutions, in which the individual is the presumed principal political actor. Such a situation led to stratified citizenship.

Table 9.1. Major Ethnic Groups in Nigeria, Rwanda and South Africa

Nigeria	%	Rwanda	%	South Africa	%
Hausa	21	Hutu	90	Africans	76.4
Yoruba	21	Tutsi	9	Coloreds	8.5
Igbo	18	Twa	1	Asians	2.5
Fulani	11	-	-	Whites	12.6
Ibibio	7	-	-	-	-
Kanuri	4	-	-	-	-
Edo	3	-	-	-	-
Tiv	2	-	-	-	-
Ijaw	2	-	-	-	-
Bura	2	-	-	-	-
Nupe	1	-	-	-	-
others	8	-	-	-	-

Source: South African Institute of Race Relations 1994; Nigerian Fact-Finder 1995; and Keesing's Record of World Events 1997.

Ethnic groups that capture a nation's majority vote do enjoy a larger bundle of rights and undertake a greater responsibility for the nation than members of the minority ethnic groups.

Political differentials, tribalism, racial supremacy, inequality, and discrimination also caused some of the grievances in these nations under study. The military action in Nigeria and Rwanda could be explained in terms of ethnic mobilization. Political competition within the context of unstable multi-ethnic coalitions and rebellions are due to dissatisfaction in the distribution of economic resources and powers between the various competing ethnic groups or citizenship. Faced with this situation, what are the prospects for containing ethno-political conflict in Nigeria, Rwanda and South Africa?

Policy Options:

Nigeria, Rwanda, and South Africa could adopt a corporate pluralism policy, in which all minority ethnic groups would be expected to adopt in full the cultural ways of the majority groups. This will enhance greater tolerance toward ethnic diversity in the nation. They should also undertake sweeping measures to foster political and economic equity among ethnic groups. Specifically, these policies should be aimed at improving the social and economic standing of the long-term victims of discrimination. Accommodative and consensual approaches that accept pluralism as legitimate and permanent sharing include federalism or regional self-government, cultural pluralism, electoral coalitions, and systems of power sharing. (Bates 1974; Rothchild 1981; Esman 1994; Sisk 1995). Accommodation approaches may occur separately or in combinations, an example of the latter being the carefully crafted pattern of ethnic regionalism and central power sharing that has evolved in Belgium and Switzerland.

Alternatively, these nations could adopt a melting pot or an assimilation policy. This will require the formulation of a hybrid culture whereby all present ethnic groups will converge. The implications of this policy however, is that out of the various ethnic groups in these countries, which group will be selected and what will be the criteria for selection? Although, formulation of a hybrid language was successful in Indonesia, the citizens of these nations might be suspicious of any government nursing this line of thought. The amalgamation or the intermixing of diverse ethnic groups in these nations would however, advance ethnic convergence.

Multi-culturalism as a government policy could recognize, respect and encourage the retention of ethnic cultures within the larger societies of these nations. Consociationalism and federalism would allow for smaller arenas of political practice in which to enact ethnic citizenship and for representation at the center, and they also provide institutional mechanisms at the national level to moderate elites exploiting or acting on ethnic obligations (Lijphart 1977 & 1984; Hyden and Bratton 1992; Halisi 1997). However, the extent to which multi-culturalism will be accommodated by these nations, and how these factors affect the development of a definite national identity is another issue this policy should address. Sustaining and enhancing multi-culturalism can only hinder the movement of the various ethnic groups into mainstream institutions, thus perpetuating the system of ethnic stratification. Multiethnic coalitions can insure that ethnic communities or factions within them participate in government.

In military or single-party regimes, where control of the state is decided by non-electoral processes, ruling elites should be careful to include representatives of constituent ethnic communities in decision-making roles to reassure them that their status is respected and that they share in benefits provided by the state. Such coalition arrangements require continuous delicate political management to appease mutually suspicious constituents.

Uncontrollable conflict is not inevitable, and the answer to the problems of democracy and ethnic conflict is not to redraw the maps of Nigeria, Rwanda, and South Africa. Rather, it lies in political structures that discourage the polarization of ethnic conflict and encourage trans-ethnic alignment and crosscutting cleavages. The crucial institutional variables in containing ethno-political conflicts are those pertaining to the party system and central local relations in government and party structures. The elites of the majority ethnic groups should be aware that reducing the fear of losing power need not involve abandoning either state expansion or democratization process. Milton Esmàn (1994), and Donald Horowitz (1990) rightfully stated that electoral systems in which politicians depend on votes only from coethnics tend to reward ethnic extremists who assert maximal demands (Kellas, 1991). Political systems in which politicians seeking election must appeal to members of more than a single ethnic community and depend on their electoral support generally produce more moderate politics and reward accommodative politicians with cross-ethnic appeals.

Political parties need stronger organization with greater input from ordinary citizens than has existed in these countries since their respective independence (Ndegwa 1997; Esman 1994; Sklar 1993; Olorunsola 1972). Such parties should encompass multi-ethnic coalitions, and should give the coalitions a greater stability by introducing effective supra-ethnic party identities, and patterns of political integration. If there is competition among parties, all need to feel that they will continue to have a fair chance to win in the future if they lose the next election. The fear that electoral competition would lead to intense conflict that would threaten the integrity of these nations was the justification most frequently given for military intervention, whose decree led to moderate decrease in non-violent protest and moderate increases in rebellion in Nigeria and Rwanda.

Redemocratization will probably rekindle non-violent ethno-political mobilization and protection to some extent. But strong parties and faith in having a fair chance to win in future should direct such mobilization into institutionalized channels, and keep it from threatening a regime's stability (Horowitz 1990; Ekeh 1976; Sklar 1993).

Delegation of power to local rather than state governments and party units needs to be both substantial and institutionalized, so that ordinary people will have an effective voice in the arena that matters most to them (van den Berghe 1975; Esman 1994; Gurr 1995). Elites in national level competition will be guaranteed the opportunity to protect their local power bases. Under these conditions both democracy and state capacity will be strengthened. There will be the sense of political security for both the leadership and the populace. This will help keep a broad multi-ethnic coalition stable and to moderate the self-perpetuating tendency of communal contention.

Institutional arrangement will make economic growth less likely to generate strong grievances (Crawford 1976; Lijphart (1977; Selassie 1992; Esman 1994; Ndegwa 1997). However, like the argument presented by the relative deprivation perspective, if economic decline is too great, of course, all political institutions will be threatened. The formation of a working class that parallels the advantaged class in drawing its membership roughly in proportion from various ethno-political groups will help to separate ethnic and class conflict.

Finally, the elimination or at least the minimization of foreign intervention will also contribute greatly to the containment of ethno-political conflict in Nigeria, Rwanda and South Africa. Settlement thus rests on mutual agreement usually based on substantive compromise.

CONCLUSION

Among multi-ethnic societies in Africa, Nigeria, Rwanda and South Africa have experienced constant cases of bloody conflict and inequalitarian pluralism. The distinguishing identities of the political units are also not obliterated. Individuals in the nations under study operate with dual citizenship, one in an ethnic group and the other in the nation-state. This duality in citizenship differs in form from those practiced in Nigeria and Rwanda compared to those in South Africa during its apartheid regime. The dual and competing citizenship practiced cannot be fully fudged; however, the tension inherent in their coexistence can be mitigated. In such situation, electoral laws could be enacted to respond to the reality of ethnic voting founded upon ethnic citizenship. This would offer incentives to ethnic elites and politicians to seek votes outside their ethnic groups of accountability. Typically, federalism, consociationalism and limited electoral engineering are the policy options suggested to accommodate ethnicity problems in pluralistic societies, such as those in Nigeria, Rwanda, and South Africa. Despite the legacy of centuries of ethnic conflicts in these nations, power sharing may yet prove to be the way out of this impasse.

Ethnic conflict and change are inherent features of a multi-ethnic nation such as the three under study. Due to significant economic, political, and social inequality among the various ethnic groups, challenges to the dominant social order arise periodically. Also cultural and religious differences among the ethnic groups may continue to impel ethnic conflict.

By combating socio-economic insecurity, which arises from scarcity and inequality, Nigeria, Rwanda and South Africa will move towards either equalitarian pluralism or corporate pluralistic nations. Pragmatic and appropriate policies associated with regional autonomy, assimilation, pluralism and power sharing have the potential for accommodating the essential interests of most disadvantaged and politically active ethnic groups. However, assimilation policy should be the long-term national goal. Recent developments in South Africa, as we have seen, illustrate that efforts in this regard may in some cases yield significant changes. If those changes can be sustained, there is a strong reason to expect that comparative change can be achieved in other societies with severe ethnic divisions.

REFERENCES

Ahmadu, Bello. 1962. My Life: Autobiography of the Sardauna. Daily Times Press, Lagos.

Aka, S.M.O. 1994. "For My Northern Neighbor". Community Concord Newspaper. Lagos-Nigeria. August 21, p.5.

Akin-Aina, Wale. 1994. "Logic in the Illogical". Newswatch News Magazine,

Lagos, Nigeria. July 25, p.9.

Anderson, Benedict. 1991. Imagined Communities: Reflections on the Origin and Spread of Nationalism. New YorK: Verso.

Awolowo, Obafemi. 1981. Awo on the Nigerian War. Tribune Press, Ibadan, Nigeria.

Awolowo, Obafemi. 1947. Path to Nigerian Freedom. University of Ibadan Press, Ibadan, Nigeria. p.28.

Banton, Michael. 1983. Racial and Ethnic Competition. Cambridge: Cambridge University Press.

Bates, Robert H. 1974. "Ethnic Competition and Modernization in Contemporary Africa". Comparative Political Studies 6, (January), 457-84.

Beinaart, William. 1994. Twentieth- Century South Africa. New York: Oxford University Press.

Bienen, Henry, and Jeffrey Herbst. 1996. "The Relationship between Political and Economic Reform in Africa." Comparative Politics 29, (October): 23-42.

Davies, James C. 1962. "Towards a Theory of Revolution". American Sociological Review, pp.5-19.

David-West, Tam. 1994. "Nigerian Federalism and The Virus of Disunity". The Guardian Press. (January 2), pp.5-6.

Deutsch, Karl. 1953. Nationalism and Social Communication: An Inquiry into the Foundation of Nationality: Cambridge, MIT Press.

Diamond, Larry. 1987. "Ethnicity and Ethnic Conflict". The Journal of Modern African Studies. Vol. 25 (1) pp.117-128.

Dibie, Robert. 1994." ECOWAS: Is Functionalism the Answer to Regional Economic Integration in West Africa." Journal of Ethno-Development, Vol. 3, #3.

Ekeh, Peter. 1975. "Colonialism and the Two Publics in Africa: A Theoretical Statement." Comparative Studies Society and History, Vol. 17, No. 1.

Esman, Milton. 1994. Ethnic Politics. Ithaca, New York: Cornell University

Press.

Funga, F. 1991. "Pouvoir, ethnies et regions" Dialogue (149) (Nov.-Dec.).

Geertz, Clifford. 1994. "Primordial and Civic Ties." Pp 29-34 in Hutchinson and Anthony D. Smith Ed., Nationalism. Oxford University Press.

Glickman, Harvey, ed. 1995. Ethnic Conflict and Democratization in Africa. Atlanta, GA: African Studies Association.

Gordon, Milton M. 1964. Assimilation in American Life: The Role of Race, Religion, and National Origins. New York: Oxford University Press.

Grosse, S. 1994. The Roots of Conflict and State Failure in Rwanda. The Political Exacerbation of Social Cleavages in a Conteext of Growing Resources Scarcity. Ann Arbor, Department of Population Planning and International Health, School of Public Health.

Gurr, Robert T. 1993. Minorities at Risk: A Global View of Ethnopolitical Conflict. United States Institute of Peace Press, Washington, D.C.

Gurr, Robert. 1970. Why Men Rebel. Princeton University Press. Princeton, New Jersey.

Halisi, C.R.D. 1997. "From Liberation to Citizenship: Identity and Citizenship in Black South Africa Political Thought." Comparative Studies in Society and History 39 (January): 66-85.

Horowitz, Donald. 1985. Ethnic Groups in Conflict. University of California Press, Los Angeles.

Horowitz, Donald. 1990. "Making Moderation Pay: The Comparative Politics of Ethnic Conlict Management." In Joseph Montvile, Conflict and Peacemaking in Multiethnic Societies. Lexington, Mass: Lexington Books.

Hyden, Goran and Micheal Bratton.(eds). 1992. Governance and Politics in Africa. Boulder, CO: Lynne Reinner Publishers.

Horton, John. 1966. "Order and Conflict Theories of Social Problems". American Journal of Sociology (May/June), pp.51-73.

Ignatief, Michael. 1993. Blood and Belonging: Journeys into the New Nationalism.

Toronto: Penguin.

Jagun, Dokun. 1993. "Nigeria: The Basis of Union". The Nigerian Guardian, Lagos. (April 8), pp.3-7.

kellas, James. 1991. The Politics of Nationalism and Ethnicity. London: Macmillan Education.

Lelyveld, Joseph. 1985. Move Your Shadow: South Africa, Black and White. New York: Penguim.

Lemarchand, Rene. 1995. "Four Models for Resolving Ethnic Conflict." African Voices 4 (Summer): 1-37.

Lemarchand, Rene.1994. Burundi: Ethnocide as Discourse and Practice. New York: Cambridge University Press.

Lijphart, Arend. 1977. Democracy in Plural Societies: A Comparative Exploration. New Haven, Connecticut: Yale University Press.

Lijphart, Arend. 1980. "Federal, Confederal, and Consociational Options for the South African Plural Society." in Robert Rotberg and John Barrat ed. Conflict and Compromise in South Africa. Lexington, Mass: Heath.

Maharaj, Gitanjali. 1999. Between Unity and Diversity. Claremont, South Africa: David Philip Publication.

Mamdani, M. 1996. Citizen and Subject. Contemporary Africa and the Legacy of Late Colonialism. Princeton, Princeton University Press.

Marger, Martin. 1997. Race and Ethnic Relations. New York: Wadsworth Publishing Company.

Melson Robert and Howard Wolpe. 1970. "Modernization and the Politics of Communalism: A Theoretical Perspective". American Political Science Review, Vol LXIV, (December).

Morrison, D.G. and Stevenson, H.M. 1972. "Cultural Pluralism, Modernization and Conflict: An Empirical Analysis of Sources of Political Instability in African Nations". Canadian Journal of Political Science. Vol. V. No.1, March, p.90.

Ndegwa, Stephen. 1997. "Citizensip and Ethnicity: An Examination of Two

Transition Moments in Kenyan Politics. American Political Science Review. Vol. 91, No. 3 (September).

Nnoli, Okwudiba. 1980. Ethnic Politics in Nigeria. Fourth Dimension Publishers, Enugu, Nigeria.

Ola, Robert and Samuel Hume. 1994. Government and Local Development inWestern Nigeria, Benin City: Ambik Press.

Olorunsola, Victor. 1972. The Politics of Cultural Sub-Nationalism in Africa. Garden City, NY: Anchor Books.

Osifo-Whisky, Onome. 1994. "The Trouble with the North". Tell Magazine. Lagos, Nigeria (August 15), p.3.

Ottaway, Marina. 1994. Democratization and Ethnic Nationalism: African and Eastern European Experiences. Washington, DC: Overseas Development Council.

Park, Robert. 1924. "The Concept of Social Distance." Journal of Applied Sociology 8: 339-344.

Parsons, Talcott. 1975. "Some Theoretical Considerations on the Nature and Trends of Change of Ethnicity" in Nathan Glazer and Daniel Moynihan (eds). Ethnicity: Theory and Experience. Cambridge: Harvard University Press.

Peled, Yoav. 1992. "Ethnic Democracy and the Legal Construction of Citizenship: Arab Citizens of the Jewish State." American Political Science Review 86 (June): 432 - 43.

Prunier, G. 1995. The Rwanda Crisis: History of a Genocide. New York: Columbia University Press.

Richard, Joseph. 1987. Democratic Challenges in Africa. The Carter Center Working Papers Series. Atlanta, GA: Carter Center.

Ross, M.H. 1993. The Culture of Conflict. Interpretations and Interests in Comparative Perspective. New Haven, London: Yale University Press.

Rothchild, Donald. 1964. Safeguarding Nigeria's Minirities. Pittsburgh, PA: Duquesne University Press.

Rothchild, Donald. 1981. Ethnopolitics: A Conceptual Framework. New York: Columbia University Press.

Sanda, A.O. 1976. Ethnic Relations in Nigeria. The Caxton Press, Ibadan, Nigeria.

Saxton Lloyd, and Walter Kaufmann. 1971. The American Scene: Social Problems of The Seventies. Belmont, Calif: Wadworth. p.2.

Schermerhorn, R. A. 1970. Comparative Ethnic Relations: A Framework for Theory and Research. New York: Random House.

Selassie, Alemante G. 1992. " Ethnic Identity and Constitutional Design for Africa." Stanford Journal of International Law. Vol. 29, No.1, pp.1-56.

Sisk, Timothy. 1995. Democratization in South Africa. Princeton, NJ: Princeton University Press.

Sklar, Richard. 1993. "The American Frontier for Political Science," in Africa and Disciplines, edited by Robert Bates, V.Y. Mudimbe, and Jean O'Barr. Chicago: University of Chicago Press.

South African Institute of Race Relations. 1997. Race Relations Survey. Johannesburg: SAIRR.

Stewart, Angus. 1995. "Two Conceptions of Citizenship." British Journal of Sociology 46 (March): 63-78.

Thompson, Leonard. 1990. A History of South Africa. New Haven, Conn.: Yale University Press.

Uvin, Peter. 1997. "The Prejudice, Crisis, and Genocide in Rwanda". African Studies Review, Volume 40, No.2. (September).

van den Berghe, Pierre. 1978. Race and Racism: A Comparative Perspective. 2nd ed. New York: Wiley Press.

Waters, Malcolm. 1989. "Citizenship and the Constitution of Structures Social Inequality." International Journal of Comparative Sociology, Vol. 30. NO. 3-4, pp.159-180.

William, Gavin and Terisa Turner. 1978. "Nigeria". In West African States: Failure and Promise. Edited by John Dun. Cambridge University Press, London.

Young, Crawford. 1976. The Politics of Cultural Pluralism. Madison, WI: University of Wisconsin Press.

Yinger, Milton. 1981. "Toward a Theory of Assimilation and Dissimilation." Ethnic and Racial Studies 4:249-264.

Chapter 10

Resolving the Problems of Diversity and Ethnic Conflict in Sub-Sahara Africa

Robert Dibie

INTRODUCTION

In sub-Saharan Africa, efforts to reconcile state and communal claims have been positioned along a broad continuum. This process range from hegemonic system – that is, from hierarchical military or civilian led, one party or multiparty systems that concede minimal scope to ethnic or national autonomy – to a number of partial or full power-sharing systems. In this study political regimes are defined as the patterns of behavior accepted by the dominant state coalitions and the general public to be the legitimate local formula for the exercise of political power. Despite the commitment of most national leaders to instill a sense of national identity, the allegiance of a large portion of African peoples to particularistic ethnic groups still surpasses their loyalty to the national community. As a consequence, achievement of greater degree of interethnic accommodation and national integration constitutes the most critical political problem facing most sub-Saharan Africa states today.

Pan-Africanists thought had been thrashed out during the period of independence movement against colonial rule in Africa is now being ignored. Indeed, it is troubling to many observers that on the threshold of the twenty-first century; political ethnicity remains one of the daunting obstacles to the democratization process in sub-Saharan Africa. Ethnic irredentism of groups attempting to overcome existing political divisions has sometimes caused internal conflict and created friction and occasional violence between states. The recent origin of many boundaries that resulted from the European scramble for Africa has also complicated the task of forging a sense of unity (Lafay 1995). Effective national administrative amalgamation in British controlled territories like Ghana, Nigeria, and Kenya occurred only after World War II, and the countries comprising French West Africa and French Equatorial Africa have only been governed as completely separate and distinct territorial entities since 1956. Somalia and Cameroon attained their present border on the eve of independence through the incorporation of separate territories formally under the control of two different colonial powers (Britain and France). Eritrea was join to Ethiopia, to constitute the present borders of that state in 1952, and it took several lives and conflicts to separate Eritrea from Ethiopia in the 1980s. Tanzania arose from the 1964 union of Tanganyika and Zanzibar subsequent to the independence of both.

Some of the best known large ethnic groups in sub-Saharan Africa, like the Yoruba, Igbo, Sukuma, kikuyu, and Kru people did not exist as self-conscious entitles prior to the colonial period. The emergence of more comprehensive ethnic unit does not, however, preclude the retention of more limited ethnic identification (Dibie 2001; Rothchild 1997). For instance, in the face of certain competitive or threatening situation, all Yorubas may join in a united front, but under different circumstances the Oyo Yoruba and the Ekiti or the Ijebu Yoruba can become competitors or even enemies.

The civil war that occurred in Nigeria, Rwanda, Burundi, the Democratic Republic of Congo, Angola, Liberia, Somalia, Sudan, Ethiopia and so forth were attributable to the clashes of ethnic groups over the control of the apparatus of government for the allocation of the national resources. Thus, we can argue that the coming of independence aggravated ethnic competition and at the same time created a greater need for unity. National sovereignty at one stroke both eliminated the necessity of acting in concert against the colonial power and produce new national political prizes for which ethnic groups could compete for (Bates 1972; Melson and Wolpe 1971).

On one hand, ethnic conflict groups in sub-Saharan Africa can be a creative force, proving material benefits and meeting such intangible needs as esteem and a sense of identity and purpose. It is normal for people to mobilize in an effort to gain organizational, ideological, political, and economic power. As long as they compete according to the rules of the political game and accept their opponent's right to participate, the result can be positive.

In the other hand, ethnicity can be a highly destructive force. Acute tension can be unleashed as group struggle over territory, cultural survival, and physical existence. Similarly, if one group controls the state and its institutions and excludes others from positions of influence, deep resentments and hostility will often surface. In worse case scenario – apartheid in South Africa, the carnage in Rwanda, and the civil war in Sudan – grim, hostile perception can result in damaging relations for all who are draw into the confrontation.

This chapter examines how leaders of sub-Saharan Africa nations can prevent harmful relations from arising and, when they occur, how diplomats and organizations can influence those involved to shift to more constructive internal systems of ethnic conflict management. The chapter argues that there is no alternative to sustained investment in a peace process that links the capabilities of a responsible and responsive state with the use of pressures and incentives by mediators. The goal must be to create new institutional constraints or to facilitate the return to regularized group interactions. The chapter also uses the analysis of noncoercive and coercive incentives to provide an innovative option that diplomats can use to alter the strategies of groups involved in ethnic conflicts.

SYSTEMS APPROACH TOWARDS RESOLVING ETHNIC CONFLICT

As Easterly and Levine (1995) state: 'High ethnic diversity may lead to increase civil strife, political instability, and destructive competition for rents by ethnic factions. This statement reflects the situation in a number of sub-Sahara Africa (SSA) countries. Most countries in SSA did not come into being as a result of a slow historical process. Rather, they were imposed from the outside by colonial powers, often with little regard for the countries' ethnic composition. As Lafay (1995) states: "... the shape of most sub-Saharan countries is simply the result of colonial border cutting." Countries characterized by people who identify primarily with the values and interests of competing ethnic groups are at a distinct disadvantage compared with countries whose people share national values and objectives.

John Stuart Mill (1862) believed that groups who had a sense of being a 'nation' should have a separate government. He stated (1862, p. 309): "Where the sentiment of nationality exists in any force, there is a *prima facie* case for uniting all members of the nationality under the same government, and a government apart." Findlay (1995) contends that ethno-religious problems among ethnic groups are not limited to SSA. They are prevalent in a number of republics of the former Soviet Union, ex-Yugoslavia, Lebanon, Malaysia, Sri Lanka, the UK and more.

Ethnic groups will tend to play according to national rules of the game and will tend to cooperate with the other ethnic groups within a given country as long as they feel that the distribution of income and wealth among the groups is somehow 'acceptable'. The larger the difference between the actual distribution and the 'acceptable' one, the stronger the incentive for the losing ethnic group to look out for its own interest rather than cooperate with the other groups. In the extreme case where the losing ethnic group can do better on its own, it may decide to secede. This may lead to civil war if the groups who benefit from the existing arrangement do not accept the partition of the country. For instance, mineral-rich regions such as Katanga (now Shaba) in the Democratic Republic of Congo and Biafra in Nigeria attempted to secede but the attempts failed, and. Biafra's attempt led to a bloody civil war.

Maintaining peace and cooperation between ethnic groups may require the redistribution of income. A case in point is Cote d' Ivoire, where coffee and cocoa are mainly produced in the south while rice an import substitute, is, mainly produced in the north by a different ethnic group. Trade taxes on imports and exports have been used to subsidize the rice-growing group by lowering the domestic terms of trade and redistributing income from the coffee and cocoa producers to the rice producers.

A number of studies have examined the growth effect of group diversity in terms of ethnicity, culture or income. Collier (1995b) divides SSA countries according to three filters. He finds that around 11 percent of SSA's population lives under civil war and fails to pass his filter of minimal conditions of peace. Another 40 percent of the population satisfies the peace condition but fails to pass the second filter of macroeconomic stability, where failure is defined as an inflation rate above 25 percent with no significant deceleration over the past 3 years. Further, another 12 percent of the population satisfy the first two filters but fail to pass the filter of an adequate resource allocation environment. Ignoring the 8 percent of the people living in middle-income countries. Collier (1995) shows that those countries which pass the three filters - and which constitute about 29 percent of SSA's population - grew at about 6% in 1993 and 1994. This is also about 6% faster than the other SSA countries. One might wonder why these other countries have not improved their policies in order to capture some of these enormous potential gains, and what constraints have kept most SSA countries in such low-growth prisoner-dilemma situations.

The impact of ethnic diversity on growth in SSA was further examined in Easterly and Levine (1995). Based on cross-country growth regressions for the period 1960-89, they show that ethnic diversity is associated with significantly lower growth and with a lower likelihood of adoption of good policies. The higher ethnic diversity in Africa explains about 0.8 percentage points of the 2.3 percentage point gap in annual growth between Africa and the rest of the world. In other words, it explains about 35 percent of that gap. And when its impact on policies is included as well, Africa's higher ethnic diversity explains 45 percent of the gap.

Easterly and Levine's (1995) finding that the ethnic diversity variable is negatively associated with growth holds even after controlling for warfare. Collier (1995b) suggests that one interpretation for that result is that the ethnic diversity variable is a proxy for the lower degree of trust in ethnically divided societies. Thus, ethnicity acts as a pole around which group members can mobilize and compete effectively for state controlled power, economic resources, positions, contracts, awards and constitutional protections. Ethnicity as used in this study refers to a subjective perception of common origins, historical memories, ties, and aspirations. (Diamond et al. 1988)

Mauro (1995) finds that corruption reduces investment and growth. He uses an ethno-linguistic fractionalization index as an instrument for corruption, thereby confirming Easterly and Levine's findings for Africa. The impact corruption has on the growth rate of a nation is examined by Shleifer and Vishny (1993). They argue that the negative effect of corruption on growth is larger than the effect of taxation because the former entails more rent-seeking activities and is more wasteful. Alesina and Rodrik (1994) use a median voter model to show that higher income inequality raises the demand for redistribution and results in more taxation and less growth.

The negative impact of corruption in Shleifer and Vishny (1993) and of taxes in Alesina and Rodrik (1994) is due to their impact on the incentives to produce, consume and seek rents under ethnic and income diversity respectively. This study contributes to the debate by examining another effect of diversity, namely the effect of inter-ethnic cooperation and political stability in an ethnically fractionalized society.

Figure 10.1 shows the systems approach to state ethnic relations. The model attempts to relate the regime strategies of hegemony, elite power sharing (including hegemonic exchange and contemporary elite power sharing arrangement), and polyarchy (both parliamentary and presidential) to the latent grievances in the environment over such concerns as insecurity, inequality, status, identity, recognition and territory. These grievances can be tapped by political elites intent upon making demands for change as well as those wishing to maintain the status quo (Azar 1983; Rothchild 1997).

Since SSA's decolonialization, the leaders of some polyarchies and elites coordinated regimes have managed to avoid the worse-case scenarios by channeling demands along predetermined paths and developing new routines and incentives for conflict avoidance. By emphasizing the tangible or distributive side of these state societal relations, these elites have defused some of the anxieties and passions of ethnic rivalry. Central government practices in many polyarchies and elite power-sharing regimes reveal a keen regard for maintaining balance among groups and subregions when recruiting for civil service or allocating revenue.

Clearly, the potential for conflict management is greater when group demand are reasonable and moderate, and when they accept the legitimacy of competing interest and do not challenge the integrity of the political order. Nonnegotiable demands for assimilation, restructuring of power, border rectification, population movement, and partition and territorial separation are likely to pose fundamental challenges to a state's organizing principles and informal rules of engagement that could cause aggressive violence.

The need to have a third party capable of applying noncoercive and coercive incentives will remain constant in sub-Saharan Africa, but the nature of the mediation process can be expected to change significantly in the years ahead. New investment in mediator capacity is necessary to deter ambitious and unscrupulous leaders who might have the potential of spreading across International borders (for example, the spread of warfare from Liberia to Sierra Leone in the early 1990s). Aside from occasional external

Figure 10.1
System Approach Model on How to Resolve Ethnic Conflict.
Source: Adopted from Rothchild, Donald. 1997. Managing Ethnic Conflict in Africa. Washington, D.C.: Brookings Institution Press.

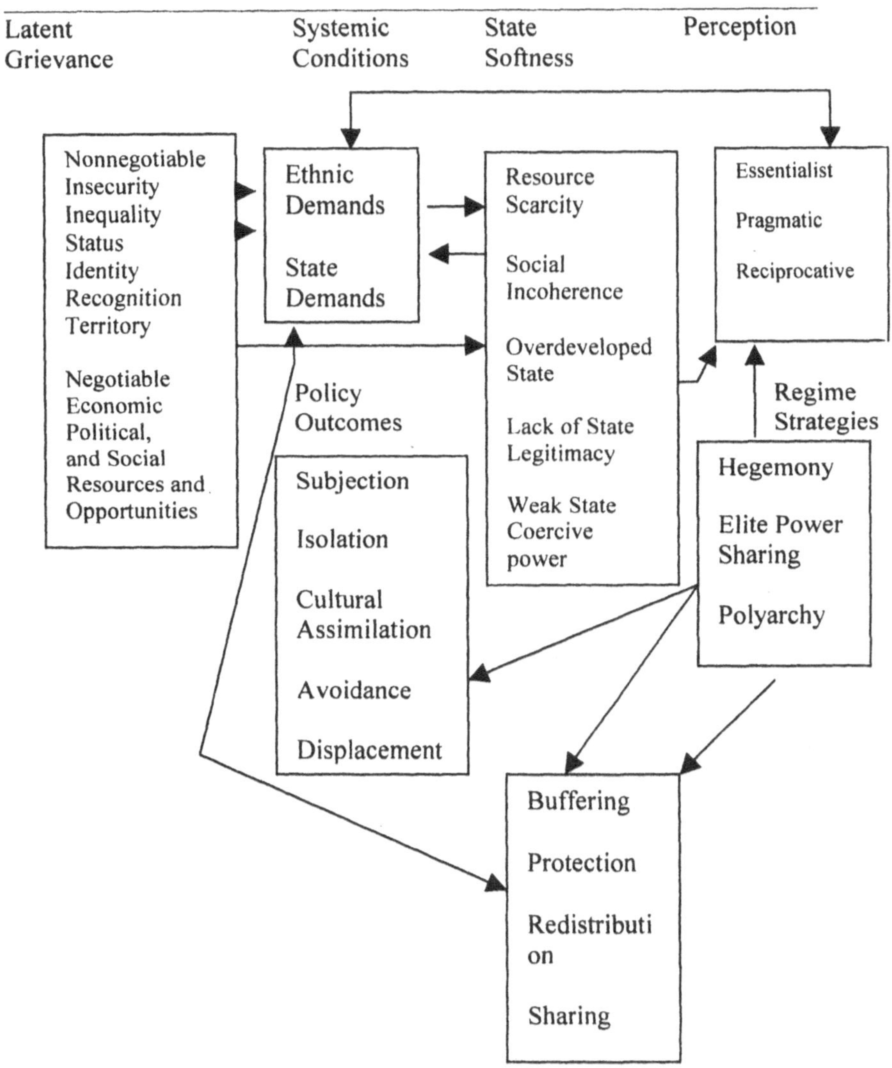

Interventions (such as ECOMOG intervention in Liberia and Sierra Leone) greater backing from the United Nations peacekeeping force is need in the subregion.

Figure 10.1 shows three perceptions – essentialist, pragmatic, and reciprocative perceptions. Reciprocative perception assumes that interethnic relations can be made less threatening when conciliatory move is made by the major actors in a dispute situation. This will lead them to seek to transform the structure of relations, by acting in a conciliatory manner to induce a similar response. Essentialist perception creates an interaction process, which is marked by fear and antagonism. This fear and antagonism later complicate the negotiation process. Where state and ethnic leaders view others as fundamentally threatening to their physical, cultural, or social survival, they tend to believe that any compromises on their part will weaken their position. Pragmatic perceptions are promoted when the incentive structure encourage leaders and groups to make moderate demands and abide by the rule of the game (Rothchild 1997; Hardin 1995)

In figure 10.1, nations will respond to ethnic demand and counter demands by applying the hegemonic, polyarchy and power-sharing strategies. States that use the hegemonic approach would consolidate power at the political center and emphasize hierarchical control by government and party. In hegemonic regimes, state elites are fearful that communal demands will be nonnegotiable and would contribute to the over politicization of the society. Therefore, they use the hierarchically based controls at their disposal to ether resist communal demands or attempt to structure societal relations in line with their preferences. This authoritarian approach is not without heavy costs. Repression, zero-sum mentality and state-ethnic deadlock or confrontations are the side effects of this approach.

Elite Power-sharing and polyarchical regimes allow a broader range for legitimate conflict among the elite representatives of ethnic, regional, and other interests. Elite power-sharing regimes are processors rather than makers of demands. They are more inclined to accept the legitimacy of autonomous social interests and in order to promote measures necessary to make ethnic groups feel secure in their relations with the state and other ethnic interest. They are also more inclined to negotiate with and accommodate these powerful social forces to achieve national unity (Hardin 1995; Rothchild 1997)

In sum, figure 10.1 is the system approach to ethnic-diversity management that attempts to give the readers some insight into conflict management as a system of interactions. Collective grievances and demands are linked to the structuring of regimes and their strategies and policies. Ethnic, regional demands and state responses are seen as interwoven and reinforcing. Demands for inclusive state coalitions and proportional distributions are accepted as negotiable and legitimate and can be handled within the political order, whereas demands for groups security and such indivisible goods as the separation of populations and secessions are generally nonnegotiable and threatening to the political system. As such, these latter demands have potentially destructive consequences for social coherence and state legitimacy.

The relationship between ethnic group demands and state response are critical because of the feedback effect and a variety of external pressures.

Democratic regimes, with their emphasis on low state control, open party competition, regular elections, and public accountability, provides features that can facilitate intergroup cooperation in SSA.

PATTERNS OF DIVERSITY AND ETHNIC CONFLICT IN SUB-SAHARAN AFRICA

It is troubling to note that at the beginning of the twenty-first century political ethnicity remains one of the daunting obstacles to the democratization process in sub-Saharan Africa. The preservation of some loyalty to particularistic groups is not necessarily incompatible with national integration. However, national integration requires that identification with the national community supersede in certain situations more limited ethnic loyalties. National cohesion thus entails the development of an integrating strand among the network of allegiances and commitments of the national community. Interaction between state and society assume a constant engagement of rival interests in the contemporary political arena among various groups that have mobilized to secure public resources from those in authority at the political center. These groups are formed along ethnic, racial, religious, regional, or class lines and have distinct origins and appeals. They also share common features such as socially constructed identity whose leaders advance demands upon the state as well encounter each other in a dynamic interplay of interest-inspired competition and collaboration. (Barrows 1976; Posen 1993).

The pattern of diversity and ethnic conflict in sub-Saharan Africa is complicated by the special historical position of one dominant ethnic community. For example the historical ascendancy of the Amharas in Ethiopia, the Americo-Liberians in Liberia, the Tutsi in Burundi and Rwanda, and the Arabs in Zanzibar has significantly influenced the conditions of contemporary political and economic life in these nations. Colonial legacies also vested some newly independent states with one privilaged community, like the Creoles in Sierra-Leone, the Baganda in Uganda, and the Barotse in Zambia (Smock and Bentsi-Enchill 1975). The refusal of the once subordinate ethnic communities to continue to acquiesce to these unequal relations has already provoked violent changes of the political order in Nigeria, Rwanda, South Africa, Uganda, Ethiopia, and Somalia, and has caused considerable instability in many other sub-Saharan African nations.

Ethnicity in the politics of Nigeria is not novel because it has, since its inception as a sovereign nation-state, remained an important variable in the country's politics. Ethnicity, however, gathered momentum when the competition for power and the survival of each ethnic group became the focal point of the republic's political leaders. The involvement of the Nigerian military in ethnic politics has been addresses by many scholars. Pita Agbese (1990) and Ike Udogu (1999), contends that the creation of states (currently 36) by the military regimes has its roots in the assumption that they would fulfill what was considered to be legitimate demands for selfdetermination. A case in point is the ethnic minority right groups, which argued for the creation of following ethnic states: Ijaw, Yoruba, Igbo, Hausa-Fulani, Ibibio, Kanuri, Edo, Nupe, Urhobo, Tiv, and Gbagyi. Although the position of this group did not prevail, it nevertheless illustrated the depth of ethnonationalism among many Nigerians and the problem it might continue to crate for democracy in the polity.

The Hutu and Tutsi ethnic groups in Rwanda and Burundi use the same language and institutions and are often very similar to each other in appearance, leading some social scientists to deny that they do, in fact, represent separate ethnic groups. Belgian colonial rule did much to foster a sense of difference and eventually led to the emergence of a sense of separate consciousness that has gained political expression in collective competition and conflict (Rothchild 1997). Whereas journalistic narration of the crisis in Rwanda and Burundi accentuate ethnicity as the causal factor of the carnage in the countries, serious analytic interpretation of the crisis shift the focus to the nation-state, that is, which ethnic group controls the nation and prior distribution of goods and services. In Rwanda and Burundi, the notion of who controls the national pie has galvanized confictual relations between the Hutu and Tutsi with the Twas and other groups sufficiently marginalized (Udogu, 1999).

The type of diversity and ethnic politics in Cameroon presents a unique case from the perspective of its tripartite characteristic. That is, anglophone, francophone and indigenous complexions. In addition to the problematic marriage of French and English traditions is this multilingual state, political competition for power tends to sharpen the ethnic walls, interests, and differences. Political parties were formed along ethnic and regional lines. Cameroon Peoples Democratic Movement (CPDM), with its support among the Beti-Pahouin Collectivity in the center, south, and east provinces; the National Union for Progress and Democracy (NUDO), Foulbe and northern-Moslem dominated (Udogu 1999). The Social democratic Front (SDF), Bamileke, Anglophone of the west province; the Movement for Defense of the Republic (MDR) drew its support from Kirdi ethnic group in the far north province (Udogu 1999; Takougang 1996). The formation of these ethnoregional parties in Cameroon was not intended to further democracy per se. Rather, they were created within the context of resource competition theory for the control of amenities and scarce resources. This was important for the improvement of the ethnic constituencies. In such political confrontations, the nation-state is only relevant to the extent that it is being used to further group interest and advantage.

In Cote d' Ivoire, former president Felix Houphouet-Boigny' and in Cameroon president Paul Biya's (and previously in Kenyatta's Kenya), a more public countenanced system of balanced inclusion and interelite reciprocities and exchange became evident. In the 1960s and 1970s, for example, Houphouet-Boigny accepted ethnic-based fear as part of the country's political reality and sought to demobilize major ethnic challengers by political carefully distributing tangible benefits to key players in the ruling coalition and cooping important patrons into his one-party government (Rothchild 1997).

In the Cameroon case, former president Ahmadou Ahidjo, despite his heavy-handed and secretive tendencies, prudently used his ministerial appointments to balance ethnoregional, linguistic, religious, and economic interests (Rothchild 1997). His successor, Paul Biya, a Catholic from the south-central region, has been even more committed to the principle of ethnic and religious proportionality, upholding the north-south balance in his executive appointments and ensuring that a northern Muslim would eventually succeed him as president.

In Kenya, the dominant political philosophy was that a one party system was more likely to further stability than a multiparty system. To encourage multipartism, single party advocates contend, could lead to deep ethnic crisis propagated by ethnically oriented parties, social and economic distemper, and political disorder. In the 1990s the IMF and World Bank put pressures on President Daniel arap Moi's regime to open up the political system. There was the apprehension that in a free and fair election, Moi was likely to lose because of his unpopular policies. Perhaps more significantly was his fear that multiparty democracy could lead to ethnic politics, and because he is a Kulenjin, an ethnic minority group, it was a foregone conclusion that the majority groups, as for instance, the Kikuyu, could defeat him. To Influence the outcome of the 1992 presidential election, some have alleged a number of ethnically instigated clashes occurred in the area of the Rift Valley. Indeed, the Kulenjin (which constitute about 4 percent of the Kenyan population) launched an attack in late 1991 and early 1992 on villages made up of Kikuyu, Luo, and Luhya ethnic groups with the loss of many lives (Nowrojee and Manby 1993; Udogu 1999). In the democratic election that occurred between arap Moi's Kenyan African National Union (KANU) against the rival parties Forum for the Restoration of Democracy (FORD), KANU won with 36 percent votes and maintained a majority of the members of parliament (108 out of the 188 seats). In fact no Kikuyu, and only one Luo in KANU won their seats and as a result the regime nominated former Members of Parliament (MPs) from those ethnic groups (as a consociational or power sharing strategy to appease these major collectivity.

In the Sierra Leone case, following the marginalization of the dominant Creoles ethnic group in the internal battle for the control of resources, the Mendes and Temnes opened another chapter of competition in the nation. The Mendes (under the banner of the Sierra Leone People's Party) (SLPP) had to lock horns with the Temnes (under the platform of the All People's Congress) (APC) for control of the apparatus of government (Udogu 1999). Following the 1988 elections, the ethnic composition of the cabinet was 5 Mendes, 12 Temnes, 4 Limbas, 3 Creoles, and 3 others (Kandeh 1992).

It could be therefore, argued that colonialism had a mixed impact in sub-Sahara Africa. Though it did radiate a set of institutions and practices to Africa that are useful, it also introduced many values that are not useful. Those values that are useful have become the frameworks for the new practices of sub-Saharan Africa various governments. Those values that are not useful have undercut Africa's autonomy from the developed West and implanted new values and identities.

How do these brief preceding analyses on political ethnicity impact on democracy and the future of sub-Saharan Africa, and what can African leaders do to prevent harmful relations from arising? An answer to this question will form the basis of the following analyses.

PUBLIC POLICY AND INCENTIVE FOR MANAGING DIVERSITY AND ETHNIC CONFLICT

In sub-Sahara Africa, state and ethnic leaders have often responded to their political environment by competing with each other according to well-understood rules. Leaders in such a situation have an incentive to pull back from the threat of extended conflict and negotiate with their rivals. This becomes the basis for a possible political settlement. This study has already examined ethnic conflicts in a number of Sub-Saharan nations. In these instances, sub-Sahara African states could reform their intrastate conflict management system and recognize that the major actors are better off with an agreement to cooperate than with no agreement at all.

What incentives and guidelines can ruling state elites or internal or external mediators use to facilitate political negotiation and reciprocity? In a domestic context where recurrent patterns of relations are present, incentives that consist of structural arrangements or distributive or symbolic rewards should be used by state to channel individual and group choice along preferred lines and to promote regular patterns of interaction between the state and societal groups. Polyarchies consciously make use of structural incentives (electoral, formal power-sharing, and federal mechanisms), distributive inducements (fiscal programs and allocative preferences), and symbolic rewards. While elite-coordinated regimes, with their extensive reliance on face-to-face encounters, tend to utilize ad hoc, internally developed system guidelines to encourage conciliation.

Guidelines that spell out suggestions for action that each state subnational group might encounter should they fail to agree to resolve the dispute in negotiable term is necessary. Guidelines are by no means inviolate markers but rather they are indicators for prudent state leadership. Such guides include not only positive decision rules on the application of principles of inclusiveness, autonomy, redistribution, and proportionality, but also such negative guides to action as threat, coercion, and punishment (Rothchild 1997). Combinations of these, the use of carrot and sticks, may also be relevant to the practical relations between state and society. These various packages of structural, distributive, and symbolic incentives and positive and negative decision rules would help political leaders to sub-Saharan Africa to manage ethnic conflict.

In essence, conflict management should involves avoiding a collapse in the norms of encounter and encouraging actors to shift their preferences (their rank ordering of outcomes) before a stalemate. This would enable them to engage in cooperative activities. Therefore, internal structural incentives that are created and well maintained by a strong and responsive state, can have a critical role in confidence building. Such incentives could encourage the parties to reevaluate their actions before undercutting the reciprocities and negotiating processes that provide for a civil society (Azarya 1994). As long as the state remains responsive to the legitimate demands of various interests (such as in South Africa following the 1994 transition to nonracial majoritarian rule), an authoritative state actor, if it exists, can play a positive role by mediating between rival internal parties. This could workout well provided that the state is not captured by one of the competing ethnic-based interests (Rothchild 1999). However, when muscle becomes essential to surmount an impasse or to enforce the terms of bargain, state and interstate initiative can be indispensable, primarily because only states have the necessary leverage to induce the parties to accept new alternatives.

One key variable for facilitating an externally guided agreement appears to be the status and power of the third party actor. The range of possible mediators (or coalitions of mediators) and their capacity to change the peace process through combinations of coercive and noncoercive incentives are striking. When a decolonizing state prepared to mediate between internal parties (as Britain was in Ghana, Kenya, and Zimbabwe), or when the great powers change their preferences and perceptions and cooperate to press the disputants to reach a compromise (as in the Angola-Namibia accords of 1988), the prospects for successful conflict management are enhanced (Kochan 1981).

Both coercive and noncoercive incentives seek to alter behavior in a cooperative direction, but they differ in their costs of application and their anticipated effect upon recalcitrant local actors. Noncoercive incentives extend benefits or rewards for compliance by a targeted actor, whereas coercive incentives punish or threaten to punish such an actor to bring it into line with preferred types of political behavior. The first set of incentives is obviously easier to apply and may well elicit a positive response to the third party intervener from the targeted state or movement.

Further, when both parties to a conflict can see some advantage to be gained from a conciliatory approach, there may be room for a mediator to manipulate the situation to facilitate a settlement. Mediator would hope that the cumulative effect of a package of positive and negative inducements will lead at least one of the parties to accept their second preference, and, therefore, to bring about some degree of mutual cooperation. Jack Snyder (1990); contend that a successful cooperation requires a push from some powerful provider of incentives to cooperate, and the creation of institutions that coordinates the participant's expectations and actions.

Power sharing and polyarchical approaches are other methods of revolving ethnic conflict in sub-Saharan Africa. These approaches allow a broader range for legitimate intergroup relations among the elite representatives of ethnic, religious, and other interests. Under such circumstances, there will be greater openness and flexibility among representatives of the various groups sharing power in one government. This could also help create a positive feedback to ethnic related demands because group leaders have reason to anticipate a greater responsiveness on the part of the state officials. By institutionalizing competitive elections and a degree of public accountability, polyarchies are certainly more effective than their elite power sharing counterparts in regularizing public access to decisionmakers (Rothchild 1997). However, because the elite power sharing regimes establish informal routines for broadly balanced and inclusive coalitions and proportional decision rules of civil service appointment and fiscal allocation, they are responding to the appeals of ethnic, regional, and other intermediaries.

In a power sharing and polyarchical governments preparedness to accommodate ethnic and subregional demands follows logically from their governing elites perception that claims on the state can generally be reconciled and therefore that the intensity of intergroup conflicts is likely to be low or moderate. Further, state elites can also choose to adopt policies of protection, granting constitutional and legal guarantees to minorities to reassure them of their status and safety in the political order (Nigeria in 1979, 1993, 1999) (Dibie et al. 2001; Rothchild 1997). Another example is the South Africa's 1994 interim constitution that gave minority parties (non-minority ethnic and racial groups as such) guarantees of inclusion in decisionmaking and provincial affairs. In nations such as Kenya, Ghana, Cote d' Ivoire, and Cameroon, despite the evident constraints of economic scarcity, state elites have pursued a strategy of redistributing fiscal resources to the less advantaged ethnoregions of their country, thereby increasing the likelihood that the people in these areas will have an incentive to support the state and comply with its regulations.

Federalism, which involves the sharing of a nation's power into central, subregional, and local governmental units, is another strategy to revolving ethnic conflict. It provides that each distinct political unit within the national government structure posse responsibility for certain specified functions (Dibie et al. 2001). Federalism is viewed as recognizing and working with ethnic differences, but as a possible price of promoting ethnic insularity and losing territory wide purpose. Federalism is one of the fullest expressions of horizontally based stratification arrangements that has won acceptance in Nigeria and in certain circle in Ethiopia and South Africa. In 1987 the Political Bureau of Nigeria recommended that Nigeria continued with its federal form of governance. The same political bureau also identified conferalism and unitarism to be dangerous for any nation with several ethnic groups (Dibie et al. 2001; Lijphart 1995).

Sub-Sahara African nations should ensure that they develop constitutional guidelines that will facilitate that all areas receive services and amenities, whether or not they have supported the ruling coalition, makes policies less threatening to political minorities. Provided ethnic demands continue to be reasonable and some adjustment is made in the proportionality arrangements to take account of demographic and other changes, it remains possible for sub-Saharan African leaders to work within the political system to meet the guidelines of fairness. Using such guidelines will compensate ethnic minority interests and thereby encourage their confidence.

CONCLUSION

The chapter has demonstrated that in attempting to create an effective conflict management system within the nations of sub-Saharan Africa, a mediator needs both leverage and legitimacy to make effective use of incentives. A strong and responsive internal state mediator can use leverage to structure incentives so as to minimize insecurity and prevent intense conflict from occurring.

To promote peace and democracy in sub-Saharan Africa in the twenty-first century, it is imperative to adhere to what Olusegun Obasanjo (1990) and Ike Udogu (1999) called strategic imperative for the promotion of the desire of the African people. Strategic imperative includes responsiveness and efficiency in governance, trust creation and confidence building that must be between the governors and the governed. It also includes decentralization of power to the grassroots, pluralism and decentralization of the economy, political communication, education and political awareness, promotion and defense of human rights, creation of appropriate political machinery, renewal of mandate and succession program, and popular participation in all aspects of the development process. Administratively, too, the preceding conjectures approximate the views of such scholars as Lijphart (1995) and Robert Dibie et al. (2001), who explored a consociational or power sharing scheme for the governance of multiethnic and divided societies such as Burundi, Rwanda, Kenya, Zimbabwe, Cameroon, Nigeria, and so forth. In fact a tenet of the 1999 Constitution of Nigeria, which provides for the rotation of the presidential system along geopolitical and geoethnic strata (Northeast, Northwest, Middle Belt, Southwest, East Central, and Southern minorities) is similar to this power-sharing mechanism.

Regardless of these practical and theoretical solutions to the problems of ethnic conflict management, SSA countries need to achieve greater efficiency of resource allocation in order to improve welfare and growth. Achieving these efficiency gains will require carefully designed economic reform programs. This study also have argued that the political constraints which are present in the case of ethnic diversity need to be taken into account in the design of these programs. More attention should be given to the distribution of political power across ethnic groups and to the composition of endowments of each ethnic group in order to better understand the impact of reform on each group's wealth and on the level of interethnic cooperation and political stability. Past reforms may not have given sufficient attention to some of the constraints imposed by ethnic diversity in SSA, which may help explain why they have been largely unsuccessful.

REFERNCES

Abgese, Pita. 1990. "The Impending Political Demise of Nigeria's Forthcoming Third Republic." Africa Today, 37 (3) 23-44.

Ake, Claude. 1973. "Explaining Political Instability in New States." Journal of Modern African Studies, vol. 11 (September), p. 356-373.

Ake, Claude. 1996. Democracy and Development in Africa. Washington, D.C.: Brooking Institute Press.

Alesina, A. and D. Rodrik. 1994. 'Distributive Politics and Economic Growth', Quarterly Journal of Economics, 109: 465-90.

Alesina, A. and R. Perotti. 1994. 'The Political Economy of Growth: a Critical Survey of the Recent Literature', World Bank Economic Review, 8 (3): 351-71.

Alesina, A. and E. Spolaore 1995. On the Number and Size of National mimeo, Harvard University and ECARE (University Libre of Bruxelles).

Azar, Edward. 1983. "The Theory of Protracted Social Conflict and the Challenge of transforming Conflict Situations, in Diana A. Zinnes, ed. Conflict Processes and the Break down of International Systems, vol. 20, no. 2. Denver, CO: University of Denver Press. Pp.92-111.

Azarya, Victor. 1994. "Civil Society and Disengagement in Africa." In John W. Harbeson Donald Rothchid, and Naomi Chazan, eds. Civil Society and the State in Africa. Boulder, CO: Lynne Rienner. Pp.83-100.

Bates, Robert. 1972. "Ethnicity and Modernization in Contemporary Africa." Social Science Working Paper 16; Pasadena: California Institute of Technology, (November).

Becker, G.S. 1996. The Making of preference and Values, Cambridge MA, Harvard University Press.

Coleman, J.S. 1987 'Norms as Social Capital', in G. Radnitzky and P. Bernholz (eds) Economic Imperialism, New York: Paragon.

Coleman, J.S. 1988 'Social Capital in the Creation of Human Capital', American Journal of Sociology, 94 (Supplement): S95-SI20.

Coleman. J.S. 1990 Foundations of Social Theory, Boston MA: Harvard University Press.

Collier, P 1995a 'The Marginalisation of Africa', Center for the Study of African Economies, Oxford University (September).

Collier, P. 1995b. 'Recent African Economic Performance and its Implications' mimeo, Kennedy School of Government, Harvard University.

Diamond Larry, Juan J. Linz, and Seymour Martin Lipset, eds. 1988. Democracy in Developing Countries: Africa. Boulder, CO: Lynne Rienner.

Dibie, Robert and Sharron Herron. 2001. Nigerian Public Administrators Perception of the Importance of Managerial Skills. International Journal of Public Administration, (forthcoming).

Duignan, Peter, and Jackson Roberts. eds. 1986. Politics and Government in African States 1960-1985. Stanford, CA: Hoover Institute Press.

Easterly, W. and R. Levine. 1995. 'Africa's Growth Tragedy: a Retrospective 1960-89', mimeo, Macroeconomic and Growth Division, World Bank, June.

Esman, Milton. 1973. "The Management of Communal Conflict." Public Policy, Vol. 21, (Winter), pp. 62-81.

Findlay, R. 1995. 'Notes on the Political Economy of Nationalism', in A. Breton, G. Galeotti, P Salmon and R. Wintrobe (eds.) Nationalism and Rationality, Cambridge: Cambridge University Press.

Hardin, Russel. 1995. One for All: The Logic of Group Conflict. Princeton, N.J.: Princeton University Press.

Kochan, Thomas. 1981. "Step-by-Step in the Middle East from the Perspective of the Labor Mediation Process. " in Jeffrey Z. Rubin , ed. Dynamics of Third Party Intervention: Kissinger in the Middle East. Westport, CT: Preager. pp. 125.140.

Lafay, J.D. 1995. 'Conservative Nationalism, and Democratic Institutions', ill A. Breton, G. Galeotti, P. Salmon and R. Wintrobe (eds.) Nationalism and Rationality, Cambridge: Cambridge University Press.

Lijphart, Arend. 1977. Democracy in Plural Societies. New Haven, CT: Yale University Press.

Lijphart, A. 1995. "Prospect for Power-Sharing in the New South-Africa." In A. Reynold (ed.), Elections 1994 South Africa: The Campaigns, Results and Future Prospects. New York: St. Martin's Press, pp. 221-231.

Mauro, P 1995. 'Corruption and Growth', Quarterly Journal of Economics, 110 (3), August.

Melson, Robert, and Howard Wolpe. 1971. Preface in Nigeria: Modernization and the Polictics of Communalism, ed. Melson and Wolpe. East Lansing: Michigan State University Press.

Mill, J.S. 1962. Consideration on Representative Government, Gateway Editions (originally published in 1862).

Obasanjo, Olusegun. 1990. "Eastern Promises." West Africa Magazine. (May 7-13), p.762

Posen, Barry. 1993. "The Security Dilemma and Ethnic Conflict, " Survival vol. 35 (Spring), p.28-41.

Putnam, R.D. 1993. Making Democracy Work in Civic Traditions in Modern Italy, Princeton: Princeton University.

Rothchild, Donald. 1986. "State and Ethnicity in Africa: A Policy Perspective." In Kennedy, Charles and Neil Navitte. eds. Ethnic Preference and Public Policy in Developing States. Boulder, CO: Lynne Rienner.

Rothchild, Donald. 1997. Managing Ethnic Conflict in Africa. Washington, D.C.: Brooking Institution Press.

Schiff, M. 1992. 'Social Capital, Labor Mobility, and Welfare. The Impact of Uniting States', Rationality & Society, 4 (2): 157-75.

Schiff M. 1995. 'Capital socio-cultural, diversite etlinique et reforme economique en Afrique Sub-Saharienne', Revue d'Economie du Developpement.

Schiff, M. and A. Valdes. 1992. The Political Economy of Agricultural Pricing Policy. Volume 4. A Synthesis of the Economics in Developing Countries, Baltimore: The Johns Hopkins University Press.

Smock, David.and Kwamena, Bentsi-Enchill. 1976. The Search for National Integration in Africa. New York: The Free Press.

Snyder, Jack. 1990. "Averting Anarchy in the New Europe," International Security, Vo. 14, (Spring), p. 30-43.

Takougang, J. 1996. The 1992 Multiparty Elections in Cameroon: Prospects for Democracy and Democratization. Journal of Asian and African Studies, 31 (1-2), 157-175.

Udogu, Ike. 1999. "The Issue of Ethnicity and Democratization in Africa: Towards the Millenium." Journal of Black Studies, Vol. 29, (6), pp.790-808.

Uzodike, U. O. 1996. "Democracy and Economic Reforms: Developing Underdeveloped Political Economies." Journal of Asian and African Studies, 31 (1-2), pp.21-38.

Chapter 11

Economic Reform Policies in Guinea, Cote d' Ivoire, Niger and Senegal

Ismail Shariff and Patrick Okonkwo

INTRODUCTION

West Africa is a sub-region rich in raw materials, cultivatable lands, and potential energy resources, but many countries in this region has the poorest economies in the world. West Africa is made up of countries with varying colonial experience such as British, French, and Portuguese. Despite these colonial experiences low per capita income, minimal energy consumption, and low standard of education and health care characterize nations in this sub-region. Since the 1970s most French speaking West African countries embarked on economic reform policies in the attempt to arrest the recession facing their nation and promote economic growth and development. Between 1970 and 1980 the average annual growth of the Gross Domestic Product (GDP) in West Africa was 3.5 percent. Cote d' Ivory and Mali had an average annual growth rate of 5.7 and 4.3 percent, respectively, as against minus 0.5 and 0.9 percent for Guinea and Niger (Nafziger, 1997). The yearly growth rate in Benin recorded an annual decline of 4.4 percent.

The reasons for this poor economic performance could be explained in seven folds: (1) political centralization and instability; (2) ethnic and regional inequalities (3) the difficulties created by drought in some countries in the sub-region; (4) lack of entrepreneurs; (5) large scale unemployment; (6) lack of infrastructural requirements for the mobilization and distribution of the factors and output of production and (7) inconsistency in the types of policy directed towards long-term agricultural production. The decreases in the international prices of crops accounted for low export revenue earnings, high flotation in local currency exchange rate, and minimal control of prices of agricultural products.

The persistence of deplorable economic problems in French speaking West Africa has been a major reason for the government of the nations to search for solutions. Under this circumstance, it became imperative that more external financial assistance would be required in order to arrest further deterioration and avoid the collapse of the economies of most sub-Sahara African nations. In recent years, this search has adapted the application of neoclassical economics concepts proposed by the World Bank and the International Monetary Fund (IMF). Policy reforms in the macroeconomic framework also enabled sub-Sahara African countries to adopt more market-based system of foreign exchange allocation and fewer administrative controls over imports.

This chapter will examine the relevance of the economic reform policy on development and sustainable growth in Guinea, Niger, Cote d' Ivoire and Senegal, which is endowed with considerable natural resources and which in the early 1960s experienced economic growth. We presented two arguments in this paper: (1) the narrow economic interests and broader economic concerns of sub-Sahara African nations are likely to be a strong influence in the mobilization process of economic reform. However, in exceptional cases such effects will be less pronounced because of the nature of domestic political institutions; (2) we also argued that adjustment alone cannot put sub-Sahara African countries on a sustained, poverty reducing growth path. That is the challenge of long-term development, which requires better economic policies and more investment in human capital, infrastructure, institution-building, along with better governance and political stability. In order to evaluate our arguments, we analyzed economic indicators and index from the World Bank and International Monetary Fund before these countries enacted their economic reform policy and after they did, and verified our findings with data from the Central Bank of the respective sub-Sahara African countries. The study concludes by examining the feasibility of self-reliance as an approach to tackling the problems of underdevelopment in sub-Sahara African.

ECONOMIC REFORM FRAMEWORK

The existing literature on growth and economic development assume that foreign aid could supplement savings and thereby enable the country to maintain the level of investment desirable for economic growth. According to White (1974) as the economy grows, and incomes increase, the nation can afford to set aside an increasing proportion of its income in the form of savings. In this context, the supplemental theories are essentially directed at the attainment of self-sustaining growth.

The assumption about the growth of the economy and the capacity to save enough for the desired level of investment to a large extent ignores some of the basic impediments to economic growth in sub-Sahara African nations. The inability to grow over the past three decades is due to lack of appropriate technology, sound economic policies and political stability. Also, while the extent and level of foreign financial assistance necessary for the attainment of self-sustaining growth in the sub-region depends on political stability, there are problems in the attainment of the envisaged appropriate level of sustainability. Inflows of financial aid are generally based on other reasons, which are mainly political and strategic, rather than in the economic interests of the sub-Sahara African countries.

Sub-Sahara African countries have suffered considerable problems of exclusion in their political system over the past three decades. Lipset (1959), Almond (1970) and Bollen (1979) have pursued studies, which stress the need for institutional continuity and harmony, as a prerequisite for economic development. They argued that development and order are critical and disorder makes development difficult, if not impossible. In democracies, we would expect economic interest groups and the society-at-large as voters to be fairly powerful in relation to the state. This constrains national leaders in democracies to pursue policies that are largely consistent with the median preferences of vested interests. It also impels them to be concerned with the prospective adjustment costs their economies would suffer in the event of a breakdown in economic ties, and to be sensitive to the effects costly security policies have on their economies. Leaders may have similar sensibilities in some non-democracies if the dominant political coalition includes the internationalist economic interest groups we would expect to see as powerful in an open political system when economic ties are extensive, or the domestic-oriented interest groups we would expect when economic ties are not extensive. In many authoritarian regimes, for instance, the leadership is quite autonomous from societal forces. The institutional framework in praetorian politics may not effectively assimilate struggles between competing groups (Huntington 1968; Gordon 1974; Snyder 1990). Thus, narrow economic and non-economic interest groups with disproportionate influence can capture national policy and shift it away from the preferences of median economic interest. According to most scholars, political capacity must consist of disciplined, competent leaders and the establishment of rule by law, rather than by arbitrary decree. Such political capacity bolsters the inventor confidence crucial for long-term economic growth (Sandbrook 1990; Essien 1990; Ihonvbere 1994).

John Prescott (1972) and Mika Vehnamaki (1998) pointed out that the model of political processes that combine the interaction between public policy and geographical factors is mostly based on societal and natural environments. Once the policy is formulated and then implemented, a number of unperceived factors of the society and natural environments tend to intervene the political process and divert the actual policy outcome from the intended one. These societal and environmental factors would force the political leader of a nation to fine-tune the policy so as to make the outcome better correspond to the intended goals. Thus, economic policy can be treated as a political process that is compatible with Prescott and Vehnamaki's model. In Senegal, Niger, Guinea and Cote d' Ivoire the political leaders formulated the structural adjustment policy on the basis of the perceived factors of the societal and natural environments. However, as the structural adjustment policy was put through actual implementation, various unperceived factors came up to distort the intended objectives. Examples of such factors are a dramatic decline in trade, rainfall, ethnic conflict and sudden drought.

This view represents a significant step away from the previous conventional wisdom that developing nations' economic troubles were often derived from too much government (Lal, 1986). The World Bank itself, for example, was a major proponent of government retrenchment during the 1980's. But as mentioned above, recent analyses have come to focus more upon the type, rather than the scope, of state intervention. Lawrence Summers and Vinod Thomas (1993) contend, that governments have done too much of the things they cannot do well - i.e., regulating markets and producing ordinary goods - and too little of things they must do well - i.e., maintaining macroeconomic stability and making necessary public investments. In a similar vein, Jeffrey Herbst (1993), Julius Ihonvbere (1994) and Wayne Nafziger (1997) stress the lack of a legal and political system which could establish an environment that promotes business confidence as a key factor to economic decline in Nigeria and Ghana.

Current conventional wisdom contends that economic crisis acts as a critical "trigger" for reform (Bates and Kruger, 1993). Yet the nature of such crisis "triggers", as well as their specific relation to reforms, remain unclear (Waterbury, 1989). Indeed, many sub-Sahara African countries endured lengthy periods of severe economic decline or crisis before any reforms were initiated. For such crises failed to trigger reform until they impinged on the pattern of politics long cultivated by African statist regimes. Clark Leith and Michael Lofchie (1995) argued that a viable opening for reform usually occurred only after the "glue" of corruption and rent-seeking cementing the government's coalition of clients began to run out. Using Ghana as an example, Leith and Lofchie demonstrate how the government's carefully rent pool became subject to a tragedy of the commons problem, as more and more political clients were allowed to access to finite and increasingly diminishing rents. Once rent-seeking opportunities dried up, the political networks supported by such rents began to disintegrate. In Cote d' Ivoire and throughout sub-Sahara African, this initial unhinging of old statist networks created an opening that allowed political entrepreneurs to seize the political agenda and initiate economic reforms.

Decision making theories, most prominently prospect theory (Payne, et al. 1992; Kahneman and Tversky 1979), and provide this missing core of a convincing explanation. The central empirical finding of prospect theory is that people tend towards risky behavior when confronted with threats to their well being, but are cautious when facing auspicious prospects. Crises trigger bold actions, while the expectation of gains induces risk aversion.

Prospect theory maintains that people do not make decisions based on absolute levels of utility as conventional rational choice approaches assume, but in terms of relative gains and losses, using the status quo as their normal point of reference. Interestingly, people display a marked aversion to losses, which they take much more seriously than gains of equal magnitude (Kahneman and Tversky 1979; Tversky and Kahneman 1992). They imbue the status quo with a special legitimacy (Kahneman, Knetsch and Thaler 1990), defending it more fiercely than seeking further improvements.

Decisions therefore hinge on whether a person faces the prospect of gains or of losses. When faced with the choice between different possibilities of gains, people tend to select risk averse options. They regularly prefer a certain gain of smaller magnitude to a less likely gain of much higher magnitude even if the expected utility of the latter option (the product of its probability times its value) exceeds that of the former. In the domain of losses, however, many people opt for risk seeking: They shun a certain loss of small magnitude and prefer instead a "lottery" that contains the promise of avoiding any loss, but also the risk of a big loss. The aversion to a certain, if moderate loss induces them to choose this risky option even if due to the low probability of avoiding all losses its expected utility is lower than the limited decline of the former option.

As these striking findings suggest, people tend towards prudence in their efforts to advance, but are frustrated in their determination to avoid setbacks. When confronted with threats, they hedge their bets on the unlikely prospect of recouping the status quo, which risky choices offer, rather than accept a certain, yet limited loss. This willingness to run extraordinary risks in order to regain one's deserved position is reinforced by the common tendency to assimilate recent losses slowly (Kahneman and Tversky 1979: 28-87). Clinging to the previous status quo as their reference point, many victims of crises see any option that falls short of recuperating their prior position as involving losses. After suffering losses, people thus tend to select risky gambles that offer the (unlikely) prospect of breaking even, eliminate all earlier losses and recoup the old status quo (Thaler and Johnson 1990). People's unwillingness to adjust their reference point downward exacerbates their tendency towards risk seeking.

Risk seeking in the domain of losses provides the central impetus for the adoption of draconian reform programs and their popular acceptance. It explains why heads of government take highly risky decisions to enact measures that orthodox economists consider economically rational, but those politicians regard as politically irrational. Leaders who face severe crises tend to enact daring counter-measures and many people endorse these bold efforts to save the country. Dramatic problems put both leaders and citizens in the domain of losses and prompt a common tendency towards risk acceptance. Leaders can use the political capital they derive from their determined attack on the crisis to push through structural reforms. If these efforts lead to economic recovery, both leaders and citizens turn to risk aversion. Leaders therefore adopt more cautious policies, and citizens prudently accept the new development model, rather than boldly pushing for drastic further improvements. In this way market-oriented reforms achieve political consolidation.

Through its systematic treatment of shifts in risk propensity, prospect theory provides the core of a convincing explanation for the adoption, endorsement, and preservation of drastic neo-classical measures. This explanation accounts for the different steps of market-oriented reforms, which start with immediate stabilization measures, proceed to structural changes in economic institutions, and then - if successful end with the consolidation of the new development model. These different steps can be grouped into four turning points, namely leaders' decision whether or not to adopt a tough stabilization program; citizens' endorsement or rejection of these painful measures; leaders' political strategy for restructuring the country's development model; and¾in addition to the economic success of neo-classical reforms leaders' tactics for garnering sustained political support for the new market-oriented model. This sequence of turning points outlines the "branching tree" of reform politics. While many paths lead to stalled reform or political failure, some combinations result in successful change.

Most Sub-Sahara African nations initiate drastic structural reforms when two conditions coincide, namely a profound economic crisis and when new leaders assume power. When a country suffers from deep problems and the danger of further deterioration looms, prospect theory predicts a tendency towards bold choices designed to save the nation, even at great risk. New leaders act on this impulse and initiate draconian measures of adjustment and restructuring, while discarding more cautious and arguably more promising alternatives. Long established leaders, however, are reluctant to admit the failure of their earlier economic policies and drastically shift course. The loss aversion found in psychological experiments suggests that continuing leaders are unwilling to disavow their past efforts. Rather, incumbents are tempted to "throw good money after bad. And try to muddle through. New leaders, by contrast, disassociate themselves from their predecessors' failures, credibly shift course, and embark on dramatic reforms. Only new leaders who face deep crises therefore adopt market-oriented shock programs.

Whether a majority of citizens accepts or rejects these stabilization measures constitutes the second turning point. Painful reforms elicit widespread support if the population faces a profound open crisis. Hyperinflation, in particular, puts large numbers of people rapidly in the domain of losses and induces them to endorse leaders' risky efforts to save the country. By contrast, if the preceding government artificially suppressed severe imminent problems, many people do not see themselves in the domain of losses and therefore fail to support the bold choices of a new leader who seeks to preempt a severe crisis.

The willingness of many people to support drastic measures gives new leaders a stock of political capital that they can use to push through structural change and limit opposition to a profound transformation of the country's development model. How skillfully leaders use this asset and pursue their reform course determines the third turning point. Leaders have different strategic options: They can draw on their mass support to gain autonomy from established political and social interests and impose reforms by fiat. At the opposite extreme, leaders can negotiate with established forces and pursue reform through transaction. Both of these extreme tactics are suddenly changing course in Niger, Senegal, Guinea and Cote d' Ivoire. Rather than converting to neo-liberalism, leaders with a longer tenure are tempted to throw good money after bad ones and persist with policies that are similar to recipes tried before. The strong aversion to losses found in innumerable psychological experiments prevents long-standing incumbents from admitting defeat and embracing radically new policies." Rather, they desperately try to bolster the established development model through limited adjustments.

The consolidation of the structural reform and development model depends on its economic success and on governmental efforts to spread the resulting benefits to large numbers of its' citizens. Such improvements put many citizens into the domain of gain and thus induce them to turn risk-averse and accept the new, neo-classical development model and its initiators. While the long-term impact of neo-classical reform is still unclear in Sub-Sahara Africa, its medium term consequences differ strikingly. Particularly, in countries that suffered from open hyperinflation, neo-classical shock policies often produce rapid stabilization. However, in countries plagued by repressed inflation economic liberalization frequently has the opposite effect by unleashing an inflationary spiral. These differences in economic structure and in the character of the initial crisis affect the chances for consolidating structural reform policy.

REASONS FOR STRUCTURAL REFORM POLICIES

The changing global political economy with the demise of the former Soviet Union and the Cold War and the rise into prominence of Western financial capital and values partly constricted Third World nations to secure economic assistance for development efforts. Growing national debt, imbalance in international trade, low technological advancement and lack of monetary stabilization are also reasons why most Third World nations looked for measures that would bring about structural change in the economy. Indeed, economic crisis critically triggered the structural reform. This crisis further impinged on the pattern of politics long cultivated by Third World nations' corrupt regimes. However, letting the economy slide further could endanger leaders' political survival by triggering social unrest or military revolt. Facing clear prospects of losses, leaders tend to opt for bold reforms by embracing neo-classical policies. The key elements of these neo-classical policies are reduced government spending, privatization of state-run enterprises, currency devaluation, deregulation, trade liberalization, reduction of subsidies, and incentives to promote production for exports. For these reasons, leaders who have held office for years and who have unsuccessfully sought to stem their country's decline continue to implement old recipes in an effort to muddle through and avoid drastic change. That they had condemned before.

In other situations, new leaders are not tied down by strong commitment to the existing development model. They therefore respond to deep crises in the risk acceptant fashion predicted by prospect theory. When facing the failures of state-interventionist, projectionist policies, they boldly adopt drastic market-oriented reform.

POLITICAL LEGACY OR CENTRALIZATION

In Senegal, Niger, Guinea and Cote d' Ivoire where economic reform has taken place, are not new democracies. For instance, the governments in Senegal, Niger, Guinea, Benin, Mali, Togo, and Burkina Faso were military backed regimes. When the general economic development of sub-Sahara African nations in the sub-region is put in perspective, political stability constitutes an important critical variable. As a matter of fact, the ideal plan for economic development is a complementary political system that develops progressively without major conflict within and among its institutions. Political parties and pressure groups as well as other political institutions should become more articulated and consolidated to enable smooth transition from one government to the other. This would guarantee the atmosphere in which development issues could be continuously and effectively addressed. However, very few nations in West Africa enjoy political stability. Beginning from the second half of the 1960's many West African nations have experienced varying forms of political instability and rule of laws. The cases of economic reform in Senegal, Niger, Guinea and Cote d' Ivoire will be illustrated.

French speaking West African countries have experienced military intervention in government. In 1974, Niger's Hamani Diori was removed from government. This experience have been repeated in Burkina Faso in 1983, when Captain Thomas Sankara assumed power; in 1978 in Mauritania, when Moktar Ould Daddah was overthrown through a coup; and in Guinea in 1984 after the death of Ahmed Sekou Toure. There have about three military interventions in Togo since 1960. The Republic of Benin has also experienced about five military coups after its achievement of independence. The major reasons given by these coup leaders are the failure of the civilian regimes to promote economic growth and development. It is however, doubtful if all these coups could be justified in the face of continuous poor economic performance across the sub-region. In most of these military regimes, waste of resources had reached an unprecedented level while corruption had assumed a very high proportion. The emergence of several millionaires among the military junta is a sign that the army has not been efficient in implementing appropriate economic policies.

The policies of the military regimes in West Africa have become increasingly controversial, as they often lack sufficient understanding of the role of international communities in development. Rapid turnover of leaders have promoted discontinuity in programs, and has led to massive failures in the implementation of well-formulated economic policies prescribed by the World Bank and IMF, thus, sending wrong signals to foreign investors. Uncertainties in economic polices of sub-Sahara African nations under the military regimes have also led to the drying up of much needed foreign investment. The following section examines the reform policies that have been the main instruments of the military and non-military governments for economic development in most West African nations from 1980 to mid 1990's.

POLICY CONVERGENCE

In the 1980s export-led economic reforms were initiated by political elites Senegal, Niger, Guinea and Cote d' Ivoire who previously benefited from import substitution industrialization. An export led reform program provided a way for such elites to revitalize their authority and control over society (Kalher, 1990). Furthermore, since many of the reforms in a structural adjustment program can be instituted by executive decrees, initial commitment to a reform program provided an effective and relatively painless way for such elites to obtain external funding from the World Bank and the International Monetary Fund.

The structural adjustment policy (SAP) has been the major economic policy that had profound impact on foreign aid, self-reliance, and economic development in Senegal, Niger, Guinea and Cote d' Ivoire since the 1980's. Many countries in the sub-region adopted structural adjustment policy after the World Bank and IMF had advised them that the only way to overcome economic recession and establish the basis for sustainable economic growth and development was to reform their economy. The assumption was that most of the previous economic policies of West Africa nations, like those of other developing countries, have been inadequate and poorly implemented. Traditionally, sub-Sahara African nations enacted policies such as government supply of public goods, encouraging natural monopolies, information asymmetries and externalities which foster non-competitive behavior in their economy and result in market failures. Since these policies have, to some extent, shifted focus from self-reliant development, there are considerable doubts about their positive impacts on economic recession and promotion of growth and development in the sub-region. Partly because of this, the degree of commitment to the implementation of the program varies from one country to another. The programs have to a large extent generated a number of undesirable and unintended economic and social problems while attempting to promote growth i.e., increase efficiency, export foreign exchange earnings and reduced stabilized prices.

Cote d' Ivoire, Senegal, Guinea and Niger, among others, have embarked on various forms of structural adjustment programs. Generally, structural adjustment programs (SAP) in West Africa have the conventional Keynesian and neoclassical economics approaches to economic development. The broad objective is, the maintenance of the level and rate of growth while maintaining external balance (Osagie, 1987). The common approaches for SAP are deregulation, privatization, trade liberalization, foreign exchange price flexibility, financial structure reforms, and international cooperation (Nafziger, 1997).

The cooperation of the international community constitutes an important part of the reform package for Sub-Sahara African countries. The paucity of capital has generally been a limitation to the implementation of economic development programs in the past. Nevertheless, increase in financial resources would be required, as new projects would be proposed in the productive sector under SAP. The cooperation of the international community is expected in the promotion of better prices for commodity exports to increase the foreign exchange earnings of the adjusting nations and assist in foreign debt reduction.

Trade liberalization policy includes tariff rationalization of import licensing, and the elimination of marketing boards. Higher tariff and non-tariff barriers generate high effective protection rates that make domestic production inefficient and noncompetitive against foreign products. The rationalization of tariff will promote efficiency in domestic industries. The discontinuation of the system of import licensing will remove the channels for corruption, but the elimination of market boards will generate fresh problems (Olukoshi et al, 1994).

Financial structure reforms would, among other things, involve the expansion of rural branch banks and the introduction of mobile banks to the weekly run rural market day and the integration of the credit unions and cooperatives into the formal financial system. Nevertheless, as regards interest rate all deposit rates would be raised above the current or expected inflation rate to yield positive real interest on deposits, for this is the only way to attract savings into the financial system (Olaniyan, 1996). The relatively higher costs of credit would ensure that only projects with higher social rate of return are undertaken.

The structural adjustment policy prescribes the deregulation of utility prices in order to achieve cost recovery in the public supply of water, energy, transportation, and communication as well as other utilities (Phillips and Ndekwu, 1987). It is assumed that excessive regulation of public utility prices constitutes an important source of budget deficits. Deregulation will reduce budget deficits. But then, it should be pointed out that one fundamental problem of cost recovery is the inevitability of negative political and social effects. The principle of equity will be lost because this will reduce the supply of basic needs to the vulnerable groups in society.

Foreign exchange rate represents the core of the structural adjustment policy for most of sub-Saharan Africa. This is well illustrated for example in cases in Cote d' Ivoire, Senegal, Niger, Guinea, Togo, Mali and Benin. It has been central to the demand management policy. The measures suggested avoid the periodic shocks of currency devaluation in favor of smooth market-oriented currency depreciation resulting in market-determined exchange rates through Central Bank auctions or Forex bureau, in which commercial banks and private vendors purchase and sell foreign exchange on the free/open market. (Central Bank Report, 1996). It is calculated firstly that if foreign exchange flexibility is achieved, it will attract the inflow of remittances and other foreign transactions away from the parallel market and reverse capital flight. As regard supply-side price incentive, the flexible exchange rate permits the raising of producer prices to stimulate production and supply of export products which, all things being equal, should lead to increased export revenues, lower import costs as demand for imports falls, and therefore of improvements in the balance of payments.

Table 11.1 shows the pattern of growth of Gross Domestic Product (GDP) of sub-Sahara African nations, which have introduced the structural adjustment policy. The table also shows that although for most nations there was increase in the growth of their GDP in the first three years after 1985, nevertheless, growth declined for almost all within the period. All the eight sub-Saharan African nations, however, experienced a decline in growth between 1988 and 1990.

Table 11.1
Growth Pattern of GDP in West African Nations 1980-1990 (in percentage)

Country	1980	1982	1984	1986	1988	1990	Aver.
1. Cote d' Ivoire	-0.9	1.6	-1.0	3.7	-1.8	-6.1	-0.8
2. Senegal	-2.7	14.8	-4.7	4.6	5.1	4.5	3.6
3. Guinea	0	1.8	-2.7	7.1	5.9	4.7	3.4
4. Niger	4.8	-1.2	-16.9	6.4	5.0	3.1	0.2
5. Togo	14.7	-3.4	5.9	3.4	5.0	1.9	4.6
6. Benin	20.9	6.8	2.0	-1.7	1.2	1.1	5.1
7. Mali	-1.3	6.7	1.3	17.9	2.4	0.3	4.6
8. Burkina Faso	-0.1	10.0	-1.8	10.0	7.4	1.7	4.5

Source: Calculated from World Bank, African Development Indicators, 1992, pp.31-33.

The Republic of Benin, Mali and Burkina Faso had very weak growth rates, compared to Cote d' Ivoire, Senegal, Guinea, Niger and Togo. Mali had significant growth in 1986 but declined in the following year. Burkina Faso also had a major growth rate of 10 percent in 1986 but this dropped to 7.4 percent in 1988. By 1990 Burkina Faso's growth had drastically declined to 1.7 percent. In general, there has been no substantial growth since the introduction of the structural adjustment policy.

Table 11.2 shows the present state of Senegal, Niger, Guinea and Cote d' Ivoire economic growth. While Guinea introduced structural adjustment programs (SAP) in 1987, Cote d' Ivoire in 1981/82, Niger in 1985, Senegal in 1979, and Mali in 1982 their economy is still indebted to foreign institutions at a range between $1.7bn (Niger) to $18bn (Cote d' Ivoire) in 1996. The average Gross Net Product (GNP) of these nations after several years of SAP is $456 per year. While Guinea is able to bring down its inflation rate to four percent, and Niger 8 percent, the inflation rate of Cote d' Ivoire has increased from 10 percent in 1975 to 26 percent. Senegal's inflation rate has also increase from about 14.3 percent in 1975 to 32 percent in 1996. The inflation rate of Mali has equally followed the increasing trend in the sub-region from 9.6 percent in 1976 to 23 percent in 1996. The debt service rate as a percentage of export for these sub-Saharan African nations range from 15 percent in Guinea to 41 percent in Cote d' Ivoire.

The variation illustrated in table 11.1 and 11.2 indicates that Senegal, Niger, Guinea and Cote d' Ivoire have considerably better chances of attaining the minimum threshold of economic development than others attain. However, the problems of achieving a sustained rate of growth of per capita income are formidable, especially in the current era of high-energy prices. The causes of inflation constitute a major area of debate and uncertainty in the sub-region, but are generally related to imbalance between excess demand for, and inadequate supply

Table 11.2
Economic Indicator of Senegal, Niger, Guinea and Cote d' Ivoire in 1996

Factor	Countries				
	Guinea	Cote d' Iv.	Niger	Senegal	Mali
Population	6.7m	14.9m	9.4m	8.7m	9.7m
Year SAP was Introduced	1987	1981-92	1985	1979	1982
GDP	$3.2bn	$8.0bn	$2.2bn	$5.8bn	$2.7bn
GNP per Capita	$500	$650	$270	$750	$270
Foreign Debt	$2.9bn	$18bn	$$1.7bn	$3.8bn	$2.7bn
Debt Service as % of Export	15%	41%	33%	29%	19%
Inflation	4%	26%	8%	32%	23%

Source: Calculated from World Bank 1996 Annual Report. Washington D. C.

of goods and services. This imbalance in the nations under study relates to rising expectations, changing tastes, to an increase in the money supply with higher propensities for consumption than savings, and to changes in terms of trade, which make imported Intermediate and finished goods more expensive with particularly serious results in economies where the price elasticity of demand for such goods is low. The real growth in these nations will depend therefore, on their ability to decrease vulnerability to such import oriented inflation and to increase domestic productivity. Next, we shall examine these nations to find out what went wrong with their reform policies.

STRUCTURAL ADJUSTMENT POLICY CASES

Guinea

After the death of President Sekou Toure in 1984, General Lansana Conte emerged as the leader of Guinea. Economic reform under Conte commenced with the PIRN (Program Interimaire de Redressement Nationale), an interim program covering the years 1985 to 1987. PIRN was subsequently elaborated into PREF (Programme de Redressement Reconomique et Financier), a general structural adjustment program recommended by the World Bank and the IMF (Arulpragasam and Sahn, 1997).

SAP in Guinea attracted a lot of funds to the nation. The World Bank, IMF, and Paris Club financed 83 percent of all projects and gave Guinea credit worth $636 million during its structural adjustment policy period. Guinea was also permitted to reschedule its Paris Club debt in 1986. A further rescheduling of $205 million debt was also agreed upon in a new Paris Club agreement in 1992 (Olaniyan, 1996). Notwithstanding Guinea's potential resources in minerals and agriculture, it is classified among the twenty-five countries with the lowest per capital incomes in the world.

The aid flow to Guinea during its structural adjustment program was directed to areas of economic priorities. In 1985, 30 percent of foreign aid was toward the production sector, 23 percent to social and administrative infrastructure, 19 percent to economic infrastructure, 13 percent program assistance, and 9 percent to technical cooperation (Arulpragasam and Sahn 1997). Although economic infrastructure suffered a decline to 6 percent in 1986, it rose to 40 percent the following year, and later declined to 28 percent in 1988. Between 1986 and 1995 Guinea introduced economic reform policies that it assumed would lead to future economic growth.

Reform in financial sector in Guinea has been extensive, including complete privatization of the banking sector and issuance of a new currency. The facing out of many parastatals, moreover, has significantly increased the share of credit extended to the private sector. Despite these reforms, the Guinea economy remains relatively unmonetized. In some instances the implementation of planned reform has been incomplete or half-hearted, in others institutional and infrastructural barriers have hampered reforms undertaken. The Guinea case shows that price reform alone is not a panacea. Measures beyond price-oriented structural adjustment must be employed.

Senegal

Abdou Diouf succeeded Leopold Senghor as president of Senegal in 1981. As soon as Diouf took over office he introduced measures to liberalize and democratize the Senegalese economic and political system. The World Bank and IMF gave full backing to proposals on structural adjustment for the country and followed it up with significant financial assistance. The ultimate aim of the World Bank has been to ensure that Senegal emerges as a successful shop case for other African countries that are hesitant to adopt SAP as the path to economic recovery and growth.

The pattern of external debt since the 1970s has been a major cog in the wheel of economic growth and development in Senegal. Senegal's external debt between 1970 and 1980 increased from $131 million to $242.3 million. The implications of the growth in external debt for the Senegalese economy were driven home by the burden of debt service payments. This rose from a low 2.9 percent in 1970 to 10 percent in 1980. This situation in the 1980s called for an urgent solution to the accelerated growth of external debt. The structural adjustment program in Senegal came about as a result of economic stabilization reforms. In 1979 the government announced a Plan de Redressment towards the implementation of the reform. The World Bank immediately encouraged the Senegalese government to seek extended fund facilities of the International Monetary Fund to ease the implementation of the reform policy.

At the ending of 1992 the Senegalese economy was yet to get out of crisis despite the SAP policy. Although the economic performance indicated some improvement in the manufacturing sector by 18 percent in 1992 from 8 percent in 1983, it decline in the agricultural sector (Olaniyan, 1996). During the SAP period external debt of Senegal increased jointly with the burden of debt service payment. This negatively affected the ability of the nation to promote economic development.

Privatization, one of the corner stones of SAP in Senegal, has on the whole had a dismal record (World Bank, 1994). The social effect of SAP in unemployment, low education and health standard, raise considerable doubt about the future and relevance of the program. The number of unemployed people has risen to a record level as a result of cut in public expenditure, agricultural reforms and privatization. Education and health have also stagnated as SAP focused the attention of the government to other sectors, especially debt servicing. Finally, these developments elicit great concern because the problems are part of the issues the structural adjustment policy was supposed to address.

Niger Republic

Niger is one of the nations in West Africa that was affected by drought between the 1970s and 1980s. It is a poor nation despite the discovery and exploitation of uranium, which brought surplus budget to Niger toward the ending of the 1970s. A drop in uranium revenues from 1980 and the drought that plagued the nation caused its economy to decline.

Foreign assistance to Niger dropped during the first half of the 1980s from $64 million in 1980 to $52 million in 1984. These financial assistance, however, increased to $130 million in 1987 before dropping to $95 million in 1989 (World Bank, 1996). Recognizing the failure of its economic policies, the government enacted a stabilization program in 1983. The IMF supported this policy. In 1985, the government formally formulated its structural adjustment policy.

Niger structural adjustment policies have been biased in favor of primary activities - agriculture, livestock rearing, and mining. It has also favored import substitution rather than export promotion activities (Berger, 1989). In 1988, the modern sector supplied 27 percent of GDP, yet it employed just 3 percent of the labor force (Olaniyan, 1996). The modern sector is composed primarily of government administration, mining, transport, and commerce, which contributed between 12 to 45 percent of modern sector activities in 1988.

At the height of the economic crisis in 1985, the flow of technical cooperation amounted to 30 percent of total Overseas Development Fund. This assistance decreased to 19 percent from 30 percent in 1988. The commitments to production decreased to 17 percent in 1987 from 23 percent in 1985, and increased to 22 percent in 1988. Agricultural production was also adversely affected by drought. All these economic problems made Niger's indebtedness to represent 32 percent of its GDP in 1982, 50 percent in 1985 and 57 percent in 1988. In 1996 the government debt still stood at $1.7bn and the GNP per capita $270. The debt service rate was limited to 30 percent. Despite Niger's almost 12 years of structural adjustment policy; the nation has been classified as a debt distressed country.

Cote d' Ivoire

Cote d' Ivoire is one of the most advanced French speaking West African nations. Between 1965 and 1980, the nation had a remarkable growth rate. The GDP grew at an average annual rate of eight percent. Agriculture grew by three percent, and industry and services grew by 11.1 percent (Olukoshi et al, 1994). The main factor for this success is the nations comparative advantage in cocoa, coffee, and timber.

The increase in earnings from cocoa and coffee in the late 1970 encouraged the government of Cote d'Ivoire to borrow from abroad. By 1988 its external debt increased to $8.5 billion from $1.7 billion in 1975 (Nafziger, 1997).

At the same time the nation's debt service ratio increased from 9 percent in 1976 to 40.8 percent in 1987.

This economic crisis led to the introduction of the structural adjustment reform program in 1981-85, 1986-1989 and 1990-1992. The goals for this policy was to bring about a drastic reduction in the budget deficit, and to balance the overall external debt as well as stabilize the debt service ratio to 30 percent. SAP in Cote d' Ivoire was supported by World Bank loan aimed at altering the balance of manufacturing production away from relatively inefficient import substitution to the processing of raw materials for export. At the middle of the 1990s none of the SAP goals were achieved (World Bank, 1996; Olukoshi et al, 1994). Collapsing export earnings, which had dropped, by 60 percent of GDP resulted in a build up internal and external debts. The ill advised cocoa export embargo created a major foreign exchange shortage, prompting the postponement of scheduled interest repayment by Cote d Ivoire to the London and Paris Clubs. The banking system in the nation was also badly squeezed by liquidity crisis stemming from a decrease in cocoa earnings.

The case of Cote d' Ivoire is that of over a decade of sustained economic crisis, the nation's hope for the future still lies in improvements in the international terms of trade for cocoa and coffee. This notion really undermines the IMF and World Banks recommendation to structurally adjust the economy to be less reliant on cocoa and coffee. After several lean years in the late 1980s, Cote d' Ivoire's economy is now flourishing, having grown at an average of 7 percent in 1995-1996, with most economists predicting similar rates for the near future. Central to the turnaround has been the nation's emergence as a leader in the privatization of inefficient government owned enterprises such as national airlines, hotels and telephone networks, which has opened the door to private investment. These reforms have been critical in attracting foreign investors and the money necessary to promote local industry. Cote d' Ivoire's exports have been booming, due to the development of a sizable manufacturing base, a rarity in a continent mostly dependent upon agricultural production.

POLICY IMPLICATION

Three reasons could be given for the economic performance of Senegal, Niger, Guinea and Cote d' Ivoire. First, as far as exchange rate policy is concerned, the standard conditions of domestic supply and demand, as well as foreign demand, which hold to make devaluation successful, are often not satisfied. This is especially so because the retrenched technological structures do not easily permit the substitution of local inputs from imported ones. In case of nations whose main exports are primary commodities that are subject to quotas and whose prices are externally determined and whose imports are essentially (medicine, petrol, building materials, capital goods, spare parts, and so on, devaluation can only have a negligible effect on the improvement of the balance of payment. Secondly, SAP is based on the assumption that markets are competitive and those resources are perfectly mobile. It was for this reason that SAP recommended liberalization, deregulation and minimization of the role of government in resource allocation. In sub-Saharan Africa, however, there is the existence of market imperfection and non-competitiveness. This makes the structural adjustment program assumptions invalid in the sub-region. Thirdly, the justification of trade liberalization derives from the classical theory of comparative advantage that is not compatible with situations in which import elasticity's far exceed those of export. In the context of the present West African nations' situation, excessive trade liberalization is not a feasible policy in view of the projectionist practices of the industrially developed countries against exports from Africa. This action by industrial countries has caused large-scale unemployment and poverty in the sub-region.

The World Bank's report grossly underestimates the impact of external factors on the economic performance of Senegal, Niger, Guinea and Cote d' Ivoire that participated in the adjustment program. The collapse of the terms of trade and increase in interest rates was considered to be unimportant. However, the fact that Sub-Saharan African nations as a group have lost market share does not necessarily imply that the declining terms of trade have been unimportant to these nations.

The measures taken by the World Bank to correct this menace include (1) compensatory actions and transitional arrangements; (2) protection of the most vulnerable groups; (3) protection of the long-term interests of the population; (4) measures to ensure that the poor effectively participate in growth process. These actions may be in part of a structural adjustment loan or a sectional adjustment loan.

After several years of adjustment policies is sub-Saharan African nations better than before? Of course the answer is no. It is interesting to note, however that sub-Saharan African nations have reached the level of development where free movement of capital out of a nation should be allowed. The appropriate policy response to capital flight is not to legalize capital flow, but to make domestic investment more attractive. Adjusting the overvalued exchange rates and providing a legal framework that sets clear rules on property rights and thereby promoting investment is more important for reducing capital flight than any government control on foreign exchange. The task of improving economic policy making and the implementation of reforms could only be undertaken by African governments themselves, through a conscious decision to improve the efficiency of public administration.

Sub-Sahara African governments should enact policies that will maintain macroeconomic stability by limiting the overall budget deficit to a level that is sustainable through available external finance, and non-inflationary borrowing from the banking system. Managing an exchange rate system is not difficult when budget deficits and inflation are under control. After an adequate initial devaluation, which would lead to a slight under-valuation of the domestic currency, a crawling position can be used to maintain a competitive exchange rate. The main challenge facing sub-Sahara African governments is to reform their tax system by improving tax administration, and imposing efficient taxes and to prioritize government expenditures to support long-term growth. Sub-Sahara African government bureaucracies have to be restructured to support rather than supplant private-sector investment and production.

Sub-Sahara African governments should also enact broad-based agricultural development. Rapid growth of agricultural incomes would stimulate the demand for manufactured goods and services. The growth of small-scale non-agricultural enterprises in rural areas depends on the dynamism of the agricultural sector. Increasing specialization and commercialization of small holder production will stimulate intra regional trade. Diversification of agricultural export should be a priority in any agriculture-based development strategies. Each nation needs to put in place policies and institutions that can support a rapid increase in new investment based on small holder producers. Agricultural research should also be encouraged in the universities and funds provided by the government.

The role of public policy in Sub-Sahara African nations is to prioritize the allocation of resources, and to provide good universal primary education, vaccination against common communicable diseases, and information about family planning and nutrition. Effective implementation of policies to promote human resource development requires grass-root participation in local communities. Therefore, improving local governance is necessary if there is to be sustainable improvement in human resource development. Most government expenditures on health go to few urban hospitals, while inexpensive lifesaving preventive medicine such as vaccination of infants is not adequately financed. Conditions in government hospitals are generally appalling, despite the relatively large share of public expenditure that goes to curative medicine. Reallocation expenditure in the health sector from hospitals to preventive medicine cannot attain improvement in the health sector.

Reform of financial system, particularly increasing the availability of credit at reasonable cost would help foster development of the private sector. The lack of a developed financial infrastructure should not be used as an excuse for failing to promote the private sector. The economic crisis facing sub-Sahara African nations should serve as a challenge to their leaders. African leader should be innovative in taking advantage of the deep-seated economic crisis as an opportunity to articulate a development vision that will provide for their people. Fundamental reform policies are therefore, required to address specific concerns of each sub-Sahara African nation.

Finally, there may be no need yet for high optimism about structural adjustment policies in sub-Sahara Africa. The instruments for sustained economic development are yet to be fully in place in the sub-region. The dynamics of the reform policy are still unpredictable and mostly depend on external forces whose values are rarely compatible to the political and cultural tenets of the region. The policy makers in the sub-region will have to come to full grips with all these foreign values if structural adjustment programs are to be relevant to economic growth and development in sub-Saharan Africa. There is the need for African nations to embrace a comprehensive development strategy which has room for a developing country that is able to serve the public purpose without being insensitive to the need for economic rationality, political accountability, and long term stability. These sub-Sahara African nations should also encourage the democratization of their national economy and society in order to check tendencies towards the monopolization of power by a single leader.

CONCLUSION

In this chapter we took the state to be a set of ongoing institutions for social control and authoritative decision making and implementation. The sub-Sahara African nations covered are conceptually different in economy and society. Their inherent interest in expanding the scope for autonomous action, asserting control over economic and social interactions, and structuring economic and social relationship with advanced industrial nations is evidence in the trade and financial support they received.

Economic and political crises had a de-stabilizing effect on all the countries we analyzed. The capability of these nations to encourage economic development and maintain social stability during their structural adjustment reform policies was severely undermined by corruption and a lack of foresight by the leaders. In considering the influence of specific political leaders, we argued that both narrow economic interests and broader economic concerns are likely to be a strong influence in the negative impact structural adjustment has had in achieving particular economic and development goals. So too, do the ways in which institutions and structure power relations and allocated political resources that can be used to shape both economic and development agendas. The 1980s and 1990s have presented governments in Senegal, Niger, Guinea and Cote d' Ivoire with challenges, but this study indicates the extent to which they lacked the scope for innovation.

The general theories of foreign aid and development have limited application as seen in the cases of structural adjustment policies in Senegal, Niger, Guinea and Cote d' Ivoire. A number of critical variable peculiar to some nations do not wholly justify the conclusion and inferences drawn from these theories. The theory of self reliance, although sounding realistic and sometimes irresistible, is loaded with a lot of difficulties even at the stipulated first stage of its operation which primarily entails reduction in external dependence in the process of economic growth. This concept appears almost impracticable given the turn of events in the international economy in the last two decade.

Finally, though the political transitions promoted by economic policy reform in the sub-region remain in early stages, policy reform should generate further democratic implications. More significantly, the sacrifices and political will necessary to put economic integration into full operation are disappointingly lacking in sub-Saharan Africa.

REFERENECS

Arulpragasam, Jehan and David Sahn. 1997. Economic Transition in Guinea: Implications for Growth and Poverty. New York: New York University Press.

Almond, G. and Coleman J. (ed). 1960. The Politics of Developing Areas. Princeton: Princeton University Press.

Ames, Barry. 1987. Political Survival: Politicians and Public Policy in Latin American. Los Angeles: University of California Press.

Anyanwu, Aham. 1992. Nigerian Structural Adjustment Program: A Multi-Sectoral Analysis. Enugu: ABIC Books and Equipment Limited.

Asante, S.K.B. 1986. The Political Economy of Regionalism in Africa. New York: Praeger.

Benien Henry and Victor Diejomaoh. 1981. The Political Economy of Income Distribution in Nigeria. New York: Holmes and Meier, pp. 373-420.

Bienen, Henry. 1971. The Military and Modernization. Princeton University Press.

Bollen, K. 1979. "Political Democracy and the Timing of Development." American Sociological Review, 44: pp.572-87.

Briggs, Jean. 1981. " A Pint of Blood? or $20". Forbes. (October 12, Issue), pp. 91-98.

Callaghy, Thomas. 1993. "Political Passion and Economic Interests: Economic Reform and Political Structure in America" in Hemmed (ed). Responses to Africa's Economic Decline. New York: Columbia University Press. p. 479.

Cammack Paul, David Pool and William Tordoff. 1993. Third World Politics: A Comparative Introduction. Baltimore: The John Hopkin University.

Central Bank of Nigeria. 1996. Annual Report and Statement of Accounts.

Cribb, Robert and Collin Brown. 1995. Modern Indonesia. New York: Longman.

Dike, Enwere. 1994. Economic Transformation in Nigeria. Zaria: Ahmadu Bello University Press.

Drake, Christine. 1989. National Integration in Indonesia. Honolulu: University of Hawaii Press.

Esmara, Hendra. 1975. "Regional Income Disparities." Bulletin of Indonesian Economic Studies 11 (March Issue), pp. 44-58.

Essien, Efiong. 1990. Nigeria Under Structural Adjustment. Ibadan: Foundation Publishers.

Friedmann, John. 1972. "A General Theory of Polarized Development," in Growth Centers in Regional Economic Development. Niles M. Hansen (ed). New York: The Free Press, pp. 82-102.

Gordon, M. 1974. "Domestic Conflict and the Origins of the First World War". Journal of Modern History 46:191-226.

Graf. William. 1988. The Nigerian State, Political Economy, State Class and Political System in Post-Colonial Era. Portsmouth: Heinemann Press.

Herbst, Jeffrey. 1993. The Politics of Reform in Ghana, 1982-1991. Los Angeles: University of California Press, p. 160.

Hill, Hall. 1984. "Survey of Recent Development". Bulletin of Indonesian Economic Studies 20 (August), pp. 1-38.

Huntington, Samuel. 1968. Political Order in Changing Societies. New Haven, CT: Yale University Press.

Ihonvbere, Julius O. 1994. Nigeria: The Politics of Adjustment and Democracy. New Brunswick: Transaction Publisher.

Imoko, Dave O. 1990. "The Development of Nigerian Manufacturing Sector." The Nigerian Interpreter. (October Issue).

Kahneman Daniel, Jack Knetsch, and Richard Thaler. 1990. "Experimental Tests of the Endowment Effect and the Coase Theorem." Journal of Political Economy 98 (December): 1325-48.

Kahneman Daniel, and Amos Tversky. 1979. "Prospect Theory." Econometric 47:2 (March): 63-91.

Krueger, Anne. 1993. "Virtous and Vicious Circles in Economic Development." American Economic Review. (May Issue).

Lal, Deepak. 1986. "The Political Economy of Economic Liberalization". The World Bank Economic Review. (Vol. 1, #2), pp. 273-299.

Lipset, S. M. 1959. "Some Social Requisites of Democracy: Economic Development and Political Legitimacy". American Political Science Review, 53:69-105.

Lipumba, Nguyuru. 1994. Africa Beyond Adjustment. Washington D.C.: Oversea Development Council.

Nafziager, Wayne. 1997. The Economics of Developing Countries. Upper Saddle River: Prentice Hall.

Odetola, Olatunde. 1982. Military Regimes and Development: A Comparative Analysis of Africa. London: George Allen Press.

Olaniyan, Omotayo. 1996. Foreign Aid, Self-Reliance, and Economic Development in West Africa. Westport CT: Praeger.

Olukoshi Adebayo, Omotayo Olaniran, and Femi Aribisala. 1994. Structural Adjustment in West Africa. Lagos: Pumark Nigerian Limited.

Olukoshi, Adebayo. 1992. The Politics of Structural Adjustment in Nigeria. London: James Carrey Publishers.

Oke, B. A. 1990. "Structural Adjustment and the Role of the Central Bank of Nigeria: The Nigerian Experience and Future Direction". Central Bank of Nigeria Economic and Financial Review. Vol. 28, No. 1, pp. 36-38.

Onimode, Bade. 1989. Alternative Development Strategies for Africa. London: Institute for African Alternatives.

Osagie, E. 1987. "Problems of Structural Adjustment Programs in West Africa". in Phillips A. O. and Ndekwu E. C. (eds)., Structural Adjustment Programs in a Developing Economy: The Case of Nigeria. Ibadan: NISER, p.236.

Oyediran, Oyeleye. 1979. Nigerian Government and Politics under Military Rule 1966-79. New York: St. Martins Press.

Payne John, James Bettman, and Eric Johnson. 1992. "Behavioral Decision Research." Annual Review of Psychology 43:87-131.

Prescott, John. 1972. Political Geography. Methuen & Co Limited, London.

Phillips Adedotun, and Olu Ajakaiye. 1993. Nigerian Economic and Society: Economic Policy and Development. Ibadan: NISER, pp.9-20.

Phillips Adedotun, and Eddy Ndekwu. 1992. Structural Adjustment Programs in a Developing Economy: The Case of Nigeria. Ibadan: NISER Publication.

Quarcoo, P.K. 1990. "Structural Adjustment Programs in Sub-Saharan: Evolution of Approaches." African Development Review, 2(2), December Issue, p. 13.

Ranis, Gustav. 1995. "Another Look at East Asian Miracle." The World Bank Economic Review. (September Issue), 509-534.

Sandbrook, Richard. 1990. "Taming the African Leviathan". World Policy Journal. (Fall Issue), pp.673-701.

Shaw, Timothy and Julius E. Okolo. 1994. The Political Economy of Foreign Policy in ECOWAS. New York: St. Martin's Press.

Snyder, J. 1990. "Averting Anarchy in the New Europe." International Security 14:5-41.

Summers, Lawrence and Vinod Thomas. (1993). "Recent Lessons of Development". The World Bank Research Observer. (July Issue), p. 249.

Thaler Richard, and Eric Johnson. 1990. Gambling with the House Money and trying to Break even." Management Science 36: 643 -60.

Vehnamaki, Mika. 1998. "The Economic Geography of Ghana's Structural Adjustment." Scandinavian Journal of Development Alternatives and Area Studies.Vol. 17, No. 2 &3, pp. 61-71.

Wade, Robert. 1990. Governing the Market: Economic Theory and the Role of Government in East Asian Industrialization. Princeton: Princeton University Press.

World Bank. (1996). The World Bank Annual Report. Washington, D.C.

World Bank. (1994). Adjustment in Africa: Reform, Results, and the Road Ahead. Oxford University Press.

World Bank. (1993). World Development Report. New York: Oxford University Press, p. 296.

World Bank. (1990). World Development Report. New York: Oxford University Press.

Chapter 12

Politics in the Democratic Republic of Congo

François Muyumba

INTRODUCTION

The theme of this chapter relates to the overall state of Political Liberalization and Democratization in Africa generally, and more specifically in the Democratic Republic of Congo (DRC), which is an integral part of what scholars refer to as "sub-Saharan African states." The overall concern of the chapter is to critically assess the state of the transition movement toward democracy, which sub-Saharan Africa has been experiencing since the late 1980s. The struggle for political liberalization and democracy in Africa can finally be regarded as a part and parcel of the global struggle for human rights, civil rights and good governance.

The task at hand is to demonstrate once for all that the struggle for democracy is one of the longest struggles sub-Saharan Africa has waged, in the most recent time. Though successes in the battle have been rare at best, and delayed at worst, the last two decades of the 20th century burst in front of us with the birth of a new world order. Its first proclivity appeared as an internal struggle within the Eastern Europe, threatening the very existence of the Soviet Union, and later destroying it as many of its states acquired their own independence and freedom. The iron curtain was quickly grumbling to the grounds while it shrunk down the wide divisions between East and West, and exposed to the entire world, the devastating socio-economic and political conditions under which Eastern Europeans lived! Second, the sudden fall of the Berlin Wall on November 9, 1989 promised the rebirth and unification of the greater German state. Thirdly, the Romanian revolts against their autocratic rule, culminating in the physical elimination of the Caucasus on December 25, 1989.

For Africa however, it was the forth and most momentous event, the liberation of Nelson Mandela from prison after twenty seven years and his immediate return to politics, that awakened and d gave hope to Congolese people as well as to the rest of sub-Saharan Africa. All these events, including the flood of Eastern Europeans into Western Europe provided a strong impetus to democracy seekers everywhere. For sub-Saharan Africa organizing into a democracy movement must now pursue the illusive democracy. Not only was the objective of such movement to challenge the autocratic regimes but also to demand their rapid replacement as apart of the new progressive search for a better life on earth. The political opposition groups so far marginalized and muffled in the region would intensify their demands to bring the established order and authorities to reason.

As the likely success of such efforts depended on the strengths and weaknesses of the anti-democratic responses provided by the autocratic regimes, most opposition parties and regimes adopted the non-violence tactics and approaches that tended to be more effective in exposing the weaknesses of the entrenched authoritarian state. All of the sudden, the lack of "democracy" and/or "democratization process" turned the continent on its head with the worsening political and economic conditions as an "Open Sore" (Soyinka 1996), on its bloodied face. Every African state could no longer ignore nor underestimate the people's quest for liberalization and democratization. It is important to posit that the quest for liberal and democratic apparatus had already been in high gears and resembled the greater quest for desalinization and liberation Africa had known in the 1960s. The new movement for democracy in sub-Saharan Africa, and in the Democratic Republic of Congo (DRCongo) itself was nevertheless not yet distinguishable from what had been the skirmish hit and run assault on the state. One needs to realize that what was new this time, was the seriousness of the commitment and sincere efforts democracy seekers and their movement exerted toward the determination to bring forth the political liberalization and democratization as "a moral imperative"(Nzongola 1998:11), and which globally could no longer be denied. People all over the sub-Saharan Africa were interested in the transition to a new socio-political and economic relationships between the different segments of one society, between and among the political actors within one nation, as well as within a region, and above all, between the old way and new way of conceptualizing and constructing a just and more progressive society.

The modest effort attempted in this chapter is to focus primarily on the case of Democratic struggle in the Democratic Republic of Congo (Zaire). I will also outline the nature of the challenge faced by both ruling autocracy and the opposition parties in their effort to create a period of transition from autocratic rule to a more open political process. The theories and practices of democracy is best described by the apparatuses of governance and their transformation and readjustment would be cautiously treated especially from the vantage point of their ability to pass the test of accountability, transparency, fairness, justice, equity and civility. This chapter cannot be completed without examining the colonial legacy and its implication for democracy in the Democratic Republic of Congo.

THEORY AND FRAMEWORK

The democratic implications of democratic society are plainly evident in the term itself. But we also have, in previous chapters, noted that there are other political ideologies that subscribe to the principles of popular sovereignty and political equality. According to Robert Dahl (1971), if political power is not equally distributed, those who exercise such political power cannot rightly claim political legitimacy.

Whatever our view of human nature, it has immediate implications for our political preferences as we shall read about Mobutu's regime. However, when a nations leader choose between democratic and authoritarian options, their choice automatically implies a view of the nature of human beings. What divides democrats from authoritarians is their conclusion about the following: the extent to which each individual is capable of self-development without the aid of superior authority. The authoritarian according to Marcus Ethridge and Howard Handelman (1994) has a dim view of what man can accomplish on his own. Plato, for example, considered that most men were uniformed about their natural capabilities. Without enlightened guidance from absolute political authority (authoritarian leader), they were unable to develop their capabilities, and consequently were unable to ensure their own happiness and justice of the larger social order.

The democrats, on the other hand, according to Robert Dahl (1971) regard man as a basically rational creature, neither mire as in sin nor dependent on a superior authoritarian leader for the fulfillment of his individual potential. The individual himself argues Robert Dahl (1971) is best able to understand his own needs and interests. The individual's continuing efforts to improve the circumstances of his/her life are also likely to contribute to the betterment of the whole society, and this in turn explain why progress is considered a major characteristic of those societies in which human beings are free to define and pursue their own welfare.

The main point of democracy was that all individuals ought to have an equal opportunity to demonstrate their particular capabilities and that their circumstances of birth should not jeopardize their chances of proving whether they have these capabilities, that in short, everyone should have an equal opportunity to show how unequal he or she is. Popular consultation is thus a key element of democracy. It means that citizens of a nation have a real opportunity to be heard and that this opportunity occurs at regular, and fairly short intervals. Thus, democracy requires the acceptance and applications of the principle of majority rule. Robert Dahl (1971) contend that democracy means that when citizens disagree about a political decision or candidate, as the virtually always do, then the decision made or the candidate selected will be in accordance with the wishes of the larger group of people.

The theory of democracy when applied in Africa should hold African leaders responsible for the present crisis in the continent (Sklar 1987; Robert and Rosberg 1985). Sub-Sahara African political leaders should focus on the means by which a democratization of the political system and a liberalization of the economy can combine to promote sustainable development that is beneficial to all citizens. To what extent did the various regimes of the Democratic Republic of Congo (former Zaire) applied the democratic theory? How have the citizens of this sub-Sahara African nation benefited from their political system since independence? These are question that are addressed in the rest of this chapter.

THE COLONIAL LEGACY

From a historical perspective, the Democratic Republic of Congo (former Zaire) was born out of the Belgian colonial empire in sub-Saharan Africa. Belgian Congo became the Republic of Congo, on June 30th, 1960. Later the country became Congo- Kinshasa, and Democratic Republic of Congo, and finally in 1971, become the Republic of Zaire. What is interesting about this change in names is that, the country was undergoing several changes reflecting the political will of the central authorities and especially distancing itself from the democratic tradition. These changes were not always welcome by the Congolese people, but they nevertheless constituted the symbolic cultural chocks that were building up until they were able clearly define the Neo-colonialist state and force citizens to speak out against them. Congo-Kinshasa, it should be recalled, emerged from the colonial era as a multiparty state. The Congolese people had since 1954 successfully and logically organized themselves along large socio-ethnic groupings, some of which such as the Alliance de Bakongo (ABAKO) became well-established socio-political organizations in the Provinces. ABAKO regrouped the Congo peoples, "Lulwa Freres" the Lulwa people, Movement Populaire Luba, all the Luba people. Many of these had small branches in different cities and towns, In the later years, especially toward 1959-60, there were National Movements such as "Le Mouvement National Congolais" (MNC), which were actually established after 1958 with Congolese delegates returned from the All African Conference organized by Kwane Nkrumah as part of the celebration of Ghana's first anniversary as an independent State. The conference prepared the African leaders from everywhere to launch their own struggle for independence. No party was ever national as longer as the Belgians were concerned, because the colonial structural arrangement considered each province was an entity by itself. So, "Le Parti Solidaire Africain of Antoine Gizenga and Cleophase Kamitatu regrouped the people from Kwilu district and from the city of Kinshasa (Léopoldville). Le Parti National du Peuple (PNP) de Jean Bolinkango etc. regrouped the people from Equatorial province. Quite often the selection of the name of the party reflected the level of projected party's scope of influence, some time the name did not symbolize anything. Other political players such as Colonel Joseph Desiré Mobutu and Laurent Desire Kabila were not anywhere closer to the centers of decision-making. And it is our understanding that both had no known membership in any of independence movements including MNC-Lumumba. Like all African political parties, Congolese political parties emerged out of the so-called "Independence Movements" and this is why it is not difficult to account for the overwhelming lack of political preparation and experience for most Congolese leaders, including Patrice Emery Lumumba in the 1960s.

The political history of the Democratic Republic of Congo unfolded in the midst of change that the ordinary citizens, and some times well-placed politicians could not themselves control. Before June 30, 1960, Congolese were becoming radically bold in their demand for immediate independence. The riot of January 4th, 1959 served as symbolic outcry for freedom. By June 30. 1959s, emerging leaders and colonial government functionary were spending a month to six months in Belgium on special training. There was an intensification of nationalist sentiments as there as well sentiments for the creation of Belgo-Congolese communities, but thereafter, the conflict of interests between Congolese and the liberal Europeans appeared. There were also the Western and Eastern blocks tensions whose offshoots affected the embryonic African worldview, and delayed the successful arrival of true democratization process. For the Democratic of Congo, (then Republic of Congo), independence would be gained through the concept of one-man one vote. Congo like other colonies was apprehensive about the potential participation of European settlers in the election of 1960. Thus, the cry for one-man one vote was calculated to guarantee the victory of the Congolese over the Belgian colonialists who might have wanted to falsify the results of the elections. Indeed often, this notion was apparently utilized in the elections of 1994 in South Africa. The African masses in all colonies supported democracy and agreed to participate massively in then first elections to express by voting their determination to see them freed from the colonial bondage. Indeed, this should not be taken lightly because the situations in Mozambique and Angola did exactly what the Congolese had avoided.

THE END OF DEMOCRACY IN CONGO

In September 14, 1960, Mobutu, then just a newly promoted to the rank of colonel and appointed Chief of Staff in the newly reorganized Armee Nationale Congolaise (ANC) --Congolese National Army advocated the abolition of multiparty political system. He succeeded, at least temporarily in convincing the Congolese that his intervention, through the September 14, 196o's coup d'Etat was prompted by his frustration with politicians and the democratization process that precipitated the decay of the governing authority, and he accused the legislators of the first Parliament for "playing politics for politics sake." Mobutu regarded the Political fiasco of the 1960-1965 era as a result of the multipartism gone mad. The young colonel Mobutu announced his intention clearly in September 1960 that he was "neutralizing all the political leaders." (Dolmas, Jeune Africa, 1960 in Heinz et al, 1969:6). This action was, according to comment attributed to President Kwame Nkrumah whose role in UN politics in the Congo was not negligible, Nkrumah affirmed that:

> "Colonel Mobutu's action was subversive, that Ileo's government was fraught with illegality, and furthermore that Kasavubu and Lumumba were the only legitimate authority in the Congo."(Heinz et al., 1969:24)

In reviewing the Congolese political history one finds that the central authority in Kinshasa was unable to control and manage the vast country in terms of security, military and police communications, without neglecting the significant problems in economic trade between Kinshasa and the rest of the country. There was also a clear lack of appreciation of the time necessary to render the democratization process more effective and functionally risk free. The process of the first elections should have been staggered to allow the masses to gradually become familiar with the art and process of elections. All was done at once, and all the sudden the power of the mass was not longer exercised to punish or reward the elected officials who might have misconduct themselves. That is there was not enough time and resources disbursed on the preparation of Congolese to understand the rules of the democratic politics.

In search of power and its legitimization, Mobutu and his young bureaucrats and Para commandos hunted down the Lumumbist and other leaders sympathetic to Lumumba and his party (MNC). The quest for liberalization and democracy became synonymous with the anti-Mobutu sentiments, and thus, the democratization process was stillborn before it had actually begun. Despite scholar's engrossment of Lumumba's significance, as a nationalist hero, his contributions in the ninety-day tenure, are meager and unknown because they cannot be documented accurately.

Mobutu's experience in the other hand, including the conflicts of 1960-1964, reinforced his determination to gain control and command of the military hardware, technology and autocratic management of the state as well as the preparation and expansion of the Armed forces so that together, they might play a decisive role in the future struggles for power. And in the defense of the nation. Consequently, the Coup d'Etat of September 14, 1960, not only succeeded to neutralize Kasavubu and Lumumba, but it also inaugurated the military intervention in liberal politics, and finally the beginning of unstable and illegitimate governments. As maintained in the official documents of the "Parti de La Revolution Populaire" (PRP):

> "At the beginning came the Coup d'Etat of September 14, 1960 which interrupted the democratic tradition of the republican institutions, leading toward the crisis, the lack of power whose consequence was the indignation and the profound disapproval by the people, a popular insurrection exploded, in 1963, in

> Kwilu, and from 1963-1966 in the eastern provinces of the country, whose end required several foreign military interventions (my translation). (PRP. 1967:1).

If anything, Mobutu's coup d'Etat led to Lumumba's untimely death in January 17,1961. The attempts to return the country toward the democratic norms were suddenly interrupted by the second "coup d'Etat" on November 24, 1965, closing the chapter on Congolese experimentation with true democratization process. (PRP. 1967:1). Joseph Kasavubu--the first President and Moise Tshombe, — the Prime Minister, had tried once again to bring the rule of law and democracy in 1964-65. It is important to remember that the 1965 elections were well organized, and people had voted massively, for Moise Tshombe and his coalition of parties (Conaco) emerged victorious. Tshombe himself had accepted to return to Congo from his exile in Europe to play an important role in reconciliation and resolution of the crisis that had separated the Lumumbist from other Congolese politicians who had promoted such structures as federalism and confederation. Tshombe had been successful in attracting investment in the Congolese economy in 1964, and in changing the overall economic situation. It was logically just that he should develop a strong ambition to head the government of the Second Republic.[i] It is also believed that he had expressed the interest to enter into the contest for the presidency. Tshombe's tenure as a transition Prime Minister was tremendously successful. He had succeeded in mobilizing an army of Congolese and mercenaries to route out the rebels in Kwilu, Kisangani and Kivu. He was also able to bring Congolese together in an attempt to forge a national integration as well as an economic program to fight inflation and ascertain some level of Congolese well being. Many Ladies in Kinshasa welcomed Tshombe's economic mirables, because the cost of living went down suddenly. Tshombe's accomplishments cannot be dismissed only on grounds of his anti-nationalist sentiments and his preference of federalism. He actually was responsible for bringing the rebellion in Kwilu, Kisangani and Kivu to an honorable end. Tshombe was thus able to carve his place in the center of Congolese politics by also bringing the Katangese army and leaders back into the Congolese Political family. This is clearly reflected by his efforts in integrating the former Katangese army into the "Armee National Congolais" (ANC) and working at reconciliation with other politicians, especially through the nomination of a new Commission charged with the task of drafting the 1964 constitution. This did not rest well with Mobutu's allies whose plan was also to have Mobutu become the military leader of the second Republic. Once again, Mobutu rose to neutralized Tshombe and Kasavubu. A careful analysis reveals the fact that with the integration of the ANC, Tshombe had succeeded to introduce some of his well-trained officers in the ANC who could have easily contested for higher ranks than Mobutu, and who could thus have replaced him as the head of the Congolese Armed Forces. Hence ended the quest for "the Second independence" by the Mule list rebels, and the prospect for democracy under a Tshombe government in the Congo.

For the next twenty years (1965-1985), The nationalist parties and their followers who had vehemently opposed Mobutu's rule, remained only in shamble, their demands for the legitimization of the governing apparatus, democratization and equitable distribution of resources now only ghost ideas. The ruling autocracies across the sub-Saharan Africa provided a comfortable platform for Mobutu to deal more readily with the solidification of the strict military systems, and experimentation with the one -party system. (Ghana, Nigeria Egypt, Malawi, and Tanzania). The autocrats were convinced that they could simply acquire power militarily and impose their patrimonial authority through decreed policies from above. This was the period of "elephant projects" which were intended to serve the external investors more so than to build lasting infrastructures that would respond to the aspirations and needs of the citizens. In the Democratic Republic of Congo (Zaire) such project as the "Inga damn on Western Congo river," and the Telecommunication center, and other skyscrapers in Kinshasa as well as the City of L' OAU in Galiema, to say less of the grandiose Gbadolite--Mobutu's North -Western home- village in Ubangi, with all its shielded bunkers, were intended to show case the prestige among the nations of sub-Saharan Africa, and the world despite the generally miserable conditions under which the Congolese/Zairian citizens lived! These costly projects closed even further the windows of opportunity for the democratic ideas to blossom. They did not promote the rule of law as the most important foundation for democracy and better governance.

In the 1990s the course towards democracy became the most difficult task for authoritarian regimes in sub-Saharan Africa, Democracy seemed to easily turn into a burden for most developing nations. Indeed, within the context of the Democratic Republic of Congo (Zaire), and the current war of aggression, there seems to be a definite effort to delay the democratization in the belligerent countries of Congo - Kinshasa, Rwanda, Burundi and Uganda. The first configuration deals with Mobutu's autocratic regime, and its existence as a product of the colonial legacy, and a real manifestation of the" anti-democratic forces in the country." The problematic of democratic politics being disruptive in the Congo-Kinshasa, spread rapidly to Nigeria, Togo, Central African Republic, and other countries. This was followed by the institutionalization of military regimes and then the One- Party system. "The Democratic of Congo," is a, misnomer since democracy has never been practiced or institutionalized in the country. Like many other sub-Saharan nations, Congo-Kinshasa failed to adopt the principled practices of democracy as suggested by Sørensen above. The second configuration is Kabila's lukewarm attitude toward democracy and yet, it appears that so far he remains apparently reluctant to accept the overwhelming demands for the institutionalization of democracy and the democratization process which, when followed rigorously, does not guarantee that those who hold power today will necessarily have it after the elections. The very important ideas about democracy and better Governance are discussed in subsequent sections below.

Kabila's three years rule does not give us enough data to consider in critical analysis of his performance and his intentions for the future of the country presently at war. Kabila carries a heavy burden presently because the country he liberated from Mobutuist is now aggressed and occupied by his former allies-- the neighboring armies of Rwanda, Uganda and Burundi. Indeed a few observers wander if the politics of self-preservation might not dictate that Kabila holds on to the mantle of leadership while the war goes on longer, and the bargaining for democracy takes second place among the other priorities. Can it be said that Kabila's presence at the helms of power has not perpetuated the status quo and delayed the arrival of the rule of law and democracy? Does democracy work well in a fragile and dysfunctional state? Where then is the choice for Kabila's State in context of world politics and the sheer sensitivity for democratization process by the people of Congo-Kinshasa?

KABILA'S STATE AND THE PROSPECT FOR DEMOCRACY

Mzee Laurent Desiré Kabila, 59, emerged in 1996 as a spokesman for an obscure organization known as "the Alliance of Democratic Forces for the Liberation of the Congo"(ADFL). The title "Mzee" reminds me of Mzee Jomo Kanyetta who as the first President of Kenya, run the country with an iron hand. Kabila was probably the oldest of all the members of this alliance. As the senior spokesman of ADFL, Kabila rapidly gained Congolese and other people's respect because of the speedy and successful execution of war whose stated objective was to overthrow the devilish Mobutu's rule. Kabila's successive victories from town to town, and from province to province, soon reached the heights that he could no longer be ignored by December 1996. Congolese intellectuals in Diaspora who had been so adamantly opposed to Mobutu, and who had been so effective in reaching the centers of decision-making in the West, were so surprised by Kabila's successes in handing Mobutu's forces defeat after defeat, and moved fast to look at him closely to determine for themselves what he was planing to do. Several high level emissaries were of the All North American Conference on Congo (ANACCO, then-- ANACZA), were dispatched to meet and talk and gather information on Kabila and determine who were his allies, what were their intentions and what were their project of the society.

By mid-January, 1997, ANACCO (then ANACOZA) had established closer business links with the Kabila, and could thus advice the opposition forces in Kinshasa, and elsewhere (Muyumba, 1997). ANACCO contributed enormously to the success of the Kabila's Long March from Kivu to Kinshasa. Kabila's life-long revolutionary activities made him Mobutu's opponent for thirty-seven years. Kabila had cut his political teeth as a follower of the nationalist leader, Patrice Emery Lumumba who becomes the first prime minister of the independent Congo in 1960 (The New York time, April 11, 1997). For almost two decades, Kabila had been known as a committed Marxist who waged a low-grade insurrection in the mountains of eastern Congo. He is a member of the

Balubakat, a Luba group from Katanga province, who quickly gained popularity wherever his movement won control. From October 1996, Kabila's Parti de la Revolution Populaire (PRP) of about 30.000 members, including well-trained men led by officers from Rwanda, Uganda and Burundi Armed forces, established the ADFL and launched their campaign Against Mobutu. Kabila signaled to the Congolese that he was not safe and that he was in danger of being killed when in a TV. Interview, he related "I am not certain whether or not I will make it to Kinshasa alive." But he did certainly make it to Kinshasa in mid May 1997; seven months after his Allied forces first entered the Congo (then Zaire). Kabila proclaimed himself President of the Democratic Republic of Congo, on May 17, 1997. If the victory against Mobutu was sweet, his self- investiture into power was never well received by the civil society, the religious communities and by the main internal opposition parties (UDPS, PALU and PDSC), and by others who know very well the political history of the Congo. So, though loudly applauded as victorious and champion commandant of ADFL forces, Kabila will immediately face sour music because his allies failed to muster the intensity and volume of the aspirations for democratization of the political apparatus.

A sophisticated and crafty internal opposition well established and well led by imminent leaders reacted vigorously, to Kabila's autocratic postures, and then created the politics of silence to allow Kabila time to formulate his agenda, and his policies. Looking back, Kabila would have wanted to meet personally with major leaders of opposition to determine exactly where they were politically, and where the nation was socially in relation to their quest for a more democratized Congolese state. Indeed there were already many things Kabila and the opposition shared: All opposition groups were united in the ideas that: Kabila wanted a free and sovereign Democratic Republic of Congo. They despised Mobutu's personification with the state, which leads to the cult of personality; they sought to disengage anti-democratic politics. The internal Opposition had feared that Kabila might be a regionalist who would push for the division of the Congo into separate states and why not smaller nations. But from the beginning, Kabila and Allies refused to meet on one-to-one with the leaders of the internal opposition. It is possible that many of Kabila's advisers are estrangement fearful of the power of the opposition, especially in the Capitol city of Kinshasa where the grassroots movements had already acquired its own mind, and could not accept a new form of dictatorship!

NEW THROBING FOR DEMOCRACY

Given their past experience with Mobutu, it seems that the internal opposition could read Kabila's actions even before he had relayed them to the people. Kinshasa is a very political city, it has been the seat of the state for almost forty years and thus true politicians do nothing less than to engage in predication of the actions of the leadership. Also, the population of Kinshasa is among the most politically educated population one can find any where in urbanized world community. Many Congolese from all walks of life retire in the city, and are able to carry on their traditional affinities as well as their professional connections. Many of these people are religiously committed to social change, and they do whatever is possible to participate in the creation of a new and dynamic society. Kinshasa with a population of almost seven millions people, is a microcosm of the Congo. It is highly integrated, and people appreciate this amalgamated culture. It is from this context that leaders of opposition emerge. These are individuals who live above the ethnic racial and religious divisions, and are committed to the idea that there is a better way of conceptualizing a better and just society. Hence they are a resource that a new comer cannot neglect to meet. Nevertheless, the opposition groups were disappointed that they could not meet privately with President Kabila. Any such meeting could not be possible without, the rings of security provided by the Rwandan and Ugandan officers. Even when Kabila solicited the meeting, contacts between him and the Congolese opposition parties were not conducive for the heart to heart exchange discourse. Already Kabila had measured the temperature about liberalization and democracy very well. Since 1982, the opposition activities had ceased to be a one party business, several parties and civil society groups including the non-government organizations (NGOs) were involved into the quest to bring about a greater liberalization of Mobutu's One-Party State, The internal opposition was no longer a business of one person, one Parti, etc. who could be removed, imprisoned, banished and relegated somewhere. Kabila's closest advisers and respected Congolese members of his inner circles ended up being old Mobutists from Katanga and other who often misadvised in his dealing with the internal opposition. For example, before the end of 1997, Kabila banished all political parties, and decreed that there will not be political parties in the Democratic Republic of Congo. He also had Tshisekedi roughed up at his residence, arrested secretively at night, interrogated, and then relegated to his village. Many outstanding citizens, and former office-holders in Mobutu regime, were arrested and kept in prisons for long time without having been judged and/or found guilty for wrong doing. Such actions did not set well with the civil society, which knew what the Sovereign National Conference has done and regulated. The above analysis appears to be severely negative. However they are mild compared to the reactions of the Congolese who knew Mobutu's political actions and who believe that Kabila was becoming another Mobutu! The relegation of Tshisekedi to Kabeya-Kamuanga, his hometown. In Kasai, can be regarded as the last drop of water on an already full bucket of water. It radicalized the internal opposition groups at home and abroad and re-launched the efforts to maintain vigilance over the conduct of the Kabila's State.

Despite cautious advises provided through back channels to the President, the expected wise responses never appeared. It should be understood that ANACCO emissaries to Kinshasa did not refrain from encouraging dialogue between Kabila and the opposition. Some of Diaspora's efforts resulted on the positive and corrective actions that led to some liberalization and release of political figures from their detentions. Although the president is still popularly regarded as hero, Kabila's political actions such as the abolition of all political parties, his creation and establishment of the " Comité Populaire du Peuple ,"--(People's Popular Committee) which indeed resemble Mobutu's MPR committees. And his reliance upon military and police to resolve politically negotiable matters, makes him resemble more and more to Mobutu, - the incarnation of anti-democratic, anti-human rights, and anti-justice President. Those who know Kabila more closely find him to a descent man, exceptionally gifted, and able to "work with everybody".

Kabila's wartime government was is an illusive institution. It has been very difficult to find many of his pronouncements and to determine policies from general observations. From August second, 1998 to the present, the country has been occupied in both North West and North East and Eastern provinces. According to international reports, tremendous violation of human rights, and women sexual abuse are committed daily by the occupying forces from Burundi, Rwanda and Uganda. All these forces were once allied with Kabila and penetrated the Congolese Armed Forces Archives, and even participated in removing from the Congo some of the sophisticated weapons the Armed Forces had acquired under Mobutu. Some Officers from the Rwanda, Burundi and Uganda, even passed for Congolese, and could thus be appointed as Chief of Staff of Congolese Armed Forces. So on August 2, 1998 when the war started, the country defense forces did not have secured channels of communication, and as it known, even the President's phone calls etc. could be monitored from afar!

On positive side, is Kabila's ability to rally the Congolese to the cause of the nation? I was impressed and moved by the president's appeal to Congolese nationalism, and his success in mobilized the different segments of the Congolese community to fall behind him. Without this support, Kabila's regime would have been out of power by July 10,1998. The regime has been shaped by the war, and therefore it is able to withstand the coordinated assaults from Rwanda, Uganda, and Burundi. Kabila's defense tactics were also impressive, as he succeeded to get a needed and crucial support from Angola, Namibia, and Zimbabwe within few days. The war and its effects is now a source of worry. First, Kabila was able to expose the Aggressors' plot, and to identify the Rwandan Tutsis led by Kagame whose intent was and is still to carve a piece of Congolese soil as part of their plan to rebuilt the old Tutsi empire. Kabila also predicted that this would be a longer war, and that the nation needed to mobilize itself to confront such challenge. While these words were being release, the Ugandan and Rwandan forces were being flown some 2,500 mile to the west coast of DRC to occupy major military basis at Kitona, occupy the city of Matadi, and the Inga dam on the Congo river basin. Kabila, created the feeling that Kinshasa population was very important in the defense of the nation, and in speaking plainly about what was at stake, he succeeded mobilize the people (Personal notes on war, 1998).

The politics of the Africa's World War I, is that almost ten African countries have sent military in the DRC to help the Congo as well as the aggressors. Both UN and the Organization of African Unity are working without break to attempt to resolve the crisis. But the way it looks now, certain Western interest groups, which are backing the aggressors, are nowhere in harry to end the war. The war is now used to deprive the Congolese government from having access to its mineral resources and use it for the reconstruction of the Congo.

The Congolese people are seriously concerned about the future of their country and are demanding that uninvited and aggressive forces from Uganda, Rwanda and Burundi withdraw from their soil. This is why, as we shall discuss below the Civil society, the non-governmental organizations (NGOs) the government, and the opposition parties got together on the February 9-11, in a consultation sponsored by the Religious and NGOs to prepare the Inter-Congolese dialogue recommended by the Lusaka Cease-fire Agreement. (IRIN)

As the result of the consultation conference, President has called for elections to take place on May 10, 2000 in the areas still controlled by the government. The opposition parties are questioning such a short notice for elections. Nevertheless, the call was delayed from may, 1999 because of the war, and it seems that the president hope to achieve his promise that he intended to the rule of law and democracy.

The liberal members of the "Legislative Council" mounted the most effective challenge against Mobutu's One-Party State. First, they managed to hold hearings on the performance of different governmental departments and used those hearings as a legitimate opportunity to question the moral, ethical, and legal ground upon which certain important decisions were made. They were able to expose through their reports and archives, the mismanagement of public funds and the betrayal of people's aspirations, trust and hopes.

Mobutu's efforts to resist this legislative intrusion into the executive domain quickened the pace toward a showdown between himself and rebellious MPR legislators who were critical of the regime. The National Legislative Council" becomes one of the more radical insiders who sought to exercise its full oversight authority over governmental affairs. In the final analysis, the theoreticians (Sørensen (1993), Nzongola (1998), Mazrui (1986), and Leslie (1993) saw the action of the Legislative Council as an effort to gradually force Mobutu's hand to liberalize not only the discourse toward democracy, but also the process within which the one-party state functioned, and perhaps later, seek to transform the entrenched Mobutu's state (MPR). The consequent results of those revandications were the adoption of the same concerns by the Congolese civil society. The opposition leaders in the other hand, suffered severely from interrogations and humiliation, beating an imprisonment, and banishment to their villages, where there were no running water, electricity, newspapers or TV stations. Many outspoken and radical opposition politicians, such as Etienne Tshisekedi, Antoine Gizenga were sent to secret prisons and tortured and they do carry on their bodies to this day, the branded insignia of Mobutu's MPR."

THE GRASSROOT MOVEMENT IN THE QUEST FOR DEMOCRACY

In Congo/Kinshasa (Zaire) "The Thirteen," as they came to be known generated a highly critical document calling for a multiparty system, free elections and Mobutu's resignation."(Leslie 1993, 55). The group quickly became the major opposition force, many of its members and allies facing imprisonment in 1981, and many tortured. Although the "Thirteen" constituted a very significant opposition group they did not get recognized as "L'Union pour la Democratie et le Progres Social (UDPS) (Union for Democracy and Social Progress.), until late. By 1988, UDPS finally established itself as the defacto second party with sizable internal and external supporters, It had attracted well educated and nationally well known members and leaders, and it had inspired the emergency of supportive grassroots movements in every province, which was able to withstood Mobutu's familiar practice of doing the impossible things to create internal division and defection in any opposition group. Furthermore, Mobutu's Armed Forces terrorized, arrested, interrogated, imprisoned and banished his political opponents. But, even after this defection, UDPS and Etienne Tshisekedi persisted as symbols of opposition in Congo-Kinshasa (Zaire). As Leslie 1993 observes:

> Tshisekedi himself has been under house arrest and exiled several times throughout the years for illegally organizing and holding mass rallies condemning the regime. Refusing to be coopted, he soon came to represent democracy for Zairian citizens (1993:56)

It is perhaps better to observe that from the very beginning, UDPS was a moderate organization in its aims. Its leaders sought "to effectively play their role as legislators and members of MPR, and strove to become an independent voice within the context of the existing apparatus. Its rise in the late 1980s was to establish itself as the second party in the country, and gave the people an opportunity to choose between itself and the dominant state party, MPR. In this way its goals included the establishment of a pluralist political system to replace the existing one-party state' (Leslie, 1993: 56). Certainly the increasing quest for liberalization and democratization elsewhere in the world was always preceded by the intensification of "oppressive and economic actions characteristic of the autocratic states of the late 1980s, The UDPS rode the tide of popular dissatisfaction, becoming one of the more radical in its demands and the ultimately call for the complete dismantling of the Mobutuist system" (Leslie, 1993: 56)

A fairly complete analysis of the Congolese quest for liberalization and democratization must therefore be weighed against two competing controversies concerning the dilemma facing the Sub-Saharan Africa and its appreciation of Democracy. Namely, the need to determine whether democracy is an alien idea that needed to be imported from somewhere, or whether, it is a universal concept that might apply differently to varying contexts and time. It should be noted that in the context of Sub-Saharan-Africa, and particularly in Congo/Kinshasa the political power remains in the hands of autocratic leaders who most of time were unwilling to yield it to any electoral process by which power could be lost, or bargained away. In Congo-Kinshasa, Mobutu's autocratic state of the late 1980s to early 1990s, did not tolerate the rise of a strong Civil Society, and therefore, the civil society was not well organized and the grassroots organizations were not recognized unless they became armed rebellions. Thus the question of whether power can be acquired by the use of the forces (coup d' Etat) or by the open elections where electors voice their choice freely and in the privacy of a booth begs for an answer.

Nzongola (1998) discusses the above controversies in regard to the feasibility of democracy and democratic governance in contemporary Africa by considering the following two important aspects: There are those who see cultural and economic obstacles to democratization in Africa. For some, "democracy is an alien phenomenon that is being imported into a society whose culture places more emphasis on the community than on the individual, and is furthermore incapable of internalizing liberal democratic values." (1998:10). Sørensen (1993) suggests that there are four possible pre-conditions that might ease the transition to democracy. Each pre-condition sets a stage during which the actors must fulfill certain things. Together the pre-conditions raise critical questions about what patterns of economic, social and cultural conditions are most favorable to the attainment of democracy. For others, "the economic preconditions for democracy, include the need for a solid middle class," creating an impossible problem for the societies where their absence abound. Nzongola (1998) posits the notion that

> "Africa is a repository of human values that are fully compatible with the very foundations of democracy as a political concept. Unfortunately, these values were undermined and thus stunted, in their development, by both colonial oppression and post colonial misrule.' (Nzongola, 1988:10).

Furthermore Nzongola argues that, "there is no need to Africanize democracy, the key demand of the moment is rather to democratize Africa." In other words, If democracy is a universal ideal, it cannot be imported or Africanize because the latter in already everywhere. (Nzongola, 1988). He points out that "Democracy is not an exclusive property of Western societies. Democratic norms and principles are universal. But the institutions which inform democracy and the concrete forces of its political practice may vary in time and space (i.e., through historical epochs and from country to country)." (Nzongola, 1988)

Elsewhere, historians have established that pre colonial, Sub-Saharan Africans, experienced a measure of democracy at the village level and, indeed, beyond in larger political communities. As in some other places in the world, in addition to tyranny and other forms of rule, African practiced democracy. As a universal form of rule with specific manifestations in time and space, democracy is a political concept rooted on three underlying ideas, namely, democracy as a value, a process and a habit-forming practice. "Democracy is above everything else a moral value or "imperative."(Nzongola 1988). It is a basic human need, a necessity, and therefore a political quest of all freedom loving human beings. "Imperative" implies a permanent aspiration of human beings for freedom, for a better social and political order, one that is more human and more or less egalitarian (Nzongola 1998:11).

Congo-Kinshasa, like all human societies, aspire and strives to improve its material conditions of life as well as its latitude of freedom--whatever the real situation might be. Such pressing need can easily become a necessity, or even a political demand for a new social project of the society, especially when people's socio-political and economic situations deteriorate, or when there are periods of unyielding crisis. (Nzongola 1988) Kwame Nkrumah used to caution Africa to seek first" the political kingdom, and everything else would be given to you."(Armah 1974). Classically, most enlightenment philosophers--Rousseau, Voltaire, Montesquieu and Diderot Nzongola (1998) says "were interested in building here on earth the Augustinian heavenly city with all the trimmings of up-to-date natural science, humanism, the ideas of progress, etc. In 19th and 20th centuries, Karl Marx came closer to creating the Augustinian city with even better, stronger and more useful material in order to attain his utopia of egalitarian and non-conflitual society. This is a society without social classes but with enough material wealth for all! This is where the progressive idea of democratic value of individual human worth and solidarity that are evident in the writing of the philosophers and Karl Marx and fit well into the mold of the African social fabrics where the individual is not only an individual but also a social beings. Nzongola also pointed out that "moral decay, together with the destruction of the economic and social fabric of our countries by postcolonial dictators, --[Such as Mobutu}--, has compelled all freedom loving people to rise up in a new social movement for political change."(Nzongola 1998: 11). Currently, the struggle for democracy in the Democratic Republic of Congo has become as a moral imperative from which neither Kabila nor Congolese citizens can escape.

DEMOCRACY AND THE PROJECT OF SOCIETY

One of the major challenge facing the Congolese government today, the absence or the appearance of such absence of a clearly defined project or vision of the Congolese society. It is important to determine whether democracy can be regarded as a perfect system or not. Scholars (Mazrui (1986), Nzongola (1998), Sorensen (1993), and other) believe that "as any other human construction, democracy is better understood as a continuous process of becoming. In this sense "perfect" implies a utopia that the people, the institutions and the people, and the governance strive for. Democracy can never be perfect, but it is ideally the best mechanism in promoting equal access to fundamental human rights, and civil liberties for all (Mongolia). 1998:12) This discussion supposes that the quest for democracy leads to the demand for the fundamental human rights of the human person to life, and security; the freedom of religion, assembly, expression, press, association... economic. Social and cultural rights. This implies that the quest for democracy is meaningless when it fails to satisfy the basic needs of the population. Above all, democracy involves the quest for the rights of the people to seek and attain their inalienable rights to self-determination. Accordingly, one must admit that the democratization process now underway in the Democratic Republic of Congo, is a logical consequence of the non-fulfillment of peoples' expectations at the independence time, and all through the long tenure of Mobutu. Such quest will not be ended by the arrival of Kabila, or any other autocratic leader. Such quest is furthermore, a reaction to the failure of the postcolonial Congolese state to realize the national project of society, namely genuine independence, national integration, economic development, and social justice (Mongolia 1988, 13). Like Africa itself, the Democratic Republic of Congo is even now, still thunderstruck by the torments of regionalism and tribalism and indeed the likely success in democratization will require democratic institutions that stand above the fray of ethnic fear and prejudice.

DEMOCRACY AS A POLITICAL PRACTICE

The Republic Democratic of Congo has not had the opportunity to involve a democratization process whose practice improves and enhances its application and implementation of the rule of law. Here I am more concerned with the deliberate decision of the society to place certain limits upon it so as to allow the system and process of democracy to become familiar to the people. It means that there must be a rule of law that governs every aspect of decision-making. From the President on down to the people, or their elected representatives, democracy should be involved in all decision- making. Inside of the political parties as well as at the level of towns, urban centers, and cities, no decision should be made arbitrarily without the full participation of the people concerned. Democracy in this manner involves the specific manner of organizing and exercising power in accordance with certain universal norms and principles. Nzongola and Lee (1998) have outlined the following universal principles of democratic governance, which can easily be applicable in the Congolese situation:

1. The notion that legitimates power or authority emanates from the people. (Ibid. 14). It is the people who exercise power either directly or indirectly through the elected assembles. Elected executives, or some other mode of representation (dignitaries in lineage heads or elders in some African societies).

2. The concept of rule of law ("Etat de droit") refers to the fact that power should not be arbitrary, and that a set of rules or regulations with respect to its limits and mode of operation must circumscribe its exercise. The parameters of state power and sphere of governmental authority and influence must be well defined and limited so as to allow other social actors to participate well (Mongolia 1988)

3. The principle that rules are chosen and are accountable to the people suggests that democracy is government by consent of the governed. It is the governed that must approve not only the rules by which they are administered, but also the rules by which they themselves live as well as their policies are latter implement (Nzongola 1988, 14)

The challenge in the latter case is the ability of a system to be accountable to the people for their acts. Accountability is so severely a part of Bantu traditions, that in some Bantu Kingdom, traditional rulers did not accept to become kings until in the late years of their life. Because a failure to be accountable...to show power and its consequence, led leaders to death. They had to pay the supreme price if they were unable to account for wind, rain--storm, lightening etc. things that caused miseries to the entire community.

4. The People's right to participate in the management of public affairs through free, transparent and democratic elections, through decentralized governmental structures; and through non-governmental organization (NGOs). This is where the right to organize freely, political and trade union pluralism, and the independence of the organizations of civil society from the state.

5. Democracy and the government: Sorensen (1993) recognizes the people's right and responsibility to change the government that no longer serves their best interest or the right to revolt against such. The American constitution makes the citizens responsible to be the watchdogs of their government. Civil War was fought to make sure that the Government of the people by the people and for the people shall not parish from the face of the world." Since democracy recognizes itself to be, a government of the people by the people and for the people, the people have the responsibility to replace it with a better government. (Nzongola et. al., 1998:14)

In the DRCongo, the rebels have used this practice to launch their opposition to autocratic power. The dilemma however has been that when armed forces are used in any struggle, the victorious military groups always want the biggest piece of the pie while they do not sometimes have a clearest vision of what kind of society they wish to create.

DEMOCRACY AND INTERNAL FACTORS:

Scholars agree that the primary stage of the struggle between the forces of the status quo and those of Change is the effect of the internal conditions and culture. The democratization process is often affected by contradictions between the deepest aspirations of the people and the leadership. Nzongola and Sorensen both agree that when the opposition is made up of deserters from the ruling circles of the old regime, the leadership tend to focus on vengeance and retributions of their former allies than in transforming the state radically by democratizing it and increasing its capacity to serve the people. Nzongola is categorical in asserting that "fanning of ethnic conflict and the destruction of economy by rulers who exploit crises to remain in office. Do constitute violence against democracy." (Nzongola 1988, 16-17). The quality of the political culture prevalent in a country defines the internal factors. The Democratic republic of Congo may have to seek the creation of a political culture that is principled by the respect for the democratic process of open debate, transparent decision-making than on deal-making among politicians, It is a serious problem when leaders fail to honor the agreements to which they subscribe in negotiations. The Western governments through their intermediary do not trust Kabila on ground that he is able to slip, out of some treat and agreements that he find disadvantageous to him and to his people. This is not bad at all if the trend does not become a familiar practice. But such practice is indeed dishonorable as already discussed above.

DEMOCRACY AND EXTERNAL FACTORS

Dependency on resources provided by external power reduces the possibility of democracy. (Sørensen, 1993:25-27). Ndengwa (1996) examine the status of the Non-governmental organizations (NGOs) and concludes that over-dependency on external resources may be anti democratic, especially as the organization looses a genuine commitment to democracy. Nzongola posits that the objective conditions of current globalization process do not favor democracy. He further explains that" dogmatic assertion of virtues of the market in face of growing inequalities and social exclusion, even in the very centers of developed capitalism, is a sign of an anti-democratic tendency to discourage an open debate on alternative economic models,"(Nzongola 1988, 17).

Accordingly, Nzongola (1998) and Sørensen (1993) believe that..."democracy does not fall from the sky," "it is brought forth by individuals and groups who fight for it (Sørensen 1993:29). Democracy movement which produced the first governments in sub-Saharan Africa, and in Congo-Kinshasa particularly, could not have been fully prepared elsewhere to quickly generate permanent and dynamic apparatus through which political relationships could be defined and maintained. Certainly the concept of " one-man -one vote" adopted in 1957 and reinforced recently in 1994 elections in South Africa provided a smooth transition from the colonial and racial autocracy to postcolonial state, but democracy could not be upheld in a society which had emerged from a divided settings, beset with ethnic fanning and regional allegiance cultivated during the colonial era. Indeed the Neo-colonial state jumped at every occasion for a chance to present its paternalistic clasp to the new power. The preconditions for democratization were subverted by the sudden interference by external forces into the Congolese internal context. While in the 1960s Mobutu, and the latent interference by Rwanda and Uganda in imposing Kabila and ADFL in the normative and progressive process of democratization. What is meant here is that any take over of power by military means interruption of the normative process, which requires peace, negotiation, persuasion and bargaining and adherence to decisions are the only reinforcements of democracy.

PROSPECT OF DEMOCRACY IN CONGO

The review of efforts of the opposition to seek Liberalization and Democratization in the Democratic Republic of the Congo requires an examination of the events that impacted the country quest for independence in the 1960 and the event that followed its attainment. One must assume that there were two major and overwhelming struggles. The struggle for equality and justice in the era of colonial domination that focused on the improvement of workers' wages, and socio- political circumstances. The Belgians did not understand the gravity of these demands and aspirations by the Congolese to build here on earth the Augustinian city. The colonial authorities failed to grasp the deep meanings of economic independence and responded only to political quest for indigenous role within the political arena, or political independence as an alternative. The Congolese first tasted elections in 1957. When urban elections were organized to elect representatives to the city councils and mayors. The second experience took place in the general elections of May and June and led to the elections of the first representatives into the national assembly. One can indeed conclude that until 1957, Congolese had not formally belonged to any political party. If they did, the case of ABAKO, they were not recognized an official party, and they did not speak about democracy and independence because those ideas and the conceptual frames of reference stood for words not tolerated in the colonial expressive language. So the period from 1957 to 1965 can be regarded as the era of mobilization and political consciousness. But not really an era of democracy. The struggle for self-determination sought equality, independence and self-expression. Hence in language as well as in attitudes and actions, the people became creatively outspoken, and they would sometimes use coded language to really communicate. Meanwhile, though the struggle for independence was successful, its most difficult stage-- democratization-- could not be conquered without a serious effort on part of the state, and in cultivating and promoting the universal principles and their practical application to political situations facing the people.

A successful attempt was made to show that Mobutu came to power with some clearly stated objectives and goals. In 1961, and again in 1965, Mobutu was led to believe that the challenge to country was to find the most acceptable formula defining the criteria for authoritarian rule. It is clear that to Congolese, the lack of democracy was the absence of a democratization process that clearly defined the rules of the game. The events that followed the granting of independence to the Belgian Congo in 1960 were not primary underwritten by tribalism or ethnic cleavages as many have attempted to claim (Young 1983:138). The external factors greatly out weighed local events, and led the way toward the divisions that were consequences of forces unseen and uncontrollable at this stage. Mobutu's behaviors, acts and policies were predominantly anti-democracy.

In the same fashion, we have attempted to show that Kabila's war against Mobutuist forces in 1996, and his preoccupation with current aggression against the DR Congo by Rwanda Burundi and Uganda can perhaps be fanned as causes for interruptions to the democratization process. A case in point has been the postponement of the elections scheduled for 1999, which are now called for to take place in May 10, 2000. Such a short notice can be very easily be construed to be a direct assault on the democratization process. According to Sørensen (1993), the term democracy comes from the combination of two Creek words: *demos* (people) and *kratos* (rule). The concept that democracy is " *rule by the people*," may sound innocently straightforward, but it immediately raises a number of problematic issues with regard to time. Context, and past history. Both Held (1987) and Sørensen (1993), suggests a critical review of the following few questions:

In the Congolese context, *those who are to be considered "the people"* generally refer everybody who is defined ethnically. The Congolese are primordial ethnic individuals; the potency of ethnic mobilization would be incomprehensible without recognition of its primordial dimension. Ethnic consciousness rests upon shared symbolic meanings, emotionally laden and deeply rooted, which can trigger fears, anxieties and animosities. The capacity of these affective symbols to apply "we" and "they" demarcations lies in their ability to project themselves as primordial attachments--however novel or ill-defined a given unit of identity may be (Young, 1985:140). If democracy is a form of government, then the DR Congo has had a major problem in determining just how the choice of one or the other form of government should be made. In most colonial territories, which sought independence in the 1960s, there was no time to question and understand the notion of democracy. Actually, African accepted the easy concept of "one-man-one vote without worrying about the complex demand that the majority accept the burden and responsibility to protect and safeguard the interests and rights of the minority. Even as we live and observe the working of democratic system in Western societies, certain countries such as Italy still stands out as sore thumbs with their complex democratic system. With over sixty political parties competing for leadership of the national government without mandate from the largest majority of the mass! Generally in Africa, political parties, like democracy itself, remain illusive, especially as their statement of purpose and self-definition fail to actualize the "rule of the people by the people for the people." That is, despite the notion that democracy existed in for of the palaver (1993), modern political apparatus still do not promote equal access to the centers of decision making!

In classical Plato's view, democracy in Athens refers us to the possibility of decay in a context where the historically marginalized poor come to power through the majority of their vote, or defeat of the righteous bourgeois and refuse to follow the established laws and order. Here Plato points to wiser men, philosophers --the educated elite-- as those who ought to provide necessary leadership. Aristotle in the other hand viewed "democracy "as the government devoted to serving the poor and argued in favor of a combination of monarchy and democracy, especially with intent to create a balance of power between the poor and the wealthy. Apparently, with the decline of Athens, the debate about democracy was put in the back-burn for a long time. It is also known that in the feudal society of Middle Age, "power was not vested on the elected bodies. It was based on rank that could be attained only through inheritance or by force (Sørensen, 1993, p.4).

The modern concept of "democracy" did not emerge until the 19th Century, and so, though democratic ideals and principled institutions existed elsewhere, they did not exist in Africa in modern forms. However I recognize that Africa's ruled by the council of elders, which in many incidences was a representative body characterized by bargaining debate by the elders where "decisions by consensus" dominated the patterns and practices by Kingdoms and Empires. Crude dictatorship and tyrannical rules were incidentally not practiced throughout Africa. Elsewhere in Western Europe however, democracy is traceable to Renaissance period. This implies that before the middle age autocracy was the form of government most found in Europe. From Renaissance to Nineteenth century, ideas about democracy took shape in the context of the new discourse between autocratic rulers and the growing free and economically self defining Civil Society, coupled with the development of modern industrial-period with its social classes and their relationships.

Given the restraining colonial conditions imposed upon the Africans, and deliberate efforts to deny access to quality education, especially political education, the principled ideals and practices of democracy as "rule by the people" could not emerge nor have a chance to be developed in colonial Africa generally, and much less in the Belgian Congo. After a period of hundred years of colonial autocracy preceded by brutal enslavement period, Congo had no chance but to familiarize itself with autocracy. As a young boy growing up in the Belgian Congo, I can still remember clearly that certain expressive terms such as *liberty and liberation, freedom and independence, equality, democracy, socialism and communism and racism* etc., constituted a group of words and concepts whose usage in daily life was very offensive to colonial rulers, and thus remained constrained if not altogether banned! Toward the late 1950s, any insinuation of these words placed one in danger of being arrested, interrogated and imprisoned, and lashed. As Adam Rothschild (1999) relates, Belgian colonial agents had a free hand and took liberty with Congolese who resisted their orders.

> To Europeans, Africans were inferior beings lazy, uncivilized, little better than animals, as beasts of burden. In any system of terror the functionaries must first of all see the victims as less than human, and Victorian ideas about race provided such a foundation (Rothschild 1999, p.121)

THE ZARIAN STATE AND DEMOCRATIZATION PROCESS

By November 1965, Mobutu's arrival into power was a total break down of the democratization process and the return to the centralized authoritarian rule imposed from above during colonialism. First of all, in 1961, Mobutu's military security officers wearing cowboy hats tortured people who were accused to be allied with Patrice Lumumba, or allied with his political party. In Yolo Sud, my neighbors were beaten and put in the trunks of black limousines and taken away never to be seen again. In 1965 it was clearly the establishment of a wedge between the Military regime and the forces of democracy. The process of class formation and political socialization, which is under girded, by the democratization process experienced serious set back. As Sørensen (1993) cites Barrington Moore whose account of the roots of democracy and dictatorship concluded that a vigorous and independent class of town dwellers has been an indispensable element in the growth of parliamentary democracy. No bourgeois, no democracy" (1993: 57). This implies that Lumumba or not, Congo's early aspirations for democracy were a wasted energy, because most Congolese did not become bourgeois over night after colonialism! The Civil wars and ethnic conflicts were the logical prolongation of the struggle for, genuine liberation that ended suddenly with the death of Patrice Emery Lumumba. The arrival of Lumumba at the head of Congolese government in 1960, interrupted plans by external forces that inspired first of all, the secession of Katanga under Moise Tshombe, and the nullification, of the sovereign decision of the people as an expression of the General elections of 1960. Mobutu having been so instrumental in Lumumba's demise, made the regime of Kasavubu vulnerable to charge of usurpation of power. Joseph Kasavubu, the First President of the independent Congo, had been elected to the leadership of ABAKO, to the leadership of the Commune of Dendale, to the House of Representative, and to the Presidency. Kasavubu the Democrat, was willing to listen to the voice of the mass, was intrigued to participate in debate and bargaining for coalition and cooperation with other leaders. As matter of fact, Mobutu from his college of Commissioners set up as a shallow government and an anti-democratic institution marginalized Kasavubu.

Mobutu's overall concern was how to legitimize his rule, stay in power longer, and manage to become a bourgeois rather than respond to a new set of quests regarding the merit of liberal democracy as a vehicle for bringing political stability and social progress. The college of commissioners represented a government of appointed officials who in fact were responsible to nobody. The *external factor* as a pre-condition to democracy reflected the support Mobutu received from the West. Hence as the country was thus divided into three leadership groups: Kasavubu in one hand, Mobutu and the college in another, and Patrice Lumumba's followers in the other. The ruling class under Mobutu had no political culture, and therefore it created its own characterized by involvement in all intrigues and physical elimination of adversaries to legitimize its claim to power, and maintain such power through all means possible. There was no precedent of success in electoral process, or by the well-established institutions that could preferably could facilitate the success of a democratization process. Hence the clash between the ruling class and the civil society emerged because Mobutu thought that politics should be run as an efficient military system.

By 1965, the Congolese Civil society was predominantly poor and powerless, and very dependent upon the centralized authority of Catholic Church and its international connection, the emerging Protestant Council with its international supports, and the determined labor organizations still in their embryonic stage. Indeed not strong basis for the democratization. The Congolese mass at large could not have been well organized into solid political parties, and its loyalty was tested by its state of being very poor and kept so much in periphery so as, to be without voice nor power to impact the centers of decision-making. For example, the colonial structure had left behind budget lines for Church schools, Lay schools and private schools in the hands of the centralized authority. Thus to pay teachers and other, schools staff, one had to beg to receive Governmental subsidies. It was not an easy task to try to rebel against such a sure sources of resources.

In the context of Mobutu revolutionary rhetoric's, democracy pursued by the political parties of the 1960s had turned the nation into political decay that went nowhere, and stopped everything from progressing. Mobutu regarded all politicians as capable of colliding in an anti- nationalist politics. Mobutu, chose autocracy and militarism as the most efficient political process in a struggle to raise the standards of life and economic progress. Hence from 1965-to 1997, Mobutu increasingly worked on establishing himself as, dictator more so than in builder practitioner of democratic way of life. Some of his early attempts at democratization failed miserably because in most cases Mobutu was the only candidate for the president, and people were forced to vote for him or against him those who voted against him faced tortures and death. A good example was the university student at Lovanium and Kisangani who always voted in red. Mobutu would send troops to torture them and sometimes he denied them scholarship as result of their stubbornness. Of course in order to legitimize himself Mobutu had to publicly hang, torture and banish leaders who contested his leadership. Who in such context would raise his/her voice in defense of democracy and the democratization process?

TSHISEKEDI AND THE QUEST FOR DEMOCRACY

The birth of the Third Republic was expected, but how does one attain liberal democracy without a clear democratization plan? Usually the conservative--forces of status quo organize to maintain autocracy. The deliberate effort by Mobutu and cronies to challenge the democratic forces, especially. Etienne Tshisekedi wa Mulumba, who demanded the institution of the rule of law as a guarantee that the rule of the game will be the same for everybody. The organization of the Sovereign Naional Conference (SNC) allowed the representatives of different interest groups to meet and establish guiding principles leading toward a full democratization process. The transition to Democracy in Zaire was a result of a long struggle for civil liberties. The Mobutuist State was very reluctant to face any organized body, which might produce a set of recommendations that may have the power of a law, which could regulate the relationship between the governance and the governed. For Zaire, it was the Sovereign National conference of 1992 that represented the first and open transition. I mean the participant had the opportunity to voice their grievance and disagreement with the Zairian state. The output of the SNC included a recommendation for SNC to establish the transition government led by a Prime Minister elected by SNC. Although this was a transitional measure, the lack of flexibility became a real threat to the entire democratization process. The conference had succeeded to bridge the difference between the state and the civil society, but they failed to convince the different interest groups to secure authority, nor to allow Mobutu to engage into real reforms wanted by the people. If the Birindwa group takes and upper hand (as it looked like they would by utilizing any necessary means), then democratic reforms in Mobutu's Zaire could not be realized.

DRCongo (then Zaire) finds itself at the fork in the pursuit of democracy or the return to autocracy. It must be admitted that both the Opposition and the established failed to realize what was at stake. For example, the question we are asking ourselves is whether "Zaire under Mobutu was ever ready for political structural change or what conditions were necessary for such to take place?

A look back to the 1990's suggests that many Zairians were ready to move toward the democratic system. It was therefore essential that policy-makers reflect on the problematic of the democratization of public administration in general, as well as regional and local administration systems. With the Zairian political system in complete disarray and based on the fact that the state had ceased to exist in Zaire, the interest of this analysis couldn't have been more timely.

As a reminder, by 1994 Zaire had become a state less society, with Mobutu as the President in decline but still very dangerously clinging to power. The school systems had been inoperative for a decade or so, the health care system was nonexistent so much that people were dying like flies in conditions unimaginable for a modern society. The courts and public prisons were empty while parallel courts and obscure prisons had mushroomed all over the country. The country's human rights had worsened. And Zaire was in the state of emergency for food and medicines. Our study of the period reveals that, the families were taking turns to eat and meals were eaten once every three days. Public fury alternating with apathy as one watches breathlessly a potentially rich nation succumbing in the hands of an oppression regime, and becoming bankrupt and slowly but surely suffocating to death. Congolese people watched powerlessly as the overwhelming situation beyond their control took over the destiny of their lives. The social fabrics was so much exploited as the forces of evil again utilized the maxim of "Divide and Conquer", a tactic used by the Belgian colonialists and now effectively being applied again by the Zairian state.

The immediate repercussion of "Divide and Conquer" happened in Katanga under Mobutu and Kyungu' s watch, where Luba-Kasai who had lived peacefully in that part of the country among the Lunda, Tshokwe, Bemba, Balamba, Baluba ba Kazambe and Nkongolo, and Basanga, for over 1/2 of a century, were suddenly being asked to leave because of their ethnic background. Old friends were becoming new enemies as result of a desperate strategy to weaken the opposition.

KABILA'S STATE AND THE TUTSI CONNECTION:

Historians believe that history is cyclical and it is at this very moment somewhat repeating itself in the Congo. In 1908, Congo, then a "Free State (1878-1908),"was a property of King Léopold. Was handed over to the Belgian Government as result of international pressure over King Léopold's exploitation of Congo and his abuse of the human rights of the Congolese people. Adam Hochschild (1999) reports that "exogenous rather than endogenous factors" contributed to the exposition of these abuses (Hochschild 1999)

In 1959, as Congolese become enthusiastic about freedom and accepted to become an independent nation, independence appeared, it gave birth to sentiment for a strong sense of national cohesion and movement for increased democracy with the purpose of organizing themselves for self-determination. Again external factors and resources including the Pan-African movement had provided the impetus for African countries to follow suite with their Asian counterparts. Pan-Africanism was, and still is, activated by a sense of African solidarity. It generated at time, a strong sense of shared suffering under colonialism, and quickly "united" Africans in the struggle for independence.

African leaders of independence movements across the continent agreed, "Africa must unite in order for to be really free". And they agreed also that the first step toward such independence should be the universal suffrage or general elections organized on basis of one man one vote--democracy; and that such should be a victory over the colonial system(Armah, 1974). Nkrumah, the first President of Ghana had insisted on Congolese leader's presence at the 1958's All African Conference in Accra. The reluctant Belgian Colonial administration, sent Patrice Lumumba, Joseph Ngalula, Gaston Diomi, but, Joseph Kasavubu and Joseph Kanza ended up there too. The colonial government fought against such an idea and decided to isolate the Congo from the rest of Africa. They designed a plan to indeed delay the granting of independence until some thirty years into the future. It is perhaps not a coincidence that the year projected would be 1990, the year Mobutu gave up the presidency of his One-Party system MPR, and pronounced it dead!

The Belgian paternalist system assumed that the Congolese would be happy enough once they knew they were being compensated for the inconveniences of forced labor by an improvement in their material conditions of life. Through the Belgian colonial maxim of Dominate in order to Serve), went even further to exploit the weaknesses of the emerging Congolese middle class whom they promised a variety of different things including, (1) improved material conditions of life, and (2) power and prestige provided by Belgium's and other international financial and economic interest groups controlled by the West. Consequently, it was evident that between 1960 and the 1990s, the relationship between major Western powers and the first and second republics was that of a benefactor and a recipient. That is the dependency system under the Belgian colonial system was handed over to their African puppets that were carefully selected, trained in military, security. And police matters, and put in power to serve Western interest groups. Such a dependency system was as matter of policy preferred by Western powers and regarded the most efficient system because decisions on urgent matters would forthcoming quickly. Such a policy was to make a Congolese someone who was assisted, insured, pensioned, instead of a Congolese who would be self-reliant and self-determining. Hence the Congolese was relegated to the individual status without taking into account the cultural basis from whence he emerged. For those who still can recall, each member of the Congolese classed moyenne (low middle class) was provided with his standardized house (with pre-determined number of rooms), mass-produced furniture, pre-determined scale of food, his free time regulated to the last detail and without a trace of imagination; on top of which, to stop him making an unwise use of his money, a part of his wages was replaced by "payment in-kind." If these descriptions correct, scholars need to ask whether or not the Congolese early leaders were really ready to assume the mantle of supreme leadership in the Congo?

It is also essential for any African country to strive to raise a good number of well trained, well behaved and much more human citizens. Former President of the United States, Mr. Jimmy Carter. Once observed that the President like any elected leaders should be the best reflection of the American society. Leaders are the best reflection of The Congolese society, and so the people have the right to expect that they will be individuals with proven ethical conducts. Leaders who will up hold democratic values and support and re-enforce their dissemination and maintenance for future generations.

It will also be important that the country be able to recycles its leaders at pre-determined time periods. Power corrupts. Congolese should place legal limits on the future rulers. They should not want leaders who want to become autocratic kings and regional dictators. Good leaders will abide by the Constitution and not be those who want to initiate constitutional changes that favor their staying in power, and above the existing law as we have seen for the past 37 years of Mobutu. This implies that the country must continue to seek to establish the rule of law and democracy.

RELIGIOUS INSTITUTION AND CIVIC SOCIETY

Evidence abounds to show that Congolese people were dehumanized throughout the colonial era. Accordingly, the defenders of Belgian paternalism, the Congolese were better fed and had better housing and medical care than all other Africans. Every village of any size had a clinic, a school and a church" (Kanza, The Rise and Fall of Patrice Lumumba, p. 7).

Therefore, the period between 1960 and 1965 symbolizes for me, a struggle between capitalism and nationalism; it was a period of experimentation with power and the tricks of the trade: intrigues and search for ways to control and maintain that power. According to Maulana Karenga (1980) this search for more power appeared normal because politics itself is defined as the art and process of gaining, maintaining and using power. " But in order to ensure the continuity of the dependency system under the so-called Neo-colonialism. Governments under the second republic, everything for all the people. Slowly but surely, the triangulation apparatuses legated to them started to loose its breath. First, the Missionary church became the national church --, the opponent rather than a collaborator in the process of the exploitation of the people. Second, the national church was co-opted (see Protestant church under Mobutu) by the state, and often it could not stand up publicly in defense of the voiceless. The church leadership needs also to be limited by governing rule of law. They should not become permanent fixtures. As nongovernmental organizations, the church needs to balance its acts from becoming too dependent on external resources and being influenced by external forces to being a source of genuine nationalist and patriotic leadership. All of these require that democratic principled tenets apply to all of our national entities.

As demonstrated by the February 29, 2000 National Dialogue, the civil society is an independent source of resources. Sometimes, the churches received "subsidies from the colonial administration to run church schools, and sometimes Catholic churches, received up to 50% of the churches operating budgets. After independence, these subsidies died off. As it happened, churches were slowly being handed over to the Congolese Clergy" (Ndegwa, 1998).

As a result of these tensions, a power struggle between the Church and the Zairian State became public. Congolese identity became an issue whereby Christian names were dropped or changed altogether under the pretext of some "Retour a l'authenticite" (Back to authentic roots through the use of one's traditional names). In addition, Congolese religious leaders became the targets for politicians unfit to handle freedom of expression exemplified by the religious elite. The climax is all well known to those in line with the Zairian history.

As the political apparatus became increasingly greedy, the business component of the triangulation was given its final blow with the policy of nationalization known as "Zairianization." Mobutu nationalized all small and medium enterprises owned by Europeans, and confiscated what he could from the Congolese he did not like. The very economic sector that had kept the country economically strong was now in Mobutu's hand. All nationalized companies were subsequently handed other to clientele politicians with no business background whatsoever. The real motive was to develop a cult of personality, and re-enforce it with new concept whereby Mobutu is deified as the "enlighten Guide". From this practice new norms such as" Ruling by prestige" were born. Clearly, as Smith points out in his book the Wasted Wealth, Mobutu wasted a great deal of national resources not only in order to maintain a system of dependency but also in cultivating a clientele system and patronage as the ramification of centralized tyrannical autocracy. As the expression dear to Mobutu's uncle, Mr. Litho, proclaimed: "Bokoliana." (A Lingala sentence meaning "people will eat one another") such statement seemed now to reach its climax when Mobutu established the system of a parallel government under the "One Party State." This redundancy in government increased the waste in management. The "animation politique" required workers to create dance groups from the lowest unit of government to the highest to praise and please the eye of the "Guide" and his chieftains who felt very much satisfied once they saw women's buttocks moving from one side to another. Mobutu used to quote Léopold Cedar Senghor's poem that said "heureux ceux qui chantent et qui dansent" (meaning happy are those who sing and dance), to justify his and his clients exploitation of the people, However in the case of Congo today, President Kabila should not allow himself or his ministers and clients to establish new banks of women among whom these leaders could choose at will. Under Mobutu, it did not matter whether these women were married or unmarried. Immorality was the law. Rape went unpunished. Corrupting minors went unpunished. And, Congolese a people could only helplessly watch when all of this was taking place.

As the most responsible institution for the moral and ethical fabrics of modern Congolese society, the religious institutions are under the auspices of the Religious authority that the Congolese search for end to the current war. Like in the colonial era, the church carries a recognized clout in its ability to stand almost neutral in the struggle to resolve the war and conflict now in its second year. The Congolese religious leadership and Civic leadership have played reconciliatory roles before, but this time, they organized a two-week national consultation that brought rebels, government, and religious and civic representatives to Kinshasa. The following are a few of their positions and recommendations:

> The national consultation convened by religious leaders in Kinshasa as a "preparatory meeting" for the national debate, stipulated in the Lusaka cease-fire agreements, ended on
>
> Saturday. Participants issued a communiqué in which they reiterated that the *Congolese people were sovereign and aspired to live in peace,* (DRC State television reported).
>
> They condemned the "war of aggression and invasion of our national territory". They also condemned the "massive killing of Congolese, the looting of natural resources and the destruction of our economic and social infrastructure, and the destruction of our environment".
>
> "We therefore call upon our brothers and sisters of the armed opposition to have a sense of patriotism, to immediately lay down their arms, and to dissociate themselves from the enemies of our people," (www.reliefweb.int/IRIN).

Current political trends, patterns of business dealing and political positions resemble so much to Mobutu, and deserve to be carefully and critically examined. Certainly Kabuli's tenure has not yet produced its white elephants, but the different contracts formulated so far have tended to favor the investment of rare capital into the same projects that have been the source of the people's miseries: Mining of precious stones and metals has never been directed toward responding to the social need of our society. Unfortunately Kabuli's state face a challenge from the war which has occupied the entire Eastern and north western parts of the Congo, and is now threatening the source of diamonds in south central Congo.

In brief, the transition from the colonial period to the political independence of the Congo had economically benefited the West and its Neo-colonialist State under Mobutu and his family. Mobutu succeeded to corrupt all sectors and fabrics of the national life. From my tour of Congo (then Zaire), in 1994, Public administration from Kinshasa to, regional, sub-regional and local administrative sectors had become dysfunctional due to the encroachment of both democratic principles, and the administrative code of conduct. Imagine having one's fingers printed, and finding out soon after that in order to wash the ink, one had to pay a bystander an amount of dollars to get the soap!

Public Administration theories and Practices, suggest that public administration and political institutions can operate either positively or negatively. In the case of Mobutu's Zaire, these institutions operated negatively all the time. The institutions became a strong regressive factor and a real barrier to development. Negatively, these institutions broke all the records: corruption became rampant; human rights abuses were and still are high; clienteles and patronage were strongly enforced and became the norms; mismanagement became a norm; inefficiency; lawlessness; impunity and traffic of influence became a model; irresponsibility, incompetence, lack of real balance of power and lack of internal audits characterized Mobutu's governance.

Since May 17, 1997, Kabila's administrative apparatus and styles are emerging, and they are attempting to operate more positively, and in sustainable fashion. Kabila appears to be interested first on the management and reconstruction of the productive industries. There is a remarkable change in the cities with their clean streets and green grass planted recently. The environment is taking precedence over many other projects, but these are essential elements in transformation of people's view of themselves. There also is improvement in the public relations sectors. These appear small achievements, but consider the first visitor's view of Congo at the Airport, where now there is air-conditioning in every waiting room, and the toilettes, light and restaurants etc. are functioning properly. Consider a welcoming youthful and intelligent immigration officers who deal with the visitor up front without requiring bribe of any kind. They speak English, French, Portuguese Swahili and other Congolese languages. It is wonderful to see change.

Nevertheless, Politically, it seems that Kabila's participation in the recent Consultation with Civil Society, sponsored by the Religious organizations, is an important step toward the coalition Kabila needs to make his government legitimate. There is also the fact that the President has relied too much upon Mobutuist from Katanga and Maniema as political resources. He sincerely needs to move away from this regional and or ethnic dependency.

Our thesis then becomes simple: the typology of governments that developed after independence, especially between 1965 and the 1996's with its sluggish, centralized, dual bureaucracies as well as their preoccupation with the personification of power and the lack of liberty as to the choice, control and audit of public officials, unable these governments to responded to the flexibility and technologies required for an active participatory public administration. These governments become politically undemocratic, ineffective and wasteful. By 1996, 37 years of independence, Congolese governments with their autocratic regimes and galloping inflation simply did not function well in the rapidly changing, information-rich, knowledge-intensive global world and economies of the 1990s.

The impetus of the democratization movement, which changed Eastern Movement, was that it created strong and unfulfilled expectation in Africa. While it seemed to have worked well for the liberation struggle in South Africa against Apartheid, in the rest of sub-Saharan Africa the governance has remained tightly in the hands of the so-called "strong men." Kabila follows the same patterns as If new models of public institutions were not available. The Democratic Republic of Congo and other sub-Saharan African societies will be condemned to continuously stay dependent upon the West which has already began to marginalize them, and might not be compelled to consider any relationship with them because of such heavy dependency.

It is with this understanding of institutional leadership that other voices begun to emerge within the Congolese communities both inside and outside of Congo. Institutions do not properly function in absence of well-informed, and carefully trained leaders. It was impossible for Mobutuist leaders to suddenly change and become "new democrats". It would also be difficult for Kabila's ministers to learn new tricks if they persist in adopting what the Mobutuist had found useful. Indeed politically, Kabila and his government do not need leaders who had destroyed the minds of Congolese youth, and killed the whole generation of future leaders. Kabila must work to create new democratic mechanisms, which facilitate the transition to democracy.

It is essential provide the Congolese with new vision of kinds of society they want rather than concentrating on the leaders they need? While this requires cooperation from all forces of change existing presently in the Congolese community, all conscientious leaders who are mentally and spiritually healthy are encouraged to rise above the fray and work toward such endeavor. Leaders emanate from the society, they are the product of a society, and in creating conditions and situations conducive to democratization process, a society the people want, will emerge, and it will engender leaders who have the interest and well-being of their people at their hearts.

The important questions for the Congolese people in 1996 and at that stage were not, how much centralization or much federalism or how much federation they must establish, but rather what were the fundamental problem facing the nation? At that moment, it was important to realize that Mobutu was the wrong type of government, the wrong image of the society and the wrong legacy to pass on to the future generations. Therefore Congolese did not need more dictators, more corruption, they needed better governance.

Kabila's task appeared to be that of providing better governance during and after the war. Unfortunately Kabila was killed by one of his bodyguards in January of 2001. He must conduct and win this war by military means as well as by diplomatic negotiations. Both instruments must be updated and given fresh air. The process of democratization must be given priority for national and local development. The Congolese people I spoke to and listened to in 1994, 1997, and 1998, did not need another colonial power, or another dictatorship. Uganda, Rwanda and Burundi have convincingly demonstrate how authoritarian they can be, they have corrupted leaders in their own countries who indeed want to spread their influence under the guise of assisting the Congolese rebels! The people of these nations are much in need of a democratic system. Their leaders, however, have ignored their quest for the rule of law and good governance. Congolese diplomatic corps and government should focus on building democracy as a weapon to fighting against these dictators and force them to withdraw from Congolese land. A governmental system that provides an environment conducive to such governance is also a defensive weapon against aggressors and invaders.

GENERAL JOSEPH KABILA: THE NEW PRESIDENT

The Congolese national hero and liberator, Laurent Desire Kabila passed away on January 16, 2001, in an assassination still to be full comprehended or accounted for by the Investigative Commission created to find out the truth and to determine the real perpetrators of the heinous crime. President Laurent-Desiré Kabila who had succeeded to liberate the country from the entrenched Mobutuist Dictatorship would be himself gunned down by one of the trusted bodyguards. Laurent D. Kabila's Government immediately selected his son, Joseph Kabila, to be the caretaker President. And then on January 26, 2001, three days after the burial of his Father, the thirty-one years old Joseph Kabila was officially installed and inaugurated as the new President of the Democratic Republic of the Congo.

Following excerpts from his first speech to the nation demonstrate clearly that President Joseph Kabila is determined to change the image of Congo and its government in the international community, and in the mind of Congolese citizens themselves. In his address to the Nation as a new President of the

Republic, Joseph Kabila emerges as an adult, mature and Pan-African nationalist who would not hesitate to align himself with, or follow the example provided by Africa's greatest leaders Nkrumah, Lumumba, Mandela, and Nyerere, Naser and his father, Laurent Desiré Kabila.

Address to the Nation by His Excellency Joseph Kabila to the Congolese People is as follow:

On the diplomatic Level:

The Democratic Republic of Congo intends to play a role more active in the international businesses. Before the expansion of wars, the aggravation, and globalization, of poverty, the Democratic Republic of the Congo intends to bring particular contribution in order to arrive at adequate solutions with the other peoples of the world.

Concerning the African continent:

I would like to make a pathetic appeal for the greatest solidarity among the people of Central, East Africa and the rest of Africa. I urge, therefore, the brothers, sisters, and peoples of Africa to re-dynamize the Organization of Unites Africaine in the spirit of the founding fathers. As expressed by Mzee Laurent-Desiré Kabila, a great panafricanist, it is necessary to renew with the redemptive flame of Kwame NKrumah, Julius Nearer, Nelson Mandela, and Lumumba.

The Democratic Republic of Congo, being physically the geo-strategic center of Africa, intends to play a role of primary importance in the revival of the Pan-African Organization.

Concerning the SADC:

The Democratic Republic of Congo calls upon all for a great integration. It will play a more active role again in Africa's integration. The Democratic Republic of Congo urges its peer countries to insure a valid representation in structures of the Organization of African Unity (OAU). It demands equally the concretization and implementation of sectarian projects, which it had submitted to in the OUA.

As for the process of peace in Burundi:

The Democratic Republic of the Congo is committed to the contribution and success of the mediation of President Nelson Mandela, and Mzee Laurent-Desiré Kabila in Libreville. The new government of The Democratic Republic of Congo is faithful to the line of conduct set up by Mzee Laurent-

Desiré Kabila, and it is concerned about the preservation of our political independence.

European Community Union:

I have the firm resolution to continue to improve the relationships and cooperation with our principal partners in the European Union. I will strive to bandage sores caused by some misunderstandings, because I am aware that the European Union has a role to play in the development of Congo.

I am thinking particularly of: (1) France to which I address, in the name of the Congolese People, all my gratitude for its numerous commitments to the United Nations Security Council in the research of solutions to specific crisis that exists in our country. I assert here, my availability and willingness to continue the amelioration of our bilateral and multisectarian relationships. (2) Belgium with which the Democratic Republic of Congo shares historical ties. I wish see and develop friendly relations of mutual understanding and accord for a more fruitful cooperation. (3) As for relationships with United States of America, I wish to recognize that there have been years of ambiguities, and that there have been moments of mutual misunderstanding with our former Administration. The Democratic Republic of Congo intends to normalize the bilateral relationships with the new Administration, based on the mutual respect and willingness to advance the interests of both of our peoples. (4) I salute fraternal relationships existing between my country and the People Popular of China, Russia, as well as others countries of Asia. I intend to strengthen our relations with them. (bmmudia@GW.ORL.ILSTU.edu/January 29, 2001)

For internal Politics, Joseph Kabila seeks an appreciation of the Congolese People. He does not hesitate to call them great People, and deserving people. It is a bit disconcerting for a President who has not reached the legal age set to become President, but the people seems to be ready for another change. Here is what he tells the Congolese about
themselves:

I salute and thank you, the Congolese people, a great people, and deserving one. That have known, overcome, and conquered many difficulties, I congratulate you to reunite and the serenity whose I have known to make proof during difficult hours and painful that crosses our Nation. I do not know how to congratulate the Constituent Assembly and the Legislative-Parliament of Transition, for having taken the highest policy decisions of historical significance during this difficult period that the nation faced. I cite particularly the fact that they have elevated the late President Laurent-Desiré Kabila to the prominence of National Heroes and to invest in me the confidence of our people.

I would like to also praise and thank the Government of Public Salvation for having known exactly how to insure the continuity in management of the State during those tragic hours. (bmmudia@GW.ORL.ILSTU.edu/January 29, 2001)

To the Congolese Armed Forces, an organization that owes a lot of loyalty to Kabila Senior. Joseph Kabila is very carefully in giving away any sign of being concerned with disloyal members of the Military. He thinks particularly of the Congolese Armed Forces and all the Security Forces. He exhorts them to exercise their patriotic duties and urges them to uphold steadfastly the national wishes that were legated by the late Mzee -Desiré Kabila. (Joseph Kabila, Jan.29, 2001.)

In regard to the national Police, Joseph Kabila promises to remain" committed to making the Congolese Police Forces into a modern police, strong, and, well equipped, respectable and respectful of rights of each, and capable to defend the nation in all circumstances." This is important for Kabila if he must remain popular figure within the National Police Organization, many of whose members are veteran soldiers.

Politically, Joseph Kabila establishes a clean connection to his Father's political organization, the so-called Popular Power Committee (PPC). Laurent Kabila had found a bit toughs to establish his own political party or to affiliate him with an existing one. So about the time of his Third year in the Office, with the growing distance between him and the eastern neighbors. Laurent Kabila sought the internal support among the masses and found that by creating the (PPC), he will have a political base. So it is logical for Joseph Kabila to also seek the PPC's support:

I salute and thank the Popular Power Committees, the Popular Forces of Defense, as well as the Territorial Forces for their remarkable contribution to the maintenance of order especially in this difficult period. I invite you in the name of this Nation to remember countries of the SADC, particularly, the Republic of Zimbabwe, the Republic of Angola, and the Republic of Namibia, as well a other friendly countries, that have always supported our country, and are concerned about finding ways and means to end the war of aggression. (bmmudia@GW.ORL.ILSTU.edu/ January 29, 2001)

Concerning the war of aggression by Rwanda and Uganda, Joseph Kabila promise to meet with Paul Kagame on his first trip to the United States. He urged "the Regular Armies of Rwanda, Uganda, and Burundi to withdraw immediately without conditions, from the Congolese territories." (Joseph Kabila 2001)

His African Policy seems to be focused on the strengthening of the Organization of African Unity (OAU), which, he regards as the mother of all African organizations. He expressed his gratitude to (OAU) for all efforts that have been deployed in order to find a negotiated settlement of the Congolese Crisis." (JK Speech) He invited OAU to solemnly implicate itself more readily in instituting the efficient process of co-facilitation of the Inter-Congolese Dialogue. Indeed the response to this request was swift, as at this writing the former President of Botswana, Sir K. Masire has intensified his consultation with the rebel groups and African States to set up the Inter-Congolese Dialogue.

To the Congolese people, Kabila related his overall assessment of the prevailing political and social conditions. He stressed the fact that "Before the Nation in peril, a broken and battered Nation, the Nation overexploited and victim of all sorts of covetousness and violence," the Congolese must form a union of all its sons and daughters, wherever they are or may be found to face the challenge of the war. Underlying this determination was a reaffirmation his father faith and trust on the different sectors of the Armed Forces, the national police, to Security Forces and all forces alive for resistance and defense of the national territory. Joseph Kabila was indeed attempting to legitimize his new administration as it can be seen in his effort to urge the Congolese politicians, the Churches, the laborers, the Congolese women, youth, and the friendly countries, and aliens who have chosen to live in the Democratic Republic of Congo, to participate in the restoration of a new and peaceful Congo, fully prosperous in the communion and reconciliation for all.

This furthermore carried by his message to the Congolese living in the territories under occupation. He sought to assure them that the nation will "remember their highest senses of sacrifice as well as their attachment and loyalty to the Homeland." He also expressed to them the nation's solidarity in the struggle that they lead, in the difficult conditions for the liberation of the country. In addition, he promised the Congolese in the occupied territories that his " military and diplomatic efforts and policies will be oriented toward your total liberation from the occupation by the aggression forces from Burundi, Rwanda Uganda and their backers." (bmmudia@GW.ORL.ILSTU.edu/January 29, 2001).

African intellectuals and Congolese analysts believe that Kabila Senior's assassination was engineered by Uganda and Rwanda with complicity from both Angola and Zimbabwe, because Kabila senior was thought, as one unnamed diplomat puts it, an obstacle to the Lusaka Peace Agreement and the overall resolution of the political crisis (personal interview).

Beyond these African countries, there was other concerned Western powers, which would have wanted Kabila Senior's quick exit. Often mentioned and feared is the United States under Bill Clinton, which regarded Kabila as a radical nationalist who resisted all initiatives by the USA. Like in the 1960's, this kind of the burden could not have been passed on to President Gorge Walker Bush. United Kingdom and its strong backing of Uganda could be also among the players.

Hence, Joseph Kabila's first international tour including France, Britain, USA, Belgium and Germany accounts as response to those worries. Within three days of his swearing in as President, Kabila met the President of Rwanda, the Secretary of State, General Collin Powell, and other in Washington DC. French President Jacques Chirac is very important. France has always wanted a big role to play in the destiny of the Democratic Republic of Congo, one of the largest Francophone countries. Of course the analysts hypothesize that the interests of Western powers have constitute a reliable basis under which the similarities between their attitudes toward Patrice Emery Lemma, and Joseph

Desire Kabila can be compared. In both of these cases, A thirty year old Mobutu will be installed in power with the assistance of CIA (Lumumba) and in later case, Joseph Kabila (a thirty-one years-old) will inherit power, leaving aside all the veteran opposition parties and their leaders. This" darlingization" of a new generation of leaders in the third world is to be watched closely. For instance, Joseph Kabila appears to be headed toward the hands of some powerful players like those that have seen to it that in Morocco, Jordan, and Syria there are fresh young faces and new politics.

Nevertheless Joseph Kabila's advisors appear to be aware that he must disassociate himself from the complex statutory issue of " inherited power" in a country whose name is "the Democratic Republic of Congo" as a characterization by the Congolese national aspiration for democracy, and not a monarchy. Kabila is thus walking "malembe-malemba," (slowly- slowly) on tight rope, always pushing away from the appearance of being only the heir of his father's power which is not easy to do, but which he must do if he has to emerge as the rightful and legitimate successor. Recent developments in Kinshasa indicate that the Government of President Joseph Kabila is moving fast moving in that direction by smoothing the relations with the UN and the International community, changing rapidly what was seen as strained and even difficult international relationships cultivated by his late Father, Mzee Laurent-Desire Kabila. Already there are signs that his inauguration speech followed by his early visits to the UN Headquarters in New York and the messages he has been personally delivering to Western capitals, Kabila is seen as having a definite effect upon his hosts and their diplomatic programs. For example, The UN Security Council has moved to stop any forms of aid and cooperation with the Rebel groups in RDC. In a statement attributed to Jeremy Greenstock of United Kingdom, and current President of the UN Security Council, it is noted that the Council resolution 1341 had called on all parties to the Lusaka cease-fire agreement to cease support for rebel groups, which are fully responsible for violence and humanitarian abuse. Greenstock insisted in a press conference that assistance has got to stop and the parties have got to come with plans that cease the activities of the armed rebel groups that are not signatories to Lusaka. For Ambassador Jeremy Greenstock observes further that: "It's a very important part of the story to come and the Council is not going to let go of it," he said. Also in a recent report from the UN secretary-general Kofi Annan there are references to the violence in some areas as having almost a genocidal character, which "cast a nasty echo back from previous history". While welcoming the progress of troop disengagement so far, members of the Council said they expected all parties to live up fully to their commitments under the agreements, cooperate unreservedly with the UN Mission in the DRC (MONUC) and draw up "realistic plans" by the 15 May for their complete withdrawal from the DRC, as requested in Security Council resolution 1304. "And we also want to see realistic plans for a demobilization, disarmament, reconciliation and reintegration process," he added. "We've seen the importance of that in the Sierra

Leone and other contexts; it's going to be vital for the DRC." (: IRIN-CEA Update 1,162 Wed, 25 Apr 2001 [2010423])

What appears to be a major change in attitude toward Congo is reflected by the expressed desire of the UN Security Council to plan bold action to counter the slow and painful armed rebel groups movement toward disengagement of troops. UN plans to make disengagement a higher priority item on the agenda of an upcoming mission by the Security Council to the DRC in mid-May 2001. Jeremy Greenstock, Security Council President said that the secretary-general, Kofi Annan, has invited the Council to a retreat on 4 to 5 May to discuss the Great Lakes region. Such a move by the UN can be seen as a positive reaction and responsive to recent diplomatic campaign by Joseph Kabila who has not only gone extra mile to meet with Western power enters in the USA, United Kingdom, France, Germany, Sweden, Belgium Switzerland, but also to seek wisdom form some of the Africa most dynamic leaders such Mohmar Kadafi of Libya, Thebo Mbeki of South Africa, Albert Mugabe, of Zimbabwe, Eduardo Dos Santos of Angola, Albert Bongo of Gabon, and many others.

In the home Front, President Joseph Kabila, has so far been meeting different sectors of the Congolese population, and listening to their concerns, grievances, and aspirations. He has therefore established himself as legitimate President and head of a new government. He asked his father Cabinet, government, and Staff of all-important Government Agency to step down. And he proceeded to nominate and appoint his cabinet, his ministers, and Staff, and it has been reported widely that he has reorganized the National security Office, and establish as such his own National Police Chief, and revamped the secret services.

In his first speech to the nation, he established a difference between himself and his father. He was interesting in ending the war, and was open to accept the Lusaka Peace Agreement as the guiding principle. He also promised to honor and respect the constitution, and to stride to establish the rule of Law. In his swearing in of the new group of members of his government, he instructed them to be the first obedient of the law, and servers of the people. Furthermore in his first and official visit to the Republic of Angola, Kabila was well received:

The Angolan president José -Eduardo Dos Santos has encouraged his Congolese visitor Joseph Kabila to extol flexibility in the implementation of the Agreement of Lusaka report peripheral radios captured in Kinshasa and which cited the joint-statement published Thursday following the first official visit to Luanda by Mr. Kabila. Furthermore, in a declaration made during his stay in the Angolan capital, President Joseph Kabila has conditioned the beginning of the democratic process in democratic Republic of Congo (RDC) to the withdrawal of those he called the Rwandan and Ugandan" occupying forces." The two leaders also announced that they would strengthen the cooperation between Angola and the RDC. (bmmudia @GW.ORL.ILSTU. EDU)

The analysis of Kabila Speech in Angolan parliament reveals that, it was Kabila's deliberate intent and aim to recognize and salute the presence of Angolan troops and other allies (Zimbabwe and Namibia) in the RDC. He asserts that the former never was on a foot of equality with the Rwandan and Ugandan troops that are supporting Congolese rebel groups they had organized themselves. The Congolese president recognized that the Republic of Angola has committed itself to the defense and protection of the sovereignty and territorial integrity of the RDC before Kabila the Angolan parliament (bmmudia @ GW.ORL.ILSTU. EDU).

Perhaps, it should be pointed out that the relationship between the Democratic Republic of Congo and the Republic of Angola goes back to the colonial days when Angolan refugees moved into the Congo and remained there until their nation was able secure its independence. In the pre-colonial days, the Portuguese had found that the Kingdom of Kongo was covering the coastal strip that spread out into the present Democratic republic of Congo, Congo Brazzaville, and Angola. So there are deep historical and ethnic connections between the two countries. Also Angola has since the beginning of war in August 2, 1998 brought a significant military assistance to the Kinshasa regime and it has maintained in this capacity important military contingents in RDC following the assassination of the late president Laurent- Desire Kabila whom, the Angolan government had helped, in 1997, to overthrow the ancient Congolese dictator, Mobutu Sees Seko.

Elsewhere Joseph Kabila still has to find a formula to break the ice with the Leaders of Congolese Liberation Front (CLF) Jean-Pierre Bemba, Wamba Dia Wamba, and other who are being pressed to accept to pull back their troops some 15 km from the frontline in Equatorial province. These leaders are still under the control of their Rwandan and Ugandan backers, and it appears that for while longer, it will be difficult to determine just when, they will be able to meet independently with Joseph Kabila. The presence of the UN peacekeeping forces in some regions is already an encouraging step toward the easing of tension, though the work has just begins for all sides. Already the deployment of 120 UNUC soldiers from Morocco in the city of Kisangani was the first positive step toward peace. Large cheering crowds of about 100,000 people, who threw flowers and shouted, 'Bon courage' to them, met the peacekeepers. The Mission's Force Commander, Lieutenant-General Montage Diallo, also greeted the troops at their arrival, which brings the total number of UN troops in the DRC to about 600. Although in comparative terms this appears to be a very small contingent, it constitutes a moral booster for the Congolese government, and a real deterrent to other atrocities in occupied territories.

One positive sign to Kabila initiatives is the recent return of the DRC's veteran opposition leader, Etienne Tshisekedi to Kinshasa. He arrived in Kinshasa in April 2001 after 16 months in exile. Confidential reports suggest that heavy security was in place for Etienne Tshisekedi's return, and that Joseph Kabila's National of Security Adviser Mbuyo himself was at the Airport to meet Tshisekedi and probably make sure that nothing would happen to create any confusion. This suggests that Joseph Kabila's government is weighing the type of relationship it must have with political leaders who have historically opposed dictatorship and stood for the democratization process. Though reports also suggest that journalists were kept at distance from Etienne Tshisekedi, while he was greeted by a delegation of his Union for Democracy and Social Progress (UDPS) party, the government recognizes his importance in the planned Inter-Congolese-Dialogue. Security vehicles and some of his supporters led Tshisekedi from the International airport to his home in Kinshasa's district of Limeté. One of the Kinshasa newspapers, 'Le Phare', which backs the UDPS, suggests that Tshisekedi was planning to meet President Joseph Kabila soon. (lundbla@sympatico.ca)

President Joseph Kabila has also been meeting with such influential group of members of the Federation of Congolese Enterprise (FEC). This group was among the first local group that President met and it not coincidental that the group is socio-professional and promises to be a source of ideas about how the economic should be handled and managed. Observer projects that a solid partnership might be forged between the State and these enterprises. (bmmudia@GW.ORL.ISTU.Edu. May 4, 2001)

In Conclusion, this brief entry captures a very brief period of Joseph Kabila first hundred days in the Office. Joseph Kabila is still haunted by the dream of his slain Father, and the burden of Leadership. His new Government is made up of technocrats, with just a few figure retained from the Government of Public Salvation. The remaining challenge is for Joseph Kabila to conquer the admiration of the people, especially in interior communities and provinces where he remains an unknown entity. His youthfulness is an advantage, and will allow him, if so desires to become very popular, especially if he can master some of Congo major languages and speak them where they are the lingua fracas. On Economic spheres he has received two major visits by the World Bank and IMF, and he has appointed a former President of the Belgian Central Bank, to be the Technical Assistant to Jean Claude Masangu, Governor of Banque Central du Congo (BCC). The Chief Financial institution. The Economy is awaiting a booster by the creation of new jobs and investment in major road building.

While in the late 50s and early 60s the motto was "Africa shall be free", in the period from 1986-1996 the motto had become "Africa shall be redeemed from dictatorship". The Congolese radical opposition leaders that emerged in later 1980s believed that governments that will be able to ensure long-lasting stability through democratic institutions, will be the only governments that will be able to generate progress. Such was the origins of the Union for Democracy and Socio-economic Progress (UDPS) for their nations. The democratic institutions that provide conditions for people to work, produce good, transport, and market their good will indeed enhance the self-actualization, and dreams of Congolese people's well being. But Congolese political parties have to transform themselves from being the oppositions parties to becoming political parties, promoters of democratic way of life, reconciliatory, managers of conflicts and crisis, and builders of democratic apparatuses. That the parties themselves should provide transparently the models of how the practice democracy within, how the give equal participation, hoe the respect and protect human rights and how the seriously honor the contracts, treaties and conventions they themselves have negotiated and agreed to.

In retrospectively, the pre-requisites for a political and institutional structural adjustment are centered around (1) the concept of democracy and (2) good governance. As already outlined by Nzongola (1998) and Sørensen (1993) above. The basic notions of democracy include (1) the universal principle that holds that humans in all human societies aspire to progressively improve from what they are to what they ought to be. Here the classical ideas were to rollback power from authoritarian rule to the people. In a military dictatorship, the might of the army keeps the leader in power. In a monarchy, people accept the tradition of having a king or a queen on a throne. In a theocracy, the leaders' authority comes from the religious belief that they speak for the gods. In a direct and pure democracy, authority is in the hands of all the people, most of whom participate directly in governance. Such direct and pure democracies are rarely efficient.

What Congolese people have wanted since 1982 was more than a "representative democracy" which meant that the decision making would be delegated to elected officials who get their power by winning the confidence and trust of the people they represent. In essence, the people grant the elected officials the power to determine who will receive certain services and who will not. Because power corrupts - Congolese have seen in the Developed nations that during the past 30 years, it is therefore essential that the people retain for themselves the authority to allocate the elective offices. The holding of office becomes in itself an important value for; large number of people would compete for public office. Again, because power corrupts, it would be essential for elected officials not to have the authority to make any decision they want. There should be a balance of powers, which keep officials from different branches in check. Most importantly, representative democracy should be backed up by a constitutional democracy. Consequently, writing a constitution that limits the ability of the people or their representatives to abuse power provided such a constitution becomes a very fabric of the society and provided it is embodied in their daily life.

Because, for a Constitution to maintain itself, it must receive an unconditional public support without which anti democratic forces would certainly destroy the very means of governance. Despite the fact that the concept of democracy sounds simple at the periphery, it is in reality of extreme complexity both on the theoretical and practical levels.

Therefore for a country like Zaire, which has been governed (and continues to be governed) under a military dictatorship, the introduction of the basic notions of democracy 101 has become a cruel if not an unpalatable experience. No one said it would be easy under democracy. Indeed, democracy has been for some especially for Americans, a human and societal experimentation. Democracy, according to FD Roosevelt "is human history". It is indeed human history made up of victories and defeats as well as hope and deception. Perhaps, Alexis de Tocqueville had said it best when he concluded that, "one must make the best out of democracy. In principle, it may not be a good thing. But there is no alternative, and therefore one must take good care of democracy".

1994 especially following the Sovereign National Conference saw democracy seen by some Congolese as a revolutionary stand against a worn out military regime in search of fresh breath. Some others considered democracy as a symbol of defiance, a protest, a liberation of self, a conflict of classes and that of generation. Some others however, have accepted the notion of democracy as the only way out for economic progress and social well-being. This is the reason why democracy has been regarded in some African settings as a disease, perhaps a contagious disease! The timing of the spread of the disease of "democracy" could not have been more coincidental. People around the world were in search of all those values that are so essential, so critical to their welfare including but not limited to the freedom of speech, freedom of the press, freedom of assembly, freedom of religion, equality towards the law and all other civil liberties that allow individuals the freedom and the pursuit of their happiness. This was and is the nature of the Opposition Parties that were led by Union Pour la Democratie et le Progrès Sociale (UDPS). The internal opposition led by veteran opposition leader, Dr. Etienne Tshisekedi wa Mulumba followed the strategy not only to acquire democracy, but also to follow closely the process of democratization. This implied that they were ready to bargain and negotiate with the established power.

In terms of political structural adjustment, all democratic government should meet all the aforementioned conditions as well as meet the following requirements:

1. Equality towards the law, which means that no one from simple citizen to a regional governor to the president, could be exempt from the law. All citizens must have equal rights and for some charges resulting from the law. Equality towards the law also pre-suppose electoral equality which allows one vote for each adult citizen during free and open elections. These elections have got to be without discrimination on the basis of fortune, religion, social origin, sex, race, and philosophical or political convictions.

2. Periodic Election of officials and if necessary limited terms for holding public office. This would allow seasonal turnovers as well as a recycling of new blood and new leadership in elective positions.

3. Legislative Bodies organized as mandated by the law under the constitution.

4. Political Liberty and Participation, which allow for political pluralism and which guarantee all civil liberties.

5. Political Party Structure, which should attract a coalition of People who choose to organize formally and cooperate to achieve, shared political goals. Political parties should not really be substantially reduced because what Congo needs is to have broad latitude in their self-expression to ensure vast participation. The two hundred plus political parties

> that existed in the 1992-1994 in Mobutu's Zaire were detrimental to a democratic political and organizational development. It was simply a disastrous experimental design for a democracy in gestation.

Furthermore, the fact that political party leaders and/or leadership strata considered themselves as the only legitimate people to run for office, such a system lacked the will to train young and future leaders. It fails short in ability to galvanize leadership. It rests upon old and tired leadership, which discourages young to evolve and inject new ideas and new dynamism to a democratic process.

It would simply be best for political party structure to rely on qualified expertise in the running of political parties. Those experts would then be responsible for recruiting, training and maintaining potential leaders of all ages, educational backgrounds, gender and religious beliefs. Potential leaders who share the same political goals and ideology would then join hands to present their ideas to the people in an electoral campaign process. The people would then decide who to keep in office, and who to vote out of office.

These and other factors are essential in building a democratic political system that is based on the principle of human dignity and that guarantees equality of its citizens and their participation in the system. A democratic political system assumes political stability and hence, encourages social and economic progress and development of the communities.

CONCLUSION

Governance was earlier defined as the process by which a people collectively solve their problems and meet their society's needs. Government is the instrument people use to provide appropriate conditions for good governance.

When one looks at the situation in Zaire for the past 40 years one can observe the following conclusions about the Zairian government: Most people do no longer believe in government. One does not look at government as necessary institution. The form of which, in Zaire is regarded as uncivilized in the hands of evil people. Government should be the mechanism people should use to make communal decisions: Where to build roads, what to do about illiterate adults, what kind of education to provide for the children. Government should be a way and means to provide services that benefit all people. In Mobutuist Zaire, government had come to be defined in the reverse. It was considered as a mechanism a cliquish group of power-hungry people must use to make decisions for personal gain: how to become rich without much efforts: Zairianization, embezzlement, shady policies; corruption, etc.

The Armed forces were utilized not for the defense and protection of all the people but rather as a means of repression of the people to maintain autocratic regimes in power. These evil regimes rather than improving infrastructures they would rather destroy them. Imagine that during the early days of independence, Congolese had more access to telecommunications than after. They produced more crops before independence than after. What is even more upsetting is the fact that Congolese first governments willingly made destructive policy decisions? Today when you pick up the phone and call Ivory Coast, Cameroon or Nigeria, the phone would ring and you would communicate without difficulty. If you decide to hang up and call again after 20 minutes, well you won't have any problems connecting at all.

The same is however, not true with Kabila's Congo. It is not that a Congolese is incapable of providing such services but that the Mobutu government was unwilling to make such services available to the people. Mobutu's regime was confining, repressive, debilitating, and controlling governance. All well-to-do government officials own cellular phones. Therefore they do not care if the people have access to the phones or not.

Most people in Zaire have come to believe that the Zairian society has been de-humanized and hence cannot function effectively within an ineffective government. We believe that government which relies on clienteles and patronage rather than expertise and knowledge and governments with centralized means of governance, are not up to the challenges of leading human kinds into a changing information society, services oriented and knowledge-based global economy.

Most people believe that both the people who work in government and the systems in which they work are the problem. It is therefore essential that Zaire, as it finds itself at the crossroads, should not waste this opportunity to carefully consider the codes of ethics of the kinds of people they will choose to represent them as well as the kinds of people those representing them will recruit to assume responsibilities which impact the general good and welfare of our society.

We believe these systems can be changed to liberate the enormous energies of the Zairian people and to heighten their ability to serve the public. We also believe in the change of the guards. We have had enough with the same old folks who are out of vision. Therefore, they all should be out of sight if we are serious about the change and if we want to be at the rendezvous of the 21st century. To quote the famous phrase by the Vice President of the United States, Al Gore, "It is time for them to go".

Some of us believe that neither dictatorship nor Federalism nor Federation has much of relevance to the problems of the country at this stage, unless the basic notions of democracy and freedom for any Zairian national to move freely and live in peace wherever he/she wants to, are embodied in the minds and daily behavior of our people. Governance through democratic means might heighten and encourage the explosion of creativity, talent, responsibility, dedication and energy for the well being of our people without distinction of ethnic background and origin.

Finally, most of us believe deeply in equity - in equal opportunity for all Congolese. We need to do away with filling in administrative and political positions with incompetence and or relatives who do not know better. Governments should also be in the business of maximizing productivity.

Ineffective utilization of the person power is simply not the best way to govern. In order to accomplish this, there is a need for a political structural adjustment.

Congolese today assume that democracy will take roots outside of drastic political modification and transformation of their basic attitude toward governance or are they simply hoping for a structural alternative, making the Kabila regime more respondents to their aspirations? In Mobutu's Zaire, there was a need for a restructuring of our administrative apparatus. Administrative reforms should have been in line with political reforms. Under Kabila, it seems there should be re-partitioned in entities that allow efficiency as well as people's participation in governance. Additionally, since the Congo is often referred to as a subcontinent. This massive territory will not simply be governable from Kinshasa by a handful of people who above all have no interest in the advancement of the nation, and the welfare of its people. We need to consider other ways of organizing and repartitioning the country. And I will leave that to Public Administration specialists.

Sørensen (1993) considers democratization to be the process that includes the search for the preconditions that must be met to ascertain the institutionalization of democracy. He observes "Democracy does not fall from heaven, it is part of human experimentation, and it must be a product of social actors who fight for it by convincing the people that it is good and a better approach to consensus decision-making. Such process requires also a period or several periods of transitions that allow people to be involved and not be on margin of the process. A split in coalition often precedes democratic openings. The best application in the transitional period is to make democracy work in re-establishing confidence in the conduct of business, especially arriving to a democratic decision-making, even though the decision may be against the democratic leaders. Therefore, beginning with the political party itself--opposition or not, there should be a clear involvement of the mass through elected representatives in the decision-making. Each cities and town should have its representative government. Critical in. this first stage would be to ensure democracy as a system of government functioning in accordance with good governance principles under a progressive set of laws that a democratic State and national governments have been able to establish. Once people develop democratic habits and expectations, they can institutionalize them and all the mechanisms necessary to re-enforce the democratic rules are put in place. To defuse the present situation, Localities should proceed with the first stage of elections for their constituent assembly. Elections should be held every two years so that people can become familiar with the process, the second level might be the elections of the district assembly, where the country could move towards the elections Provincial assemblies that are to allow for a clear decentralized system of government. Whether the country will evolve to become a federalist state or a federation should be a long-term goal, which will require a lot of planning and strategizing to avoid situations such as the ones that took place in Katanga in 1993-1994. The inherent right for each citizen to live anywhere in the country

should override the rights of regional apparatus. In other words, each citizen belongs to the nation before he can belong to the state or region.
The challenge facing the Congolese people are numerous, however, the lack of citizens participation in the political system is very critical. Military men and women, as well as their leaders, should represent the best of all the citizens of the nation. The future of Congo lies in its children; therefore government should provide a better education system that would help galvanized sustainable development in the long run. In absence of major investment in good health services, quality schools and institutes of Higher education, Colleges and Universities, our future is indeed at stake. The continued absence of democratization mechanisms will forever make democracy and development impossible to attain.

REFERENCES

Armah, Kwesi. 1974. Ghana: Nkrumah's Legacy. London: Rex Collings Ltd.

Boissonnade, Euloge. 1998. Kabila Clone de Mobutu. Editions Moreux, Paris-France.

Carter, Gwendolen M. and Patric O'meara. 1985. (Eds.) African Independence: The First Twenty-five Years. Indiana University Press, Bloomington

Chabal, Patrick. 1994. Power in Africa. New York: St. Martin's Press.

Clark, Leon. 1970. Through African Eyes Cultures In Change. The Rise Nationalism: Freedom Regained. No. V. Westport, CT: Praeger.

Dahl, Robert. 1971. Polyarchy: Participation and Opposition. New haven, CT: Yale University Press

Ethridge, M., and Howard Handelman. 1994. Politics in a Changing World. New York: St. Martin's.

Fanon, Frantz.. 1963. The Wretched of the Earth. New York:. Grover Press.

Harrison, Lawrence. 1985. Underdevelopment is A State of Mind: The Latin American Case, Lanham, MD: Harvard University and Madison Books.

Hochschild, Adam. 1999. King Léopold's Ghost : A Story of Greed, Terror, and Heroism in Colonial Africa. First Marine Book--Hounghton Miffin Co

Jackson Robert, and Carl Rosberg. 1985. "Democracy in Tropical Africa: Democracy versus Autocracy in African Politics." Journal of International Affairs, 38, 2, 231-256.

Kanza, Thomas 1996. The Rise and Fall of Patrice Lumumba. KIMPWANZA (UHURU) -No 29, avril /mai. p. 7.

Kabila, Laurent -Desire. 1967. Naufrage du Processus de Re-democratisation. Parti de la Revolution Populaire (PRP) Makanga, Kivu,. Congo-Kinshasa.

Leslie, Winsome J. 1993. Zaire: Continuity and Political Change in Oppressive State. Westview Press, Boulde.

Mazrui, Ali. 1986. The African Experience: Triple Heritage. New York: Oxford University Press.

Ndegwa, Stephen. 1998.. The two faces of Civil Society: NGOs and Politics in Africa. Kamerian Press, West Hartford, Connecticut.

Nzongola-Ntalaja. 1982. Class Struggles and national liberation in Africa: Essays on the Political Economy of Neocolonialism. Roxbury, Mass: Omenana,.

Nzongola-Ntalaja, Georges and Margaret C. Lee. 1997. The State and Democracy in Africa. Ed. Trenton, NJ: Africa World Press, Inc

Reno, William. 1998. World Politics and African States. Boulder, Colorado: Lynne Rienner Publishers.

Sklar, Robert. 1987. "Developmental Democracy." Comparative Studies in Socity and History, 29, 4, and 35-61.

Sonyika, Wole.1996. The open Sore of a Continent: A Personal Narrative of Nigerian Crisis. New York: Oxford University Press.

Sørensen, George. 1993. Democracy and Democratization: Dilemma in World Politics. Westview Press.

Sudan, François et al. 1998. "Kabila: Un an apres la chutte de Mobutu, où en est le nouveau Congo?--Un dossier exceptionnel." Jeune Afrique No. 1948, Du 12 au 18 Mai,. pp. 85-224.

United Nations Office for the Coordination of Humanitarian Affairs 2000. "Report on Consultation on War in the Democratic Republic of Congo." February 29 to March 11, p.25 –27.

Willame, Jean Claude. 1999. L'Odyssée Kabila: Trajectoire Pour un Congo Nouveau, Karthala, Paris.

Young, Crawford, and Thomas Turner. 1985. The Rise and Decline of the Zairian State. Madison, WI: University of Wisconsin Press.

bmmudia@GW.ORL.ISTU.Edu. May 4, 2001.

bmmudia@GW.ORL.ILSTU.edu/January 29, 2001.

lundbla@sympatico.ca

Chapter 13

Pan Africanism and Colonial Legacy

Robert Dibie and Babatunde Agiri

INTRODUCTION

Between 15 November 1884 and 26 February 1885, leading European countries with urgent desires for colonial acquisition in Africa met at a conference in Berlin with Otto von Bismarck. Bismarck, the German Chancellor, served as the chairman and laid down the ground rules for the achievement of European goals in Africa and avoided open conflicts among themselves. Thereafter, from 1885 to 1900, Germany, Britain, France, Portugal, Italy and Belgium severely conquered and partitioned Africa, and established European colonial rule.

Contrary to the theory promoted by some writers that classified the defeated Africans as "resisters" or "collaborators", all African nations are now known to have resisted European conquest. The strategy of resistance varied from one African community to another. None openly welcomed the European intruders as "friends". Indeed, almost immediately after the conquest, many of the so-called "collaborators" were among the first to break out in open rebellions against the alien administration (Boahen, 1990).

The partition of Africa by the Europeans led to the present 54 nation states in modern Africa with a plethora of problems: nationalism, ethnicity, irredentism and boundary problems on the one hand; economic development, regional co-operation and continental unity on the other. Pan-Africanism as an ideology has been offered as a solution to these daunting problems confronting African states. Why has the ideology failed to achieve the desired goals and success?

Our first step is to understand what is Pan-Africanism? It is a modern ideology that has its origins in the 19th century among the enslaved Africans in the US and the Caribbean. It began as a conscious protest by the blacks against the brutal conditions of slavery and the continued de-humanization and social degradation of their persons even after the abolition and emancipation. It called for unity among Africans in Diaspora against racism and all forms of social injustice and repression in the New World. Later, it became relevant as an ideology against European conquest and barbaric exploitation of Africa. The common cause between Africans in the Diaspora and their kith and kin in Africa was easily seen in the human sufferings of the African race in the hands of European imperialists and aristocracy. The early leaders of the movement understandably came from the US and the Caribbean; namely Marcus Garvey from Jamaica, WEB DuBois from the US, Henry Sylvester Williams from Trinidad and others (Jacobs 1981; Martin 1985).

It can therefore be argued that Pan-Africanism is a direct result of the colonial partition of Africa. But could Africans have achieved regional co-operation or dream of continental unity if the Europeans had not come to divide up the continent?

PRE-COLONIAL POLITICAL SETTING

At the beginning of the 19th century, Africa comprised a wide range of both big and small autonomous polities among which there was no political cooperation. Inter-state politics especially among the larger states rested upon the demands for territorial and economic expansion. Bilateral treaties where they existed were observed in accordance to the realities of power politics, in other words, of the balance of military power among the states. For example, the contest between Buganda and Bunyoro for the lost counties; between the Asante and the Fante on the Gold Coast (now Ghana); and between the Sokoto Caliphate and Borno kingdom (Adeleye 1971; Boahen 1974; Kiwanuka 1971, Oyeleye et al. 1999). This was also true of the relations between the bigger and more powerful states and the smaller and decentralized ones. Regional cooperation tended to be based upon the expansion of the stronger at the expense of the weaker.

The nineteenth century in some parts of Africa witnessed the evolution of new bigger states or empires that incorporated larger areas of the continent, yet this did not lead to the formation of new political unions. In the sudanic zone from the Senegambia area in the west to the Red Sea in the east, there emerged the following Islamic states: Futa Toro, Futa Jallon, the Tukulor empire and the empire of Samori Ture; the Sokoto Caliphate and the revitalized Borno Kingdom, the kingdom of Darfur and the Mahdist State. There was no coordinated effort to bring this vast area of Africa under one ruler or to form a political union among these Islamic states. Rather, driven apart by doctrinal differences and the personalities of their rulers, these states warred against one another: the Tukulor against its predecessor, the Hamdullahi caliphate and Sokoto against Borno, which eventually made the states easy preys to European conquest. The feeble political and diplomatic co-operation between the Tukulor empire and the Sokoto caliphate did not save them from European conquest (Oloruntimenhin, 1972; Oyeleye et al. 1999).

A new state building process was also evident among Islamic states in North Africa. Except Algeria which was conquered by the French in 1830, Morocco an independent sovereign monarchy under the Filali dynasty and the Turkish dependencies in Tunisia under the Husaynid dynasty and in Egypt under the dynasty of Muhammad Ali redefined their national interests and took their first steps towards modernization. As in the case of post independent African states, these states became heavily indebted to European financiers and bankers. Britain and Morocco-and Tunisia occupied Egypt by France. Libya later came under Italy. European imperialism in the Middle East at the period encouraged the growth of Pan -Arabism that sought to promote unity among the Arab nations and combat European cultural and economic imperialism. But the North African states rejected Pan Arabism and emphasized individual territorial nationalism.

The disunity among African states was also visible in other parts of the continent. In South Africa, the Zulu experiment of new nation building left in its wake much human and material destruction among the surrounding African groups but led to the growth of new African states formed by the refugees from the Zulu wars. These states, Botswana, Swaziland and Lesotho were separated from one another and could not therefore form any strong resistance against European attacks and loss of territories. The Zulu nation although remarkable by its military machine did not receive the support of its African neighbors because of its martial excesses (Cooper 1965; Guy 1979).

North of the Zambezi, the Zulu mode of state formation continued and smaller communities was fused together under a new type of political leadership that emphasized militarism and strong social cohesion. Yet the new states were very independent one from the other. A significant development in this area was the establishment of the Ndebele kingdom, which was soon at loggerheads with the Shona that had preceded it. Cecil Rhodes and his men later exploited the rivalry between these two powerful African states. He defeated the Ndebele and Shona people and created the British colony of Southern Rhodesia now Zimbabwe. The disunity among the Africans could also be seen in the East African hinterland (Ranger 1967).

Notwithstanding the lack of unity among African states and peoples, each demonstrated evidence of strong nationalism and patriotism that was rekindled later by Pan-Africanism. Among African nations and communities, the existence and acknowledgement of common traditions of origins, traditional cultures and values ensured social cohesion, patriotism and nationalism. For example, the Asante employed the "spirit" of the golden stool to evolve, maintain and retain the Asante Union until the British broke up the kingdom and introduced ethnicity into Asante politics (Boahen, 1974). Similarly among the Yoruba even after the collapse of Oyo Kingdom, the Oduduwa story of creation was strong and each ruler believed that the other was a brother. This is what Akinjogbin (1967) has described as the "Ebi" (kinship) theory. Agaja Trudo, the founder of the New Kingdom of Dahomey imposed a new ideology on the Aja-speaking peoples emphasizing the contribution of each citizen to the political and social unity of the kingdom. Similarly in Benin, Buganda and other centralized states, the cultural or the ideology of kingship reinforced the socio-political institutions. The ruler represented the founding ancestor of the kingdom. In the islamized states, Islam provided the founding ideology whereas in Ethiopia, the Ethiopian Orthodox Church provided the ideological base of the nation. Thus each kingdom or state had strong cultural bases in its religion that welded the socio-political institutions together.

Among societies with decentralized political institutions, the kinship system provided a strong bond. An exogamous marriage system reinforced the tradition of common brotherhood. All these welded the people together as a society, ensuring patriotism and nationalism which some of these communities demonstrated in cases of their strong resistance to alien administration (Afigbo, 1973; Oyeleye et al. 1999). Thus, the appeal to socio-political ties in the case of the centralized kingdoms or to socio-cultural connections in the case of polities with decentralized political institutions remained crucial to the sustenance of social cohesion and unity among each African community. Nonetheless, it is difficult not to accept that there were potential ethnic or sub-ethnic divisions that could easily be exacerbated by internal wars (the Yoruba civil wars of the 19th century, for example). Yet, the success of nationalism and patriotism by pre-colonial African nations could be measured in the direct absence of major ethnic problems until the arrival of European rule that thrived upon the policy of divide and rule.

That the concept of continental unity did not appear to have been widespread, if it existed at all, in pre-colonial Africa, is not extra-ordinary. Examples from the history of other continents show that there was no active concept of a European Community or of Asian unity until after 1945. So, the Pan African ideology it could be argued, remains the first of the ideals of a continental unity to be actively prosecuted by Africans in the Diaspora and those on the continent in the history of the world even though its concepts and achievements have been ridiculed by some authors (Geiss, 1974).

Despite the lack of unity among African states and peoples during the pre-colonial period, there were active trading activities among the various regions. West Africa constituted an economic region with trade in indigenous commodities such as kolanuts and gold from the forest zone to the sudanic zone and through to North Africa and Egypt. During the 19th century, the Asante kingdom was the bridge of this trade, which went to Hausaland and Bornoland from there to North Africa and Egypt. In return, the people of the sudan exported cattle and varieties of rock salt including potash to the inhabitants of the states in the forest zone. Not even the existence of other forms of trade between the Europeans on the coast and the Africans was allowed to jeopardize the trade to the hinterland. And every community ensured the safety of the traders and the trade routes even in times of wars (Agiri 1985; Austin, 1995).

Similarly, trade and trade routes flourished in East, Central and South Africa linking the various African communities. There were long caravans of traders between the East Coast and its hinterland up to the headwaters of the Congo River. Trade routes also linked Angola in the west to Mozambique in the east (Gray et al 1970). The existence of these vast trading regions of Africa was what excited the cupidity of the Europeans. The continent was cut up into new economic regions based upon the European trading activities and it is yet an uphill task to reverse the situation.

THE COLONIAL PERIOD

The fact that Pan Africanism did not achieve or could not have achieved any of its major goals during the colonial period in Africa should not come as a surprise. Initially, as stated above, its leading protagonists were located outside of Africa, in the United States and Caribbean. Secondly, the movement lacked the physical force to compel the European colonialists to listen and accede to its views. It relied on moral force that was discounted by the Europeans in favor of their own policy. Its outcry and opposition against Italian aggression and conquest of Ethiopia in 1935 went unheeded by the Western Powers. The Italian-Ethiopian war taught Pan Africanists two important lessons: first that direct military force not moral persuasion meant everything to the Europeans imperialists. Second, it became obvious that before the Pan African ideology can be effective on the African continent, colonialism must be defeated and African peoples regain their independence.

The next stage in the development of Pan Africanism therefore was the transfer of effective leadership of the movement from the US and Caribbean to Africa. The battle had to be fought on the African Continent itself.

In 1900, the first Pan African Conference was held in London; it was followed by 4 congresses of the movement in 1919, 1921, 1923 and 1927. Meanwhile, a new generation of Africans was being educated in the US, Britain and France who was to become the leaders of the movement and eventually of nationalist and independence struggles in Africa. Some of these men were present and, in fact, took part in organizing, the 1945 Pan African Congress in Manchester in the United Kingdom. They included Kwame Nkrumah, Jomo Kenyatta and nearly all the *dramatis personae* that led African countries to independence, beginning with Ghana in 1957. The 1945 Manchester Pan African Congress brought African-Americans and Africans effectively together to draw ups a new blueprint for African nationalism and accelerated the decolonization process. But it was at the first All-African Peoples Conference held in Accra in 1958 that

African nationalism received its greatest boost as an area of Pan Africanism. The nationalist struggle in Africa was now clearly defined: "seek ye first the political kingdom and all things shall be added unto you." Armed struggle against recalcitrant European rule in Africa, for example in Algeria, Kenya, Central African Federation of Rhodesia and Nyasaland, Mozambique and Angola and South Africa was now actively encouraged. This sent a signal to the Western Powers that African nationalist struggle had now reached a new age. The proclamation of unity of Africa that did not recognize the colonial boundaries caused consternation among some African leaders who regarded it as an incitement to rebellion by their citizens against their states (Ajala, 1974).

It is important to stress that African nationalism was now rediscovered on a new concept. At first, idealized ancient stories of Africa provided an ideology for the new nations e.g., Ghana, Mali and later Zimbabwe and others. Local patriotism associated with pre-colonial kingdoms and communities that were now integral parts of the new states became suspected as being hindrances to the sustenance of the new nationalism. They were tolerated only to the extent that they did not clash with the new nationalist ideas. Where they did, the new governments forcibly suppressed them. To this extent, the old ideas of patriotism became divisive within the new political set up and African leaders blamed this development upon colonialism. The question was how to put the old wine into a new bottle. It marked an important stage in the process of historical development of African nations.

If the new nations were having what has now been described as ethnic problems, how had the colonial administration been able to survive that problem? First, the colonial administration was distant from the people despite the location of their administrative officers in many districts in their territories. This made it possible for it to play the role of an arbiter in the internal politics of these territories. When it desired, it played one group interest against the other. More importantly, it controlled the effective use of force: when challenged on some occasions by local civil outbursts, such revolts were ruthlessly put down to demonstrate to the people where power ultimately lay (Rotberg, 1971).

It was, however, different with the independent states. The peoples believed that this was *their* government and it must cater not only to their needs but also redress *their* "wrongs" even if to do so would create more problems. Each African leader then sought solutions in what he believed to be the African ideal--a single party organization that allowed some form of consensus among the people. Others went over to socialism but only a few were outrightly Marxist. The nation was taken to be a village in which every section had a direct contribution to policy formulation and decision making. Consensus rather than division of opinions were encouraged (or rigidly enforced).

The fact that the one party government has not worked well in all cases is evident in the introduction of new programs for democracy all over Africa today. The Western Powers have enforced this new trend as they linked one party government systems with the failure of economic programs in each African country. Here we need to analyze two important issues. First, did Pan Africanism and nation building in Africa imply authoritarian regimes in form of one party organizations? Second, is there a logical link between one party states and failure of economic programs?

Pan Africanism only preached and supported the re-achievement of African independence. It does not lay down the specific system of government to consummate this idea. The 1945 Manchester Pan African Congress suggested the mobilization of the masses but not the political ideology of each state. Thus, Pan Africanism cannot be blamed for the excesses of some African leaders in this matter. Neither can it be said to have failed as a result of colonial legacy. Once each African nation regained its independence, the ideology of the nation and the structure of government were left to the leaders to fashion out. Pan Africanism had provided the avenue for the re-gaining of African independence. It did not provide a political formula about how each African State should be ruled. And it could not have done so; and if it had, it could not have succeeded in effecting its implementation. Africans became disillusioned when their new government used excessive power, just as the colonial rulers had done, to maintain peace. We can then conclude that the authoritarian posture of African government emanated from the colonial experience.

Furthermore, it is arguable that there is a direct link between the existence of one party state organizations and the failure of economic programs in Africa. In other words, democratization does not necessarily bring about deregulation and privatization of the economy. What do many protagonists of democratization of the political process often overlook, deregulation and privatization of the economy is that from 1960 industrialized nations promoted investment in African economies only if such an investment went into the public sector. If it involved the private sector, then the African government had to guarantee the investment. Thus, public sector investment became the order of the day. African governments became directly involved whether they became one party state or not (Green, 1981).

Thus, it erroneous to single out one party state, because multi-party states also have problems of centralized economies since they too controlled the public sector. It is yet to be seen if democratization will produce a magic solution to deregulation and privatization. What is essential is the creation of a productive middle class rather than a reenter state and a collaborative middle class. Again, this is beyond the tenets of Pan Africanism.

PAN AFRICANISM AND ECONOMIC INTEGRATION

Today, Pan Africanism is almost synonymous with African unity and economic integration. But as with the case of African nationalism and nation building, this ideology did not spell out in details the forms that African unity and economic integration should take. Would it be gradual or a one step measure leading to an economic unity? The same is true with African unity. The fact that leaders disagreed among themselves about the procedure and not the end result demonstrates the validity of the ideology. The history of the inauguration of the Organization of African Unity (OAU) in 1963 illustrates the divergent views among African leaders. In the final analysis the federalists or moderates won and the Unitarians or radicals lost. And so, the structure of the OAU has been patterned more or less after that of the United Nations Organization, without a Security Council (Ajala 1974; Mazui 1993).

It is in the area of economic integration that the colonial legacy has been very strong and undoubting. As indicated earlier on, the pre-colonial economic regions of Africa were completely disrupted and replaced by others based upon European trading activities. The political and economic nature and structure of each colonial territory followed the same pattern of dependency upon the colonial metropolis. Based upon an exploitative theory of economic internationalization, African economies supplied raw materials for European industries in return for European manufactures. Where emergency circumstances compelled as it happened during World War II, this policy was changed to allow some light and agricultural industries in the colonies. This later became known as the *import substitution theory*. This process allowed for the setting up of industries in colonial territories where there was a well-profaned demand for particular manufactures. When the maximum stage of production for the market is reached, the next stage would be the purchase of intermediate capital goods, e.g. manufacturing parts to improve the quality of production, now for export. This crucial stage is necessary for the industry to survive and be productive for the whole economy. It also carries along with it the training of local technical expertise in the industry (Hirscham, 1958; Oyeleye et al. 1999).

Unfortunately, this import substitution strategy has not been allowed full growth in any African country. Once the first stage had been attained, the second and the most important stage were hardly implemented because the financial and technological investments were controlled by European multinationals. The cost of the goods became more exorbitant and the local buyers were compelled to buy because the industry now monopolized the market. The profits are repatriated overseas. Thus, African countries that tried to follow the liberal capitalist process of industrialization have found themselves in an economic quandary.

Where African countries adopted a socialist path of production in which the major heights of the economy were nationalized, economic progress was still hampered when the products were not competitive in world market. Thus, African governments with their concern to improve the social well-being of their peoples found it very difficult to move forward to achieve this goal as a result of the colonial legacy and the fact that it is difficult to extricate their economies from a world capitalist economy.

More importantly is the attitude of African entrepreneurial class to economic production. Having been reared in the retail trade complex of the colonial economy, this class looked forward to quick returns on their investment ventures. Only very few would like to have a long-term productive investment.

Furthermore, African countries failed to reckon with the counterpanes of the West. Even before the OAU was inaugurated in 1963, the United Nations had in 1958 established the Economic Commission for Africa (ECA) with a similar objective to achieve an African Common Market. The actual reasons for the inauguration of this body have never been fully told, yet it is on record that for many years of its existence, at least until the 1970s, it seems to have served as diversionary to the real intents and purposes of the OAU. The ECA claims to be a body to provide technical and scientific information on economic integration of Africa, yet it was the independent African States that in 1960 first called for the establishment of an African Development Bank among others to promote self-reliance in economic matters. Since that institution was established, its directors have been controlled from the West and its lending powers by the industrially advanced nations (Diaku, 1985). Here again the wind was taken out of the African bag.

The ECA as an organ of the United Nations has claimed parity with the OAU. It has refused to be subordinated to institutions set up by that body to achieve economic integration. The old idea that Africans lacked the competence in economic matters may have been a major reason for the attitude of the ECA up to the 1970s. The ECA lacked the political will to carry out its plans except with the full collaboration of African leaders. It was the African countries that brought to the attention of the world the need for a New International Economic Order. African countries with support from the Caribbean, Latin American and Asian regions decried the continued imbalance in world trade against producers of primary products that further widened the gap between the industrialized and non-industrialized nations. African countries have realized that it would require some political intervention to resolve their economic problems. And they have continuously used their membership in the non-aligned movement, the United Nations Conference on Trade and Development (UNCTAD) and the United Nations (UN) to focus attention on their problem (Mazrui, 1993).

While African leaders have realized the importance of political pressure and will to push for desirable economic ends in international trade and economy, they have not been forthcoming to use this process to achieve regional economic integration within Africa. Here, the ECA has been doing well since the 1980s in encouraging African nations to work together to achieve regional economic cooperation. Some of Africa's leaders still persist to recognize and pursue economic links with their former colonial masters. The conflict between the existence of two regional economic bodies in West Africa, namely Economic Community of West African States (ECOWAS) devoted to the attainment of a full economic and political union of West African States and Economic Community of West Africa (ECWA) that has strong financial and economic ties with France is a case in point. The move to have a common West African currency to aid further intra-West African trade in ECOWAS is thwarted by ECWA that has its currency, the local franc, tied directly to the French Franc. The adoption of a common currency by the European Union may not necessarily resolve this problem.

Can ECOWAS achieve its objective in reducing the economic dependency of West African countries? Asante (1993) has convincingly argued this cannot be unless and until the provisions of the ECOWAS treaty are modified to introduce an "institution or machinery which is empowered" to negotiate with external actors [foreign investors] on behalf of the Community. The foreign investors should be willing to provide the necessary investment and divestment or an institution to control the importation of technology.

The South African Development Coordination Conference (SADDC) inaugurated in April 1980 by Angola, Botswana, Mozambique, Tanzania, Zambia, Lesotho, Malawi, Swaziland and Zimbabwe was initially to control the economic influence of South Africa upon this region. All these countries except Tanzania and Angola had a long history of labor migration of their peoples to the South African mines. Thus, these countries had contributed to the economic development and wealth of South Africa and the sustenance of the apartheid system. SADDC, then, was one of the Pan-Africanist measures against colonialism and apartheid. On the positive side, SADDC was concerned about transport problems in this region of Africa. At the same time, the Preferential Trade Area for Eastern and Southern Africa (PTA) was established to replace the defunct East African Economic Community and include Ethiopia, Somalia, and the countries in the SADDC to foster inter-regional trade. Since the inauguration of these regional economic bodies, South Africa has been under a new government that has dismantled apartheid with the Africans sharing power in government. It is yet to be seen what impact this will have on an economic union from South Africa to the Horn of Africa. What role will South African economy, as a fully industrialized market economy, play on the economies of the other African States? Will it lead to another incidence of dependency in which the South African economy is the center and the other African economies, the periphery? The answer to these questions will depend on the structures of the internal economies of the African States, the movement towards self-reliance in industrialization and production.

Other regional economic cooperation schemes sponsored by ECA are Economic Community of Central States comprising the Central African Republic, Congo, Chad, Gabon and the United Republic of Cameroon. These states were former members of the French Equatorial Africa and despite political vicissitudes, they are closely attached to their former colonial master. It is difficult to see how they would free themselves and form an independent Central African Common Market.

Similarly, the projected Economic Community of the Great Lakes Countries bringing together the Democratic Republic of Congo (formerly Zaire), Burundi and Rwanda suffers from the vertical economic link between these countries with France and Belgium (Adedeji, 1993). The path towards an economic integration is fraught with problems of existing ties based on the old colonial connections. In North Africa, nationalist economic integration policies have made the achievement of regional economic integration a mirage.

THE COLONIAL LEGACY

In this concluding section I shall try to demonstrate how colonialism has influenced sub-Sahara Africa nations post-independent politics. Two aspects of this legacy and its aftermath are noteworthy. The first is the patterns of public administration, education and legal systems. The second is what we will refer to as the economic legacy.

When the colonial authority departed the Third World nations little had been done to bridge the differences between the tribes and ethnicity's. The political system that was supposed to sustain the nations in their developing years had been hastily improvised and in no way met the challenges represented by a diverse humanity, espousing different values, traditions, and practices. Neither were the sub-Sahara Africa nations political leaders up to the task of transforming the colonial legacy into a coherent national political experience. Burdened by Westminster parliamentary, Semi-presidential, and federal models, Third World only marginally understood, the politicians who had received the transfer of power were inclined to promote their regional and ethnic interests, and they diverted attention from the tasks of becoming national.

Colonialism is generally held by Europeans to have progressively improved sub-Sahara Africa nations productive capacity through the introduction of modern technology, and total per capita output. Belgium, Britain, France, Portugal and Spain would point to the wider provision of education, health care facilities, roads and other services as an indication of spreading social benefits to Third World nations during the post-independence period. However, the colonial administrators fail to compare the exploitation rate with the development they created in their formal colonies. The national product of these colonies was not distributed equally by the Europeans, and it was certain that the real incomes and levels of welfare of the broad mass of the population did not improve. Post-independence financial loan to sub-Sahara Africa nations have failed to produce development because much of it had been channeled to support corrupt and authoritarian allies of the First World rather than to promote development. The question then is: how did colonialism develop the sub-Sahara Africa nations?

When Europeans terminated their colonial rule in sub-Sahara Africa between 1955 and 1965, they left behind a considerable common heritage in culture, language and inter-territorial institutions which had previously facilitated cooperation between Europe and the people of sub-Sahara Africa nations. The British, French, Spanish, Portuguese and Belgian left behind their respective systems of education, administration, legal, language and currency. During colonial periods, the British imposed indirect rule of administration on its colonies.

They maintained that indirect rule was designed to protect and preserve sub-Sahara Africa nations political systems, traditions, and cultures, however, the consequence of indirect rule was that it reinforced separate ethnic identity and stunted the development of a national and tribal political consciousness. This pattern of government served the British colonial interest very well, permitting them to play ethnic groups against each other. Meaningful political participation was not encouraged. Political discourse which is important in any system but perhaps more so in one that was evolving, was not nurtured during the colonial regime.

British rule exacerbated differences of class, region and community in sub-Sahara Africa nations. The emergent nationalist movement in sub-Sahara Africa nations inherited this values and was led by elites of business people, professionals and rural peasants who promoted what they were expected to gain economically and politically from independence. This pattern spilled over to the post-independence political era. Hence, it is unrealistic for anyone to expect ethnic groups that had been played one against the other for so long by British colonial administration, to know how to forge one nation suddenly when they were granted independence. Thus, inter-ethnic political violence in former British colonies can be partly traced to indirect rule.

The British imposition of parliamentary system of government in almost all its former colonies at independence is another vital legacy. Independent sub-Sahara Africa nations who inherited the British parliamentary system - the Westminster Model - with multi-party structure, government opposition party, independent judiciary and civil service, found out later that their ethnic and regional divisions made it difficult to debate differences while also functioning cooperatively in national politics.

The Belgians, Spanish, French, Germans and Portuguese excised a highly centralized or "direct" type of administration. This means that European rule was imposed on the people of sub-Sahara Africa nations regardless of the existing political relationship among the citizens. The result of this centralized administration was that the nations were governed without any regard to existing ethnic stratification. The French imposed forced interaction and equal subjugation. Reinforcement of ethnic fragmentation did not occur. This is not to say that ethnic conflict did not or does not exist in French or Portuguese colonies. It simply suggests that it is less pronounced in French areas, but salient in Portuguese-ruled ones. Indeed the Portuguese colonial policy clearly alienated the majority of Third World colonies they ruled over.

German colonial administration was highly centralized. They went into sub-Sahara Africa colonies with the idea of economically expiating the areas and maximizing there economic power as fast as possible. Military officers and private entrepreneurs were given power and responsibility, but their political ineptitude soon became evident when they encountered local resistance and suppressed it harshly (Khpoya, 1994; Oyeleye et al. 1999). Due to bitterness and resistance from the people of Tanganyika (now Tanzania in Africa), the Germans decided to introduce some reform policy called "scientific colonialism". Under this policy the German colonial administration constructed several capital projects such as roads, railroads, and trade centers.

The Belgian colonial administration encouraged massive transfer of wealth from what is now Democratic Republic of Congo to Belgium. Their colonized citizens in sub-Sahara Africa nations received only limited education that would allow them to read the Bible take orders efficiently from the missionaries and function at best as clerks in the colonial bureaucracy. The colonized people were not prepared to assume control of their nation at independence. Between 1955 and 1965 when most of the sub-Sahara Africa nations were granted independence, they were left with a high literacy rate. An interesting irony is that some of the Third World nations became exemplified in evangelical success for the missionaries. Yet they were the least prepared for self-rule. Sub-Sahara Africa nations continue to be among the worst governed, and the poorest despite having the world's largest reserve of precious minerals.

The Christianity and education are also part of the colonial legacy in sub-Sahara Africa nations. After colonial administration was established, the missionaries and the colonial authorities forged a very close working relationship (Mazrui 1986; Khapoya 1994). Schools were staffed and ran by missionaries but subsidized in varying degrees by colonial regimes, whose interest in colonial education simply was to ensure that enough sub-Sahara Africa citizens were educated to meet the limited need for semi-skilled workers in colonial bureaucracies. According to Ali Mazrui (1986), European religion instilled submissiveness by stressing that life on earth was temporary, to be used only as exercise for eternal life. To qualify for eternal life, one was taught to exercise Christian virtues of forgiveness, submissiveness, and patience. Humiliation and suffering, such as were being endured by sub-Sahara Africa nations during colonialism, were thought to be enabling and spiritually cleansing. The church ran the school system, and put major emphasis on religious education rather than the kind of education that would have permitted sub-Sahara Africa citizens to play a greater role in the future political affairs of their nation. Therefore, we could tie the relationship between the church missions and the colonial regimes as truly a conspiracy to under develop the people of sub-Sahara Africa nations.

Frank Gunder (1969) sees the deindustrialization of India under British colonialism, and the disruption of African society by slave trade and subsequent colonialism, and the total destruction of sub-Sahara Africa civilization by Spanish and Portuguese conquistadors as example of creation of underdevelopment. The imposition of European economic, political and social institutions model on Third World nations caused underdevelopment. Frank Gunder argued that sub-Sahara Africa nations serve as economic satellites of the highly developed regions of Northern America and Western Europe in the international capitalist system. He further argued that the development of sub-Sahara Africa nations will be stimulated by indiscriminately transferring capital, institutions, and values from Europe and North America to their former colonies. He suggested that sub-Sahara Africa nations can develop only by withdrawing from the world capitalist system. Such a withdrawal means a large reduction in trade, aid, and investment, and technology from developed capitalist countries.

Many scholars (Mazrui 1986; Dordon 1996, Khapoya 1994; Mamadani 1996; Nafziger 1997) agree with Frank Gunder that former colonial colonies paid dearly for economic dependency under European rule. Sub-Sahara Africa nations development was not self-directed. Production was directed toward external rather than domestic needs, economic policies inhibited local industrial activity and led to uneven ethnic and regional economic progress. The manifestations of dependence include over-reliance on European and American markets, susceptibility to faultiness in commodity prices, the growth of foreign debt, the dominant position of multinational companies within the economy, and the alleged willingness of the post-independence political and administrative elites to cooperate with former colonial regime interest in Europe. Dependence permits the exploitation of the region by Europeans, even after the end of former colonial authority particularly through the repatriation of profits by Western multinational corporations operating in sub-Sahara Africa nations. The full potential of sub-Sahara Africa nations resources was not realized under the colonial regimes and in the majority of post-independence governments.

The major point in this book is that sub-Sahara Africa nations social, economic and political problems are only partly its own making. Britain, France, Belgium, Spain, Germany, Portugal and North America should face their own complicity in creating and maintaining sub-Sahara Africa nations plight. After almost six hundred years of exploiting the sub-Sahara Africa, an indiscriminate relationship between these European countries and sub-Sahara Africa nations to erase the legacies of colonialism and post-independence dominance or neo-colonialism seems long overdue. This discourse suggests that the manipulation and exploitation of sub-Sahara Africa nations by the Africans to secure economic and political dominance has been ineffectual if not counter productive. Mutual and equitable cooperation between the First World and sub-Sahara Africa nations in economic, political, education and social development without exploitation could have enhanced the latter's development and stability.

CONCLUSION

While Pan Africanism has led directly to freeing Africans from the shackles of European colonial rule and domination, it has only been partially successful in achieving continental economic integration and freedom. The colonial period is more than a transition in the life of Africa; it is an epoch when new economic institutions that are still with us were set up. It has been difficult to free African economies from the clutches of dependency and marginalization in world economy because the options opened to African nations are few. They cannot go into an economic cyst, to protect themselves and build up their economies as China, Russia, and even Japan have done. The socialist economic system has not succeeded because of economic pressure from the West to which the African economies traded. The African economies found it difficult to eat from the tables of two diametrically opposed donors.

Now that the Cold War is over, Africa's economic problems can be reduced to three major issues: (1) the lack of political will by Africa's leaders to achieve economic cooperation among themselves, (2) the restructuring of the internal economies to allow for regional economic integration and, (3) the rise of a new set of African entrepreneurial class devoted to economic production. The arrival of such a private sector will achieve economic progress in a market economy.

REFERNCES

Adedeji, Adebayo. 1993. "Comparative Strategies of Economic Development in Africa", in Ali Mazrui (ed) Africa Since 1935. London: Heinemann. pp. 393-431.

Adedeji, R. A. 1971. Power and Diplomacy in Northern Nigeria, 1804-1906: The Sokoto Emirate and Its Enemies. London: Longman.

Afigbo, A. E. 1973. "Patterns of Igbo Resistence to British Conquest. London: Longman.

Agiri, Babatunde. 1985. "Kola Trade in West Africa" in G. Volger et al. Volz: Koln. pp. 528-532.

Ajala, A. 1974. Pan-Africanism: Evolution, Progress and Prospects. New York: St. Martins Press.

Akinjogbin, I. A. 1967.Dahomey and Its Neighbors 1708-1818. New York: Cambridge University Press.

Asante, S. K. 1993. "Pan Africanism and Regional Integration" in Ali Mazrui (ed), Africa Since 1935.

Austin, G. 1995. Asante's Response to the ending of the Slave trade, in R.C. Law,

From Salve trade to Legitimate Commerce, The Commercial Transition in 19th Century West Africa. Cambridge, MA: Cambridge University Press. Pp. 93 –118.

Boahen, Adu. 1974. "Politics in Ghana 1800-1974" in Ade Ajayi and Crowder M. (ed.) History of West Africa, Vol II. London: Longman.

Boahen, Adu A. 1990. Africa Under Colonial Domination 1880-1935. Unesco General History of Africa. Vol. VII. London: James Currey.

Cooper, Omer. 1979. The Zulu Aftermath. London: Longman.

Diaku, I. 1985. "African Development Bank and African Development Fund: Problems and Prospects" in Onwuka R. I. and Asefa Sesay (ed) The Future of Regionalism in Africa. New York: St. Martin's Press.

Geiss, Imanuel. 1974. The Pan African Movement: A History of Pan_Africanism in America. New York: Africana Publishing Company.

Gondon A. and Gondon, Donald. 1996. Understanding Contemporary Africa. Boulder: Lynne Rienner Publishers.

Gray, Richard and David Birmingham (ed), 1970. Precolonial Africa Trade. London: Macmillan.

Green, Reginald. 1981. "Foreign Direct Investment and African Political Economy: In Adebayo Adedeji (ed) Indigenization of African Economics. New York: African Publishing Company.

Hirscham, Albert. 1958. The Strategy of Economic Development. New Haven: Yale University Press.

Jacobs, Sylvia. 1981. The African Nexus Black American Perpectives on the European Partitioning of Africa 1880-1920. Westport: Greenwood Press.

Khapoya, Vincent. 1994. The African Experience: An Introduction. New Jersey: Prentice Hall.

Kiwanuka, S. 1971. A History of Buganda. London: Longman.

Mamadani, Mahmood. 1996. Citizen and Subject: Contemporary Africa and The legacy of Late Colonialism. Princeton University Press.

Martin, Tony. 1985. The Pan African Connection, From Slavery to Garvey and Beyond. Boston, MA: The Majority Press.

Mazrui, Ali. 1986. The African: A Triple Heritage. London: BBC Publication

Mazrui, Ali. (ed.) 1993. Africa Since 1935, Unesco General History of Africa, Vol VIII, London: Heinemann.

Nafziger, Wayne. 1997. The Economics of Developing Countries. Upper Saddle River: Prentice Hall.

Oloruntimehin, B.O. 1972. The Segu Tukular Empire. London: Longman.

Oyeleye, Oyediran, and Adigun Agbaje. 1999. Nigeria: Politics of Transition and Governance 1986-1996. Senegal, Dakar: CODESRIA.

Ranger, T. O. 1967. Revolt in Southern Rhodesia 1896-1897. London: Heinemann.

Rotberg, Robert (ed). 1971. Rebellion in Black Africa. New York: Oxford University Press.

World Bank. 1996. World Development Report. New York: Oxford University Press.

SELECTED BIBLIOGRAPHY

Abgese, Pita. 1990. "The Impending Political Demise of Nigeria's Forthcoming Third Republic." Africa Today, 37 (3) 23-44.

Aborisade, O. and R. Mundt. 1998. Politics in Nigeria. New York: Longman.

Adams, Ian. 1993. Political Ideology Today. Manchester: Manchester University press, pp.82-83.

Adedeji, Adebayo. 1993. "Comparative Strategies of Economic Development in Africa", in Ali Mazrui (ed.) Africa Since 1935. London: Heinemann. pp. 393-431.

Adedeji, R. A. 1971. Power and Diplomacy in Northern Nigeria, 1804-1906: The Sokoto Emirate and Its Enemies. London: Longman.

Adelman, L. Kenneth. 1979. Liberia: "Hosting the O.A.U." Africa Report, (July-August). Africa News, (1980) April 21.

Afigbo, A. E. 1973. "Patterns of Igbo Resistence to British Conquest. London: Longman.

Agiri, Babatunde. 1985. "Kola Trade in West Africa" in G. Volger et al. Volz: Koln. pp. 528-532.

Ahmadu, Bello. 1962. My Life: Autobiography of the Sardauna. Daily Times Press, Lagos.

Ajala, A. 1974. Pan-Africanism: Evolution, Progress and Prospects. New York: St. Martins Press.

Aka, S.M.O. 1994. "For My Northern Neighbor". Community Concord Newspaper. Lagos-Nigeria. August 21, p.5.

Ake, Claude. 1973. "Explaining Political Instability in New States." Journal of Modern African Studies, vol. 11 (September), p. 356-373.

Ake, Claude. 1996. Democracy and Development in Africa. Washington, D.C.: Brooking Institute Press.

Akin-Aina, Wale. 1994. "Logic in the Illogical". Newswatch News Magazine, Lagos, Nigeria. July 25, p.9.

Akinjogbin, I. A. 1967.Dahomey and Its Neighbors 1708-1818. New York: Cambridge University Press.

Alesina, A. and D. Rodrik. 1994. 'Distributive Politics and Economic Growth', Quarterly Journal of Economics, 109: 465-90.

Alesina, A. and R. Perotti. 1994. 'The Political Economy of Growth: a Critical Survey of the Recent Literature', World Bank Economic Review, 8 (3): 351-71.

Alesina, A. and E. Spolaore 1995. On the Number and Size of National mimeo, Harvard University and ECARE (University Libre of Bruxelles).

Allen, Susan. 1973. "President Tolbert: Exclusive Interview," Africa Development 8 (July).

Almond, G. A. 1978. Comparative Politics (2nd edition) New York: Little, Brown & Co.

Almond, G. and Coleman J. (ed). 1960. The Politics of Developing Areas. Princeton: Princeton University Press.

Ames, Barry. 1987. Political Survival: Politicians and Public Policy in Latin American. Los Angeles: University of California Press.

Amin, Samir. 1967. Développement du capitalisme en Côte d'Ivoire, Paris.

Amin, Samir. 1972. Unequal Development, New York: Monthly Review Press.

Amin, S. 1976. Unequal Development. New York: Monthly Review Press.

Ammendola, Curtris, Blonddish, and Kommers Lancaster, Western European Government and Politics, New York: Longman, 1997.

Anderson, Benedict. 1991. Imagined Communities: Reflections on the Origin and Spread of Nationalism. New YorK: Verso.

Andre, Gunder, Frank. 1969. Latin America: Underdevelopment or Revolution? New York: Monthly Review Press.

Anyanwu, Aham. 1992. Nigerian Structural Adjustment Program: A Multi-Sectoral Analysis. Enugu: ABIC Books and Equipment Limited.

Apter, David. 1965. The Politics of Modernization. Chicago: University of Chicago Press.

Armah, Kwesi. 1974. Ghana: Nkrumah's Legacy. London: Rex Collings Ltd.

Arulpragasam, Jehan and David Sahn. 1997. Economic Transition in Guinea: Implications for Growth and Poverty. New York: New York University Press.

Asante, S. K. 1993. "Pan Africanism and Regional Integration" in Ali Mazrui (ed), Africa Since 1935.

Asante, S.K.B. 1986. The Political Economy of Regionalism in Africa. New York: Praeger.

Austin, G. 1995. Asante's Response to the ending of the Slave trade, in R.C. Law, From Salve trade to Legitimate Commerce, The Commercial Transition in 19th Century West Africa. Cambridge, MA: Cambridge University Press. Pp. 93 –118.

Awolowo, O. 1946. Path To Nigerian Freedom. London: Faber and Faber Ltd.

Awolowo, Obafemi. 1947. Path to Nigerian Freedom. University of Ibadan Press, Ibadan, Nigeria. p.28.

Awolowo, Obafemi. 1981. Awo on the Nigerian War. Tribune Press, Ibadan, Nigeria.

Awolowo, O. 1987. Adventures in Power (Book Two): The Travails of Democracy and the Rule of Law. Ibadan: Evans Brothers (Nig. Pub.) Ltd.

Ayittey, George B. N. 1991. *Indigenous African Institutions.* New York: Transnational Publishers, Inc.

Azar, Edward. 1983. "The Theory of Protracted Social Conflict and the Challenge of transforming Conflict Situations, in Diana A. Zinnes, ed. Conflict Processes and the Break down of International Systems, vol. 20, no. 2. Denver, CO: University of Denver Press. Pp.92-111.

Azarya, Victor. 1994. "Civil Society and Disengagement in Africa." In John W. Harbeson Donald Rothchid, and Naomi Chazan, eds. Civil Society and the State in Africa. Boulder, CO: Lynne Rienner. Pp.83-100.

Bach, Daniel. 1999. (ed.). Regionalization in Africa: Integration and Disintegration. Bloomington, IN: Indiana University Press.

Banton, Michael. 1983. Racial and Ethnic Competition. Cambridge: Cambridge University Press.

Barkan, Joel D. ed. 1994. Beyond Capitalism vs. Socialism in Kenya and Tanzania, Boulder, Lynne Rienner Publishers.

Bates, Robert. 1972. "Ethnicity and Modernization in Contemporary Africa." Social Science Working Paper 16; Pasadena: California Institute of Technology, (November).

Bates, Robert H. 1974. "Ethnic Competition and Modernization in Contemporary Africa". Comparative Political Studies 6, (January), 457-84.

Becker, G.S. 1996. The Making of preference and Values, Cambridge MA, Harvard University Press.

Bédié, Henri Konan. 1992. "The Speech of the first ordinary opening session of the Parliament" in Abidjan, Côte d'Ivoire, on April 29.

Beinaart, William. 1994. Twentieth- Century South Africa. New York: Oxford University Press.

Bello, A. 1962. My Life. Cambridge: The University Press.

Benien Henry and Victor Diejomaoh. 1981. The Political Economy of Income Distribution in Nigeria. New York: Holmes and Meier, pp. 373-420.

Bernstein, H. (ed.) 1973. Underdevelopment and Development. Boltimore:Penguin Press.

Betts, Richard K. (ed.) 1994. Conflict After The Cold War: Arguments on Causes of War and Peace, New York, Macmillan Publishing Company.

Bienen, Henry. 1971. The Military and Modernization. Princeton University Press.

Bienen, Henry, and Jeffrey Herbst. 1996. "The Relationship between Political and Economic Reform in Africa." Comparative Politics 29, (October): 23-42.

Boahen, Adu. 1974. "Politics in Ghana 1800-1974" in Ade Ajayi and Crowder M. (ed) History of West Africa, Vol II. London: Longman.

Boahen, Adu A. 1990. Africa Under Colonial Domination 1880-1935. Unesco General History of Africa. Vol. VII. London: James Currey.

Bollen, K. 1979. "Political Democracy and the Timing of Development." American Sociological Review, 44: pp.572-87.

Booker, Salih. 1998. "Thinking Regionally: Priorities for U.S. Policy Toward Africa" (http://www/africapolicy.org/bp/region.htlm). Background paper (Internet source).

Bratton, Michael 1998. "Second Elections in Africa", Journal of Democracy, Vol. 9, No 3, July, pp. 51-66.

Briggs, Jean. 1981. " A Pint of Blood? or $20". Forbes. (October 12, Issue), pp. 91-98.

Burkey, Ingvild (1991) "People's Power in Theory and Practice: the Resistance Council System in Uganda". Unpublished paper, Yale University.

Callaghy, Thomas. 1993. "Political Passion and Economic Interests: Economic Reform and Political Structure in America" in Hemmed (ed). Responses to Africa's Economic Decline. New York: Columbia University Press. p. 479.

Cammack Paul, David Pool and William Tordoff. 1993. Third World Politics: A Comparative Introduction. Baltimore: The John Hopkin University.

Cardoso, F. and E. Faletto. 1979. Dependency and Underdevelopment in Latin America, Berkeley, Los Angeles, University of California Press.

Carter, Gwendolen M. and Patric O'meara. 1985. (Eds.) African Independence: The First Twenty-five Years. Indiana University Press, Bloomington

Central Bank of Nigeria. 1996. Annual Report and Statement of Accounts.

Cetron, Marvin. And Oven Davis. 1991. Crystal Globe the Haves and have-nots of the New World Order. New York: St. Martin's, pp.185 - 205.

Chazan, Naomi. 1992. "Africa's Democratic Challenge." World Policy Journal. 9/2 (spring) 279 – 305.

Chabal, Patrick. 1994. Power in Africa. New York: St. Martin's Press.

Chepkwony, A.1987. The Role of NGOs in Development: A study of the NCCK 1963-78 Uppsala: Scandinavian Institute of Africa Studies.

Chilcote, H. Ronald. ed. 1982. Dependency and Marxism: Toward a Resolution of the Debate, Boulder, Colorado: Westview Press.

Chilcote, R.H. and Johnson D. L. (ed.). 1983. Theories of Development: Mode of Production or Dependency? Beverly Hills: Sage Publications.

Christian Science Monitor (The) 19 June 1997 "New Rulers, U.S. Plan Give Africa a Future", (Judith Matloff).

Christian Science Monitor (The), 1 April 1998, "Africa's Dreams Begin to Take Root", (Kate Dunn), p. 1.

Chweya, L. et al. 1996. "Political Communication: Its Role in State-Civil Society contest in Kenya", in African Council for Communication Education Biennial Conference, Cape Town, Cape Town, South Africa, November, 1996.

Clark, Leon. 1970. Through African Eyes Cultures In Change. The Rise Nationalism: Freedom Regained. No. V. Westport, CT: Praeger.

Clower, Robert et al. 1966. Growth Without Development: An Economic Survey of Liberia, Evanston: Northwestern University Press.

CODESRIA Bulletin .1993. No. 1.

Coleman, J. S. 1986. Nigeria: Background To Nationalism. Benin-City, Katrineholm: Broburg and Wistrom.

Coleman, J.S. 1987 'Norms as Social Capital', in G. Radnitzky and P. Bernholz (eds) Economic Imperialism, New York: Paragon.

Coleman, J.S. 1988 'Social Capital in the Creation of Human Capital', American Journal of Sociology, 94 (Supplement): S95-SI20.

Coleman. J.S. 1990 Foundations of Social Theory, Boston MA: Harvard University Press.

Coleman, J. S. and Roseberg, C. G. Jr. (eds.) (1966). Political Parties and national Integration in Tropical Africa. Berkeley and Los Angeles: University of California Press.

Collier, P 1995a 'The Marginalisation of Africa', Center for the Study of African Economies, Oxford University (September).

Collier, P. 1995b. 'Recent African Economic Performance and its Implications' mimeo, Kennedy School of Government, Harvard University.

Construire l''Afrique: le Magazine panafricain de la politique et de l'enterprise 1994. No-21-Aôut-Novembre

Conteh-Morgan, Earl. 1997. *Democratization in Africa: The Theory and Dynamics of Political Transitions*. Westport: Praeger.

Cooper, Omer. 1979. The Zulu Aftermath. London: Longman.

Crawford, Young. 1994. The African Colonial Sate in Comparative Perspective. New Haven: Yale University Press.

Cribb, Robert and Collin Brown. 1995. Modern Indonesia. New York: Longman.

Curtin, Philip, Steven Feierman, Leonard Thompson, and Jan Vansina. 1994. *African History from the Earliest Times to Independence*. London: Longman.

Czempiel, Ernest-Otto. 1983. "America-Germany: A Particular Relations," German Foreign Affairs Review. Vol. 34, 78 - 101.

Czempiel, Ernest-Otto. 1983. "America-Germany: A Particular Relations," German Foreign Affairs Review. Vol. 34. Ethnicity and Politics in Liberia,

Dahl, Robert. 1971. Polyarchy: Participation and Opposition. New haven, CT: Yale University Press.

Dahl, Robert. 1983. Dilemmas of Pluralist Democracy. New Haven, CT: Yale University Press.

Dahl, Robert. 1989. Democracy and its Critics. New Haven, CT: Yale University Press.

Daily Nation, October 14, 1996.

Daily Telegraph (The), 9 May 1996 "Ugandan President seeks Poll Approval after 10 Years in Power", (Louise Tunbridge) p. 15.

Davidson, Basil. 1992. *Black Man's Burden: Africa and the Curse of the Nation-State*. New York: Times Books.

David-West, Tam. 1994. "Nigerian Federalism and The Virus of Disunity". The Guardian Press. (January 2), pp.5-6.

Davies, James C. 1962. "Towards a Theory of Revolution". American Sociological Review, pp.5-19.

Decalo, Samuel. 1990. *Coups and Army Rule in Africa.* New Haven: Yale University Press

Deutsch, Karl. 1953. Nationalism and Social Communication: An Inquiry into the Foundation of Nationality: Cambridge, MIT Press.

Diaku, I. 1985. "African Development Bank and African Development Fund: Problems and Prospects" in Onwuka R. I. and Asefa Sesay (ed) The Future of Regionalism in Africa. New York: St. Martin's Press.

Diamond, Larry. 1987. "Ethnicity and Ethnic Conflict". The Journal of Modern African Studies. Vol. 25 (1) pp.117-128.

Diamond Larry, Juan J. Linz, and Seymour Martin Lipset, eds. 1988. Democracy in Developing Countries: Africa. Boulder, CO: Lynne Rienner.

Diamond, Larry, Juan J. Linz, and Martin Lipset (Eds.) Politics of Developing Countries: Comparing Experiences with Democracy, Boulder, COLO: Lynne Rienner, 1995.

Diamond, L. 1988. Class, Ethnicity, and Democracy in Nigeria: The Failure of the First Republic. Syracuse: Syracuse University Press.

Dibie, Robert. 1994." ECOWAS: Is Functionalism the Answer to Regional Economic Integration in West Africa." Journal of Ethno-Development, Vol. 3, #3.

Dibie, Robert. 2000. Understanding Public Policy in Nigeria. Westport, CT: Greenwood Press.

Dibie, Robert and Sharron Herron. 2001. "Nigeria Public Administrators Perception of Managerial Skills." International Journal of Public Administration. (forthcoming).

Dicey, A. V. 1982. Introduction to the Study of Law of the Constitution. Indianapolis: Library Classic, pp. 107 – 179.

Dicklitch, Susan (1995) "Indigenous Non-governmental Organizations, Civil Society and Democratic Transition in Uganda: 1986-1994". Ph.D. Dissertation, University of Toronto.

Dicklitch, Susan (1995-96) "Uganda: a microcosm of crises and hope in sub-Saharan Africa", International Journal, Vol. LI, winter, pp. 103-125.

Dicklitch, Susan (1998) The Elusive Promise of NGOs in Africa: Lessons from Uganda. London and New York: Macmillan and st. Martin's.

Dike, Enwere. 1994. Economic Transformation in Nigeria. Zaria: Ahmadu Bello University Press.

Dos Santos, T. 1970. "The Structure of Dependence". American Economic Review #60, pp. 231-6.

Drake, Christine. 1989. National Integration in Indonesia. Honolulu: University of Hawaii Press.

DuBois, W.E.B. 1990. *The Soul of Black Folk.* New York: Vintage.

Duignan, Peter, and Jackson Roberts. eds. 1986. Politics and Government in African States 1960-1985. Stanford, CA: Hoover Institute Press.

Dunn, D. Elwood. 1979. The Foreign Policy of Liberia During Tubman Era: 1944 -1971, Benham, Hutchinson Pub. Group.

Durant, W. J. 1924. The Story of Philosophy: The Lives and Opinions of the Greater Philosophers. Garden City: Garden City Publishing Co.

Duverger, M. 1959. Political Parties: Their Organization and Activity in the Modern State. London, Methuen and Co. Ltd.

Easterly, W. and R. Levine. 1995. 'Africa's Growth Tragedy: a Retrospective 1960-89', mimeo, Macroeconomic and Growth Division, World Bank, June.

Eastman, Ernest. 1983. The Speech on "Liberia's new role in Africa." Georgetown University, November 29. Washington, D.C.

Eckstein, H. 1968. "Parties, Political Party Systems," International Encyclopedia of Social Sciences, Vol. 11, pp. 436-453.

Ekeh, Peter. 1975. "Colonialism and the Two Publics in Africa: A Theoretical Statement." Comparative Studies Society and History, Vol. 17, No. 1.

Eldersveld, S. 1982. Political Parties in American Society. New York: Basic Books.

Emerson, R. 1966. Parties and National Integration in Lapalombara, J. and Weiner, M. (eds.) Political Parties and Political Development. Princeton: Princeton University Press.

Epstein, L. D. 1967. Political Parties in Western Democracies. New York: Prager.

Epstein, L. D. 1975. "Political Parties," in Fred Green stein and Nelson Polsby, ed., The Handbook of Political Science. Vo. 4, Nongovernmental Politics. Reading. Mass.: Addison-Wesley.

Esmara, Hendra. 1975. "Regional Income Disparities." Bulletin of Indonesian Economic Studies 11 (March Issue), pp. 44-58.

Esman, Milton. 1973. "The Management of Communal Conflict." Public Policy, Vol. 21, (Winter), pp. 62-81.

Esman, Milton. 1991. Management Dimensions of Development. West Hartford: Kumarian Press.

Esman, Milton. 1994. Ethnic Politics. Ithaca, New York: Cornell University Press.

Essien, Efiong. 1990. Nigeria Under Structural Adjustment. Ibadan: Foundation Publishers.

Fanon, Frantz.. 1963. The Wretched of the Earth. New York:. Grover Press.

Financial Times (The), 5 February 1996, "Uganda Asians start up again: An Enterprising Community Six Years after it was Allowed to Return", (Michael Wrong), p. 7.

Findlay, R. 1995. 'Notes on the Political Economy of Nationalism', in A. Breton, G. Galeotti, P Salmon and R. Wintrobe (eds.) Nationalism and Rationality, Cambridge: Cambridge University Press.

Fleischman, Janet. 1994. Easy Prey: Child Soldiers in Liberia, New York: Human Rights Watch.

Friedmann, John. 1972. "A General Theory of Polarized Development," in Growth Centers in Regional Economic Development. Niles M. Hansen (ed). New York: The Free Press, pp. 82-102.

Funga, F. 1991. "Pouvoir, ethnies et regions" Dialogue (149) (Nov.-Dec.).

Furtado, Celso. 1970. Economic Development of Latin America: A Survey from Colonial Times to the Cuban Revolution. Cambridge University Press.

Geertz, Clifford. 1994. "Primordial and Civic Ties." Pp 29-34 in Hutchinson and Anthony D. Smith Ed., Nationalism. Oxford University Press.

Geiss, Imanuel. 1974. The Pan African Movement: A History of Pan_Africanism in America. New York: Africana Publishing Company.

Gellner, Ernest. 1983. Nations and Nationalism. London: Oxford University Press

Gertzel, Cherry (1990) "Uganda's Continuing Search for Peace", Current History, Vol. 89, No. 547, May, pp. 205-208, 231-232.

Gifford, Paul. 1994. Christianity and Politics in Does' Liberia, Cambridge, New York: Cambridge University Press.

Ginsburg, Mark B. Ed. 1992. Understanding Educational Reform in Global Context :Economy. State and Ideology, New York: Garland Publishing, Inc.

Gitonga, A. K. 1987. "The Meaning and Foundations of Democracy" in Oyugi, W.O. et al, (eds) Democratic Theory and Practice in Africa. Nairobi: Heinemann.

Gitonga, Afrifa K (1988) in Walter Oygui O., A tieno Odhiambo, Michael Chege and Afrifa K. Gitonga (eds). Democratic Theory and Practice in Africa.

Glickman, Harvey, ed. 1995. Ethnic Conflict and Democratization in Africa. Atlanta, GA: African Studies Association.

Goldstein, Joshua. 1994. International Relations. Harper Collins College Publishers, pp. 392-93.

Gondon A. and Gondon, Donald. 1996. Understanding Contemporary Africa. Boulder: Lynne Rienner Publishers.

Gordon, Milton M. 1964. Assimilation in American Life: The Role of Race, Religion, and National Origins. New York: Oxford University Press.

Gordon, M. 1974. "Domestic Conflict and the Origins of the First World War". Journal of Modern History 46:191-226.

Graf. William. 1988. The Nigerian State, Political Economy, State Class and Political System in Post-Colonial Era. Portsmouth: Heinemann Press.

Gray, Richard and David Birmingham (ed), 1970. Precolonial Africa Trade. London: Macmillan.

Green, Reginald. 1981. "Foreign Direct Investment and African Political Economy: In Adebayo Adedeji (ed) Indigenization of African Economics. New York: African Publishing Company.

Grosse, S. 1994. The Roots of Conflict and State Failure in Rwanda. The Political Exacerbation of Social Cleavages in a Conteext of Growing Resources Scarcity. Ann Arbor, Department of Population Planning and International Health, School of Public Health.

Guardian (The) (London). 22 June 1998, "Guerrillas Intensify Uganda Terror Raids", (Anna Borzello), p.14.

Gurr, Robert. 1970. Why Men Rebel. Princeton University Press. Princeton, New Jersey.

Gurr, Robert T. 1993. Minorities at Risk: A Global View of Ethnopolitical Conflict. United States Institute of Peace Press, Washington, D.C.

Gur, Robert and Barbara Harff. 1994. Ethnic Conflict in World Politics: Dilemmas in World Politics. Boulder, CO: Westview

Haas, Ernst. 1964. Beyond the Nation-State: Functionalist and International Organization. Stanford: Stanford University Press.

Haas, Ernest. 1970. International Organization Vol. 24, #4. Berkeley: University of California.

Halisi, C.R.D. 1997. "From Liberation to Citizenship: Identity and Citizenship in Black South Africa Political Thought." Comparative Studies in Society and History 39 (January): 66-85.

Hansen. H. B. and M. Twaddle. 1996. "Uganda: The Adent of No-Party Democracy in The New Struggle for Democracy in Africa, edited by J. Wiseman. Avebury, England: Aldershot.

Hardin, Russel. 1995. One for All: The Logic of Group Conflict. Princeton, N.J.: Princeton University Press.

Harowitz, I. L. 1981. "Military Origins of Third World Dictatorship and Democracy" in Third World Quarterly Vol.3, 1981 pp. 37-47.

Harris, P. B. 1979. Foundations of Political Science. London: Hutchinson and Co. (Publishers) Ltd.

Harrison, Lawrence. 1985. Underdevelopment is A State of Mind: The Latin American Case, Lanham, MD: Harvard University and Madison Books.

Hauser, Ellen (1997) "Donors and Democracy in Uganda: An Analysis of the Role of Western Donors in Democratization Efforts in Uganda", Ph.D., Dissertation, University of Wisconsin-Madison.

Herbst, Jeffrey. 1993. The Politics of Reform in Ghana, 1982-1991. Los Angeles: University of California Press, p. 160.

Herskovits, Melville J. 1967. *The Human Factor in Changing Africa.* New York: Vintage Books.

Hill, Hall. 1984. "Survey of Recent Development". Bulletin of Indonesian Economic Studies 20 (August), pp. 1-38.

Hirscham, Albert. 1958. The Strategy of Economic Development. New Haven: Yale

University Press.

Hlophe, Stephen. 1979. Class, Ethnicity and Politics in Liberia, Washington, D.C.

Hochschild, Adam. 1999. King Léopold's Ghost : A Story of Greed, Terror, and Heroism in Colonial Africa. First Marine Book--Hounghton Miffin Co

Hodgkins, T. 1953. Political Parties in British and French West Africa. Information Digest, Africa Bureau, No. 10: London.

Horowitz, Donald. 1985. Ethnic Groups in Conflict. University of California Press, Los Angeles.

Horowitz, Donald. 1990. "Making Moderation Pay: The Comparative Politics of Ethnic Conlict Management." In Joseph Montvile, Conflict and Peacemaking in Multiethnic Societies. Lexington, Mass: Lexington Books.

Horton, John. 1966. "Order and Conflict Theories of Social Problems". American Journal of Sociology (May/June), pp.51-73.

Hough, Jerry. 1986. The Struggle for the Third World, Soviet Debates and American Option. Washington, D. C. The Brooking Institute.

Houston Chronicle (The), 22 March 1998, "Ugandan Leader's vast Popularity Marred by 'No-Party' Democracy," (Scott Staus), p. 9.

Howard, Lawrence 1988. Involvement in Africa South of Sahara, 1800-1860, New York: Garland Publishers.

Human Rights Watch, World Report 2000: Africa Section, New York, New York: Human Watch, December 1999.

Huntington, Samuel. 1968. Political Order in Changing Societies. New Haven, CT: Yale University Press.

Hyden, Goran and Micheal Bratton.(eds). 1992. Governance and Politics in Africa. Boulder, CO: Lynne Reinner Publishers.

Ignatief, Michael. 1993. Blood and Belonging: Journeys into the New Nationalism. Toronto: Penguin.

Ihonvbere, Julius. 1994. "The Irrelevant State: Ethnicity and the Quest for Nationhood. Africa Ethnic and Racial Studies 17 (1), pp.42-40.

Ihonvbere, Julius O. 1994. Nigeria: The Politics of Adjustment and Democracy. New Brunswick: Transaction Publisher.

Ihonvbere, J. 1996. "Elections and Conflicts in Nigeria's Non-Transition to Democracy." Africa Demos 3 no.5, May: 8-11.

Ihonvbere. J. and O. Vaughan. 1995. Nigeria: Democracy and Civil Society. The Nigerian Transition Program, 1985-1993 in J.A. Wiseman (ed), Democracy and Political Change in Sub-Saharan Africa. London: Routledge, pp. 132 - 153.

Iliffe, John. 1995. *Africans: The History of a Continent.* New York: Cambridge University Press.

Imoko, Dave O. 1990. "The Development of Nigerian Manufacturing Sector." The Nigerian Interpreter. (October Issue).

Independent (The) (London), 10 June 1993, "Museveni takes Measured Route to Democracy: Uganda President Explains why he Resists West's Pressure for Change", (Richard Dowden) p. 13.

Isichei, Elizabeth. 1997. *A History of African Societies to 1870.* New York: Cambridge University Press.

Jackson, Robert, and Carl Roseberg. 1985. "Democracy in Tropical Africa: Democracy versus Autocracy in African Politics." Journal of International Affairs, 38 2, 231 –256.

Jackson, Robert, and Carl Rosberg. 1986. "The United States of East Africa: Tanzania, Uganda and Kenya," in Politics and Government in African States 1960-1985, (eds.) by Peter Duignan and Robert Jackson. Stanford, CA: Hover Institute Press.

Jacobs, P. E. and Teune, H. 1964. The Integrative Process: Guidelines for Analysis of the Bases of Political Community in Jacob, P.E. and Toscano, J. V. (eds.) Integration of Political Communities. New York: J.P. Lippincott Company.

Jacobs, Sylvia. 1981. The African Nexus Black American Perpectives on the European Partitioning of Africa 1880-1920. Westport: Greenwood Press.

Jagun, Dokun. 1993. "Nigeria: The Basis of Union". The Nigerian Guardian, Lagos. (April 8), pp.3-7.

Joseph, Richard. 1998. "Africa, 1990-1997: From Abertura to Closure", Journal of Democracy, Vol. 9, No. 2, pp. 3-17.

Joseph, Richard. 1997. "Democratization in Africa after 1989: Comparative and Theoretical Perspectives", Comparative Politics, April, pp. 363-382.

Kabila, Laurent -Desire. 1967. Naufrage du Processus de Re-democratisation. Parti de la Revolution Populaire (PRP) Makanga, Kivu,. Congo-Kinshasa.

Kahneman Daniel, and Amos Tversky. 1979. "Prospect Theory." Econometric 47:2 (March): 63-91.

Kahneman Daniel, Jack Knetsch, and Richard Thaler. 1990. "Experimental Tests of the Endowment Effect and the Coase Theorem." Journal of Political Economy 98 (December): 1325-48.

Kanza, Thomas 1996. The Rise and Fall of Patrice Lumumba. KIMPWANZA (UHURU) -No 29, avril /mai. p. 7.

Kasfir, Nelson (1994) "Uganda Politics and the Constituent Assembly Elections of March 1994", Paper presented at the Workshop on "Developing Uganda", Lyngby Lungbrosskole, Denmark, 2-5 June.

Kasfir, Nelson (1998) "No-Party Democracy" in Uganda", Journal of Democracy, Vol. 9, No. 2, pp. 49-63.

Kautsky, John. 1968. "Nationalism" in Kebschill Harvey (ed), "Politics in Transitional Societies: The Challenge in Asia, Africa and Latin America. New York: Appleton-Century-Crafts, pp.112-113.

kellas, James. 1991. The Politics of Nationalism and Ethnicity. London: Macmillan Education.

Kenyatta, Jomo. 1938. *Facing Mount Kenya.* London: Secker and Warburg.

Key, V. O. 1961. Public Opinion and American Democracy, New York: Alfred A. Knopf.

Khapoya, Vincent. 1994. The African Experience: An Introduction. Englewood Cliffs, N.J.: Prentice Hall.

Khapoya, Vincent. 1994. The African Experience: An Introduction. New Jersey: Prentice Hall.

Khapoya, Vincent. 1998. The Afican Experience: An Introduction. Upper Saddle River: Prentice Hall.

Kilson, Martin, and Mitchell Cohen. 1992. " Africa: Crisis and Change." Dissent summer, pp. 293 - 295.

Kiwanuka, S. 1971. A History of Buganda. London: Longman.

Klare, Michael and Peter Kornblush eds. Low Intensity Warfare. New York: Pantheon Press.

Kochan, Thomas. 1981. "Step-by-Step in the Middle East from the Perspective of the Labor Mediation Process. " in Jeffrey Z. Rubin , ed. Dynamics of Third Party Intervention: Kissinger in the Middle East. Westport, CT: Preager. pp. 125.140.

Kodourie, Elie. 1971. Nationalism. London: Longman.

Kohn, Hans. 1929. A History of Nationalism in the East. London: Longman.

Krasner, Stephen. 1985. Structural Conflict: The Third World Against Global Liberalism. Berkeley: University of California Press.

Krueger, Anne. 1993. "Virtous and Vicious Circles in Economic Development." American Economic Review. (May Issue).

Lafay, J.D. 1995. 'Conservative Nationalism, and Democratic Institutions', ill A. Breton, G. Galeotti, P. Salmon and R. Wintrobe (eds.) Nationalism and Rationality, Cambridge: Cambridge University Press.

Lal, Deepak. 1986. "The Political Economy of Economic Liberalization". The World Bank Economic Review. (Vol. 1, #2), pp. 273-299.

LaPatombara, J. and Weiner, M. (eds.) 1966. op. cit.

Lasswell, H., Lerner D. and Rothwell, C. E. 1952. The Comparative Study of Elites. Stanford, CA: Stanford University Press.

Lawyers Committee for Human Rights, 1991. First Steps: Rebuilding the Justice System in Liberia. New York, N.Y.: Lawyers Committee for Human Rights.

Lelyveld, Joseph. 1985. Move Your Shadow: South Africa, Black and White. New York: Penguim.

Lemarchand, Rene.1994. Burundi: Ethnocide as Discourse and Practice. New York: Cambridge University Press.

Lemarchand, Rene. 1995. "Four Models for Resolving Ethnic Conflict." African Voices 4 (Summer): 1-37.

Leslie, Winsome J. 1993. Zaire: Continuity and Political Change in Oppressive State. Westview Press, Boulde.

Lewis P, P. Robinson, and B. Rubin. 1998. Stabilizing Nigeria: Sanctions, Incentives and Support for Civil Society. New York: The Century Foundation Press.

Lijphart, Arend. 1977. Democracy in Plural Societies: A Comparative Exploration. New Haven, Connecticut: Yale University Press.

Lijphart, Arend. 1980. "Federal, Confederal, and Consociational Options for the South African Plural Society." in Robert Rotberg and John Barrat ed. Conflict and Compromise in South Africa. Lexington, Mass: Heath.

Lijphart, A. 1995. "Prospect for Power-Sharing in the New South-Africa." In A. Reynold (ed.), Elections 1994 South Africa: The Campaigns, Results and Future Prospects. New York: St. Martin's Press, pp. 221-231.

Lipset, S. M. 1959. "Some Social Requisites of Democracy: Economic Development and Political Legitimacy". American Political Science Review, 53:69-105.

Lipumba, Nguyuru. 1994. Africa Beyond Adjustment. Washington D.C.: Oversea Development Council.

Los Angeles Times, 11 July 1995, "Ambition and Dread in Uganda: The Nation is Struggling to Escape its Bloody Past and Become the Pride of Africa", (John Balzar), p. 3.

Los Angeles Times, 12 July 1998, "Horn of Africa: A Blow to Africa's Renaissance", (Chris Landsberg), p. 2.

Lowenkopf, Martin. 1976. Politics in Liberia: The Conservative Road to Development. Stanford, California: Hoover Institution Press.

Lumumba-Kasongo, Tukumbi. 1991. Nationalistic Ideologies, Their Policy Implications and The Struggle for Democracy in African Politics, New York: Edwin Mellen Press.

Lumumba-Kasongo, Tukumbi. 1992 "Clinton and Africa" Africa Notes (December).

Lumumba-Kasongo, Tukumbi. 1992. "Clinton and Africa." Africa Notes (December), 18 – 31..

Lumumba-Kasongo, T. 1995. "Towards A Political Re-definition of Africa." (SAPEM) Volume 8, No.6 March: 33-36.

Lumumba-Kasongo, T. 1998. The Rise of Multipartyism and Democracy in the Context of Global Change: The Case of Africa, Westport, CONN: Praeger.

Macridis, Roy. 1992. Contemporary Political Ideology Movements and Regimes. New York: Harper Collin Publishers, p. 191.

Maharaj, Gitanjali. 1999. Between Unity and Diversity. Claremont, South Africa: David Philip Publication.

Makinda, Samuel M (1996) "Democracy and Multi-party Politics in Africa", The Journal of Modern African Studies, Vol. 34, No. 4, Cambridge University Presses pp. 555-573.

Mamadani, Mahmood. 1996. Citizen and Subject: Contemporary Africa and The legacy of Late Colonialism. Princeton University Press.

Maren, M.P. 1987. "Kenya: The Dissolution of Democracy" in Current History. Africa Report, May 1987 pp. 209-212.

Marger, Martin. 1997. Race and Ethnic Relations. New York: Wadsworth Publishing Company.

Martin, Tony. 1985. The Pan African Connection, From Slavery to Garvey and Beyond. Boston, MA: The Majority Press.

Mauro, P 1995. 'Corruption and Growth', Quarterly Journal of Economics, 110 (3), August.

Mazrui, Ali. 1986. The Africans: A Triple Heritage. Boston: Little Brown and Company.

Mazrui, Ali. 1986. The African: A Triple Heritage. London: BBC Publication

Mazrui, Ali. 1986. Legacy of Lifestyle: The African Triple Heritage, Washington D.C. Broadcasting Service.

Mazrui, Ali. 1986. *The Africans.* London: BBC Publications.

Mazrui, Ali. (ed.) 1993. Africa Since 1935, Unesco General History of Africa, Vol VIII, London: Heinemann.

McGreal, C. 1996. "Museveni Swear by his No-Party Panacea." The Observer (May12), p. 19.

McLaughlin, V. Russe. 196l. Foreign Investment and Development in Liberia, New York and London: Frederick A. Praeger, Publishers.

Mehmet, Ofay. 1978. Economic Planning and Social Justice in Developing Countries, New York: St. Martin's Press.

Melson Robert and Howard Wolpe. 1970. "Modernization and the Politics of Communalism: A Theoretical Perspective". American Political Science Review, Vol LXIV, (December).

Melson, Robert, and Howard Wolpe. 1971. Preface in Nigeria: Modernization and the Polictics of Communalism, ed. Melson and Wolpe. East Lansing: Michigan State University Press.

Mill, J.S. 1962. Consideration on Representative Government, Gateway Editions (originally published in 1862).

Mitrany, David. 1966. A Working Peace System. Chicago: Quadrangle Books.

Mitrany, David. 1975. The Functional Theory of Politics. London: The London School of Economics Press.

Monitor (The), 6 June 1999, "Parties, Referendum Bills Split Parliament" (Kampala), p.1-3.

Morgenthaus, Hans and Kenneth Thompson. 1985. Politics Among Nations: The Struggle for Power and Peace 6th ed. New York: Knopf.

Morrison, D.G. and Stevenson, H.M. 1972. "Cultural Pluralism, Modernization and Conflict: An Empirical Analysis of Sources of Political Instability in

African Nations". Canadian Journal of Political Science. Vol. V. No.1, March, p.90.

MPEA, 1973. Indicative Manpower Plan of Liberia for the Period 1972-1982, (Monrovia, June).

Murdock, George P. 1959. *Africa: Its Peoples and Their Culture History*. New York: McGraw-Hill.

Murungi, K. (1997. "Parliament Need Not be so Toothless" in Sunday Nation, April 20, 1997 p.9.

Mutibwa, Phares (1992) Uganda Since Independence: A Story of Unfulfilled Hopes. London and Kampala: Fountain Publisher Ltd., and C. Hurst and Co., Publishers Ltd.

Mutoro, H. et al. 1996."Political Leadership and the Crisis of Development in Africa: Lessons From Kenya" in International Conference on 'Good Governance as a Precondition for Sustainable Development', Center for Development Studies, The University of Western Australia, Perth, Australia, October 1996.

Nabudere, D. W. 1979.Essays on the Theory and Practice of Imperialism. London: Onyx Press.

Nafziger, Wayne. 1997. The Economics of Developing Countries. Upper Saddle River: Prentice Hall Press.

Ndegwa, Stephen. 1997. "Citizensip and Ethnicity: An Examination of Two Transition Moments in Kenyan Politics. American Political Science Review. Vol. 91, No. 3 (September).

Ndegwa, Stephen. 1998.. The two faces of Civil Society: NGOs and Politics in Africa. Kamerian Press, West Hartford, Connecticut.

Nehru, B.K. 1980. "Western Democracy and the Third World: A Further Comment", in Third Word Quarterly Vol. II pp. 126-130.

Nimley, Anthony J. 1991. Government and Politics in Liberia, Nashville, Tenn., Nashville, Academic Publishers International.

Nkrumah, Kwame. 1964. *Consciencism: Philosophy and Ideology for De-Colonisation*. London: Panaf Books.

Nkrumah, Kwame. 1971. Neo-Colonialism: Last Stage of Imperialism. New York: International Publishers.

Nnoli, Okwudiba. 1980. Ethnic Politics in Nigeria. Fourth Dimension Publishers, Enugu, Nigeria.

Norbu, Dawa. 1992. Culture and the Politics of Third World Nationalism. London: Routledge Press, p. 29.

North, Douglass. 1994. "Economic Performance Through Time". American Economic Review #84, (June Issue), pp. 359-68.

Nye, Joseph. 1975. "International Interdependence and Integration" in Fred Greenstein and Nelson Polsby (ed). Handbook of Political Science, Vol. 8. Addison Wesley Publishing Company, pp. 363-414.

Nzongola-Ntalaja. 1982. Class Struggles and national liberation in Africa: Essays on the Political Economy of Neocolonialism. Roxbury, Mass: Omenana,.

Nzongola-Ntalaja, Georges and Margaret C. Lee. 1997. The State and Democracy in Africa. Ed. Trenton, NJ: Africa World Press, Inc

Nzongola-Ntalaja, Georges. 1987. Revolution and Counter-Revolution in Africa :Essays in Contemporary Politics. London and New Jersey, Zed books.

Obasanjo, Olusegun. 1990. "Eastern Promises." West Africa Magazine. (May 7-13), p.762

Odetola, Olatunde. 1982. Military Regimes and Development: A Comparative Analysis of Africa. London: George Allen Press.

Ofcansky, Thomas. 1997. The Tarnished Pearl of Africa. Boulder: Westview Press.

Ojo, Olatunde. 1981. " The Impact of Personality and Ethnicity on the Nigerian Election of 1979," Africa Today, Vol.2, no. 3: 47-58.

Oke, B. A. 1990. "Structural Adjustment and the Role of the Central Bank of Nigeria: The Nigerian Experience and Future Direction". Central Bank of Nigeria Economic and Financial Review. Vol. 28, No. 1, pp. 36-38.

Ola, Robert and Samuel Hume. 1994. Government and Local Development inWestern Nigeria, Benin City: Ambik Press.

Olaniyan, Omotayo. 1996. Foreign Aid, Self-Reliance, and Economic Development in West Africa. Westport CT: Praeger.

Olaniyi, J. O. 1995. "Education as a Means of Achieving National Integration." Ilorin Journal of Education, Vol. 16.

Oloka-Onyango, Joe. 1991. "The National Resistance Movement, "Grassroots Democracy" and Dictatorship in Uganda" in Robin Cohen and Harry Goulbourne (eds). Democracy and Socialism in Africa. Boulder: Westview Press, pp. 125-141.

Oloka-Onyango, Joe. 1993. "Popular Justice, Resistance Committee Courts and the Judicial Process in Uganda: 1988-1992", Beyond Law, (Legal Pluralism), Vol. 3, No. 7, and July.

Oloo, A.G. R. 1996. "The Doctrine of Mutual Control and Accountability: The Case of the Legislature and Executive in Kenya", in African Association of Political Science (Kenya Chapter) Conference on `Democracy and the Constitutional Process in Kenya', Nairobi, July 1996.

Olorunsola, Victor. 1972. The Politics of Cultural Sub-Nationalism in Africa. Garden City, NY: Anchor Books.

Oloruntimehin, B.O. 1972. The Segu Tukular Empire. London: Longman.

Olukoshi, Adebayo. 1992. The Politics of Structural Adjustment in Nigeria. London: James Carrey Publishers.

Olukoshi Adebayo, Omotayo Olaniran, and Femi Aribisala. 1994. Structural Adjustment in West Africa. Lagos: Pumark Nigerian Limited.

Onimode, Bade. 1989. Alternative Development Strategies for Africa. London: Institute for African Alternatives.

Osagie, E. 1987. "Problems of Structural Adjustment Programs in West Africa", in Phillips A. O. and Ndekwu E. C. (eds)., Structural Adjustment Programs in a Developing Economy: The Case of Nigeria. Ibadan: NISER, p.236.

Osifo-Whisky, Onome. 1994. "The Trouble with the North". Tell Magazine. Lagos, Nigeria (August 15), p.3.

Ottaway, Marina. 1994. Democratization and Ethnic Nationalism: African and Eastern European Experiences. Washington, DC: Overseas Development Council.

Oyediran, Oyeleye. 1979. Nigerian Government and Politics Under Military Rule 1966-79. New York: St. Martins Press.

Oyeleye, Oyediran, and Adigun Agbaje. 1999. Nigeria: Politics of Transition and Governance 1986-1996. Dakar, Senegal: CODESRIA.

Packenham, A. Robert. 1976. Liberal America and the Third World: Political Development Ideas in Foreign Aids and Social Sciences, Princeton, N.J.: Princeton University Press.

Park, Robert. 1924. "The Concept of Social Distance." Journal of Applied Sociology 8: 339-344.

Parsons, Talcott. 1975. "Some Theoretical Considerations on the Nature and Trends of Change of Ethnicity" in Nathan Glazer and Daniel Moynihan (eds). Ethnicity: Theory and Experience. Cambridge: Harvard University Press.

Payne John, James Bettman, and Eric Johnson. 1992. "Behavioral Decision Research." Annual Review of Psychology 43:87-131.

Peled, Yoav. 1992. "Ethnic Democracy and the Legal Construction of Citizenship: Arab Citizens of the Jewish State." American Political Science Review 86 (June): 432 - 43.

Phillips Adedotun, and Eddy Ndekwu. 1992. Structural Adjustment Programs in a Developing Economy: The Case of Nigeria. Ibadan: NISER Publication.

Phillips Adedotun, and Olu Ajakaiye. 1993. Nigerian Economic and Society: Economic Policy and Development. Ibadan: NISER, pp.9-20.

Pittsburgh Post-Gazette, 22 July 1998, "Uganda Olive Branch", p.9.

Plekhanov, George. 1940. The Materialist Concept of History, New York: International Publishers.

Posen, Barry. 1993. "The Security Dilemma and Ethnic Conflict, " Survival vol. 35 (Spring), p.28-41.

Prunier, G. 1995. The Rwanda Crisis: History of a Genocide. New York: Columbia University Press.

Putnam, R.D. 1993. Making Democracy Work in Civic Traditions in Modern Italy, Princeton: Princeton University.

Pye, L. 1966. Aspects of Political Development. Boston: Little Brown and Company.

Quarcoo, P.K. 1990. "Structural Adjustment Programs in Sub-Saharan: Evolution of Approaches." African Development Review, 2(2), December Issue, p. 13.

Ramsay, Jeffress. 1999. *Africa*. Guilford: Dushkin/McGraw-Hill.

Ranger, T. O. 1967. Revolt in Southern Rhodesia 1896-1897. London: Heinemann.

Ranis, Gustav. 1995. "Another Look at East Asian Miracle." The World Bank Economic Review. (September Issue), 509-534.

Ranney, A. and Kendal, W. 1969. Basic Principle for a Modern Democracy. In C. Crnudde and D. E. Neubauer (eds.) Empirical Democratic Theory. Chicago: Markham. pp.41-63.

Renan, Ernest. 1929. "What is a Nation? in Hans Kohn (ed), Nationalism: Its Meaning and History. London: Longman.

Reno, William. 1998. World Politics and African States. Boulder, Colorado: Lynne Rienner Publishers.

Reuters, 1995. "Ugandans Reject Party System." Financial Times (London), 22 June. p. 7-9.

Reuters, 19 February 1996, "Ugandan Groups Lobbies Donors on Debt Reduction." p.1-2.

Reuters, 21 February 1996, "IMF Praises Uganda's Economic Reforms." P.3-4.

Reuters, 17 March 1996, "Ugandan Leader Faces Dilemma over Rebel Challenge" (Edmond Kizito). P.3.

Reuters, 12 May 1996, "Uganda's Triumphant Museveni to be Sworn in." (Peter Smerdon).

Reuters, 21 May 1996. "Uganda Steps up Publicity Drive for Privatization" (Edmond Kizito). P. 1-2.

Richard, Joseph. 1987. Democratic Challenges in Africa. The Carter Center Working Papers Series. Atlanta, GA: Carter Center.

Richardson, R. Nathaniel. 1959. Liberia's Past and Present, London: The

Diplomatic Press and Publishing Co.

Roberts, G. and Edwards, A. 1991. A New Dictionary of Political Analysis. London: Edward Arnold.

Ross, M.H. 1993. The Culture of Conflict. Interpretations and Interests in Comparative Perspective. New Haven, London: Yale University Press.

Rostow, Walt. 1970. The Stages of Economic Growth. Cambridge: Cambridge University Press.

Rotberg, Robert (ed). 1971. Rebellion in Black Africa. New York: Oxford University Press.

Rothchild, Donald. 1964. Safeguarding Nigeria's Minirities. Pittsburgh, PA: Duquesne University Press.

Rothchild, Donald. 1981. Ethnopolitics: A Conceptual Framework. New York: Columbia University Press.

Rothchild, Donald. 1986. "State and Ethnicity in Africa: A Policy Perspective." In Kennedy, Charles and Neil Navitte. eds. Ethnic Preference and Public Policy in Developing States. Boulder, CO: Lynne Rienner.

Rothchild, Donald. 1997. Managing Ethnic Conflict in Africa. Washington, D.C.: Brooking Institution Press.

Rothchild, Donald and Victor A. Olorunsola. 1983 *State Versus Ethnic Claims: African Policy Dilemmas*. Boulder: Westview Press.

Rothgells, John. 1992. Defining Power: Influence and Force in the Contemporary International System. New York: St. Martin's.

Ruiz, Hiram A. 1992. Uprooted Liberians: Casualties of A Brutal War, Washingrton, D.C.: U.S. Committee for Refugees

Saha, Santosh C. 1990. A History of Agriculture in Liberia, 1882-1970: Transference of American Valuea, Lewiston, New York: Edwin Mellen Press.

Sanda, A.O. 1976. Ethnic Relations in Nigeria. The Caxton Press, Ibadan, Nigeria.

Sandbrook, Robert, 1988. "Liberal Democracy in Africa: A Socialist-Revisionist Perspective." Canadian Journal of African Studies, Vol. 22, no.2, 240 -

267.

Sandbrook, Richard. 1990. "Taming the African Leviathan". World Policy Journal. (Fall Issue), pp.673-701.

Sartori, G. 1965. Democratic Theory. New York: Praeger.

Sawyer, Amos, 1992. The Emergence of Autocracy in Liberia: Tragedy and Challenge, Francisco, California, Institute for Cotemporary Studies.

Saxton Lloyd, and Walter Kaufmann. 1971. The American Scene: Social Problems of The Seventies. Belmont, Calif: Wadworth. p.2.

Schermerhorn, R. A. 1970. Comparative Ethnic Relations: A Framework for Theory and Research. New York: Random House.

Schiff, M. 1992. 'Social Capital, Labor Mobility, and Welfare. The Impact of Uniting States', Rationality & Society, 4 (2): 157-75.

Schiff M. 1995. 'Capital socio-cultural, diversite etlinique et reforme economique en Afrique Sub-Saharienne', Revue d'Economie du Developpement.

Schiff, M. and A. Valdes. 1992. The Political Economy of Agricultural Pricing Policy. Volume 4. A Synthesis of the Economics in Developing Countries, Baltimore: The Johns Hopkins University Press.

Schlesinger, A. 1967. A Thousand Days, New York: Fawcett World Library.

Schumpetter, J. 1960. Capitalism Socialism and Democracy. New York: Harper and Brothers.

Selassie, Alemante G. 1992. " Ethnic Identity and Constitutional Design for Africa." Stanford Journal of International Law. Vol. 29, No.1, pp.1-56.

Seyom, Brown. 1995. New Forces Old Forces and the Future of World Politics: Post-Cold War Edition. New York: Harper Collin.

Seyon, Patrick. 1985. "Liberis: Threat to Democracy," West Africa, No. 3528 (8 April).

Sharer, R., C. Schiller and M. Ahmad (1994) IMF Survey, 24 January, pp. 21-24.

Shaw, Timothy and Julius E. Okolo. 1994. The Political Economy of Foreign Policy in

ECOWAS. New York: St. Martin's Press.

Shettima, K. Ahmed. 1994. "Engendering Nigeria's Third Republic." African Studies Review 38 no.3 (December), 61-98.

Shillington, Kevin. 1995. *History of Africa.* New York: St. Martin's Presss.

Sisk, Timothy. 1995. Democratization in South Africa. Princeton, NJ: Princeton University Press.

Sklar, R. 1964. Nigerian Political Parties. Princeton, N.J.: Princeton University Press.

Sklar, Robert. 1979. "The Nature of Class Domination in Africa." Journal of Modern African Studies, vol. 17, no. 4, 540 - 552.

Sklar, R. 1979. The Nature of Class Domination in Africa. Journal of Modern Africa Studies, Vol, 17, no. 4, pp. 560- 571.

Sklar, R. L. 1983. Nigerian Political Parties: Power in an Emergent African Nation. Enugu: NOK Publishers (Nig.) Ltd.

Sklar, Richard. 1993. "The American Frontier for Political Science," in Africa and Disciplines, edited by Robert Bates, V.Y. Mudimbe, and Jean O'Barr. Chicago: University of Chicago Press.

Smith, Stewart. 1974. U.S. Neo-colonialism in Africa, New York: International Publishers. Survey of Current Business, August 1963, October 1968 and 1971.

Smock, David. 1976. The Search for National Integration in Africa. New York: The Free Press.

Smock, David.and Kwamena, Bentsi-Enchill. 1976. The Search for National Integration in Africa. New York: The Free Press.

Snarr Micheal, and Neil Snarr. 1998. (ed.) Introducing Global Issues. Boulder, CO: Lynne Rienne.

Snyder, J. 1990. "Averting Anarchy in the New Europe." International Security 14:5-41.

Snyder, Jack. 1990. "Averting Anarchy in the New Europe," International Security, Vo. 14, (Spring), p. 30-43.

Sonyika, Wole.1996. The open Sore of a Continent: A Personal Narrative of the Nigerian Crisis. New York: Oxford university Press.

Sørensen, Georg. 1993. Democracy and Democratization: Dilemma in World Politics Westview Press.

South African Institute of Race Relations. 1997. Race Relations Survey. Johannesburg: SAIRR.

Soyinka, W. 1996. The Open Sore of a Continent: A Personal Narrative of the Nigerian Crisis. New York: Oxford University Press.

Starr, J. B. 1973 Ideology and Culture. New York: Harper and Row.

Stewart, Angus. 1995. "Two Conceptions of Citizenship." British Journal of Sociology 46 (March): 63-78.

Suberu, R. 1994. "The Democratic Recession in Nigeria," Current History, 3, 215-232.

Sudan, François et al. 1998. "Kabila: Un an apres la chutte de Mobutu, où en est le nouveau Congo?--Un dossier exceptionnel." Jeune Afrique No. 1948, Du 12 au 18 Mai,. pp. 85-224.

Summers, Lawrence and Vinod Thomas. (1993). "Recent Lessons of Development". The World Bank Research Observer. (July Issue), p. 249.

Takougang, J. 1996. The 1992 Multiparty Elections in Cameroon: Prospects for Democracy and Democratization. Journal of Asian and African Studies, 31 (1-2), 157-175.

Tarr, Byron. 1993 "The ECOMOG Initiative in Liberia: A Liberian Perspective," Issue: A Journal of Opinion, Volume XXI/1-2.

Thaler Richard, and Eric Johnson. 1990. Gambling with the House Money and trying to Break even." Management Science 36: 643 -60.

Theen, R., and F. Wilson. 1996. Comparative Politics. Upper Saddle River: NJ: Prentice Hall.

Thompson, Leonard. 1990. A History of South Africa. New Haven, Conn.: Yale University Press.

Tordoff, Williams. 1997. Government and Politics in Africa. 3rd ed. Bloomington,

IN: Indiana University Press.

Townsend, E. R. (ed.) 1955. President Tubman of Liberia, (London: Consolidated Publications, Co., Ltd.

Toyin, F. and J. Ihonvbere. 1985. The Rise and Fall of Nigerian's Second Republic 1979-1984. London: Zed Books.

Udogu, Ike. 1997. (ed.) Democracy and Democratization in Africa: Toward the 21st Century. Leiden, The Netherlands: E. J. Brill.

Udogu, Ike. 1999. "The Issue of Ethnicity and Democracy in Africa: Toward the Millennium." Journal of Black Studies. Vol. 29, (6), 790-808.

UN Office for the Coordination of Humanitarian Affairs 2000. "Report on Consultation on War in the Democratic Republic of Congo." February 29 to March 11, p.25 -27.

United States Congress, House Committee on Foreign Affairs Sub-Committee on Africa. 1994. U.S. Policy in Liberia: Hearing before the Sub-Committee on Africa of the Committee on Foreign Affairs, House of Representatives, One hundred Third Congress, Second Session, Washington, D.C.: GPO.

U. S. AID Report on a brief history of development assistance to Liberia by the United States government (1946-1980).

U.S. Department of State. 1998. Uganda Country Report on Human Rights Practices for 1997. Washington: D.C: U.S. Dept. of State.

U.S. Department of State. 1999. Uganda Country Report on Human Rights Practices for 1998. Washington: D.C.: U.S. Dept. of State.

Uvin, Peter. 1997. "The Prejudice, Crisis, and Genocide in Rwanda". African Studies Review, Volume 40, No.2. (September).

Uzodike, U. O. 1996. "Democracy and Economic Reforms: Developing Underdeveloped Economies." Journal of Asian and African Studies, 31 (1-2), 21-38.

Van Buren, L. 1994 "Uganda: Economy", Africa South of the Sahara 1994. (21st Edition). London: Europa Publication.

van den Berghe, Pierre. 1978. Race and Racism: A Comparative Perspective. 2nd ed. New York: Wiley Press.

Van Dyke, V. 1996. Introduction to Politics. 3th ed. Chicago, IL: Nelson-Hall.

Wade, Robert. 1990. Governing the Market: Economic Theory and the Role of Government in East Asian Industrialization. Princeton: Princeton University Press.

Wallerstein, Immanuel. 1973. "Class and Class Conflict in Contemporary Africa." Canadian Journal of African Studies,Vol. 7, No. 3. 34 - 55.

Wallerstein, Immanuel. 1984. The World Politics of the World Economy: The States, The Movements and the Civilizations, New York, Cambridge University Press.

Washington Post. 15 March 1995 "Uganda, in Comeback, Attracts Investors; Aid Donors", (Stephen Buckley).

Washington Post. 9 May 1996, "Ugandan Vote to Test 'No-Party' System: Fears of Violence Precede Presidential Poll", (Stephen Buckley), p. 31.

Waters, Malcolm. 1989. "Citizenship and the Constitution of Structures Social Inequality." International Journal of Comparative Sociology, Vol. 30. N0. 3-4, pp.159-180.

Watson , Catherine. 1994. "No to Multi-Party", Africa Report, May-June: 24-26.

Weekly Review, (Nairobi) July 12, 1991.

Were, G. S. 1971."Politics, Religion, and Nationalism in Western Kenya, 1942 1962: Dini Ya Msambwa Revisited", in Historical Association of Kenya Annual Conference.

West Africa. 1985. No. 3529 (April 15), 457 - 469.

West Africa. 1997. "Africa in the Changing World" No. 4179 (April 15).

William, Gavin and Terisa Turner. 1978. "Nigeria". In West African States: Failure and Promise. Edited by John Dun. Cambridge University Press, London.

Wiseman, J.A. 1996. The New Struggle for Democracy in Africa. Avebury, England: Aldershot.

Wodié, Francis. 1992. "Problématique de la transition démocratique en Afrique," paper presented at Seventh General Assembly of CODESRIA, Dakar, Senegal, 10-14 February.

World Bank. 1990. World Development Report. New York: Oxford University Press.

World Bank. 1993. World Development Report. New York: Oxford University Press, p. 296.

World Bank. 1994. Adjustment in Africa: Reform, Results, and the Road Ahead. Oxford University Press.

World Bank. 1996. World Development Report. New York: Oxford University Press.

World Bank. 1996. The World Bank Annual Report. Washington, D.C.

World Bank 1997. "World Bank Approves Debt Relief Package for Uganda", News Release No. 97/1324-s, 23 April.

World Bank. 1998. Annual Report. New York: Oxford University Press.

World Trade Information Service. 1951. Part 1, No. 58, 45-58.

Yinger, Milton. 1981. "Toward a Theory of Assimilation and Disassimilation." Ethnic and Racial Studies 4:249-264.

Young, Crawford. 1976. The Politics of Cultural Pluralism. Madison, WI: University of Wisconsin Press.

Young, Crawford, and Thomas Turner. 1985. The Rise and Decline of the Zairian State. Madison, WI: University of Wisconsin Press.

Zakaria, Fareed 1997 "The Rise of Liberal Democracy", Foreign Affairs, November/December, pp. 22-43.

Zolberg.A. R.1966. Creating Political Order: The Party States of West Africa. Chicago: Rand McNally

Zolberg, Aristide. 1993. "The Specter of Anarchy: Africa States Verging on Dissolution."

List of Contributors

Robert Dibie, Ph.D., Western Michigan University, public administration and comparative political systems. Professor Dibie teaches public administration and African Politics at California State University Fresno. He previously taught at Indiana State University, Southern Illinois University at Carbondale, Wayne State University Detroit, and the University of Detroit Mercy. He has published numerous articles and three books.

Francois N. Muyumba, Ph.D., Indiana University, English Education and Curriculum, M.A., Linguistics. Dr. Muyumba is Associate Professor of African-American Studies at Indiana State University. He has authored several publications, reviews and articles and was co-editor of From Third World to One World: the Pan-African Perspective and North-South Dialogue: New Directions. Dr. Muyumba is the founding director and organizer of the Annual Pan-African Studies Conference at Indiana State University. His research interests include language and culture, Pan-Africanism and political education, interdisciplinary approaches to global education, African-American Studies and African traditions and culture.

Andrew Conteh is Professor of Political Science at Moorhead State University Minnesota. His publications are in comparative politics and structural adjustment policies in Sub-Saharan Africa. Dr. Conteh research interests include international law, relationships of Africa's Afro-Marxist states, Russian Federation and the

United States.

Leonard Gadzekpo, Ph.D., Bowling Green University, Ohio, African Arts and Culture. Dr. Gadzekpo is Assistant Professor of African-American Studies at Southern Illinois University Carbondale. His research interests include African Arts and designs, African-American Studies, African traditions and culture.

Ernest Uwazie is Associate Professor of Criminal Justice at California State University Sacramento. Dr. Uwazie is also the Director of the Center for African Peace and Conflict Resolution, and African Studies Coalition Program.

Tukumbi Lumumba-Kasongo is a Professor at the Department of City and Regional Planning at Cornell University New York. Dr. Lumumba-Kasongo is also the President of Pan-African World Congress. Dr. Kasongo is the editor of Journal of Comparative Education and International Relations in Africa. He has consulted for both the United Nations and the United States on issues concerning Africa.

Ismail Shariff is Professor and Chair of the Department of Economics at the University of Wisconsin, Green-Bay. His research and publications are in development economics. He has consulted for the United Nations in Africa, Latin America and Asia.

Patrick Okonkwo is a Professor of Marketing at Central Michigan University. Dr. Okonkwo's research and publications are in international marketing and logistics. He has been a consultant for General Motors and SCOA Nigerian Limited. Before joining Central Michigan University, he was the Chair of the Department of Marketing at the University of Jos, Nigeria.

Samory Rashid, Ph.D., University of Chicago, International Political Economy. Dr. Rashid is Associate Professor and Chairperson of Political Science at Indiana State University. His research and teaching have been in Organizational Behavior, Islam in America, Economic Reform policies in Africa and politics in the Middle East. His recent publications include “Toward Understanding America’s Islamic Legacy.”

Babatunde Agiri is Associate Professor of African History at Norfolk State University and former Director of African Studies at Kalamazoo College, where he was also a visiting Professor in African History. Dr. Agiri taught at the University of Lagos-Nigeria, for over 25 years. While in was in Nigeria, he served as the Editor of the Nigerian Journal of American Studies for several years. He also served as the President of American Students Association, and consulted for various state governments’ Historical and Museum Boards in Nigeria.

Shadrack Nasong'o is a Lecturer at the University of Nairobi. Dr. Nasong'o is currently a visiting scholar at the University of Boston, United States. He has coordinated several political and economic development projects for the Kenyan government.

Sharron Herron, Ph.D., Mississippi State University, public administration and public policy. Dr. Herron is Assistant Professor of Public Administration at California State University Fresno. She is also the director of the Maddy Institute of Public Affairs at CSU-Fresno. Her research interests include African-American politics public policy, and women Studies.

Index

www.ingramcontent.com/pod-product-compliance
Lightning Source LLC
LaVergne TN
LVHW090304210926
848480LV00001B/127